ECHO
OF THE SEA

Echoes of the Sea

SCOTLAND AND THE SEA
AN ANTHOLOGY

Edited by
BRIAN D. OSBORNE
&
RONALD ARMSTRONG

CANONGATE

First Published in Great Britain in 1998 by
Canongate Books Ltd.,
14 High Street, Edinburgh EH1 1TE

10 9 8 7 6 5 4 3 2 1

Copyright © editors and contributors severally, 1998
For a full list of copyright material see page 419

British Library Cataloguing-in-Publication Data
A catalogue record for this book is available on request
from the British Library

The publishers gratefully acknowledge subsidy from the
Scottish Arts Council towards the publication of this volume.

ISBN 0 86241 783 X

Typeset by Palimpsest Book Production Limited
Polmont, Stirlingshire

Printed and bound in Finland by
WSOY

Contents

NOTE: Titles given in quotation marks do not appear in the original and have
been provided by the editors.

Foreword

And weel I lo'e the land, my lads,
That's girded by the sea

Scotland Yet Henry Scott Riddell (1798–1870)

Scotland's relationship with the sea is an ancient and all-pervading one – from Celtic monks and their curraghs, Norse raiders and their dragon ships through the merchant ships of the medieval burghs trading with the Baltic and the Low Countries to the Fifies and Zulus of the nineteenth century East coast fishing fleet and the oil-rig support vessels of the late twentieth century. It is hardly surprising in a country where one is never very many miles from salt water that the influence of the sea should be so significant and should have been so potent a source of inspiration and imagination through the centuries.

The sea has been a source of wealth, a communication route, a larder, a battlefield and a demanding mistress. It has also been a playground for many – from Sir Thomas Lipton pursuing his dream of winning the *America's* Cup with his succession of *Shamrock* racing yachts to J.J. Bell's Wee Macgreegor and his plaintive cry 'Can I get oarin', Paw' as he and his family row around Rothesay Bay and enjoying 'a wee shoogy-shoo wi' thon steamboat's waves'.

With all these connections and influences it is little wonder that so many of Scotland's writers have responded to the sea and have been inspired to some of their finest and most characteristic work by the maritime dimension to Scotland's story. We have attempted to gather some of this rich harvest in this anthology to serve as an introduction and sampler to a rich and varied literature. Our selections have been chosen to provide both a balanced view of the sea in all its moods and functions and, as far as is possible, self-contained and satisfying pieces of writing. Where extracts from longer works have been used we have attempted to provide sufficiently long extracts to give both a sense of the whole and enjoyable and worthwhile reading experiences in themselves. For most of the passages we have also provided a brief introduction aimed at setting the passage and its author in their context and explaining any useful background information.

In researching and selecting material for this anthology seven broad themes emerged and we have grouped our chosen texts under these headings: Myth and Legend, War at Sea, A Living from the Sea, Voyages, Perils of the Sea, Pleasures of the Sea, The Age of Steam and Iron. At the beginning of each of these chapters we introduce the theme and the extracts gathered within it, highlighting other events and texts of interest and relevance. We hope that the combination of fiction, poetry and non-fiction in each section creates illuminating and attractive crosscurrents and connections.

We have taken a broad interpretation of 'Scotland and the Sea', and, in consequence, there are works both by Scots and about Scots. We have been encouraged in this approach by the thought that one of the most famous literary sailors, Daniel Defoe's Robinson Crusoe, was, although English and created by an English writer, based on the Fife seaman, Alexander Selkirk. The original account of Alexander Selkirk's adventures, although related by an English narrator, is included here as an appropriate and revealing record of a more than usually thrawn and argumentative Scot.

What gives all the varied texts in this anthology – drawn from centuries of writing and oceans of experience – a unity and a common core is, of course, the age-old fascination of mankind's relationship with the sea – a relationship seldom better explored than in Rudyard Kipling's sympathetic portrayal of the old Scots engineer McAndrew, who recollects in his night watch a lifetime at sea, its temptations, satisfactions and dangers.

Brian D. Osborne
Ronald Armstrong
February 1998

It's no child's play to go
Steamin' to bell for fourteen days o' snow an' floe an' blow.
The bergs like kelpies overside that girn an' turn an' shift
Whaur, grindin' like the Mills o' God, goes by the big South drift.
(Hail, Snow and Ice that praise the Lord. I've met them at their work,
An' wished we had anither route or they anither kirk.)

from McAndrew's Hymn by Rudyard Kipling

1
MYTH AND LEGEND

The myths and legends of the Sea are intertwined with those of the land of Scotland and successive layers of Pictish, Gaelic, Scots and Norse myth lie on top of each other in a way resembling rock strata. The analogy breaks down in that we cannot be certain about the chronological sequence of story and legend in the way that geologists describe the major divisions of geological time.

We shall therefore simply choose to begin with one of the most famous of ballads in Scots – a haunting medley of legend and what sounds like recorded history. *Sir Patrick Spens* tells of a relationship with the sea that could be true of any sea-girt nation – a wariness and respect for the power and fickleness of the sea:

> O wha is this has done this deed,
> And tauld the king o' me,
> To send me out at this time of the year
> To sail upon the sea?

The sea has a dreaded quality summed up in the stanza:

> They hadna sailed a league, a league,
> A league but barely three,
> When the lift grew dark, and the wind blew loud,
> And gurly grew the sea.

Unusually among ballads, it shows the development of a story: a veteran sea captain agrees to bring a princess back from Norway in winter and against his better judgement. On their return across the North Sea a storm destroys his ship with all on board. In some versions there is an episode at the court of Norway, but then, inexorably, we pass to the resolution of the situation, the doom which we feel certain has been in Sir Patrick's heart from the beginning. The American writer, MacEdward Leach, describes the power of the ballad form and its peculiar appropriateness for telling a story:

In one way this is the ultimate in dramatic expression, for here is the universal. Here is man in his dramatic moment. Here is *a* man becoming man and facing the one moment in life that destroys all or reveals all.

There is too a striking economy about ballads; we do not actually see the end but move from the crew's despairing attempts to staunch the wounded ship – 'but still the sea came in' – to the tremendous irony of the fashionable courtiers' epitaph:

> O laith, laith were our gude Scots lords
> To weet their cork-heel'd shoon;
> But lang or a' the play was play'd,
> They wat their hats aboon.

Ballads were part of an oral tradition, 'handed down from lip to ear', and no anachronistic notion of cliché should be allowed to stand in the way of a telling phrase.

This section deals initially with mythic or legendary stories about the sea in Scots, and this reflects the dominant linguistic force for much of our history. Without any attempt to force these anthology selections into a strictly chronological framework, the Celtic and Norse elements of myth and legend are also represented. Here too there are roots in oral tradition, and we include from the Gaelic ballad tradition the *Sea Prayer*. This was collected and translated by Alexander Carmichael of Lismore in the second half of the nineteenth century in *Carmina Gadelica*, handed down orally by 'men and women throughout the Highlands and Islands of Scotland, from Arran to Caithness, from Perth to St Kilda. It is the product of far-away thinking come down on the long stream of time. Who the thinkers and whence the stream, who can tell?' Although wary of ascribing an exact provenance to oral material and without benefit of later archaeology, Dr Carmichael goes on to speculate: 'Some of the hymns may have been composed within the cloistered cells of Derry and Iona, and some of the incantations among the cromlechs of Stonehenge and the standing stones of Callarnis. These were composed by the learned, but they have not come down through the learned, but through the unlearned.'

Which brings us to the great literary puzzle of James Macpherson and the poems of the legendary Ossian. A flurry of recent writing about the controversy has clarified some of the facts and it no longer seems possible – if it ever did – that Macpherson had gathered significant fragments of a lost Gaelic epic poem of the third century before publishing his 'translations' *Fingal* and *Temora* in 1761 and 1763. At the same time there has been a degree of rehabilitation of Macpherson as a writer and the prose poem we include, *Carthon*, in which a hero escapes from 'Balclutha' or Dumbarton by swimming to his waiting galleys, has some telling passages which perhaps go some way to explaining his enormous reputation at the time.

The Norse tradition of myth and legend is represented by four pieces. An old ballad, *The Great Silkie of Sule Skerry*, is followed by a short story, *Sealskin Trousers*, dealing with a repeating myth about close connections between humans and the silkies or seal-people. The latter piece, by Orcadian Eric Linklater, demonstrates the writer as mythmaker's ability to relate age-old tales and insights even into contemporary terms. Next comes John Buchan's story, *Skule Skerry*, which has Hitchcock-like images of seabirds and a meeting between myth and remote places – 'the Curdled Ocean with its strange beasts'. A second Linklater extract, this time in a chapter from *The Ultimate Viking*, shows the convergence beween myth and history in a chronicle of Orkney, resplendent with saga heroes like Ivor the Boneless and the Giant of Dovre.

We conclude this section with Robert Southey's version of a legend of later times, *The Inchcape Rock*. Which title is perhaps excuse enough to return to the geological metaphor – rock and water are agents of change in the landscape and seascape of Scotland, and resemble the ability of the human mind to constantly make and remake new visions, new myths and legends.

Sir Patrick Spens

ANONYMOUS

The king sits in Dunfermline town,
  Drinking the blood-red wine:
'O where will I get a skeely skipper,
  To sail this new ship of mine?'

O up and spake an eldern knight,
  Sat at the king's right knee:
'Sir Patrick Spens is the best sailor
  That ever sail'd the sea.'

Our king has written a braid letter,
  And seal'd it with his hand,
And sent it to Sir Patrick Spens,
  Was walking on the strand.

'To Noroway, to Noroway,
  To Noroway o'er the faem;
The king's daughter of Noroway,
  'Tis thou maun bring her hame.'

The first word that Sir Patrick read,
  Sae loud, loud laughèd he;
The neist word that Sir Patrick read,
  The tear blinded his e'e.

'O wha is this has done this deed,
  And tauld the king o' me,
To send me out at this time of the year
  To sail upon the sea?

'Be it wind, be it weet, be it hail, be it sleet,
  Our ship must sail the faem;
The king's daughter of Noroway,
  'Tis we must fetch her hame.'

They hoysed their sails on Monenday morn,
    Wi' a' the speed they may;
They hae landed in Noroway,
    Upon a Wodensday.

They hadna been a week, a week
    In Noroway but twae,
When that the lords o' Noroway
    Began aloud to say:

'Ye Scottishmen spend a' our king's goud,
    And a' our queenis fee!'
'Ye lie, ye lie, ye liars loud,
    Fu' loud I hear ye lie!

'For I brought as much white monie
    As gane my men and me,
And I brought a half fou o' gude red goud
    Out o'er the sea wi' me.

'Make ready, make ready, my merry men a',
    Our gude ship sails the morn':
'Now, ever alake! my master dear,
    I fear a deadly storm!

'I saw the new moon late yestreen,
    Wi' the auld moon in her arm;
And if we gang to sea, master,
    I fear we'll come to harm.'

They hadna sailed a league, a league,
    A league but barely three,
When the lift grew dark, and the wind blew loud,
    And gurly grew the sea.

The ankers brak, and the topmasts lap,
    It was sic a deadly storm,
And the waves came o'er the broken ship,
    Till a' her sides were torn.

'O where will I get a gude sailor,
    To take my helm in hand,
Till I get up to the tall topmast,
    To see if I can spy land?'

'O here am I, a sailor gude,
   To take the helm in hand,
Till you go up to the tall topmast,
   But I fear you'll ne'er spy land.'

He hadna gane a step, a step,
   A step but barely ane,
When a bout flew out of our goodly ship,
   And the salt sea it came in.

'Gae fetch a web o' the silken claith,
   Another o' the twine,
And wap them into our ship's side,
   And let na the sea come in.'

They fetched a web o' the silken claith,
   Another o' the twine,
And they wapped them roun' that gude ship's side,
   But still the sea came in.

O laith, laith were our gude Scots lords
   To weet their cork-heel'd shoon;
But lang or a' the play was play'd,
   They wat their hats aboon.

And mony was the feather-bed
   That flottered on the faem,
And mony was the gude lord's son
   That never mair cam hame.

The ladies wrang their fingers white,
   The maidens tore their hair,
A' for the sake of their true loves,
   For them they'll see nae mair.

O lang, lang may the ladies sit,
   Wi' their fans into their hand,
Before they see Sir Patrick Spens
   Come sailing to the strand.

And lang, lang may the maidens sit,
   Wi' their goud kames in their hair,
A' waiting for their ain dear loves,
   For them they'll see nae mair.

Half owre, half owre to Aberdour
  'Tis fifty fathoms deep,
And there lies gude Sir Patrick Spens,
  Wi' the Scots lords at his feet.

Sea Prayer

from Carmina Gadelica

TRADITIONAL
Translation by
Alexander Carmichael of Lismore

Helmsman: Blest be the boat.
Crew: God the Father bless her.
Helmsman: Blest be the boat.
Crew: God the Son bless her.
Helmsman: Blest be the boat.
Crew: God the Spirit bless her.
All: God the Father,
                    God the Son,
                    God the Spirit,
                       Bless the boat.
Helmsman: What can befall you
                    And God the Father with you?
Crew: No harm can befall us.
Helmsman: What can befall you
                    And God the Son with you?
Crew: No harm can befall us.
Helmsman: What can befall you
                    And God the Spirit with you?
Crew: No harm can befall us.
All: God the Father,
                    God the Son,
                    God the Spirit,
                       With us eternally.
Helmsman: What can cause you anxiety
                    And the God of the elements over you?
Crew: No anxiety can be ours.
Helmsman: What can cause you anxiety
                    And the King of the elements over you?
Crew: No anxiety can be ours.
Helmsman: What can cause you anxiety
                    And the Spirit of the elements over you?

Crew: No anxiety can be ours.
All: The God of the elements,
                The King of the elements,
                The Spirit of the elements,
                Close over us,
                    Ever eternally.

Sealskin Trousers

ERIC LINKLATER (1899–1974)

Linklater returns in this short story to a legend which occurs in many forms throughout the Northern Isles (and the Hebrides) – that of the silkies or sea-people. The essential story can be found in the ballad on the preceding pages, The Great Silkie of Sule Skerry, *and is probably of great age; in it we learn of these enchanted creatures who resemble the mermen of other climes, but who have the power to go without their seal skins in order to pass as humans. They can take human partners – indeed some island families claim to trace their descent from such liaisons. Even to the modern sceptic the soulful eyes of a seal can have human appeal, and, interestingly, biologists tell us that seals represent a reversion to aquatic habitat from ancestral land-dwelling mammals.*

Linklater, as an Orcadian, was familiar with the legend and here turns it to his own purposes, making a wry commentary on manners and relationships. He sets the seduction of human girl by sea-man within the heavily ironic, nightmarish account of an observer, but gives the story flashes of humour like the explanation given by the silkie – 'the only seal-man who has ever become a Master of Arts of Edinburgh University' – of the 'trouser-convention':

'I needn't tell you,' he said, 'the conventional reasons for wearing trousers. There are people, I know, who sneer at all conventions, and some conventions deserve their sneering. But not the trouser-convention. No, indeed! So we can admit the necessity of the garment, and pass to consideration of the material.'

There is satirical comment, too, on human society and we can read the silkie as a metaphor for a world unspoiled by human interference, as well as Linklater's delightful symbol of freedom:

Human beings have to carry their weight about, and they don't know how blissful it is to be unconscious of weight: to be wave-borne, to float on the idle sea, to leap without effort in a curving wave, and look up at the dazzle of the sky through a smother of white water.

I am not mad. It is necessary to realise that, to accept it as a fact about which there can be no dispute. I have been seriously ill for some weeks, but that was the result of shock. A double or conjoint shock: for as well as the obvious concussion of a brutal event, there was the more dreadful necessity of recognising the material evidence of a happening so monstrously implausible that even my friends here, who in general are quite extraordinarily kind and understanding, will not believe in the occurrence, though they cannot deny it or otherwise explain – I mean explain away – the clear and simple testimony of what was left.

I, of course, realised very quickly what had happened, and since then I have more than once remembered that poor Coleridge teased his unquiet mind, quite unnecessarily in his case, with just such a possibility; or impossibility, as the world would call it. 'If a man could pass through Paradise in a dream,' he wrote, 'and have a flower presented to him as a pledge that his soul had really been there, and if he found that flower in his hand when he woke – Ay, and what then?'

But what if he had dreamt of Hell and wakened with his hand burnt by the fire? Or of Chaos, and seen another face stare at him from the looking-glass? Coleridge does not push the question far. He was too timid. But I accepted the evidence, and while I was ill I thought seriously about the whole proceeding, in detail and in sequence of detail. I thought, indeed, about little else. To begin with, I admit, I was badly shaken, but gradually my mind cleared and my vision improved, and because I was patient and persevering – that needed discipline – I can now say that I know what happened. I have indeed, by a conscious intellectual effort, *seen and heard* what happened. This is how it began . . .

How very unpleasant! she thought.

She had come down the great natural steps on the sea-cliff to the ledge that narrowly gave access, round the angle of it, to the western face which to-day was sheltered from the breeze and warmed by the afternoon sun. At the beginning of the week she and her fiancé, Charles Sellin, had found their way to an almost hidden shelf, a deep veranda sixty feet above the white-veined water. It was rather bigger than a billiard-table and nearly as private as an abandoned lighthouse. Twice they had spent some blissful hours there. She had a good head for heights, and Sellin was indifferent to scenery. There had been nothing vulgar, no physical contact, in their bliss together on this oceanic gazebo, for on each occasion she had been reading Héaloin's *Studies in Biology* and he Lenin's *What is to be Done?*

Their relations were already marital, not because their mutual passion could brook no pause, but rather out of fear lest their friends might despise them for chastity and so conjecture some oddity or impotence in their nature. Their behaviour, however, was very decently circumspect, and they already conducted themselves, in public and out of doors, as if they had been married for several years. They did not regard the seclusion of the cliffs as an opportunity for secret embracing, but were content that the sun should warm and colour their skin; and let their anxious minds be soothed by the surge and cavernous colloquies of the sea. Now, while Charles was writing letters in the little fishing-hotel a mile away, she had come back to their sandstone ledge, and Charles would join her in an hour or two. She was still reading *Studies in Biology*.

But their gazebo, she perceived, was already occupied, and occupied by a person of the most embarrassing appearance. He was quite unlike Charles. He was not only naked, but obviously robust, brown-hued, and extremely hairy. He sat on the very edge of the rock, dangling his legs over the sea, and down his spine ran a ridge of hair like the dark stripe on a donkey's back, and on his shoulder-blades grew patches of hair like the wings of a bird. Unable in her disappointment to be sensible and leave at once, she lingered for a moment and saw to her relief that he was not quite naked. He wore trousers of a dark brown colour, very low at the waist, but sufficient to cover his haunches. Even so, even with that protection for her modesty, she could not stay and read biology in his company.

To show her annoyance, and let him become aware of it, she made a little impatient sound; and turning to go, looked back to see if he had heard.

He swung himself round and glared at her, more angry on the instant than she had been. He had thick eyebrows, large dark eyes, a broad snub nose, a big mouth. 'You're Roger Fairfield!' she exclaimed in surprise.

He stood up and looked at her intently. 'How do you know?' he asked.

'Because I remember you,' she answered, but then felt a little confused, for what she principally remembered was the brief notoriety he had acquired, in his final year at Edinburgh University, by swimming on a rough autumn day from North Berwick to the Bass Rock to win a bet of five pounds.

The story had gone briskly round the town for a week, and everybody knew that he and some friends had been lunching, too well for caution, before the bet was made. His friends, however, grew quickly sober when he took to the water, and in a great fright informed the police, who called out the lifeboat. But they searched in vain, for the sea was running high, until in calm water under the shelter of the Bass they saw his head, dark on the water, and pulled him aboard. He seemed none the worse for his adventure, but the police charged him with disorderly behaviour and he was fined two pounds for swimming without a regulation costume.

'We met twice,' she said, 'once at a dance and once in Mackie's when we had coffee together. About a year ago. There were several of us there, and we knew the man you came in with. I remember you perfectly.'

He stared the harder, his eyes narrowing, a vertical wrinkle dividing his forehead. 'I'm a little short-sighted too,' she said with a nervous laugh.

'My sight's very good,' he answered, 'but I find it difficult to recognise people. Human beings are so much alike.'

'That's one of the rudest remarks I've ever heard!'

'Surely not?'

'Well, one does like to be remembered. It isn't pleasant to be told that one's a nonentity.'

He made an impatient gesture. 'That isn't what I meant, and I do recognise you now. I remember your voice. You have a distinctive voice and a pleasant one. F sharp in the octave below middle C is your note.'

'Is that the only way in which you can distinguish people?'

'It's as good as any other.'

'But you don't remember my name?'

'No,' he said.

'I'm Elizabeth Barford.'

He bowed and said, 'Well, it was a dull party, wasn't it? The occasion, I mean, when we drank coffee together.'

'I don't agree with you. I thought it was very amusing, and we all enjoyed ourselves. Do you remember Charles Sellin?'

'No.'

'Oh, you're hopeless,' she exclaimed. 'What is the good of meeting people if you're going to forget all about them?'

'I don't know,' he said. 'Let us sit down, and you can tell me.'

He sat again on the edge of the rock, his legs dangling, and looking over his shoulder at her, said, 'Tell me: what is the good of meeting people?'

She hesitated, and answered, 'I like to make friends. That's quite natural, isn't it? – But I came here to read.'

'Do you read standing?'

'Of course not,' she said, and smoothing her skirt tidily over her knees, sat down beside him. 'What a wonderful place this is for a holiday. Have you been here before?'

'Yes, I know it well.'

'Charles and I came a week ago. Charles Sellin, I mean, whom you don't remember. We're going to be married, you know. In about a year, we hope.'

'Why did you come here?'

'We wanted to be quiet, and in these islands one is fairly secure against interruption. We're both working quite hard.'

'Working!' he mocked. 'Don't waste time, waste your life instead.'

'Most of us have to work, whether we like it or not.'

He took the book from her lap and, opening it, read idly a few lines, turned a dozen pages and read with a yawn another paragraph.

'Your friends in Edinburgh,' she said, 'were better-off than ours. Charles and I, and all the people we know, have got to make our living.'

'Why?' he asked.

'Because if we don't we shall starve,' she snapped.

'And if you avoid starvation – what then?'

'It's possible to hope,' she said stiffly, 'that we shall be of some use in the world.'

'Do you agree with this?' he asked, smothering a second yawn, and read from the book: '*The physical factor in a germ-cell is beyond our analysis or assessment, but can we deny subjectivity to the primordial initiatives? It is easier, perhaps, to assume that mind comes late in development, but the assumption must not be established on the grounds that we can certainly deny self-expression to the cell. It is common knowledge that the mind may influence the body both greatly and in little unseen ways; but how it is done, we do not know. Psychobiology is still in its infancy.*'

'It's fascinating, isn't it?' she said.

'How do you propose,' he asked, 'to be of use to the world?'

'Well, the world needs people who have been educated – educated to think – and one does hope to have a little influence in some way.'

'Is a little influence going to make any difference? Don't you think that what the world needs is to develop a new sort of mind? It needs a new primordial directive, or quite a lot of them, perhaps. But psychobiology is still in its infancy, and you don't know how such changes come about, do you? And you can't foresee when you *will* know, can you?'

'No, of course not. But science is advancing so quickly—'

'In fifty thousand years?' he interrupted. 'Do you think you will know by then?'

'It's difficult to say,' she answered seriously, and was gathering her thoughts for a careful reply when again he interrupted, rudely, she thought, and quite irrelevantly. His attention had strayed from her and her book to the sea beneath, and he was looking down as though searching for something. 'Do you swim?' he asked.

'Rather well,' she said.

'I went in just before high water, when the weed down there was all brushed in the opposite direction. You never get bored by the sea, do you?'

'I've never seen enough of it,' she said. 'I want to live on an island, a little island, and hear it all round me.'

'That's very sensible of you,' he answered with more warmth in his voice. 'That's uncommonly sensible for a girl like you.'

'What sort of a girl do you think I am?' she demanded, vexation in her accent, but he ignored her and pointed his brown arm to the horizon: 'The colour has thickened within the last few minutes. The sea was quite pale on the skyline, and now it's a belt of indigo. And the writing has changed. The lines of foam on the water, I mean. Look at that! There's a submerged rock out there, and always, about half an hour after the ebb has started to run, but more clearly when there's an off-shore wind, you can see those two little whirlpools and the circle of white round them. You see the figure they make? It's like this, isn't it?'

With a splinter of stone he drew a diagram on the rock.

'Do you know what it is?' he asked. 'It's the figure the Chinese call the T'ai Chi. They say it represents the origin of all created things. And it's the sign manual of the sea.'

'But those lines of foam must run into every conceivable shape,' she protested.

'Oh, they do. They do indeed. But it isn't often you can read them. – There he is!' he exclaimed, leaning forward and staring into the water sixty feet below. 'That's him, the old villain!'

From his sitting position, pressing hard down with his hands and thrusting against the face of the rock with his heels, he hurled himself into space, and straightening in mid-air broke the smooth green surface of the water with no more splash than a harpoon would have made. A solitary razorbill, sunning himself on a shelf below, fled hurriedly out to sea, and half a dozen white birds, startled by the sudden movement, rose in the air crying 'Kittiwake! Kittiwake!'

Elizabeth screamed loudly, scrambled to her feet with clumsy speed, then knelt again on the edge of the rock and peered down. In the slowly heaving clear water she could see a pale shape moving, now striped by the dark weed that grew in tangles under the flat foot of the rock, now lost in the shadowy deepness where the tangles were rooted. In a minute or two his head rose from the sea, he shook bright drops from his hair, and looked up at her, laughing. Firmly grasped in his right hand, while he trod water, he held up an enormous blue-black lobster for her admiration. Then he threw it on to the flat rock beside him, and swiftly climbing out of the sea, caught it again and held it, cautious of its bite, till he found a piece of string in his trouser-pocket. He shouted to her, 'I'll tie its claws, and you can take it home for your supper!'

She had not thought it possible to climb the sheer face of the cliff, but from its forefoot he mounted by steps and handholds invisible from above, and pitching the tied lobster on to the floor of the gazebo, came nimbly over the edge.

'That's a bigger one than you've ever seen in your life before,' he boasted. 'He weighs fourteen pounds, I'm certain of it. Fourteen pounds at least. Look at the size of his right claw! He could crack a coconut with that. He tried to crack my ankle when I was swimming an hour ago, and got into his hole before I could catch him. But I've caught him now, the brute. He's had more than twenty years of crime, that black boy. He's twenty-four or twenty-five by the look of him. He's older than you, do you realise that? Unless you're a lot older than you look. How old are you?'

But Elizabeth took no interest in the lobster. She had retreated until she stood with her back to the rock, pressed hard against it, the palms of her hands fumbling on the stone as if feeling for a secret lock or bolt that might give her entrance into it. Her face was white, her lips pale and tremulous.

He looked round at her, when she made no answer, and asked what the matter was.

Her voice was faint and frightened. 'Who are you?' she whispered, and the whisper broke into a stammer. 'What are you?'

His expression changed and his face, with the water-drops on it, grew hard as a rock shining undersea. 'It's only a few minutes,' he said, 'since you appeared to know me quite well. You addressed me as Roger Fairfield, didn't you?'

'But a name's not everything. It doesn't tell you enough.'

'What more do you want to know?'

Her voice was so strained and thin that her words were like the shadow of words, or words shivering in the cold: 'To jump like that, into the sea – it wasn't human!'

The coldness of his face wrinkled to a frown. 'That's a curious remark to make.'

'You would have killed yourself if – if—'

He took a seaward step again, looked down at the calm green depths below, and said, 'You're exaggerating, aren't you? It's not much more than fifty feet, sixty perhaps, and the water's deep. – Here, come back! Why are you running away?'

'Let me go!' she cried. 'I don't want to stay here. I – I'm frightened.'

'That's unfortunate. I hadn't expected this to happen.'

'Please let me go!'

'I don't think I shall. Not until you've told me what you're frightened of.'

'Why,' she stammered, 'why do you wear fur trousers?'

He laughed, and still laughing caught her round the waist and pulled her towards the edge of the rock. 'Don't be alarmed,' he said. 'I'm not going to throw you over. But if you insist on a conversation about trousers, I think we should sit down again. Look at the smoothness of the water, and its colour, and the light in the depths of it: have you ever seen anything lovelier? Look at the sky: that's calm enough, isn't it? Look at that fulmar sailing past: he's not worrying, so why should you?'

She leaned away from him, all her weight against the hand that held her waist, but his arm was strong and he seemed unaware of any strain on it. Nor did he pay attention to the distress she was in – she was sobbing dryly, like a child who has cried too long – but continued talking in a light and pleasant conversational tone until the muscles of her body tired and relaxed, and she sat within his enclosing arm, making no more effort to escape, but timorously conscious of his hand upon her side so close beneath her breast.

'I needn't tell you,' he said, 'the conventional reasons for wearing trousers. There are people, I know, who sneer at all conventions, and some conventions deserve their sneering. But not the trouser-convention. No, indeed! So we can admit the necessity of the garment, and pass to consideration of the material. Well, I like sitting on rocks, for one thing, and for such a hobby this is the best stuff in the world. It's very durable, yet soft and comfortable. I can slip into the sea for half an hour without doing it any harm, and when I come out to sun myself on the rock again, it doesn't feel cold and clammy. Nor does it fade in the sun or shrink with the wet. Oh, there are plenty of reasons for having one's trousers made of stuff like this.'

'And there's a reason,' she said, 'that you haven't told me.'

'Are you quite sure of that?'

She was calmer now, and her breathing was controlled. But her face was still white, and her lips were softly nervous when she asked him, 'Are you going to kill me?'

'Kill you? Good heavens, no! Why should I do that?'

'For fear of my telling other people.'

'And what precisely would you tell them?'

'You know.'

'You jump to conclusions far too quickly: that's your trouble. Well, it's a pity for your sake, and a nuisance for me. I don't think I can let you take that lobster home for your supper after all. I don't, in fact, think you will go home for your supper.'

Her eyes grew dark again with fear, her mouth opened, but before she could speak he pulled her to him and closed it, not asking leave, with a roughly occludent kiss.

'That was to prevent you from screaming. I hate to hear people scream,' he told her, smiling as he spoke. 'But this' – he kissed her again, now gently and in a more protracted embrace – 'that was because I wanted to.'

'You mustn't!' she cried.

'But I have,' he said.

'I don't understand myself! I can't understand what has happened—'

'Very little yet,' he murmured.

'Something terrible has happened!'

'A kiss? Am I so repulsive?'

'I don't mean that. I mean something inside me. I'm not – at least I think I'm not – I'm not frightened now!'

'You have no reason to be.'

'I have every reason in the world. But I'm not! I'm not frightened – but I want to cry.'

'Then cry,' he said soothingly, and made her pillow her cheek against his breast. 'But you can't cry comfortably with that ridiculous contraption on your nose.'

He took from her the horn-rimmed spectacles she wore, and threw them into the sea.

'Oh!' she exclaimed. 'My glasses! – Oh, why did you do that? Now I can't see. I can't see at all without my glasses!'

'It's all right,' he assured her. 'You really won't need them. The refraction,' he added vaguely, 'will be quite different.'

As if this small but unexpected act of violence had brought to the boiling-point her desire for tears, they bubbled over, and because she threw her arms about him in a sort of fond despair, and snuggled close, sobbing vigorously still, he felt the warm drops trickle down his skin, and from his skin she drew into her eyes the saltness of the sea, which made her weep the more. He stroked her hair with a strong but soothing hand,

and when she grew calm and lay still in his arms, her emotion spent, he sang quietly to a little enchanting tune a song that began:

> *'I am a Man upon the land,*
> *I am a Selkie in the sea,*
> *And when I'm far from every strand*
> *My home it is on Sule Skerry.'*

After the first verse or two she freed herself from his embrace, and sitting up listened gravely to the song. Then she asked him, 'Shall I ever understand?'

'It's not a unique occurrence,' he told her. 'It has happened quite often before, as I suppose you know. In Cornwall and Brittany and among the Western Isles of Scotland; that's where people have always been interested in seals, and understood them a little, and where seals from time to time have taken human shape. The one thing that's unique in our case, in my metamorphosis, is that I am the only seal-man who has ever become a Master of Arts of Edinburgh University. Or, I believe, of any university. I am the unique and solitary example of a sophisticated seal-man.'

'I must look a perfect fright,' she said. 'It was silly of me to cry. Are my eyes very red?'

'The lids are a little pink – not unattractively so – but your eyes are as dark and lovely as a mountain pool in October, on a sunny day in October. They're much improved since I threw your spectacles away.'

'I needed them, you know. I feel quite stupid without them. But tell me why you came to the University – and how? How could you do it?'

'My dear girl – what is your name, by the way? I've quite forgotten.'

'Elizabeth!' she said angrily.

'I'm so glad, it's my favourite human name. – But you don't really want to listen to a lecture on psychobiology?'

'I want to know *how*. You must tell me!'

'Well, you remember, don't you, what your book says about the primordial initiatives? But it needs a footnote there to explain that they're not exhausted till quite late in life. The germ-cells, as you know, are always renewing themselves, and they keep their initiatives though they nearly always follow the chosen pattern except in the case of certain illnesses, or under special direction. The direction of the mind, that is. And the glands have got a lot to do in a full metamorphosis, the renal first and then the pituitary, as you would expect. It isn't approved of – making the change, I mean – but every now and then one of us does it, just for a frolic in the general way, but in my case there was a special reason.'

'Tell me,' she said again.

'it's too long a story.'

'I want to know.'

'There's been a good deal of unrest, you see, among my people in the last few years: doubt, and dissatisfaction with our leaders, and scepticism about traditional beliefs – all that sort of thing. We've had a lot of discussion under the surface of the sea about the nature of man, for instance. We had always been taught to believe certain things about him, and recent events didn't seem to bear out what our teachers told us. Some of our younger people got dissatisfied, so I volunteered to go ashore and investigate. I'm still considering the report I shall have to make, and that's why I'm living, at present, a double life. I come ashore to think, and go back to the sea to rest.

'And what do you think of us?' she asked.

'You're interesting. Very interesting indeed. There are going to be some curious mutations among you before long. Within three or four thousand years, perhaps.'

He stooped and rubbed a little smear of blood from his shin. 'I scratched it on a limpet,' he said. 'The limpets, you know, are the same to-day as they were four hundred thousand years ago. But human beings aren't nearly so stable.'

'Is that your main impression, that humanity's unstable?'

'That's part of it. But from our point of view there's something much more upsetting. Our people, you see, are quite simple creatures, and because we have relatively few beliefs, we're very much attached to them. Our life is a life of sensation – not entirely, but largely – and we ought to be extremely happy. We were, so long as we were satisfied with sensation and a short undisputed creed. We have some advantages over human beings, you know. Human beings have to carry their own weight about, and they don't know how blissful it is to be unconscious of weight: to be wave-borne, to float on the idle sea, to leap without effort in a curving wave, and look up at the dazzle of the sky through a smother of white water, or dive so easily to the calmness far below and take a haddock from the weed-beds in a sudden rush of appetite. – Talking of haddocks,' he said, 'it's getting late. It's nearly time for fish. And I must give you some instruction before we go. The preliminary phase takes a little while, about five minutes for you, I should think, and then you'll be another creature.'

She gasped, as though already she felt the water's chill, and whispered, 'Not yet! Not yet, please.'

He took her in his arms, and expertly, with a strong caressing hand, stroked her hair, stroked the roundness of her head and the back of her neck and her shoulders, feeling her muscles moving to his touch, and down the hollow of her back to her waist and hips. The head again, neck, shoulders, and spine. Again and again. Strongly and firmly his hand gave her calmness, and presently she whispered, 'You're sending me to sleep.'

'My God!' he exclaimed, 'you mustn't do that! Stand up, stand up, Elizabeth!'

'Yes,' she said, obeying him. 'Yes, Roger. Why did you call yourself Roger? Roger Fairfield?'

'I found the name in a drowned sailor's pay-book. What does that matter now? Look at me, Elizabeth!'

She looked at him, and smiled.

His voice changed, and he said happily, 'You'll be the prettiest seal between Shetland and the Scillies. Now listen. Listen carefully.'

He held her lightly and whispered in her ear. Then kissed her on the lips and cheek, and bending her head back, on the throat. He looked, and saw the colour come deeply into her face.

'Good,' he said. 'That's the first stage. The adrenalin's flowing nicely now. You know about the pituitary, don't you? That makes it easy then. There are two parts in the pituitary gland, the anterior and posterior lobes, and both must act together. It's not difficult, and I'll tell you how.'

Then he whispered again, most urgently, and watched her closely. In a little while he said, 'And now you can take it easy. Let's sit down and wait till you're ready. The actual change won't come till we go down.'

'But it's working,' she said, quietly and happily. 'I can feel it working.'

'Of course it is.'

She laughed triumphantly, and took his hand.

'We've got nearly five minutes to wait,' he said.

'What will it be like? What shall I feel, Roger?'

'The water moving against your side, the sea caressing you and holding you.'

'Shall I be sorry for what I've left behind?'

'No, I don't think so.'

'You didn't like us, then? Tell me what you discovered in the world.'

'Quite simply,' he said, 'that we had been deceived.'

'But I don't know what your belief had been.'

'Haven't I told you? – Well, we in our innocence respected you because you could work, and were willing to work. That seemed to us truly heroic. We don't work at all, you see, and you'll be much happier when you come to us. We who live in the sea don't struggle to keep our heads above water.'

'All my friends worked hard,' she said. 'I never knew anyone who was idle. We had to work, and most of us worked for a good purpose; or so we thought. But you didn't think so?'

'Our teachers had told us,' he said, 'that men endured the burden of human toil to create a surplus of wealth that would give them leisure from the daily task of breadwinning. And in their hard-won leisure, our teachers said, men cultivated wisdom and charity and the fine arts; and became aware of God. – But that's not a true description of the world, is it?'

'No,' she said, 'that's not the truth.'

'No,' he repeated, 'our teachers were wrong, and we've been deceived.'

'Men are always being deceived, but they get accustomed to learning the facts too late. They grow accustomed to deceit itself.'

'You are braver than we, perhaps. My people will not like to be told the truth.'

'I shall be with you,' she said, and took his hand. But still he stared gloomily at the moving sea.

The minutes passed, and presently she stood up and with quick fingers put off her clothes. 'It's time,' she said.

He looked at her, and his gloom vanished like the shadow of a cloud that the wind has hurried on, and exultation followed like sunlight spilling from the burning edge of a cloud. 'I wanted to punish them,' he cried, 'for robbing me of my faith, and now, by God, I'm punishing them hard. I'm robbing their treasury now, the inner vault of all their treasury! – I hadn't guessed you were so beautiful! The waves when you swim will catch a burnish from you, the sand will shine like silver when you lie down to sleep, and if you can teach the red sea-ware to blush so well, I shan't miss the roses of your world.'

'Hurry,' she said.

He, laughing softly, loosened the leather thong that tied his trousers, stepped out of them, and lifted her in his arms. 'Are you ready?' he asked.

She put her arms round his neck and softly kissed his cheek. Then with a great shout he leapt from the rock, from the little veranda, into the green silk calm of the water far below . . .

I heard the splash of their descent – I am quite sure I heard the splash – as I came round the corner of the cliff, by the ledge that leads to the little rock veranda, our gazebo, as we called it, but the first thing I noticed, that really attracted my attention, was an enormous blue-black lobster, its huge claws tied with string, that was moving in a rather ludicrous fashion towards the edge. I think it fell over just before I left, but I wouldn't swear to that. Then I saw her book, the *Studies in Biology*, and her clothes.

Her white linen frock with the brown collar and the brown belt, some other garments, and her shoes were all there. And beside them, lying across her shoes, was a pair of sealskin trousers.

I realised immediately, or almost immediately, what had happened. Or so it seems to me now. And if, as I firmly believe, my apprehension was instantaneous, the faculty of intuition is clearly more important than I had previously supposed. I have, of course, as I said before, given the matter a great deal of thought during my recent illness, but the impression remains that I understood what had happened in a flash, to use a common but illuminating phrase. And no one, need I say? has been able to refute my intuition. No one, that is, has found an alternative explanation for the presence, beside Elizabeth's linen frock, of a pair of sealskin trousers.

I remember also my physical distress at the discovery. My breath, for several minutes I think, came into and went out of my lungs like the hot wind of a dust-storm in the desert. It parched my mouth and grated in my throat. It was, I recall, quite a torment to breathe. But I had to, of course.

Nor did I lose control of myself in spite of the agony, both mental and physical, that I was suffering. I didn't lose control till they began to mock me. Yes, they did, I assure you of that. I heard his voice quite clearly, and honesty compels me to admit that it was singularly sweet and the tune was the most haunting I have ever heard. They were about forty yards away, two seals swimming together, and the evening light was so clear and taut that his voice might have been the vibration of an invisible bow across its coloured bands. He was singing the song that Elizabeth and I had discovered in an album of Scottish music in the little fishing-hotel where we had been living:

> '*I am a Man upon the land,*
> *I am a Selkie in the sea,*
> *And when I'm far from any strand*
> *I am at home on Sule Skerry!*'

But his purpose, you see, was mockery. They were happy, together in the vast simplicity of the ocean, and I, abandoned to the terror of life alone, life among human beings, was lost and full of panic. It was then I began to scream. I could hear myself screaming, it was quite horrible. But I couldn't stop. I had to go on screaming . . .

Skule Skerry

from The Runagates Club

JOHN BUCHAN (1875–1940)

In this short story, taken from the collection, The Runagates Club
*(1928), Buchan takes for a setting the northern latitudes which figure
in many of his stories and novels. He infuses the tale with his usual
intense sense of place; for example: 'that curious quality of light that
you get up in the North . . . a sort of essence of light, cold and pure
and distilled'.*

*Actually, though, the location of the story, in the 'Norland Islands', is an
invention – a sort of distilled essence of Orkney, Shetland and other places,
with placenames invented or transplanted by Buchan. Even the islet in the
title, Skule Skerry, is a reworking of the Sule Skerry of the old ballad.
Along with the cod-topography there is some clever cod-scholarship.
Antony Hurrell, one of Buchan's typical spinners of 'yarns' who has
spent much of his life 'in places so remote that his friends could with
difficulty find them on the map' (here Buchan seems to be letting us in
on the spoof), makes reference to a dubious 'Saga of Earl Skuli' alongside
the real 'Adam of Bremen'.*

*In many ways this is a light piece, suitable for telling to Runagates
cronies like Lord Lamancha, who have all knocked around the world
a bit, and there is some of Buchan's usual pseudo-science – 'By some
alchemy of nature, at which I could only guess, [Skule Skerry] was on
the track by which the North exercised its spell, a cableway for the
magnetism of that cruel frozen Uttermost'. However, it is never less
than gripping, and this story, by the minister's son born in Perth, has at
times a touch of the grand alienation of his masterpiece, the posthumous*
Sick Heart River*:*

> It was like being in a small boat in mid-Atlantic – but worse, if you
> understand me, for that would have been loneliness in the midst of
> a waste which was nevertheless surrounded and traversed by the
> works of man, whereas now I felt I was clean outside man's ken.
> I had come somehow to the edge of that world where life is, and
> was very close to the world which has only death in it.

Mr Anthony Hurrell was a small man, thin to the point of emaciation, but erect as a ramrod and wiry as a cairn terrier. There was no grey in his hair, and his pale far-sighted eyes had the alertness of youth, but his lean face was so wrinkled by weather that in certain lights it looked almost venerable, and young men, who at first sight had imagined him their contemporary, presently dropped into the 'sir' reserved for indisputable seniors. His actual age was, I believe, somewhere in the forties. He had inherited a small property in Northumberland, where he had accumulated a collection of the rarer wildfowl; but much of his life had been spent in places so remote that his friends could with difficulty find them on the map. He had written a dozen ornithological monographs, was joint editor of the chief modern treatise on British birds, and had been the first man to visit the *tundras* of the Yenisei. He spoke little and that with an agreeable hesitation, but his ready smile, his quick interest, and the impression he gave of having a fathomless knowledge of strange modes of life, made him a popular and intriguing figure among his friends. Of his doings in the War he told us nothing; what we knew of them – and they were sensational enough in all conscience – we learned elsewhere. It was Nightingale's story which drew him from his customary silence. At the dinner following that event he made certain comments on current explanations of the super-normal. 'I remember once,' he began, and before we knew he had surprised us by embarking on a tale.

He had scarcely begun before he stopped. 'I'm boring you,' he said deprecatingly. 'There's nothing much in the story ... You see, it all happened, so to speak, inside my head ... I don't want to seem an egotist ...'

'Don't be an ass, Tony,' said Lamancha. 'Every adventure takes place chiefly inside the head of somebody. Go on. We're all attention.'

'It happened a good many years ago,' Hurrell continued, 'when I was quite a young man. I wasn't the cold scientist then that I fancy I am to-day. I took up birds in the first instance chiefly because they fired what imagination I possess. They fascinated me, for they seemed of all created things the nearest to pure spirit – those little beings with a normal temperature of 125°. Think of it. The goldcrest, with a stomach no bigger than a bean, flies across the North Sea! The curlew sandpiper, which breeds so far north that only about three people have ever seen its nest, goes to Tasmania for its holidays! So I always went bird-hunting with a queer sense of expectation and a bit of a tremor, as if I were walking very near the boundaries of the things we are not allowed to know. I felt this especially in the migration season. The small atoms, coming God knows whence and going God knows whither, were sheer mystery – they belonged to a world built in different dimensions from ours. I don't know what I expected, but I was always waiting for something, as much in a flutter as a girl at her first ball. You must realise that mood of mine to understand what fellows.

'One year I went to the Norland Islands for the spring migration. Plenty of people do the same, but I had the notion to do something a little different. I had a theory that migrants go north and south on a fairly narrow road. They have their corridors in the air as clearly defined as a highway, and keep an inherited memory of these corridors, like the stout conservatives they are. So I didn't go to the Blue Banks or to Noop or to Hermaness or any of the obvious places, where birds might be expected to make their first landfall.

'At that time I was pretty well read in the sagas, and had taught myself Icelandic for the purpose. Now it is written in the Saga of Earl Skuli, which is part of the Jarla Saga or Saga of the Earls, that Skuli, when he was carving out his earldom in the Scots islands, had much to do with a place called the Isle of the Birds. It is mentioned repeatedly, and the saga-man has a lot to say about the amazing multitude of birds there. It couldn't have been an ordinary gullery, for the Northmen saw too many of these to think them worth mentioning. I got it into my head that it must have been one of the alighting places of the migrants, and was probably as busy a spot to-day as in the eleventh century. The saga said it was near Halmarsness, and that is on the west side of the island of Una, so to Una I decided to go. I fairly got that Isle of Birds on the brain. From the map it might be any one of a dozen skerries under the shadow of Halmarsness.

'I remember that I spent a good many hours in the British Museum before I started, hunting up the scanty records of those parts. I found – I think it was in Adam of Bremen – that a succession of holy men had lived on the isle, and that a chapel had been built there and endowed by Earl Rognvald, which came to an end in the time of Malise of Strathearn. There was a bare mention of the place, but the chronicler had one curious note. "Insula Avium," ran the text, "quae est ultima insula et proxima Abysso." I wondered what on earth he meant. The place was not ultimate in any geographical sense, neither the farthest north nor the farthest west of the Norlands. And what was the "abyss"? In monkish Latin the word generally means Hell – Bunyan's Bottomless Pit – and sometimes the grave; but neither meaning seemed to have much to do with an ordinary sea skerry.

'I arrived at Una about eight o'clock in a May evening, having been put across from Voss in a flit-boat. It was a quiet evening, the sky without clouds but so pale as to be almost grey, the sea grey also but with a certain iridescence in it, and the low lines of the land a combination of hard greys and umbers, cut into by the harder white of the lighthouse. I can never find words to describe that curious quality of light that you get up in the North. Sometimes it is like looking at the world out of deep water – Farquharson used to call it "milky", and one saw what he meant. Generally it is a sort of essence of light, cold and pure and distilled, as if it were reflected from snow. There is no colour in it, and it makes thin shadows. Some people find it horribly depressing – Farquharson said it reminded him of a churchyard in the early morning where all his friends were buried – but personally I found it tonic and comforting. But it made me feel very near the edge of the world.

'There was no inn, so I put up at the post office, which was on a causeway between a fresh-water loch and a sea voe, so that from the doorstep you could catch brown trout on one side and sea-trout on the other. Next morning I set off for Halmarsness, which lay five miles to the west over a flat moorland all puddled with tiny lochans. There seemed to be nearly as much water as land. Presently I came to a bigger loch under the lift of ground which was Halmarsness. There was a gap in the ridge through which I looked straight out to the Atlantic, and there in the middle distance was what I knew instinctively to be my island.

'It was perhaps a quarter of a mile long, low for the most part, but rising in the north to a grassy knoll beyond the reach of any tides. In parts it narrowed to a few yards' width, and the lower levels must often have been awash. But it was an island, not a reef, and I thought I could make out the remains of the monkish cell. I climbed Halmarsness, and there, with nesting skuas swooping angrily about my head, I got a better view. It was certainly my island, for the rest of the archipelago were inconsiderable skerries, and I realised that it might well be a resting-place for migrants, for the mainland cliffs were too thronged with piratical skuas and other jealous fowl to be comfortable for weary travellers.

'I sat for a long time on the headland looking down from the three hundred feet of basalt to the island half a mile off – the last bid of solid earth between me and Greenland. The sea was calm for Norland waters, but there was a snowy edging of surf to the skerries which told of a tide rip. Two miles farther south I could see the entrance to the famous Roost of Una, where, when tide and wind collide, there is a wall like a house, so that a small steamer cannot pass it. The only sign of human habitation was a little grey farm in the lowlands toward the Roost, but the place was full of the evidence of man – a herd of Norland ponies, each tagged with its owner's name – grazing sheep of the piebald Norland breed – a broken barbed-wire fence that drooped over the edge of the cliff. I was only an hour's walk from a telegraph office, and a village which got its newspapers not more than three days late. It was a fine spring noon, and in the empty bright land there was scarcely a shadow . . . All the same, as I looked down at the island I did not wonder that it had been selected for attention by the saga-man and had been reputed holy. For it had an air of concealing something, though it was as bare as a billiard-table. It was an intruder, an irrelevance in the picture, planted there by some celestial caprice. I decided forthwith to make my camp on it, and the decision, inconsequently enough, seemed to me to be something of a venture.

'That was the view taken by John Ronaldson, when I talked to him after dinner. John was the post-mistress's son, more fisherman than crofter, like all Norlanders, a skilful sailor and an adept at the dipping lug, and noted for his knowledge of the western coast. He had difficulty in understanding my plan, and when he identified my island he protested.

'"Not Skule Skerry!" he cried. "What would take ye there, man? Ye'll get a' the birds ye want on Halmarsness and a far better bield. Ye'll be blawn away on the skerry, if the wund rises."

'I explained to him my reasons as well as I could, and I answered his fears about a gale by pointing out that the island was sheltered by the cliffs from the prevailing winds, and could be scourged only from the south, south-west, or west, quarters from which the wind rarely blew in May. "It'll be cauld," he said, "and wat." I pointed out that I had a tent and was accustomed to camping. "Ye'll starve" – I expounded my proposed methods of commissariat. "It'll be an ill job getting ye on and off" – but after cross-examination he admitted that ordinarily the tides were not difficult, and that I could get a rowboat to a beach below the farm I had seen – its name was Sgurravoe. Yet when I had said all this he still raised objections, till I asked him flatly what was the matter with Skule Skerry.

'"Naebody gangs there," he said gruffly.

'"Why should they?" I asked. "I'm only going to watch the birds."

'But the fact that it was never visited seemed to stick in his throat, and he grumbled out something that surprised me. "It has an ill name," he said. But when I pressed him he admitted that there was no record of shipwreck or disaster to account for the ill name. He repeated the words "Skule Skerry" as if they displeased him. "Folk dinna gang near it. It has aye had an ill name. My grandfather used to say that the place wasna canny."

'Now your Norlander has nothing of the Celt in him, and is as different from the Hebridean as a Northumbrian from a Cornishman. They are a fine, upstanding, hard-headed race, almost pure Scandinavian in blood, but they have as little poetry in them as a Manchester Radical. I should have put them down as utterly free from superstition, and, in all my many visits to the islands, I have never yet come across a folk-tale – hardly even a historical legend. Yet here was John Ronaldson, with his weather-beaten face and stiff chin and shrewd blue eyes, declaring that an innocent-looking island "wasna canny", and showing the most remarkable disinclination to go near it.

'Of course all this only made me keener. Besides, it was called Skule Skerry, and the name could only come from Earl Skuli; so it was linked up authentically with the oddments of information I had collected in the British Museum – the Jarla Saga and Adam of Bremen and all the rest of it. John finally agreed to take me over next morning in his boat, and I spent the rest of the day in collecting my kit. I had a small tent, and a Wolseley valise and half a dozen rugs, and, since I had brought a big box of tinned stuffs from the Stores, all I needed was flour and meal and some simple groceries. I learned that there was a well on the island, and that I could count on sufficient driftwood for my fire, but to make certain I took a sack of coals and another of peats. So I set off next day in John's boat, ran with the wind through the Roost of Una when the tide was right, tacked up the coast, and came to the skerry early in the afternoon.

'You could see that John hated the place. We ran into a cove on the east side, and he splashed ashore as if he expected to have his landing opposed, looking all the time sharply about him. When he carried my stuff to a hollow under the knoll, which gave a certain amount of shelter, his head was always twisting round. To me the place seemed to be the last word in forgotten peace. The swell lipped gently on the reefs and the little pebbled beaches, and only the babble of gulls from Halmarsness broke the stillness.

'John was clearly anxious to get away, but he did his duty by me. He helped me to get the tent up, found a convenient place for my boxes, pointed out the well and filled my water bucket, and made a zareba of stones to protect my camp on the Atlantic side. We had brought a small dinghy along with us, and this was to be left with me, so that when I wanted I could row across to the beach at Sgurravoe. As his last service he fixed an old pail between two boulders on the summit of the knoll, and filled it with oily waste, so that it could be turned into a beacon.

'"Ye'll maybe want to come off," he said, "and the boat will maybe no be there. Kindle your flare, and they'll see it at Sgurravoe and get the word to me, and I'll come for ye though the Muckle Black Silkie himsel' was hunkerin' on the skerry."

'Then he looked up and sniffed the air. "I dinna like the set of the sky," he declared. "It's a bad weatherhead. There'll be mair wund than I like in the next four-and-twenty hours."

'So saying, he hoisted his sail, and presently was a speck on the waters towards the Roost. There was no need for him to hurry, for the tide was now wrong, and before he could pass the Roost he would have three hours to wait on this side of the Mull. But the man, usually so deliberate and imperturbable, had been in a fever to be gone.

'His departure left me in a curious mood of happy loneliness and pleasurable expectation. I was left solitary with the seas and the birds. I laughed to think that I had found a streak of superstition in the granite John. He and his Muckle Black Silkie! I knew the old legend of the North which tells how the Finns, the ghouls that live in the deeps of the ocean, can on occasion don a seal's skin and come to land to play havoc with mortals. But *diablerie* and this isle of mine were worlds apart. I looked at it as the sun dropped, drowsing in the opal-coloured tides, under a sky in which pale clouds made streamers like a spectral *aurora borealis*, and I thought that I had stumbled upon one of those places where Nature seems to invite one to her secrets. As the light died the sky was flecked as with the roots and branches of some great nebular tree. That would be the "weatherhead" of which John Ronaldson had spoken.

'I set my fire going, cooked my supper, and made everything snug for the night. I had been right in my guess about the migrants. It must have been about ten o'clock when they began to arrive – after my fire had died out and I was smoking my last pipe before getting into my sleeping-bag. A host of fieldfares settled gently on the south part of the skerry. A faint light lingered till after midnight, but it was not easy to distinguish the little creatures, for they were aware of my presence and did not alight within a dozen yards of me. But I made out bramblings and buntings and what I thought was the Greenland wheatear; also jack snipe and sanderling; and I believed from their cries that the curlew sandpiper and the whimbrel were there. I went to sleep in a state of high excitement, promising myself a fruitful time on the morrow.

'I slept badly, as one often does one's first night in the open. Several times I woke with a start, under the impression that I was in a boat rowing swiftly with the tide. And every time I woke I heard the flutter of myriad birds, as if a velvet curtain were being slowly switched along an oak floor. At last I fell into deeper sleep, and when I opened my eyes it was full day.

'The first thing that struck me was that it had got suddenly colder. The sky was stormily red in the east, and masses of woolly clouds were banking in the north. I lit my fire with numbed fingers and hastily made tea. I could see the nimbus of seafowl over Halmarsness, but there was only one bird left on my skerry. I was certain from its forked tail that it was a Sabine's gull, but before I got my glass out it was disappearing into the haze towards the north. The sight cheered and excited me, and I cooked my breakfast in pretty good spirits.

'That was literally the last bird that came near me, barring the ordinary shearwaters and gulls and cormorants that nested round about Halmarsness. (There was not one single nest of any sort on the island. I had heard of that happening before in places which were regular halting-grounds for migrants.) The travellers must have had an inkling of the coming weather and were waiting somewhere well to the south. For about nine o'clock it began to blow. Great God, how it blew! You must go to the Norlands if you want to know what wind can be. It is like being on a mountain-top, for there is no high ground to act as a windbreak. There was no rain, but the surf broke in showers and every foot of the skerry was drenched with it. In a trice Halmarsness was hidden, and I seemed to be in the centre of a maelstrom, choked with scud and buffeted on every side by swirling waters.

'Down came my tent at once. I wrestled with the crazy canvas and got a black eye from the pole, but I managed to drag the ruins into the shelter of the zareba which John had built, and tumble some of the bigger boulders on it. There it lay, flapping like a sick albatross. The water got into my food boxes, and soaked my fuel, as well as every inch of my clothing . . . I had looked forward to a peaceful day of watching and meditation, when I could write up my notes; and instead I spent a morning like a Rugger scrum. I might have enjoyed it, if I hadn't been so wet and cold, and could have got a better lunch than some clammy mouthfuls out of a tin. One talks glibly about being "blown off" a place, generally an idle exaggeration – but that day I came very near the reality. There were times when I had to hang on for dear life to one of the bigger stones to avoid being trundled into the yeasty seas.

'About two o'clock the volume of the storm began to decline, and then for the first time I thought about the boat. With a horrid sinking of the heart I scrambled to the cove where we had beached it. It had been drawn up high and dry, and its painter secured to a substantial boulder. But now there was not a sign of it except a ragged rope-end round the stone. The tide had mounted to its level, and tide and wind had smashed the rotten painter. By this time what was left of it would be tossing in the Roost.

'This was a pretty state of affairs. John was due to visit me next day, but I had a cold twenty-four hours ahead of me. There was of course the flare he had left me, but I was not inclined to use this. It looked like throwing up the sponge and confessing that my expedition had been a farce. I felt miserable, but obstinate, and, since the weather was clearly mending, I determined to put the best face on the business, so I went back to the wreckage of my camp, and tried to tidy up. There was still far too much wind to do anything with the tent, but the worst of the spindrift had ceased, and I was able to put out my bedding and some of my provender to dry. I got a dry jersey out of my pack, and, as I was wearing fisherman's boots and oilskins, I managed to get some slight return of comfort. Also at last I succeeded in lighting a pipe. I found a corner under the knoll which gave me a modicum of shelter, and I settled myself to pass the time with tobacco and my own thoughts.

'About three o'clock the wind died away completely. That I did not like, for a dead lull in the Norlands is often the precursor of a new gale. Indeed, I never remembered a time when some wind did not blow, and I had heard that when such a thing happened people came out of their houses to ask what the matter was. But now we had the deadest sort of calm. The sea was still wild and broken, the tides raced by like a mill-stream, and a brume was gathering which shut out Halmarsness – shut out every prospect except a narrow circuit of grey water. The cessation of the racket of the gale made the place seem uncannily quiet. The present tumult of the sea, in comparison with the noise of the morning, seemed no more than a mutter and an echo.

'As I sat there I became conscious of an odd sensation. I seemed to be more alone, more cut off, not only from my fellows but from the habitable earth, than I had ever been before. It was like being in a small boat in mid-Atlantic – but worse, if you understand me, for that would have been loneliness in the midst of a waste which was nevertheless surrounded and traversed by the works of man, whereas now I felt that I was clean outside man's ken. I had come somehow to the edge of that world where life is, and was very close to the world which has only death in it.

'At first I do not think there was much fear in the sensation – chiefly strangeness, but the kind of strangeness which awes without exciting. I tried to shake off the mood, and got up to stretch myself. There was not much room for exercise, and as I moved with stiff legs along the reefs I slipped into the water, so that I got my arms wet. It was cold beyond belief – the very quintessence of deathly Arctic ice, so cold that it seemed to sear and bleach the skin.

'From that moment I date the most unpleasant experience of my life. I became suddenly the prey of a black depression, shot with the red lights of terror. But it was not a numb terror, for my brain was acutely alive ... I had the sense to try to make tea, but my fuel was still too damp, and the best I could do was to pour half the contents of my brandy flask into a cup and swallow the stuff. That did not properly warm my chilled body, but – since I am a very temperate man – it speeded up my thoughts instead of calming them. I felt myself on the brink of a childish panic.

'One thing I thought I saw clearly – the meaning of Skule Skerry. By some alchemy of nature, at which I could only guess, it was on the track by which the North exercised its spell, a cableway for the magnetism of that cruel frozen Uttermost, which man might penetrate but could never subdue or understand. Though the latitude was only 61°, there were folds and tucks in space, and this isle was the edge of the world. Birds knew it, and the old Northmen, who were primitive beings like the birds, knew it. That was why an inconsiderable skerry had been given the name of a conquering Jarl. The old Church knew it, and had planted a chapel to exorcise the demons of darkness. I wondered what sights the hermit, whose cell had been on the very spot where I was cowering, had seen in the winter dusks.

'It may have been partly the brandy acting on an empty stomach, and partly the extreme cold, but my brain, in spite of my efforts to think rationally, began to run like a dynamo. It is difficult to explain my mood, but I seemed to be two persons – one a reasonable modern man trying to keep sane and scornfully rejecting the fancies which the other, a cast-back to something elemental, was furiously spinning. But it was the second that had the upper hand ... I felt myself loosed from my moorings, a mere waif on uncharted seas. What is the German phrase? *Urdummheit* – Primal Idiocy? That was what was the matter with me. I had fallen out of civilisation into the Outlands and was feeling their spell ... I could not think, but I could remember, and what I had read of the Norse voyagers came back to me with horrid persistence. They had known the outland terrors – the Sea Walls at the world's end, the Curdled Ocean with its strange beasts. Those men did not sail north as we did, in steamers, with modern food and modern instruments, huddled into crews and expeditions. They had gone out almost alone, in brittle galleys, and they had known what we could never know.

'And then, I had a shattering revelation. I had been groping for a word and I suddenly got it. It was Adam of Bremen's "*proxima Abysso*". This island was next door to the Abyss, and the Abyss was that blanched world of the North which was the negation of life.

'That unfortunate recollection was the last straw. I remember that I forced myself to get up and try again to kindle a fire. But the wood was still too damp, and I realised with consternation that I had very few matches left, several boxes having been ruined that morning. As I staggered about I saw the flare which John had left for me, and had almost lit it. But some dregs of manhood prevented me – I could not own defeat in that babyish way – I must wait till John Ronaldson came for me next morning. Instead I had another mouthful of brandy, and tried to eat some of my sodden biscuits. But I could scarcely swallow; the infernal cold, instead of rousing hunger, had given me only a raging thirst.

'I forced myself to sit down again with my face to the land. You see, every moment I was becoming more childish. I had the notion – I cannot call it a thought – that down the avenue from the North something terrible and strange might come. My nervous state must have been pretty bad, for though I was cold and empty and weary I was scarcely conscious of physical discomfort. My heart was fluttering like a scared boy's; and all the time the other part of me was standing aside and telling me not to be a damned fool . . . I think that if I had heard the rustle of a flock of migrants I might have pulled myself together, but not a blessed bird had come near me all day. I had fallen into a world that killed life, a sort of Valley of the Shadow of Death.

'The brume spoiled the long northern twilight, and presently it was almost dark. At first I thought that this was going to help me, and I got hold of several of my half-dry rugs, and made a sleeping-place. But I could not sleep, even if my teeth had stopped chattering, for a new and perfectly idiotic idea possessed me. It came from a recollection of John Ronaldson's parting words. What had he said about the Black Silkie – the Finn who came out of the deep and hunkered on this skerry? Raving mania! But on this lost island in the darkening night, with icy tides lapping about me, was any horror beyond belief?

'Still, the sheer idiocy of the idea compelled a reaction. I took hold of my wits with both hands and cursed myself for a fool. I could even reason about my folly. I knew what was wrong with me. I was suffering from *panic* – a physical affection produced by natural causes, explicable, though as yet not fully explained. Two friends of mine had once been afflicted with it: one in a lonely glen in the Jotunheim, so that he ran for ten miles over stony hills till he found a saeter and human companionship; the other in a Bavarian forest, where both he and his guide tore for hours through the thicket till they dropped like logs beside a highroad. This reflection enabled me to take a pull on myself and to think a little ahead. If my troubles were physical then there would be no shame in looking for the speediest cure. Without further delay I must leave this God-forgotten place.

'The flare was all right, for it had been set on the highest point of the island, and John had covered it with a peat. With one of my few remaining matches I lit the oily waste, and a great smoky flame leapt to heaven.

'If the half-dark had been eerie, this sudden brightness was eerier. For a moment the glare gave me confidence, but as I looked at the circle of moving waters evilly lit up all my terrors returned . . . How long would it take John to reach me? They would see it at once at Sgurravoe – they would be on the look-out for it – John would not waste time, for he had tried to dissuade me from coming – an hour – two hours at the most . . .

'I found I could not take my eyes from the waters. They seemed to flow from the north in a strong stream, black as the heart of the elder ice, irresistible as fate, cruel as hell. There seemed to be uncouth shapes swimming in them, which were more than the flickering shadows from the flare . . . Something portentous might at any moment come down that river of death . . . Someone . . .

'And then my knees gave under me and my heart shrank like a pea, for I saw that the someone had come.

'He drew himself heavily out of the sea, wallowed for a second, and then raised his head and, from a distance of five yards, looked me blindly in the face. The flare was fast dying down, but even so at that short range it cast a strong light, and the eyes of the awful being seemed to be dazed by it. I saw a great dark head like a bull's – an old face wrinkled as if in pain – a gleam of enormous broken teeth – a dripping beard – all formed on other lines than God has made mortal creatures. And on the right of the throat was a huge scarlet gash. The thing seemed to be moaning, and then from it came a sound – whether of anguish or wrath I cannot tell – but it seemed to be the cry of a tortured fiend.

'That was enough for me. I pitched forward in a swoon, hitting my head on a stone, and in that condition three hours later John Ronaldson found me.

'They put me to bed at Sgurravoe with hot earthenware bottles, and the doctor from Voss next day patched up my head and gave me a sleeping draught. He declared that there was little the matter with me except shock from exposure, and promised to set me on my feet in a week.

'For three days I was as miserable as a man could be, and did my best to work myself into a fever. I had said not a word about my experience, and left my rescuers to believe that my only troubles were cold and hunger, and that I had lit the flare because I had lost the boat. But during these days I was in a critical state. I knew that there was nothing wrong with my body, but I was gravely concerned about my mind.

'For this was my difficulty. If that awful thing was a mere figment of my brain, then I had better be certified at once as a lunatic. No sane man could get into such a state as to see such portents with the certainty with which I had seen that creature come out of the night. If, on the other hand, the thing was a real presence, then I had looked on something outside natural law, and my intellectual world was broken in pieces. I was a scientist, and a scientist cannot admit the supernatural. If with my eyes I had beheld the monster in which Adam of Bremen believed, which holy men had exorcised, which even the shrewd Norlanders shuddered at as the Black Silkie, then I must burn my books and revise my creed. I might take to poetry or theosophy, but I would never be much good again at science.

'On the third afternoon I was trying to doze, and with shut eyes fighting off the pictures which tormented my brain. John Ronaldson and the farmer of Sgurravoe were talking at the kitchen door. The latter asked some question, and John replied:

'"Aye, it was a wall-ross and nae mistake. It cam ashore at Gloop Ness and Sandy Fraser has gotten the skin of it. It was deid when he found it, but no long deid. The puir beast would drift south on some floe, and it was sair hurt, for Sandy said it had a hole in its throat ye could put your nieve in. There hasna been a wall-ross come to Una since my grandfather's day."

'I turned my face to the wall and composed myself to sleep. For now I knew that I was sane, and need not forswear science.'

The Earldom

from The Ultimate Viking

ERIC LINKLATER (1899–1974)

Eric Linklater dedicated The Ultimate Viking *(1955) to his father and grandfather, who had 'trafficked under sail in many seas', and in so doing he was evoking the spirit of the Vikings or Norsemen who had such an impact on his beloved Orkney – he preferred the term to that of 'Orkneys'. Linklater's range was wide: he wrote in all twenty-three novels, various radio and other plays, and also made forays into non-fiction material like this, in which he set out to chronicle the history of these northern isles and use the unique fund of boasting and poetry that are the sagas, in particular* The Orkneyinga Saga. *As his central figure he took Sweyn Asleifsson as a kind of symbol of the restless yet creative temper of the Norse people in their 'heroic years'. The freebooting Sweyn he sums up as a man who 'felt, as it seems, a recurrent need to save from oblivion some poor empty page of the year by inscribing on it a memorable action'.*

The image of the raiding longship is familiar in tales of the Vikings, but Linklater also makes a picture of an island people who took from their neolithic predecessors a love of building and welcomed the cathedral builders, who brought Christianity with them and 'raised their minsters and cloud-reaching steeples'. The book's introduction is an account of the author's return to Orkney seeking inspiration, after a spell away from the islands:

> I had defined my task, and in the euphory of a northern spring – beside the glass-grey sea on which, and in the same years and perhaps within hailing distance of each other, had sailed Sweyn's careless vikings and the stone-masons coming from Durham to build a cathedral – in such a neighbourhood I had no doubt of its accomplishment.

The first of the Norsemen, known by name, to come west-over-sea into Orkney was Ragnar Lodbrok: Ragnar Hairy-breeks, greatest of all the vikings, who was said to have fought in fifty-one pitched battles, and being at last defeated by Ælla, King of Northumbria, was thrown into a snake-pit where he died. Ragnar is a kind of historical centaur, half man and half fable, but his human parts were real enough to beget his terrible sons, Halfdan, Ubbi, and Ivar the Boneless, who in 866 invaded England, perhaps to avenge their father, and began that thirty years' war which, despite the valour of King Alfred and the stubbornness of Wessex, left a great part of England under Danish rule.

According to more sober chronicles than that which records his death in a snake-pit, Ragnar laid siege to Paris in 845, and died in the same year. His arrival in Orkney is undated, but apparently he subdued the islands and left in command a man called Fridleif. It is possible that the Earldom was established about the middle of the century by some member of the powerful family of Möre, and in the beginning was independent of Norway; but the commonly accepted story is that it was created by King Harald Fairhair soon after the battle of Hafrsfjord in 872. There he defeated the last of the petty kings who opposed him, and established his dominion throughout Norway. But his realm was still troubled by vikings who came every summer from the Scottish isles and harried his shores, so presently he gathered a fleet and sailed westward to destroy their nests. This he did, and according to the saga of the Kings of Norway, and the saga of the Earls of Orkney, subdued Shetland, Orkney, and the Hebrides, and laid waste the Isle of Man.

One of his chief supporters was Rognvald, Earl of Möre, called the Mighty, whose son Ivar was killed in battle during the campaign; in compensation for whose death Rognvald got Orkney and Shetland. He came of a family that preceded history and was destined to rule one of the great empires of history; and the preface to the Earls' saga is a fabulous account of his descent from a king called Fornjot who – perhaps in the time of Beowulf – ruled a land between the Gulf of Bothnia and the White Sea. He had a son called Kari, who was the father of Frosti, who was the father of Snow the Old. Snow's son was Thorri, who had two sons called Nor and Gor, and a daughter, Goi. One winter, at the midwinter sacrifice, Goi disappeared, and three years later her brothers set out to look for her. Gor took ship and searched the islands in the Gulf of Bothnia, the coasts of Denmark, and the southern fjords of Norway. His brother, when the Gulf was frozen, went up into Lapland and down through Norway, and fought a battle on the Sogne fjord. After the battle the brothers met and divided the land between them – the mainland to Nor, the islands to Gor – and continuing their search found their sister in Hedmark: she was married to a king called Hrolf, whose father was the Giant of Dovre. After an inconclusive duel Nor married Hrolf's sister and

settled down to rule the lands he had won, which presently were divided,
and subdivided, among rapidly increasing descendants. But Gor held the
islands and became a sea-king, and his sons Heiti and Beiti were sea-kings
after him, and very overbearing men. They harried their cousins ashore,
and Beiti took much of their land. But Heiti kept to his ships and bred a
son of his own kind, whose longship was his home and kingdom, who
never slept under sooty rafter or drank at the hearth ingle. He was Sveidi
the sea-king, and Sveidi's son was Halfdan the Old . . .

This cold, transparent tale of the discovery of Norway – transparent
as if printed by frost on a window-pane – is embedded in the genealogy
of Earl Rognvald; and while there is no good reason for believing it,
there is no good argument for dismissing it altogether. Something of the
sort may have happened. It is likely, indeed, that something of the sort
did happen; for if Fornjot was a contemporary of Beowulf he lived at a
time when men were restless, and many little kingdoms were about to
be made, and deeds were being done that would become myths in time.
Myth has a background of reality, and in the foreground steps across
an invisible threshold into reality again: Halfdan the Old is almost an
historical figure, and though nothing is known of him but his name, his
name is a reasonable name and genealogists admit him to their tables.
His son, Earl Ivar of the Uplands, stands a little more firmly: he has
a local habitation. And Ivar had a son who is wholly real and nearly
audible: he was called Eystein the Loud Talker – and his son was Earl
Rognvald of Möre, whose seed would go swimming down the main
stream of history.

Rognvald had a son called Rolf or Rollo, who in his youth took to
the sea and became a viking. He was so huge a man that no horse could
carry him, and on his landward travels he had to walk. William Morris,
in his translation of the Kings' saga, gives him the resounding name of
Rolf Wend-afoot; but he is also known as Rolf the Ganger. He had
harried the lands in the eastern part of the Baltic without much offence
to anyone who mattered, but a bloody raid in the Oslo fjord roused
Harald Fairhair's anger, and Rolf was outlawed. In the customary manner
he went west to Orkney and the Hebrides, and continuing his voyage to
Normandy, compelled Charles the Simple, King of France, to give him
land enough, about Rouen and the estuary of the Seine, for the hazardous
beginning of a dukedom. As well as these rich fields Rolf acquired the
daughter of a Count Berenger, a girl with the friendly name of Poppa,
and by her became the father of a son known as William Longsword.
William was killed by a Count of Flanders, but left a son Richard, two
of whose grandsons grew famous as Robert the Devil and Edward the

Confessor. Robert the Devil, Duke of Normandy, fell in love with a tanner's daughter, who responded to his passion with such good will that their son was doubly endowed, with appetite and genius too. He defeated Harald Godwinsson at the battle of Hastings, the rude by-name of his boyhood was forgotten, and he was called William the Conqueror. He acquired for himself and his successors the realm of England, and founded a dynasty that would sometime reign over a comity of nations spread across the world from the Polar Sea to the Antipodes.

The tale of Earl Rognvald's descent from Fornjot, who ruled a land of silver birches and glittering lakes beyond the Gulf of Bothnia, is less improbable than the true tale of his descendants and the empire that grew about their throne in Westminster; and the first Earl of Orkney demands respectful attention. For he was the first of his family to win a title to land within the isles of Britain. He was precursor as well as progenitor of all our kings for nine hundred years.

Earl Rognvald gave his new Earldom to his brother Sigurd, who in alliance with Thorstein the Red, son of a Norse king of Dublin, attempted with gratifying success the conquest of the northern parts of Scotland. He died after battle with a Scots earl, and was buried near Dornoch. His heir died a year later, and Earl Rognvald then gave the Earldom to his own son Hallad, who set up house on the Mainland of Orkney, but was quickly appalled by the dangers of life there, and the constant depredation of vikings. So, amid loud laughter – which the saga faithfully records – he stepped down from his eminence and retired to Norway to live out his life as a simple squire.

Two Danish vikings, Thorir Tree-beard and Kalf Scurvy, settled in the islands, but Earl Rognvald was determined that his family should not lose them. Rolf the Ganger, had he been at home, might well have been given Orkney and kept out of Normandy; but he was cruising somewhere in the Baltic. Three other sons were summoned, and after an ill-tempered debate the Earldom was awarded to Einar, the youngest of them, who had the triple blemish of being ugly, one-eyed, and base-born. His mother was a thrall, and all her forebears had been thralls. But Einar was a tall man, a man of his hands and a poet, and his one eye was keen-sighted. He set sail for the islands, at once sought battle with the Danish vikings, and killed them both. He acquired a homely yet honourable nickname, not in battle, but by an economic discovery of major importance. He found an inexhaustible supply of hotly burning fuel in the spongy black soil of the peat-bogs that covered so much of his domain; and in a country without timber that was a discovery of moment. If the saga speaks truly, it was near Tarbatness, in Easter

Ross, that he cut his first peats and became known, in local history, as Turf Einar.

It was also his fortune – but his character made his fortune – to avenge the death of his father, the great Earl of Möre, who in his old age was attacked, and burnt alive in his own house, by two rebellious sons of Harald Fairhair. One of them, Halfdan Longlegs, fled to Orkney, and because his father was King of Norway, and men still thought of loyalty as a convenience rather than a guiding principle, he seduced many who owed allegiance to Turf Einar and quickly gathered strength enough to give himself a new crown. Turf Einar had prudently retired to his other realm in Scotland; but when he had mustered a fleet he returned to Orkney and defeated Halfdan, who, as night was falling, jumped from his ship and swam to the little flat island of North Ronaldsay. He was found there, early the next morning, and Turf Einar colours a page of the saga with the fearful poetry of his vengeance. He cut a blood-eagle on Halfdan's back – that is to say, he severed ribs from backbone and pulled out the lungs to lie like red wings on the corpse – and standing above the ruin of a man, he boasted of his deed. But he boasted in verse: the hard, intricate verse of heroic fashion. He was a good poet – good enough to bequeath his name to a metrical pattern – and after the battle he had mocked in verse his brothers who, living idly in Norway, left to him the burden of revenge. Now he proclaimed his satisfaction and his pride:

> Many a bearded man, for stealing a sheep,
> Has lived out his life as an outlaw.
> But I have slain the young son
> Of a proud king, while my kinsmen cackle of peril.
> I am unafraid. I say that in Fairhair's shield
> I have hacked a hole.

Though the mutilation of Halfdan's sea-chilled body is to our apprehension revolting, Halfdan himself was a young man of intemperate brutality, and the violence of Turf Einar's deed is a true reflexion – though in a savage mirror – of his love and reverence for Earl Rognvald, and as such does credit both to the father and his bastard son. King Harald, it appears, was not unduly distressed by Halfdan's death, but did not neglect to take his profit; he imposed on the Earl a fine of sixty gold marks. Einar ruled thereafter for many years, and died peacefully in his bed.

In the second half of the 10th century the annals of the Earldom are confused by two destructive Norwegian visitors, and their daughter who survived them. Eric Blood-axe, King for a couple of years, took two of Turf Einar's sons to war in England, where all were killed; and then his Queen Gunnhilda and her sons found refuge in Orkney, and brought trouble with them. A prospect of war in Denmark presently invited them to leave, but Gunnhilda left her infamous daughter Ragnhild behind her, whose habit was to consummate her marriages with murder. Earl Thorfinn ruled the islands, who was Turf Einar's surviving son, and he when he died left five sons. Ragnhild married three of them in turn, and seducing a nephew and a cousin also, infected her lovers with bloody intention and was the death of four notable men and an unknown number of their anonymous followers. Her last husband died fighting in Caithness, and Sigurd the Stout succeeded to the Earldom. He, a great-grandson of Turf Einar, was a redoubtable warrior who held Caithness against the Scots, and every summer led a viking host to the Southern Isles and Ireland. In his life were commingled witchcraft, Christian conversion, and high politics.

Sigurd's mother was Edna, daughter of the Irish king Kjarval, and she, with a skill in magic to make her more formidable, was one of those dominating and bloody-minded women who play so large a part in the sagas. It happened one summer that Sigurd was challenged to a pitched battle in Caithness by Findlaec, Earl of Moray, whose larger importance in the history of human affairs grew from his begetting a son who, when the time was ripe for it, defeated and killed Duncan, King of Scots; whose imagined virtues, pleading like angels against the deep damnation of his taking-off, gave Shakespeare the occasion to write his tragedy of *Macbeth*. Findlaec, in or about the year 995, was a dangerous enemy, and Sigurd told his mother that if he accepted the challenge the odds against him would be seven to one. To which she replied, 'I would have brought you up in my wool-basket if I had known you expected to live for ever! It is fate that governs a man's life, not his own comings and goings; and it is better to die with honour than live in shame.' Then she gave him a raven-banner, finely embroidered, and Sigurd, in a black temper, gathered an army and went to battle at Skitten Mire in Caithness. Three men who carried his banner were killed, but Sigurd was victorious.

A year or two later, with three ships, he set out on a viking cruise, and in a bay called Kirk Hope, that looks down across the Pentland Firth at Scotland, he met Olaf Tryggvisson, a great-grandson of Harald Fairhair and later, for a brilliant lustrum, King of Norway. Olaf, after harrying the English coast for several years, had become a Christian and is said to have received baptism in the Scilly Isles. His faith was ardent, his habit vigorous. He invited Sigurd aboard his ship and promptly told him, 'It is my wish that you should be baptised, and all those under you. Otherwise you will die here, at once, and I shall carry fire and sword through the islands.'

The saga charmingly says that Sigurd left the choice in Olaf's hands; and in consequence was baptised, and Christianity became the nominal faith of all Orkney. I reserve for another chapter comment on the immediacy of Sigurd's conversion, for a missionary of Olaf's expected an equally sudden transference of faith, under comparable menace, in Iceland; and the instant perception of divine truth under the bright edge of a sword cannot always be dismissed with scorn as mere opportunism. The old gods were dying for lack of faith, and a life without faith may seem worse than a house with an open roof.

Olaf, sailing to Norway and his kingdom, took as hostage a son of Earl Sigurd, but the boy soon died, and Sigurd renounced his allegiance to King Olaf. He made a political marriage with a daughter of Malcolm II, King of Scots, and in 1014, having left his son Thorfinn with the boy's grandfather at the Scottish court, set sail for Ireland and war against Brian Boru. He carried with him the raven-banner that his Irish mother had embroidered, and on Good Friday, at Clontarf, fought a battle which became, throughout the north, synonymous with the doom of a great hope. And that hope, so blackly disappointed, requires an explanation.

The Inchcape Rock

ROBERT SOUTHEY (1774–1843)

No stir in the air, no stir in the sea,
The ship was as still as she could be,
Her sails from heaven received no motion,
Her keel was steady in the ocean.

Without either sign or sound of their shock
The waves flow'd over the Inchcape Rock;
So little they rose, so little they fell,
They did not move the Inchcape Bell.

The Abbot of Aberbrothok
Had placed that bell on the Inchcape Rock;
On a buoy in the storm it floated and swung,
And over the waves its warning rung.

When the Rock was hid by the surge's swell,
The mariners heard the warning bell;
And then they knew the perilous Rock
And blessed the Abbot of Aberbrothok.

The sun in heaven was shining gay,
All things were joyful on that day;
The sea-birds scream'd as they wheel'd round,
And there was joyaunce in their sound.

The buoy of the Inchcape Bell was seen,
A darker speck on the ocean green;
Sir Ralph the Rover walk'd his deck,
And he fixed his eye on the darker speck.

He felt the cheering power of spring;
It made him whistle, it made him sing;
His heart was mirthful to excess,
But the Rover's mirth was wickedness.

His eye was on the Inchcape float;
Quoth he, 'My men, put out the boat,
And row me to the Inchcape Rock,
And I'll plague the Abbot of Aberbrothok.'

The boat is lower'd, the boatmen row,
And to the Inchcape Rock they go;
Sir Ralph bent over from the boat,
And he cut the Bell from the Inchcape float.

Down sunk the Bell with a gurgling sound,
The bubbles arose and burst around;
Quoth Sir Ralph, 'The next who comes to the Rock
Won't bless the Abbot of Aberbrothok.'

Sir Ralph the Rover sail'd away,
He scour'd the seas for many a day;
And now grown rich with plunder'd store,
He steers his course for Scotland's shore.

So thick a haze o'erspreads the sky
They cannot see the sun on high;
The wind hath blown a gale all day,
At evening it hath died away.

On the deck the Rover takes his stand,
So dark it is they see no land.
Quoth Sir Ralph, 'It will be lighter soon,
For there is the dawn of the rising Moon.'

'Canst hear,' said one, 'the breakers roar?
For methinks we should be near the shore.'
'Now where we are I cannot tell,
But I wish I could hear the Inchcape Bell.'

They hear no sound, the swell is strong;
Though the wind hath fallen, they drift along,
Till the vessel strikes with a shivering shock,—
'O Christ! it is the Inchcape Rock!'

Sir Ralph the Rover tore his hair;
He curst himself in his despair;
But the waves rush in on every side,
The ship is sinking beneath the tide.

But even in his dying fear
One dreadful sound could the Rover hear,
A sound as if with the Inchcape Bell,
The Devil below was ringing his knell.

2
WAR AT SEA

For some reason the naval dimension to Scotland's warlike past never seems to attract quite as much attention as the military. The 'Scottish Soldier' is more famed in song and story than is the 'Scottish Sailor'. Nevertheless Scotland's naval history has its literary and historical record – and Scotland's naval tradition deserves appropriate recognition in this anthology.

Scotland, with her long seaboard and archipelagos of islands was always fruitful territory for seaborne raiders, invaders, pirates and privateers. George Mackay Brown's poem *Ships of Julius Agricola Sail into the Pentland Firth* reminds us that the Romans depended as much on their fleet as on the legions for their success. From the days when the monks of Iona prayed to be spared from the terror of the Norsemen down to the nineteenth and twentieth century there have been few periods, in peace or war, when all that faced a ship leaving a Scottish port were the normal perils of the sea. Even Walter Scott, in his pleasure cruise on the lighthouse yacht *Pharos* in 1814, had to run the risk of American privateers:

> We then learn that we have been repeatedly in the route of two American privateers, who have made many captures in the Irish Channel, particularly at Innistruhul, at the back of Islay, and on the Lewis.

One of Scott's motives in going on his cruise in the *Pharos* was to visit the location for his epic poem of 1815 *The Lord of the Isles*. This tells of the contribution made by the clans of the Western Isles to the national struggle which culminated in Bruce's victory at Bannockburn in 1314. Scott's experience of the wartime perils of the sea was little different to the lot of the fifteenth century merchants whose problems with English raiders led to Sir Andrew Wood's epic battle with Stephen Bull, described by Robert Lindsay of Pitscottie.

Lindsay also gives a vivid description of the pride of James IV's navy – the *Great Michael* – the ultimate warship of her day, and a vessel whose use and possession was eagerly competed for by the Kings of France and England. For most of Scotland's history purpose-built warships like the *Great Michael* were the exception and merchant vessels were equipped for war when need arose. In 1598 James VI decided on an expedition to Kintyre and ordered all the shipowners and skippers of the Clyde ports to hold their ships in readiness to allow the most suitable vessel to be chosen. A ship and a skipper from Ayr being chosen, the other shipmasters had to lend guns and 'the best and maist able marineris' to equip and man the royal vessel. By the end of the seventeenth century matters were somewhat more advanced and two frigates and some smaller vessels formed the Scottish Navy – a force which seems to have had as many problems with the English Navy as with foreign foes – as a letter of 1706 indicates.

Scotland's bold, but disastrous, attempt at the end of the seventeenth century to set up a trading colony in Central America resulted in heightened tension between Scotland and England. A tragic consequence of this was the trial and execution of members of the crew of the *Worcester*, an English ship which had come into harbour in the Forth. The *Worcester*'s crew were suspected of having piratically captured the Scottish trading vessel *Speedy Return* and in a mood of mob anger and hysteria the captain, mate and gunner were executed.

After the Union in 1707 Scots began to play an increasing role in the Royal Navy. One Scot who followed this route was Tobias Smollett. Smollett had trained as a doctor in Glasgow, then moved to London intent on a literary career but was obliged to take a post as a surgeon's mate on a naval vessel – an experience he turned to good, if stomach-turning, account in his novel *Roderick Random*.

The role of sea power in the success and failure of the Jacobite risings was crucial – the landing of the Seven Men of Moidart from *Le du Teillay* and the reluctance of many Highland chiefs to support such a forlorn hope is linked to the forced withdrawal of the Prince's second ship *L'Elisabeth* and the loss of the men and supplies it carried. The rescue of the Prince in 1746 by *L'Heureux* from Loch nan Uamh makes a fittingly nautical conclusion to the last throw of Jacobitism. The story of Charles Edward Stuart is also linked with a much smaller ship – the boat in which Flora MacDonald carried the Prince, an event which has been immortalised and romanticised over the centuries, not least by Sir Harold Boulton in *The Skye Boat Song*. Flora MacDonald's role, however, remains well summed-up by that intrepid voyager on the Sea of the Hebrides, Dr Samuel Johnson:

A name that will be mentioned in history, and if courage and fidelity be virtues, mentioned with honour.

Scots were also instrumental in developing the naval forces of other countries – the role of Scottish admirals in the Russian navy being noteworthy and, of course, the Kirkcudbrightshire gardener's son, John Paul Jones, is recognised as the father of the United States Navy – and the author of the immortal phrase 'I have not yet begun to fight' – his defiant answer to a call to surrender when his ship the *Bonhomme Richard* engaged HMS *Serapis*. One of Jones's more questionable exploits was a raid on his own native parts in 1778 in an attempt to kidnap the Earl of Selkirk. Jones wanted to hold the Earl, whom he saw as having great influence with the British Government, as a hostage against the safety and good treatment of captured American seamen.

The Royal Navy of the French Revolutionary and Napoleonic wars was full of distinguished Scots. These included the unconventional Thomas Cochrane, who after a brilliant but controversial career and being dismissed from the service went off to command the Chilean navy and then became an Admiral in the Brazilian and Greek navies before being restored to the British navy list and dying an Admiral. More conventional careers were enjoyed by men such as Adam Duncan, created Viscount Camperdown after his victory over the Dutch fleet in 1797, and George Keith Elphinstone, Lord Keith, who was variously commander-in-chief of the Cape of Good Hope, North Sea and Channel squadrons.

In two world wars in this century Scotland saw much naval action off her coasts. John Buchan's First World War spy-novel *Mr Standfast*, set in part on the west coast of Scotland, gives an interesting account of the restrictions placed on civilian travel by the wartime controls. The Home Fleet bases in the Forth, Invergordon and Scapa Flow emphasised Scotland's strategic importance and the internment of the German High Seas Fleet at Scapa in 1918 underlined this fact. The loss of HMS *Hampshire* off Orkney, while carrying the Minister of War, Lord Kitchener to Russia in 1916, is still a subject of some controversy.

The sinking of the Donaldson liner *Athenia*, outward bound from the Clyde at the start of the Second World War, with the loss of 112 lives had a particular impact in Scotland, with many of the passengers being Scots. The *Aberdeen Journal* reflected the local dimension to the sense of outrage and loss, felt in towns and cities throughout Scotland, to this attack without warning on a civilian vessel:

More than a score of passengers from Aberdeen were on board the *Athenia* when the liner was torpedoed. They are natives of the city returning to their homes in Canada and United States. All of them, with the exception of one man, were women and children. Several of them were mothers taking their families home.

The torpedoing of the battleship *Royal Oak* and the loss of 833 of her crew as she lay at anchor in the Home Fleet base in Scapa Flow, the use of Scottish ports for assembling convoys, and the conversion of the Clydebank built liners *Queen Mary* and *Queen Elizabeth* into troopships, are merely some of the other incidents and events which underscored Scotland's naval role and strategic position.

Few events, in either war, had quite the poignancy of the loss of the Admiralty yacht *Iolaire* off Stornoway on New Year's Day 1919. Crowded with naval ratings, servicemen returning home to Lewis on New Year holiday leave, *Iolaire* ran on rocks just a few hundred yards from safety and over 200 men were drowned. The particular horror of drowning within sight of harbour and home, and dying in the first days of peace after surviving years of war, together with the impact of a heavy death toll on a small community, gives the *Iolaire* tragedy particular force, a sentiment to which the Lewis poet Iain Crichton Smith responded in his moving poem 'Iolaire'. A contemporary newspaper report gives a factual account of the disaster.

'Sir Andrew Wood'
and 'The *Great Michael*'

from Historie and Cronicles of Scotland

ROBERT LINDSAY OF PITSCOTTIE (c. 1532–80)

Lindsay, an otherwise obscure Fife laird, compiled a valuable, if not entirely reliable, chronicle of events in Scotland, extending from the 1430s (the period of James II) to his own time – the 1570s. This work, Historie and Cronicles of Scotland, *draws on earlier histories such as that of Hector Boece, as well as incorporating material derived from Lindsay's own first-hand experience and accounts of events passed on to him by others. The second of our two extracts shows Lindsay conscientiously citing his sources and giving evidence for his statements on the size of James IV's giant warship, the* Great Michael.

The first passage comes from the early years of the reign of James IV. A series of truces between Scotland and England had done little to stop privateering and piracy at sea. In 1489 English ships were attacking Scottish commerce in the Firth of Forth – or the Scottish Firth as Lindsay calls it. Sir Andrew Wood of Largo took his two ships, merchant vessels converted to warships, the Flower *and the* Yellow Carvel, *and defeated five English raiders in a battle off Dunbar. The English riposte came with the dispatch of a squadron of three ships under Stephen Bull charged with capturing Wood. Bull and Wood met off the Isle of May and after a two day running fight which took them round the Fife coast and into the Tay the Scottish captain was again victorious and able to hand over Bull as prisoner to the King.*

Wood was perhaps the most famous Scottish seaman of the period, although his contemporaries Andrew and Robert Barton also won great reputations as merchant seamen and privateers. Wood was to command the Great Michael *while Robert Barton served as her sailing master.*

Lindsay uses a colourful vernacular Scots for his history. Some modernisation of the text has been attempted in order to make his narrative and technical terms more intelligible to a modern audience, hopefully without losing all the flavour and character of the original.

'Sir Andrew Wood' (1489)

This same year, certain English ships came in our Scottish firth, and despoiled our merchants and all other travellers that came in their way. Of this the King and Council thought great ill, and desired effectuously to be revenged thereof; but they could get no man, neither captains, mariners, nor skippers, that would take in hand to pass forth upon them; till at the last, they sent for Sir Andrew Wood, knight of Largo, and desired him to pass forth upon the said Englishmen, and to that effect he would be well furnished with men, victuals and artillery, and he should have the king's favour and be rewarded richly for his travail.

Of this Sir Andrew Wood was well content, and passed furth of the firth, with two ships well manned and gunned, to pass upon the said Englishmen, whom he foregathered with at the castle of Dunbar, where they fought very cruelly on either side, with victory uncertain for a long time, nothwithstanding the Englishmen were five, and he but two, as is said, to wit, the *Yellow Carvel* and the *Flower*. Yet the said Sir Andrew Wood prevailed by his singular manhood and wisdom, and brought all his five ships to Leith as prisoners, and delivered the captains thereof to the King's grace, for which notable act the said Captain Wood was well rewarded. This was he of whom we spoke before; so he was held in great estimation by the King and all the nobility thereafter.

But immediately, when the King of England heard tell of their news, that his ships had fought and were taken by Sir Andrew Wood, he was greatly displeased therewith, and made proclamations through all England, that whosoever would go to sea, and fight with Sir Andrew Wood, and if he succeeded in taking him prisoner, and bring him to him, he should have for his reward, one thousand pounds sterling of income each year. There were many who refused, because they knew Sir Andrew Wood to be such a captain on the sea, and very fortunate in battle, wherefore they had no will to assail him. Nevertheless a captain of war, a gentleman called Stephen Bull, took in hand to go to sea and fight with Sir Andrew Wood, and bring him prisoner to the King of England, either quick or dead; whereat the King of England was greatly rejoiced, and caused the said Captain to be provided with three great ships well furnished with men and artillery.

After this the Captain passed to the sea, and sailed till he came to the Scottish Firth, that is to say, to the back of the Isle of May, beyond the Bass, and captured many of our boats that were fishing to win their living and took many of them to give him knowledge of where Sir Andrew Wood was. At the last, a little before daybreak, upon a Sunday morning, one of the English ships perceived two ships coming under sail by St Cobe's Head; then the English captain caused some of the Scottish prisoners pass to the mast-tops of the ships, that they might see or spy if it was Sir Andrew Wood or not; but the Scotsmen dissembled, and said they knew not who it was, till at the last, the Captain promised to free them without ransom if they told the truth if it was Captain Wood or not, and they certified that it was him indeed. Then the Captain was very blithe, and had wine poured and drank to all the skippers and captains that were under him, praying them to take good courage, for their enemies were at hand; for which reason he ordered his ships to war stations, and set the quarter master and captains, every one in his own post, and, like a good and stout captain caused the gunners to charge and put all in order.

On the other side, Sir Andrew Wood came boldly forward, knowing no impediment of enemies to be in his way, till at the last, he perceived two ships coming under sail and making fast towards them in a warlike manner. Then Captain Wood, seeing this, exhorted his men to battle, beseeching them to be fierce against their enemies, who had sworn and vowed to make them prisoners of the King of England:

'But by the will of God they shall fail of their purpose. Therefore set yourselves in order, every man to his own post, and let your guns and crossbows be ready. But above all, use the fireballs well in the tops of the ships, and let us defend our upper deck with two-handed swords, and every good fellow do and think on the welfare of the realm, and his own honour, and God willing, for my own part, I shall show you good example.'

So he caused the wine to be broached, and every man drank to the other. By this time the sun began to rise and shine brightly on the sails, so the English ships appeared very awful in the sight of the Scots, as their ships were great and strong and well furnished with great artillery.

Yet the Scots feared nothing, but cast themselves forward on the Englishmen, who seeing that, shot two great cannons at the Scots, thinking that they should have struck sail at their threat. But the Scotsmen, not frightened by this, came stoutly forward upon the windward side to Captain Stephen Bull, and grappled with them and fought there from the rising of the sun till the going down of the same, in the long summer's day, till all the men and women that dwelled near the coast stood and beheld the fighting, which was terrible to see.

Yet notwithstanding the night severed them, that they were forced to depart from each other till the morning and the day began to break and their trumpets blew on either side, and made them join battle again, grappling and fighting so cruelly, that neither skippers nor mariners took heed of their ships but fought on till the ebb tide and south wind bore them to Inchcape, before the mouth of the Tay. The Scotsmen seeing this, they took such courage and boldness, that they doubled on the strokes on the Englishmen, and there took Stephen Bull and his three ships, and brought them up to the town of Dundee, and there remained till their hurt men were cured, and the dead buried; and thereafter took Stephen Bull, and brought him to the King's Grace as a prisoner.

And the King received him gladly, and thanked Sir Andrew Wood greatly, and rewarded him richly for his labours and great proof of his manliness, and thereafter rewarded the English captain richly, and all his men, and sent them all safely home, their ships and all their equipment, because they had shown themselves such stout and hardy warriors. He sent them all back to the King of England, to let him understand that they had as manly men in Scotland as he had in England; therefore he desired him to send no more of his captains in time coming. But the King of England hearing of their news, was discontented, when his men said to him, that the King of Scotland had told them, if they came again in such a way to perturb his coasts, that it might be they would not be so well entertained, nor run home so dry shod. In any event the King of England accounted himself obliged to the King of Scotland, for the safe deliverance of his men and entertaining them.

'The Great Michael' (1511)

In the same year the King built a great ship called the *Michael*, which was a very monstrous great ship; for this ship took so much timber that she wasted all the woods in Fife, except Falkland wood, besides the timber that came out of Norway. Many of the shipwrights in Scotland wrought at her, wrights of other countries had their share in her; and all worked busily the space of one year at her. The ship was twelve score feet in length, thirty six feet within the walls, she was ten foot thick within the walls of oak planks, so that no cannon could do at her; she troubled all Scotland to get her ready for the sea and when she was committed to the sea, and under sail, she had cost the King £40,000 besides the ordnance and cannons that she bore. She had three hundred mariners to sail her, six score gunners to use her artillery, and a thousand men of war, besides captains, skippers and quarter masters. When this ship passed to the sea, and was lying in the road, the King caused a cannon to be shot at her, to see if she was stoutly constructed, but the cannon did her no damage. And if any man believes that this ship was not as we have shown, let him pass to the Place of Tullibardine, where he will find the breadth and length of her set with hawthorn; my informant was Captain Andrew Wood, principal captain of her, and Robert Barton, who was master skipper.

The Toll of the *Speedy Return*

from The Riddle of the Ruthvens; and other Studies

WILLIAM ROUGHEAD (1870–1952)

William Roughead was an Edinburgh lawyer who early in his career developed a fascination with murder cases and the by-ways of Scottish legal history. He edited ten volumes in the Notable British Trials *series as well as over a hundred other accounts of Scottish criminal cases collected in fourteen volumes of his work. Roughead's account of the 1909 Oscar Slater murder case was of considerable importance in eventually remedying a gross miscarriage of justice.*

His account of the loss of the Speedy Return, *a ship of the Scots Darien Company, and the trial and execution of the officers of the English ship* Worcester *in 1705, sets the story of the events at sea and in the Scottish High Court of Admiralty firmly in the context of the political climate of the time and the pre-Union manoeuvring and public emotions. As one contemporary wrote, when the question of a Royal pardon for the* Worcester's *crew arose, 'If the Queen shall grant them remissions it . . . will so exasperate the nation as may render it difficult to make them join with England upon any terms whatever.'*

Roughead's conclusion is that the Worcester's *crew were guilty of piracy, but that their trial fell some way short of justice.*

For the patriotic Scot, if the term be not tautological, there is no more dismal reading in the history of his native land than the chapter dealing with the affair of Dairen, but painful as is the story of that ill-fated enterprise its main features must briefly be recalled for a better understanding of the strange sequel with which we are here concerned.

Ever since James the Sixth forsook the throne of his ancestors for the more lucrative post made vacant by the death of Elizabeth, Scotland, poor, proud, and neglected, had watched with jealous eyes the commercial prosperity of England. Not, however, until after the Revolution, when our Dutch deliverer sat firm in his father-in-law's seat, did Scotsmen make any determined attempt to challenge their neighbours' mercantile supremacy. In 1693 the Scots Parliament passed an Act for encouraging foreign trade, declaring that companies might be formed to trade with the East and West Indies and other countries. This measure was designed to pave the way for an attack upon the monopoly of Indian trade so long the undisputed privilege of the East India Company. Two years later a scheme conceived in the fertile brain of William Paterson, the projector of the Bank of England, and fostered by Fletcher of Saltoun and other patriots, materialised in an Act of the Scots Parliament establishing *The Company of Scotland Trading to Africa and the Indies*, better known as the Darien Company of unhappy memory. King William was then with his army in France, and the Act received the Royal Assent from his Lord High Commissioner, the Marquess of Tweeddale. Probably the concession was intended as a sop to the national resentment aroused by the King's attitude in the Glencoe business three years earlier. It was proposed to fix the Company's capital at £600,000, one half to be reserved for Scotland and the other to be offered in London. The information imparted to those invited to subscribe was meagre, for Paterson, anticipating a principle since but too familiar to modern investors, held that 'if we [the promoters] are not able to raise the Fund by our Reputation, we shall hardly do it by our Reasons.' The London list was open only nine days when the entire issue of £300,000 was subscribed. The old East India Company quickly took alarm; Parliament was petitioned against the proposed infringement of its rights; the King complained that he had been ill-served in Scotland, and dismissed Tweeddale; but the Scots Act could not be repealed. The Commons threatened the directors with impeachment, and the Lords introduced a Bill to prohibit under severe penalties English subjects from investing in the Scots Company and from building, manning, or repairing its ships. As the result of these menaces the English contributors withdrew their subscriptions.

This, financially and commercially, was a fatal blow; but the spirit of Scotland was roused, and the nation to a man determined that in spite of injury, insult, and bad faith the enterprise should not be abandoned. The capital, reduced to £400,000, was subscribed in less than six months – a wonderful feat in view of the relative poverty of the country; the subscriptions ranged from £3000 to £100, and almost every class was represented in the list. Such was the national enthusiasm that many people, having subscribed for far more stock than they could carry, were afterwards unable to meet their calls.

Paterson's scheme was, in a word, to establish on the Isthmus of Darien a trading colony to operate both in the Pacific and Atlantic Oceans, and by means of the overland route to anticipate those benefits now expected to flow from the Panama Canal. After two years' delay and mismanagement the Company's fleet of five vessels sailed from Leith Roads on 26th July 1698, carrying emigrants and material for the establishment of the new colony of Caledonia, and on 1st November they arrived off Golden Island in the Gulf of Darien. With the fortunes of the settlement on the Isthmus I cannot here deal. The whole business woefully miscarried. The climate proved no less inhospitable than the Spaniards, who already occupied the country and constantly harassed the settlers; and though thus encompassed by enemies, the governors and council of the infant state quarrelled perpetually among themselves. No help came from Scotland, where the directors were busy erecting in Edinburgh, near the Bristo Port, spacious warehouses in which to store the hopeful harvest of the future. After the Company's collapse these buildings were, not inappropriately, employed as a refuge for pauper lunatics.

In May 1699 the English Government dealt the hapless colony its *coup de grâce*. On instructions secretly sent out to the colonial governors of Jamaica, Barbadoes, and New York, proclamations were issued in the King's name forbidding His Majesty's subjects at their utmost peril to hold any correspondence with, or give any assistance to the Scots settlement at Darien. Thus isolated, and beset by the allied foes Spain and fever, with no supplies coming from home, and confronted equally by famine and by disease, the disheartened survivors, after a seven months' struggle, took to their ships, and abandoning the settlement, set sail for the first port to which Providence might carry them. One vessel only, the *Caledonia*, returned to Scotland; the Spaniards and the perils of the deep accounted for the rest.

The Company meanwhile had fitted out a second expedition and the new fleet reached Darien in November. They found the colony deserted, and its capital, New Edinburgh, like Martin Chuzzlewit's thriving city of Eden, only a collection of rotting huts in a pestilential swamp. Nevertheless with native pluck and persistence the disillusioned settlers attempted to carry out the original plan; but attacked by the Spaniards on land and sea, and decimated by disease, they too in turn succumbed to fate. In April 1700 the worn-out remnant weighed anchor for the last time, and the colony was finally deserted. Of the four ships forming the second fleet not one ever reached Scotland; two were lost in a hurricane off Carolina, the others were respectively wrecked on the Cuban coast and taken by the Spaniards.

Thus died the national dream, which in the end cost some 2000 lives and upwards of £200,000 sterling.

Although many causes, including the incompetence and folly of those
responsible for its management, had contributed to the Company's
downfall, the Scottish people laid the whole blame of the disaster at the
door of England, whose hostile and jealous attitude alone had damned a
scheme which otherwise would have set the country financially on her
feet. 'Nothing could be heard throughout Scotland,' writes Sir Walter
Scott, 'but the language of grief and of resentment; indemnification,
redress, revenge were demanded by every mouth.' Never before was
there such a ferment of popular feeling – of anger and determination to
get back, in the modern phrase, some of their own. The years brought
no abatement of this settled purpose; King William died in 1702, and
Queen Anne found the Darien business still the main obstacle to a
treaty of union between the two kingdoms. In 1704 the Scots Parliament
passed the famous Act of Security, and the relations of the sister countries
became more strained than ever.

Now, it happened that one of the Darien Company's surviving vessels,
the *Annandale*, had been seized in the Downs by order of the East India
Company, to whom after long litigation, ship and cargo were forfeited
by the English Court of Exchequer. While still smarting under this fresh
affront the citizens of Edinburgh, looking down upon the Firth from their
incomparable eyrie, beheld a stout ship, flying the foreign flag of England,
enter the roadstead, having been driven by foul weather to refit in the
Forth. She proved to be the *Worcester*, a vessel of 200 tons, mounting
20 guns, with a crew of 36 men, commanded by Captain Thomas Green.
The rumour quickly ran through the city that she belonged to the hated
East India Company, though in fact she was the property of a rival
concern. Plainly Providence had delivered the *Worcester* into their hands
in response to the national prayer to be avenged for the rape of the
Annandale; but officialdom was cautious, and did not see its way safely
to assist Providence in the matter.

Early on Saturday afternoon, 12th August, 1704, the High Street of
Auld Reekie was busy with the wonted crowd of holiday idlers. About
the Cross, where the press was thickest, there might have been observed
– in the phrase of old-fashioned fiction – a man clearly charged with some
mysterious business, passing from group to group, scanning narrowly the
faces of each, and time and again beckoning apart 'such genteel pretty
fellows' as seemed best suited to his secret requirements. His purpose,
as appeared, was hospitable if eccentric; would they take their Saturday
dinner with him somewhere in the country to meet a friend or two of
his? This invitation was variously received; the prudent, being refused
further particulars, declined with thanks; the timid hastened to plead a

prior engagement. At last, having secured the fellowship of a score of likely lads, the Unknown set out for Leith, and while the company walked thither he spoke separately to each 'with more or less freedom, according as he found their several pulses beat'. As a result of these communications certain of his guests thought better of their bargain, and like those of Mr Morris in *The Suicide Club*, withdrew from so hazardous an adventure; but when Leith was reached the host found himself captain of a picked eleven – 'as good gentlemen, and (I must own) much prettier fellows than I pretend to be' – who made up in zeal and courage for what they lacked in numbers.

After dinner measures were concerted, swords, pistols, and bayonets distributed, and with the first of the evening tide the leader and three of his men set sail from Leith in a boat well laden with the brandy, limes, and sugar requisite for brewing a mighty jorum of Mr Micawber's favourite beverage. Four more followed soon after, embarking from the neighbouring port of Newhaven, while the remaining four in a third boat made for an English warship lying in the Roads, and asked to see the captain, whom they knew to be ashore. After being allowed to view the vessel they directed their course towards the *Worcester*, then riding at her anchorage within gunshot of the man-of-war. That pleasure-parties of citizens should on a fine summer evening come out as sightseers to a deep-sea ship, aroused in the guileless bosoms of the *Worcester*'s officers no shadow of suspicion. While these discussed with the occupants of the first boat 'a hearty bowle' in the cabin, the second and third boats drew severally alongside, and their occupants also asked permission to come aboard. Curiously enough, the three parties did not appear to recognise each other, but those first in possession courteously offered, as the accommodation of the *Worcester* was limited, to resign their places in favour of the newcomers, and proposed to return ashore. But this the ship's hospitable officers would by no means permit; so, there being ample liquor for all, 'with abundance of thanks, ceremony, and complement' the fresh arrivals were introduced to the original revellers, and punch and harmony were the order of the hour. The sailors, too, were not forgotten, the crew being 'lulled into a full security with drinking, singing, etc.'

The termination of this entertainment is best described in the words of the chief performer, as given from his own account by Mr Hill Burton, who discovered the MS. in an old oak chest in a cellar of the Advocates' Library: 'At my first coming on board, I took (as it were) out of curiosity a survey of the ship's condition, and would needs see what conveniences they had got between decks, in the gun-room and forecastle, etc. Some of my companions were now and then for an amusement stepping out upon deck, and we agreed upon a watchword, when we should plant ourselves thus: two to guard the gun-room door, two on the main-deck by the forecastle, two on the quarter-deck, and the other five with myself in the cabin. And really were you to be entertained with all the several humours and little pleasant interludes that happened before, at, and after the time of our going on board till the end of the show (besides their mistaking me, forsooth, for some lord, and their treating me as such, and my taking upon me accordingly), I am persuaded you'd think the whole a most compleat scene of a comedy, acted to the life; and to conclude the story, I may say the ship was at last taken with a Scots song.' Some of the crew gave their guests 'a pretty rugged chorus', but they were soon overpowered, and by nine o'clock that night the visitors were in possession of the vessel. The captured crew were put ashore, the officers kept as witnesses, and the hatches and lockfast repositories having been duly sealed with the official seal of the Darien Company, Mr Roderick Mackenzie, its active and energetic secretary, discarding his incognito, concluded the labours of an eventful day.

Surely never in the history of 'the Twelfth' was so remarkable a bag secured.

The amazing feat thus achieved by this resourceful civilian, seemingly so foreign to his peaceful function, proceeded upon a warrant of his court of directors, authorising him to seize the *Worcester* for having infringed their privileges by trading in Scottish waters, and also in reprisal, as belonging to the East India Company, but the methods adopted to carry out their orders were due to his native genius. Possible his family tree had already brought forth piratical fruit.

Next day a prize crew was obtained from Leith, and by Monday the *Worcester* was towed, for lack of wind, across the Firth and safely laid up in Burntisland Harbour, 'without sail or rudder, as secure as a thief in a mill'. Eight of her guns were landed and trained on the harbour mouth, experienced gunners were hired to man them day and night, and then Mr Mackenzie, with a mind at ease, sat down to make due report to his directors.

One wonders what the English man-of-war was about all this time, and how her captain regarded the secretary's naval victory. Whatever his views, the directors at any rate were enthusiastic in their approval, and proceedings were commenced forthwith before the High Court of Admiralty in order to secure condemnation of the ship and cargo as lawful prize by reprisal, the Scots Privy Council allowing the company a fair field, but taking no part in the proceedings.

The manifold and great losses sustained by the Darien Company included the disappearance of one of their ships, incongruously named the *Speedy Return*, on a voyage to the Indies some three years earlier, since when no tidings of her had been received. Her master was one Captain Thomas Drummond, whose name is frequently mentioned by Paterson in connection with the Darien expedition; her officers and crew mostly hailed from Leith. It was feared that she had been taken by pirates and that all on board had perished. Now, an examination of the *Worcester*'s papers, together with sundry odd expressions 'dropt' by members of her crew, led to the suspicion that they and their captain, Thomas Green, had been guilty of some very unwarrantable practices. Andrew Robertson, the gunner's mate, was heard to characterise the seizure of the ship as the just judgment of God upon them all for the wickedness that had been committed in her; and George Haines, the steward, when in his cups, declared to a numerous company, 'Lord God! our sloop was more terrible upon the coast of Malabar' – than that of a certain captain whose exploits were under discussion. Mackenzie, who was present, taking Haines aside, asked him of he knew anything of Captain Drummond and the *Speedy Return*. 'You need not trouble your head about 'em,' replied the steward, 'for I believe you won't see 'em in haste.' Pressed to explain himself, Haines said he understood they had turned 'pirrats'.

Among the belles of Burntisland, by whom the stranded crew were kindly entreated, none had such influence with Haines – especially when he was overtaken with drink – as a certain Miss Anne Seton, a damsel of nineteen, to whom the susceptible steward communicated 'the secrets of his heart to a far greater degree than Mr Mackenzie', and no wonder. Through the indiscretion of this young lady these confidences 'took vent', and reaching the ears of his shipmates caused them so to threaten Haines and his mistress that they were thereafter 'shy in owning anything of the premises', either to Mackenzie or others. One Mrs Wilkie, whose son had sailed as surgeon in the *Speedy Return*, came over from the Canongate of Edinburgh to make inquiries; she had an interview with Haines, of which more hereafter. 'The matter was in everybody's talk,' and the High Street hummed with the news that Captain Green and his crew were pirates, and that the capture of the *Speedy Return*, with the murder of every soul on board, formed an item in the bloody catalogue of their crimes.

The Privy Council began at last to move; the *Worcester*'s cargo was overhauled, her crew and other witnesses were judicially examined, and as a result of their investigations, the Council, on 13th February, 1705, ordered that Captain Thomas Green, John Madder, chief mate, John

Reynolds, second mate, and fifteen of the crew should be tried by the
High Court of Admiralty of Scotland for the crimes of piracy, robbery,
and murder. Others of the crew were, upon the recommendation of the
Council, admitted as Queen's evidence.

Accordingly on 5th March the trial began before James Graham,
Judge Admiral, and five members of the Privy Council sitting as
assessors, namely, the Earl of Loudoun, Lord Belhaven, Sir Robert
Dundas of Arniston, Sir John Home of Blackadder, and John Cockburn
of Ormiston. There was a formidable array of counsel as befitted
the importance of the case, including, for the prosecution, Sir James
Stewart, Lord Advocate; Sir David Dalrymple, Her Majesty's Solicitor;
Sir Patrick Home, Sir Gilbert Elliot, and Francis Grant, most of whom
were afterwards to adorn the judicial bench; Sir David Thoirs, Sir
Walter Pringle, and four other advocates conducted the defence. The
indictment, which was at the instance of Alexander Higgins, advocate,
Procurator-Fiscal to the High Court of Admiralty, was a document of
vast bulk, setting forth not only the alleged crimes, but the evidence
whereby these were sought to be established. Briefly, the charges were
that in the months of February, March, April, or May, 1703, the pannels,
having sailed from England in the *Worcester* on pretence of trading to
the East Indies, encountered another ship, bearing a red flag and manned
by Englishmen or Scotsmen, off the coast of Malabar, near Calicut; that
they, without any lawful warrant or just cause, attacked the said ship in
a hostile manner by shooting of guns and otherwise, boarded her, killed
her men, threw them overboard, and carried away the goods that were
on board of her to their own vessel; and that they then disposed of the
said ship by selling her ashore on the said coast. It will be observed that
while the pirates' prey was not actually alleged to have been the *Speedy
Return*, the jury were quite capable of drawing their own conclusions.
Then followed a minutely-detailed account of the circumstances from
which the pannels' guilt in the premises was inferred, but as these will
appear upon the proof they need not now detain us.

On 7th March began the elaborate pleadings as to the relevancy of
the indictment, which even for those spacious days are exceptionally
verbose and tedious. One or two points, however, may be noted. It
was argued for the pannels that the crimes libelled being alleged to have
been committed by Englishmen on the coast of Malabar, the Court had
no jurisdiction, and therefore the accused should be remitted for trial to
the proper Courts of Law in England. To this it was answered that the
jurisdiction of the Court in all maritime causes, civil and criminal, and
against all persons foreign or domestic, was established by statute, and

that by common law pirates were liable to be tried in the country where they were apprehended. Again, it was contended that the crew could not be put on trial until their captain, under whose command they acted, had previously been tried; further, that the captain should not be tried before the crew, some of whom he had cited as witnesses, as, if they were acquitted, he was entitled to the benefit of their evidence. It was replied that this was arguing in a circle, and that the pannels were all indicted together as *socii criminis*. Much more weight attaches to other objections, viz., that the libel was too general and indefinite, that it did not specify the name of the ship alleged to have been pirated, the designation of the captain, the names of those said to have been murdered, nor any circumstances by which the ship in question might specially be distinguished; and that this was the more necessary as Captain Green held a commission under the Great Seal of England empowering him to act in hostility against pirates, in respect of which he might lawfully have taken a ship and killed her crew. To this it was answered that the libel was laid as specially as the circumstances of this remote crime would permit; piracy and murder were crimes alike punishable by the laws, whatever might be the name of the vessel pirated or to whatever nation she might belong; and that his commission afforded a strong presumption of the pannel's guilt, as he was thereby required to enter in his journal particulars of any such attack, and that his journal as produced contained no entry to that effect.

On 13th March the Court repelled all the objections, found the crimes libelled, 'being proven by plain and clear evidence,' relevant to infer the pains of death, and remitted the whole to the knowledge of an assize. Next day a jury was empannelled, and the prosecutor adduced his proof. One-third of the jury was composed of Forth shipmasters – not in the circumstances the most impartial tribunal, the first on the list being Archibald Drummond, skipper in Leith, who, if a kinsman of the missing captain, would be apt to form a biassed judgment. Only one of the jury, however, seems to have been a shareholder of the Darien Company.

I can here but very briefly consider the purport of the evidence led. The trial was published, by authority, in folio (Edinburgh: Heirs of Andrew Anderson, 1705); and owing to its more than local fame was reprinted in the same form (London: Andrew Bell and Hugh Montgomery, 1705), a marginal glossary of the more difficult Scotticisms being added 'for the benefit of Common Readers'. Another report will be found in the *State Trials* (XIV., No. 438), and a sufficient abridgment is given by Arnot in his *Criminal Trials*.

The first witness called was the sea cook of the *Worcester*, Antonio Ferdinando, a man of colour, less euphemistically termed in the record, a black.

It was objected against Antonio that he was not worth ten pounds Scots, besides being a heathen whose evidence was inadmissible, but the Court repelled these objections. He swore that he believed in God, was born of pious parents, and himself, like Sir Thomas Browne, 'dared without usurpation assume the honourable Stile of a Christian'. Some two and half years earlier he had joined the *Worcester* at Callicoiloan (Quilon) on the Malabar coast, being engaged by Mr Loveday, the purser. The *Worcester* had then a sloop with her. Off that coast, between Tellicherry and Calicut, the *Worcester* and her sloop attacked another ship, sailed by white men speaking English, which ship 'did bear English colours'. The engagement, which was by way of a running fight, lasted two days; on the third day the stranger was boarded, her crew were killed with hatchets and thrown overboard, and her cargo was transhipped to the *Worcester*. She was then manned by some of the *Worcester*'s crew, who sailed her to Callicoiloan and there sold her to one Coge Commodo, acting on behalf of a king of that country. In the engagement the witness received a wound, which he exhibited to the Court, and the coat he then wore was, he declared, his share of the spoils. This coat, in the judgment of Crown counsel, was of 'Scots rugg'. He was told by Madder, the mate, that he would be killed if he mentioned the affair to any person, either white or black. During the engagement eight of the pannels were aboard the *Worcester*, and the others, including witness, on the sloop, except Reynolds, who was ashore. The captured ship carried about twenty guns.

Charles May, surgeon of the *Worcester*, said that he went ashore at Callicoiloan – apparently to attend certain patients unidentified – and remained a fortnight, during which time he heard the firing of guns at sea, and met Coge Commodo and Francisco de Olivera, the ship's 'linguister' (interpreter), who told him that the *Worcester* had gone out and was fighting another ship. Next morning the witness saw from the shore the *Worcester* in her former berth some four miles out, with a strange vessel riding at her stern. The ship's longboat came presently ashore in haste, and her crew told him the captain had sent them for water, because they had spilt and staved all their water aboard; that they had been 'busking' all night, and that they had brought a ship in with them. He then returned to Callicoiloan, where his patients were. A few days later, on going aboard to get some medicines he required, he found the *Worcester*'s deck lumbered with goods and casks, and said to Madder, 'What have you got there? You are full of business!' whereupon the mate 'did curse him, and bid him go mind his plaister box.' He afterwards learned that the prize was sold to Coge Commodo, who, as the 'linguister' informed him, complained he had bought the ship too dear. May dressed Ferdinando's wound, which, in his opinion, was occasioned by a gun-shot. Two of the other sailors also required his surgical aid, but when he asked how they came by their wounds the mate told him to ask no questions, and forbade the men to answer any upon their peril. On May persisting in his inquiries an altercation arose, and Madder ordered him to be put on shore. It was discovered that the *Worcester* had sprung a leak, but instead of having her repaired at any port on that coast, Captain Green sailed her to Bengal, a five weeks' voyage – preferring, as appears, rather to risk the loss of his ship than court inquiry by putting into Goa or Surat. All this happened in January or February 1703.

Antonio Francisco, Captain Green's black servant, was next called, to whom it was objected that he was not only worth nothing, but was 'slave to Captain Green' and had no religion. The Court, however, admitted his evidence. The witness swore that he enjoyed the same spiritual privileges as his coloured colleague. He joined the ship at Delagoa. Off the Malabar coast he heard firing from the *Worcester* but saw nothing of the engagement, being at the time chained and nailed to the floor of the forecastle – why, he does not inform us. Two days afterwards he saw goods brought aboard, which, Ferdinando told him, were from a captured ship, whose men had been killed after she was taken. Ferdinando exhibited his wound received in the fight, and told Francisco to say nothing about the engagement. The witness remained chained in the forecastle for two months.

James Wilkie, tailor, burgess of Edinburgh, stated that in October, after the cutting out of the *Worcester*, he accompanied his mother to Burntisland with a design to learn some news of his brother Andrew, who had sailed as surgeon in the *Speedy Return*. At the house of Mrs Seton they fell in company with the prisoner Haines, who in answer to his inquiries replied, 'Damn me, what have I to do with Captain Drummond?' but 'after that they had taken some cups about', Haines became more communicative, and said that when upon the Malabar coast he heard from a Dutch vessel that Drummond had turned pirate. Haines added that he had in his custody at the time the *Worcester* was seized in the Roads of Leith that which he would not have fallen in the seizers' hands for twice the value of the ship, and that he threw it overboard after the ship was taken, saying, 'Let them seek it now in the bottom of the sea!' What 'that' was we shall learn later.

Kenneth Mackenzie, indweller in the Canongate, said that he was present on the occasion referred to by the last witness. He heard Mrs Wilkie entreat Widow Seton to obtain from the *Worcester*'s crew some news of her son, and next day Anne Seton told him that Haines fell in a passion when she questioned him, swearing, not without reason, that they had a design to pump him, but he would tell nothing.

William Wood, gunner of Her Majesty's artillery, described his meeting at Burntisland with Haines, who having drunk 'pretty warmly', fell into a melancholy fit which he accounted for as follows: – 'It is a wonder that since we did not sink at sea, God does not make the ground open and swallow us up when we are come ashore, for the wickedness that has been committed during this last voyage on board that old bitch *Bess*' – pointing to the dismantled ship. Thereafter, as they walked upon the Links, Wood, with some lack of taste, observed that Madder's uncle had been boiled in oil at Amsterdam for piracy, whereupon Haines rejoined that if what Madder had done during the voyage were known, he deserved as much as his uncle.

John Henderson, writer in Edinburgh, who was present, corroborated; and Anne Seton – to whose evidence the curious objection taken that she could not be a witness because she was a woman, was repelled – confirmed the story, omitting with maiden modesty the nautical term of endearment applied by Haines to his ship. She also had heard his reference to the *pièce de conviction* which he had committed to the deep. Haines told her he knew more of Captain Drummond than what he would express at that time.

John Brown and Archibald Hodge, both skippers in Leith, said they assisted at the discharge of the *Worcester*'s cargo when she was 'rummadged' by order of the Privy Council. They found upon the goods no such marks or numbers as was customary for identifying the owners to whom these were consigned. The goods, however, were regularly enough stowed.

John Glen, goldsmith in Leith, stated that the second day after the *Worcester* arrived in the Roads he visited that ship. In the cabin Madder took a seal out of his pocket, and asked Glen what he thought of the Scots African Company's arms. Glen examined the seal, 'and found thereon the St Andrew's Cross, a Dromedarie or Camel with a Castle on the back of it, and a ship with a Rising-Sun above the Helmet, and two wild Men as Supporters' – in a word, the official blazon of the Darien Company. The seal was the size of an English halfcrown, with a handle of lignum vitae, and was quite different from that now produced in Court by the defence.

The proof for the prosecution closed with the putting in of certain instructions and letters found among Captain Green's papers, from which it appeared that his owners had given him unusual and suspicious orders regarding the conduct of the voyage. He was to write to them in cypher only, without title, date or signature, and under cover to a third party, 'the names of any dead' to be appended at the end of his letters without comment; he was to allow no letters whatever to be sent to England by any other of the ship's company; and when the *Worcester*'s cargo was 'provided', he was to sell the sloop for what she would fetch. The care and secrecy of the crew would be rewarded at the voyage's end by a month's pay gratis, and also by a share in the benefits accruing from 'the whale fishing' – which, in view of the latitudes selected for carrying on that interesting industry, would, one thinks, be highly problematical. Such sailing orders are scantly consistent with the ostensible pursuit of peaceful trading, and give additional colour to the evidence of the blacks and the crapulous babblings of Haines. The nature and value of her outward cargo – arms and ammunition worth under £1000 – are remarkable for a 200-ton ship of 20 guns, with a crew of 36. Whatever the *Worcester*'s game may have been, she was plainly not the simple merchantman she seemed.

No witnesses were called for the defence, and the proof having lasted twelve hours, counsel on both sides of the bar addressed the jury, only the speech for the prosecution being preserved. At the conclusion of the evidence the jury asked the Court's direction on the law as to the proviso in the interlocutor of relevancy that the charges must be proven by 'clear and plain evidence'. The Court directed that though the crimes libelled were not proved by direct probation, yet if they were made out by the qualifications and circumstances, even if each of these were not proved by two direct witnesses, the same should be held as clear and plain evidence. In other words, the jury could go as they pleased. The speech of the Solicitor-General, Sir David Dalrymple, in later life the erudite Lord Hailes, need not detain us; in its recapitulation of the evidence it reminds one rather of the stereotyped judicial charge. He assumed throughout that the ship destroyed was Captain Drummond's, and in conclusion observed, 'Consider how much light the providence of God has discovered in so dark a crime committed in a place so distant and solitary, and I am confident you will conclude with me that the murder and piracy is proven.' It was the way of Crown counsel in those days to throw the *onus probandi* upon Providence, especially when they found their case come out a trifle thinner than they could wish. The jury were then enclosed till the next day at ten o'clock, when they delivered their verdict in the following terms: – 'They by plurality of votes find that there is one clear witness as to the piracy, robbery, and murder libelled, and that there are accumulative and concurring presumptions proven for the piracy and robbery so libelled; but find that John Reynolds, second mate of the said ship, was ashore at the time of the action libelled.' Thereafter David Forbes, advocate, on behalf of the Darien Company, protested in advance against the ship and cargo being confiscated to the Crown, they having previously been adjudged to the said Company by way of reprisal for the seizure of the *Annandale*. The diet was then continued till 21st March. On that date the judge and assessors, by the mouth of John Park, dempster of Court, sentenced Captain Green, Madder, and three of the crew to be hanged within floodmark on the Sands of Leith upon 4th April, four others on the 11th, and the remaining five on the 18th; ordained the *Worcester* and her cargo to be escheat and inbrought to Her Majesty's use; and assoilzied (discharged) the said John Reynolds.

Thomas Linstead, the supercargo, though included in this sentence, was recommended for reprieve. He had, it appears, on 16th March emitted a declaration in presence of the Lord Advocate to the effect that when the *Worcester* was at Callicoiloan in January 1703 he went ashore to look after the goods they had sold, the ship proceeding with her sloop to Calicut. A week later he heard from some fishermen that they had seen the *Worcester* fighting at sea with another ship. He then sent a message to Calicut asking what had happened, and was told, in reply, to mind his own business. Later Coge Commodo took him on board the prize, which he (Coge) had purchased – a vessel of about 100 tons, mounting 12 or 13 guns, and, in Linstead's opinion, of Scottish build. Whether this was an accurate description of the *Speedy Return* we cannot tell. When he rejoined his ship he could get no information regarding the action. He proceeded with her to Bengal.

On 27th and subsequent days of March two others of the condemned, George Haines and George Bruckly, emitted long confessions in presence of the Judge Admiral, fully admitting their part in the taking of the vessel and the murder of her crew as set forth in the indictment, but with many corroborative details upon which I have not space to enter. Both men alleged that the ship was in very deed Captain Drummond's, a fact well known among the *Worcester*'s crew. If the statement of these penitents be accepted, no doubt as to the pannels' guilt is possible. Haines said he had kept a particular note of the matter in his journal, which, when the

Worcester was seized, he threw overboard, lest it should furnish evidence of the crime.

Whatever was thought of the verdict at the time, in the considered judgment of our historians, Captain Green and his men were no white-robed victims of a blind and unreasoning resentment. Mr Hill Burton concludes 'that the crew of the *Worcester* had been guilty of some acts of violence of the kind then so common on the high seas'; and Mr Andrew Lang pithily sums up, 'the *Worcester* had been guilty of piracy'. Whether such evidence would to-day be held to warrant a conviction is a different question.

Angry eyes across the Border had been watching the progress of these judicial doings, and we may imagine with what indignation the verdict was received in London. 'This business of Green is the devil and all,' wrote Mr Secretary Johnstone of Waristoun to his friend Baillie of Jerviswood: 'It has spoiled all business [*i.e.* as to the Union]. I am told it was two hours in the Cabinet.' In short, no Englishman believed in Green's guilt: 'Nay, in my opinion, faith, too, in this matter must be the gift of God, for I doubt much that it's in the power of man to convince this nation of it.' The witnesses, it was said, were suborned, the confessions induced by threats of torture, and the whole affair was a Jacobite plot. There were transmitted from London to the authorities in Edinburgh the affidavits of two sailors, Israel Phippany – prime name for a pirate – and Peter Freeland, who alleged that on 26th May 1701 they had sailed from Glasgow in the *Speedy Return* upon her last voyage. At Maritan in Madagascar, on a date unspecified, while Captain Drummond and his officers were ashore, the ship was taken by pirates, who compelled the crew to sail her to Rajapore, where she was burnt, the crew escaping in another vessel. They knew nothing of the *Worcester* till their return to England. Of the character and credibility of these mariners we have now no means of judging. As they stated that everyone escaped unhurt, it is curious that no other member of the ship's company ever found his way home. The Scots Privy Council retorted by sending to England the confessions of Haines and Bruckly. We shall hear again of Captain Drummond in Madagascar.

On 25th March intimation was received of the Queen's desire that the executions should be delayed till her pleasure was known. The Privy Council protested that the trial had been strictly regular, the confessions removed any doubt of the prisoner's guilt, and they begged that no interference with the sentence might be attempted. 'If the Queen shall grant them remissions,' wrote Baillie to Secretary Johnstone, 'it will spoil the business of Parliament [*i.e.* the Union], and I'm afraid will so exasperate the nation as may render it difficult to make them join with England upon any terms whatever.' The day before that fixed for the first executions, however, her Majesty commanded a reprieve until further inquiry, and the Council postponed the ceremony for a week.

The fateful day was the 11th of April. The Privy Council met on the 10th to decide what was to be done. The High Street was thronged by excited crowds, swollen by those who had come in from the country to see the law take its course, as did their heirs and successors a generation later in the affair of Captain Porteous. The Council, saving the Queen's grace, were between the devil and the deep sea; they feared to move either in mercy or justice. Early next morning 'a flying packet' arrived from London, and the rumour spread that the prisoners were pardoned. In the 'laigh' counsel-room below the Parliament Hall the Council met at nine o'clock to consider the Royal message; Anne, while urging further delay, left the decision in their hands. From without the chamber doors the fierce clamour of a formidable mob besieging the council-house broke in upon their deliberations, the uproar continuing for two hours. The people's demand for vengeance could no longer safely be withstood – it was a case of sacrificing to the popular fury either Captain Green or themselves; so they signed an order for the first executions to proceed, and at eleven o'clock 'word came out of the Council that three were to be hanged.' 'This appeased the mob,' says Wodrow in his *Analecta*, 'and made many post away to Leith, where many thousands had been [assembled], and were on the point of coming up in a great rage. When the Chancellor came out, he got many huzzas at first; but at the Tron Kirk, some surmised to the mob that all this was but a sham; upon which they assaulted his coach, and broke the glasses, and forced him to come out and go into Mylne's Square, and stay for a considerable time.' Having in this characteristic manner relieved their feelings, the populace flocked down to Leith, where on three gibbets set up in the sands were presently suspended for their satisfaction the bodies of Captain Green, Madder the mate, and Simpson the gunner. Wodrow, who was a spectator, thus describes the scene: – 'The three prisoners were brought with the Town-guards, accompanied with a vast mob. They went through all the Canongate, and out at the Water-port to Leith. There was a battalion of foot-guards, and also some of the horse-guards, drawn up at some distance from the place of execution. There was the greatest confluence of people there that ever I saw in my life, for they cared not how far they were off, so be it they saw. Green was first execute, then Simpson, and last of all Mather [Madder]. They every one of them, when the rope was about their necks, denied they were guilty of that for which they were to die. This indeed put all people to a strange demur. There's only this to alleviate it, that they confessed no other particular sins more than that, even though they were posed anent their swearing and drunkenness, which was weel known.'

So was the *Speedy Return* finally avenged. No further victim was offered in expiation of her fate, for the remaining prisoners were afterwards set free. The international ill-feeling aroused by this unfortunate business became, curiously enough, a factor in the promotion of the union effected two years later between the kingdoms; but had the Queen persisted in reprieving Green, there is little doubt that the Porteous tragedy would not have lacked a precedent.

Among the crowd that jeered and jostled at the gallows' foot stood a young man in deep mourning, a law student of twenty who had attended the trial, 'was sensible with what injustice it was carried on', and to whom Green's only crime seemed that of being an Englishman. He waited patiently until the body was cut down, when, as a last mark of respectful sympathy, he 'carried the head of Captain Green to the grave.' This solitary mourner was Mr Duncan Forbes of Culloden – *clarum et venerabile nomen* – then about to leave Scotland for Leyden to pursue those studies in the Civil Law which led him in due course to the President's chair. Thirty years later Forbes, as Lord Advocate, was to witness an even more striking outburst of the unruly passions of his countrymen when inflamed by resentment of foreign interference with their lawful prey: what respect the Edinburgh mob paid to Queen Caroline's reprieve of Captain Porteous history relates. In the debate in the House of Commons in 1737 on the motion for the commitment of the Provost's Bill, the measure by which the Government sought to punish the citizen's enthusiasm for abstract justice, Forbes made a brilliant and patriotic speech, and in rebutting the charges brought against the City Guard he referred to the case of Captain Green, and his own connection with it as already mentioned. 'In a few months after [the executions],' he declared, 'letters came from the captain for whose murder, and from the very ship for whose capture, the unfortunate persons suffered, informing their friends that they were all safe. These letters, sir, were of a date much later than the time when the crimes for which Green was condemned were pretended to be perpetrated.' The dates of these letters, whence they were written, and to whom addressed, Forbes told neither to the House nor to posterity, and historians have failed to trace in the records of the time any other reference to their receipt. Yet if documents of such interest and importance *did* come to hand, one would expect to find more than this single casual allusion to the fact. I think it probable that Forbes was merely repeating a current rumour to that effect, and that he had no personal knowledge of their existence. In a letter to his brother, dated 20th April 1705, printed by Mr Hill Burton in his *Life of Duncan Forbes of Culloden*, Forbes writes:

> The news of the town is the discovery of the oath of piracy taken as is alleged by Captain Green and his men, which George Haines, one of the men that has confessed, says to have been thus: – That Captain Green and the rest of the crew, were let blood of (by Samuel Wilcocks, surgeon, mate of the ship) in one bowl, that their several bloods together with a little claret wyne were mixed, and they made to sitt on their knees; that they were made to eat a little bread with the liquor, and in this fashion take a sacramental oath of secrecy in the horridest tearmes that could be devised. Upon this discovery Haines and Wilcocks were confronted before the Advocate, where the one alledged and the other denyed most pointedly. Its alledged, also, that there is a watch found which Captain Green had given to a Miss of his in Town with T. D. the two first letters of Captain Drummond's name engraved on it. What truth is in this I know not.

Neither of these points – the latter, if true, would have been a vital one – was mentioned at the trial, and I suspect that the letters from the *Speedy Return* existed, as they did, but in the news of the town.

There is inserted as a pendant to the report of Green's case in the *State Trials* an account of the Campden Wonder, the well-known mystery of Joan Perry and her two sons, hanged in 1660 for the murder of a venerable gentleman who turned up later safe and sound – a signal instance of the danger of convicting without due proof of the *corpus delicti,* to say nothing of the *corpus vile.* Captain Green has been held a not less notable example, mainly upon the statements contained in a work entitled *Madagascar, or Robert Drury's Journal*, published in 1729. Drury alleged that as a boy of fourteen he was wrecked in the *Degrave,* East Indiaman, upon the coast of Madagascar, John Bembo (Benbow), son of the famous admiral, being fourth mate. There he found, holding high office under the native king, one Captain Drummond, a Scotsman, whose ship had been taken by pirates. During most of Drury's fifteen years' sojourn Drummond played an adventurous and varied part in the island politics, to which he literally devoted his life, being slain by a member of the opposition, as Drury afterwards learned. 'But they told me one remarkable piece of news,' he adds, 'for the truth of which I must refer my readers to further inquiry. They said that this Captain Drummond was the very same man for whose murder and his crew's one Captain Green, commander of an East India ship, was hanged in Scotland.' Drummond, as appears, had not deemed the fact worth mentioning to Drury, though they were closely associated for several years. Drury 'understood that Mr Bembo got to England'; he himself returned in 1720, published, like many a wiser man, his volume of reminiscences, and died before 1750. A posthumous edition of his book concludes with the following note: 'N.B. – The Author (for some Years before his Death) was to be spoken with every Day at *Old Tom*'s Coffee-house in *Birchin Lane*; at which Place several inquisitive Gentlemen have receiv'd from his own Mouth the Confirmation of those Particulars which seem'd dubious, or carried with them the least Air of a ROMANCE.' One would gladly have taken advantage of this guarantee to put certain points to the traveller, but for many years historians – though inquisitive gentlemen enough – have rested satisfied with his good faith. The last edition of the *Journal* (London, 1890), edited with an introduction and notes by Captain Pasfield Oliver, R.A., author of a history of Madagascar, disposes, however, of Drury's claim to strict veracity, so that, after all, his adventures are to be ranked with those recounted in a more famous work 'which treateth of the Way towards Hierusalem and of Marvayles of Inde'. He was, as appears, a pirate; and his *Journal* was edited either by Defoe or by some sedulous ape to that ingenious author, the materials being, appropriately enough, stolen from French sources.

Benbow, at least, was genuine, and from certain anecdotes of him given in the *Gentleman's Magazine* for April 1769, it seems that he was in fact shipwrecked in the *Degrave*. He, too, kept a journal, which was accidentally destroyed by fire in 1714. 'Mr Benbow's narrative (to those who have read it) is a strong confirmation of the truth of this [Drury's] journal, with which (as far as it went) it exactly tallied,' says the writer of the memoir; but, as Mr Andrew Lang remarks, Drury's editor may have known and used Benbow's MS., which would account for the coincidence. Be that as it may, the story told of the *Speedy Return's* commander by Messrs. Phippany and Freeland was, of course, common knowledge and available as copy; but there is no evidence that Benbow mentioned Drummond. The writer also tells us that Drury was after his return employed as porter at the East India House, a situation unlikely to foster kindly feeling towards the Darien Company. The appointment is significant.

That Green and his crew *were* guilty of piracy plainly appears from *A New Account of the East Indies*, by Captain Alexander Hamilton

(Edinburgh, 1727). In February 1703, at Calicut, Green came on board Hamilton's ship at sunset 'very much overtaken with Drink, and several of his Men in the same condition'. He wanted to dispose of some small arms, powder, and shot, the balance of his cargo brought from England, the greater part of which he had already sold to good advantage among the pirates of Madagascar, but Hamilton declined to trade and advised him to hold his tongue. Then Madder the mate came aboard, expressing a desire to transfer his services to Captain Hamilton, and, being in the condition technically termed 'greetin' fu'', declared with tears that if the deeds done on their voyage should come to light it would bring them all to shame and punishment, adding with prophetic truth – for it was indeed by the strong waters of earth that the *Worcester* was finally overwhelmed – 'he was assured that such a Company of Drunkards as their Crew was composed of could keep no Secret, tho' the Discovery should prove their own Ruin.' Hamilton replied that he heard at Callicoiloan they had sunk a sloop, with ten or twelve Europeans in her, off that port – the episode, he assumed, which was troubling the conscientious mate – and that the fact was no secret there. This Madder did not deny. Next day to Hamilton, as he walked 'along the Sea Side', came May the surgeon, offering his services in exchange for a passage home: Madder, he said, had treated him with blows for asking a pertinent question of some wounded men, who were hurt in the engagement with the aforementioned sloop. But Hamilton had heard too much to be contented with their conduct, so for the remainder of his stay he 'shunn'd their Conversation', Of the justice of their subsequent conviction he expresses no opinion; 'I have heard of as great Innocents condemned to Death as they were,' is his elegy for the martyrs of the *Worcester*.

The gentle heart of Duncan Forbes, that indefatigable golfer, who was wont to play on Leith sands when the Links were white with snow, must, Mr Lang gracefully suggests, often have been touched by the sight of Captain Green's 'wuddie', Had his lordship's library contained a copy of Hamilton's instructive treatise he might have enjoyed his game with a quiet mind.

'A Matter of Protocol'

from The Old Scots Navy

Letter from CAPTAIN THOMAS GORDON
to David, Earl of Wemyss, Lord High Admiral of Scotland

On the eve of the Treaty of Union tensions ran high between Scotland and England. The two countries might share a common sovereign, Queen Anne, but this did not guarantee a harmonious working relationship between Her Majesty's government in Scotland and that in England, nor between the military, naval and civil servants of the Crown in the two Kingdoms.

Scotland's two frigates, the Royal William *and the* Royal Mary, *were in English waters when the incident reported by the Captain of the* Royal William *took place. The* Dunwich, *whose Captain Jones so objected to the Scottish Captain's flying his distinguishing pennant in English waters was, of course, a vessel of the English Royal Navy. The English Board of Admiralty had also issued instructions that Scottish naval vessels should strike their colours and salute English warships – a breach of naval protocol which Captain Gordon was not prepared to countenance without specific orders from his political masters.*

The Lord High Admiral, doubtless with an eye on the Treaty negotiations, sought a common-sense solution: 'The expedient proposal is that, being all the Queen's subjects in her own ships, that there be no dissension amongst them, but as one English man of war comes to another.'

Royal William lying at Tynemouth Haven.
June, 1706.

My Lord,

Having received a letter signed by several masters of our vessels from London, who had put in here and have aboard some valuable goods of the nobility and commissioners of the Union, to give them convoy from this home, I took the first opportunity with Captain Hamilton, commander of the *Royal Mary*, to comply with their desire.

The wind proved cross most of the way; and, having sprung the head of my foremast, I was obliged to put into harbour, where, without any previous notice, I was saluted by Captain Jones, commander of the

Dunwich, with a sharp great shot. I immediately sent my lieutenant on board him to know the meaning of such rashness. He complained of my spreading a broad pendent in English waters, and gave that for the reason. Now, my Lord, I have done nothing in this case but what the English are doing in our rivers, and what the Dutch do also in their and our waters in company of the Queen's ships. Captain Jones takes amiss also my firing an evening and morning gun, altho' the English and Dutch do the same when with us, and also the Dutch too in the very Thames; and my doing so is only with regard to the ships under my command. Captain Jones sends an account of the affair to the Prince of Denmark by this post, therefore I judged it my duty to inform your Lordship at the same time thereof; wherein I hope I'll be found to have done nothing unwarrantably.

My Lord, this case may give occasion to the regulation of the memorial between us and England, as well as foreigners; and I wish it may, for, my Lord, if we shall happen to meet with English frigates of greater force than ourselves, who no doubt will pretend the submission of striking saluting of which we cannot yield without particular instructions, the consequence may prove fatal, which by all means ought to be prevented for the good of both.

I beg, my Lord, now when so many honourable and knowing persons of our country are at London, who can assist in this affair, that the opportunity be not lost of rendering things of this nature distinct between our neighbours and us.

I cannot omit to tell your Lordship on this occasion that Captain Ramsay, commander of the *Bon Adventure*, who conveyed our recruits to Holland, told me in the road of Leith that he should be sorry of meeting me without the Island of May, since he had orders from the Board of England to make our frigates strike and salute. This makes it still the more necessary that matters be timeously adjusted, and we fully instructed how to carry out such cases, for I am firmly resolved not to yield one jot, while I have the honour to command, without particular orders, which are impatiently waited for by him, who is, my Lord, your Lordship's most obedient and most humble servant,

THOMAS GORDON.

'The Fleet Sails for Cartagena'

from Roderick Random

TOBIAS SMOLLETT (1721–71)

This is Chapter 28 from Roderick Random, *Smollett's long first novel, based in part on his own voyage to the West Indies as a surgeon in the Cartagena expedition against the Spanish. In the novel Roderick Random joins a fictional ship in the same fleet, the* Thunder, *but more accidentally than Smollett, having been 'assaulted on Tower Hill by a press-gang'. The ship sails from Spithead to the Americas and in this chapter we are treated to a vivid picture of life at sea on a full-rigged man-of-war.*

> I was wakened by a most horrible din, occasioned by the play of the gun carriages upon the deck above, the cracking of cabins, the howling of the wind through the shrouds, the confused noise of the ship's crew, the pipes of the boatswain and his mates, the trumpets of the lieutenants, and the clanking of the chain pumps.

In Smollett's racy picaresque manner, the colourful personal history of Roderick Random provides the main driving force of the novel, and we see an extension to ship-board of the same kind of knockabout adventures and encounters with rogues and eccentrics that we have already met with in Random's travels from his native Scotland. Among the eccentrics is numbered the Welsh surgeon's mate, Morgan, first of a line of Welsh comic characters which ends with the inimitable Win Jenkins in Smollett's last novel, Humphry Clinker. *We also read of the unpleasant captain of the* Thunder *and the even more unpleasant Doctor Mackshane, together with the brave Jack Rattlin, whose fall from the yard-arm occasions much frantic to-ing and fro-ing and arguments among the sawbones about the advisability of amputating his leg, in the gruesome surroundings of the surgeon's cock-pit.*

In such a frantic narrative, it is uncertain whether Smollett had a didactic or satirical intent, but in these, the early stages of the novel in English, his lively descriptions set a standard for the naturalistic novel to come.

⚜

The captain was carried into his cabin, so enraged with the treatment he had received, that he ordered the fellow to be brought before him, that he might have the pleasure of pistolling him with his own hand; and would certainly have satisfied his revenge in this manner, had not the first lieutenant remonstrated against it, by observing, that, in all appearance, the fellow was not mad but desperate; that he had been hired by some enemy of the captain to assassinate him, and therefore ought to be kept in irons till he could be brought to a court-martial, which, no doubt, would sift the affair to the bottom, by which means important discoveries might be made, and then sentence the criminal to a death adequate to his demerits. This suggestion, improbable as it was, had the desired effect upon the captain, being exactly calculated for the meridian of his intellects; more especially as Doctor Mackshane espoused this opinion, in consequence of his previous declaration that the man was not mad. Morgan, finding there was no more damage done, could not help discovering by his countenance, the pleasure he enjoyed on this occasion; and while he bathed the doctor's face with an embrocation, ventured to ask him, whether he thought there were more fools or madmen on board? But he would have been wiser in containing this sally, which his patient carefully laid up in his memory, to be taken notice of at a more fit season. Meanwhile, we weighed anchor, and on our way to the Downs, the madman, who was treated as a prisoner, took an opportunity, while the sentinel attended him at the head, to leap overboard, and frustrate the revenge of the captain. We stayed not long at the Downs, but took the benefit of the first easterly wind to go round to Spithead; where having received on board provisions for six months, we sailed from St Helen's in the grand fleet bound for the West Indies, on the ever-memorable expedition of Carthagena.

It was not without great mortification I saw myself on the point of being transported to such a distant and unhealthy climate, destitute of every convenience that could render such a voyage supportable; and under the dominion of an arbitrary tyrant, whose command was almost intolerable. However, as these complaints were common to a great many on board, I resolved to submit patiently to my fate, and contrive to make myself as easy as the nature of the case would allow. We got out of the Channel with a prosperous breeze, which died away, leaving us becalmed about fifty leagues to the westward of the Lizard. But this state of inaction did not last long; for next night our main-top sail was split by the wind, which in the morning increased to a hurricane. I was wakened by a most horrible din, occasioned by the play of the gun carriages upon the deck above, the cracking of cabins, the howling of the wind through the shrouds, the confused noise of the ship's crew, the pipes of the boatswain and his mates, the trumpets of the lieutenants, and the clanking of the chain pumps. Morgan, who had never been at sea before, turned out in a great hurry, crying, 'Cot have mercy and compassion upon us! I believe we have got upon the confines of Lucifer and the d–d!' while poor Thomson lay quaking in his hammock, putting up petitions to Heaven for our safety. I rose and joined the Welshman, with whom (after having fortified ourselves with brandy) I went above; but, if my sense of hearing was startled before, how must my sight have been appalled in beholding the effects of the storm! The sea was swelled into billows mountain high, on the top of which our ship sometimes hung as if it was about to be precipitated to the abyss below! Sometimes we sunk between two waves that rose on each side higher than our topmast head, and threatened, by dashing together, to overwhelm us in a moment! Of all our fleet, consisting of a hundred and fifty sail, scarce twelve appeared, and these driving under their bare poles, at the mercy of the tempest. At length the mast of one of them gave way, and tumbled overboard with a hideous crash! Nor was the prospect in our own ship much more agreeable; a number of officers and sailors ran backward and forward with distraction in their looks, hallooing to one another, and undetermined what they should attend to first. Some clung to the yards, endeavouring to unbend the sails that were split into a thousand pieces flapping in the wind; others tried to furl those which were yet whole, while the masts, at every pitch, bent and quivered like twigs, as if they would have shivered into innumerable splinters! While I considered this scene with equal terror and astonishment, one of the main braces broke, by the shock whereof two sailors were flung from the yard's arm into the sea, where they perished, and poor Jack Rattlin was thrown down upon the deck, at the expense of a broken leg. Morgan and I ran immediately to his assistance, and found a splinter of the shin-bone thrust by the violence of the fall through the skin. As this was a case of too great consequence to be treated without the authority of the doctor, I went down to his cabin to inform him of the accident, as well as to bring up dressings, which we always kept ready prepared. I entered his apartment without any ceremony, and by the glimmering of a lamp, perceived him on his knees, before something that very much resembled a crucifix; but this I will not insist upon, that I may not seem too much a slave to common report, which indeed assisted my conjecture on this occasion, by representing Doctor Mackshane as a member of the Church of Rome. Be this as it will, he got up in a sort of confusion, occasioned, I suppose, by his being disturbed in his devotion, and, in a trice, snatched the subject of my suspicion from my sight.

After making an apology for my intrusion, I acquainted him with the situation of Rattlin, but could by no means prevail upon him to visit him on deck, where he lay. He bade me desire the boatswain to order some of the men to carry him down to the cock-pit, and in the meantime, said he, I will direct Thomson to get ready the dressings. When I signified to the boatswain the doctor's desire, he swore a terrible oath, that he could not spare one man from the deck, because he expected the mast would go by the board every minute. This piece of information did not at all contribute to my peace of mind; however, as my friend Rattlin complained very much, with the assistance of Morgan, I supported him to the lower deck, whither Mr Mackshane, after much entreaty, ventured to come, attended by Thomson, with a box full of dressings, and his own servant, who carried a whole set of capital instruments. He examined the fracture and the wound, and concluding, from a livid colour extending itself upon the limb, that a mortification would ensue, resolved to amputate the leg immediately. This was a dreadful sentence to the patient, who, recruiting himself with a quid of tobacco, pronounced, with a woeful countenance, 'What! is there no remedy, doctor? – must I be dock'd? – can't you splice it?' 'Assuredly, Doctor Mackshane,' said the first mate, 'with submission, and deference, and veneration, to your superior abilities, and opportunities, and stations, look you, I do apprehend, and conjecture, and aver, that there is no occasion nor necessity to smite off this poor man's leg.' 'God Almighty bless you, dear Welshman!' cried Rattlin, 'may you have fair wind and weather wheresoever you're bound, and come to an anchor in the Road of Heaven at last.' Mackshane, very much incensed at his mate's differing in opinion from him so openly, answered, that he was not bound to give an account of his practice to him; and, in a peremptory tone, ordered him to apply the tourniquet; at the sight of which, Jack, starting up, cried, 'Avast, avast! d–n my heart, if you clap your nippers on me, till I know wherefore! Mr Random, won't you lend a hand towards saving my precious limb? Odds heart, if Lieutenant Bowling was here, he would not suffer Jack Rattlin's leg to be chopped off like a piece of old junk.' This pathetic address to me, joined to my inclination to serve my honest friend, and the reasons I had to believe there was no danger in delaying the amputation, induced me to declare myself of the first mate's opinion, and affirm, that the preternatural colour of the skin was owing to an inflammation occasioned by a contusion, and common in all such cases, without any indication of an approaching gangrene. Morgan, who had a great opinion of my skill, manifestly exulted in my fellowship, and asked Thomson's sentiments of the matter, in hopes of strengthening our association with him too; but he, being of a meek disposition, and either dreading the enmity of the surgeon, or speaking the dictates of his own judgment, in a modest manner, espoused the opinion of Mackshane, who, by this time, having consulted with himself, determined to act in such a manner as to screen himself from censure, and at the same time revenge himself on us for our arrogance in contradicting him. With this view he asked if we would undertake to cure the leg at our peril – that is, be answerable for the consequence. To this question Morgan replied, that the lives of his creatures are in the hands of Cot alone; and it would be great presumption in him to undertake for an event that was in the power of his Maker, no more than the doctor could promise to cure all the sick to whom he administered his assistance; but if the patient would put himself under our direction, we would do our endeavour to bring his distemper to a favourable issue, to which, at present, we saw no obstruction. I signified my concurrence; and Rattlin was so overjoyed, that, shaking us both by the hands, he swore nobody else should touch him, and if he died, his blood should be upon his own head. Mr Mackshane, flattering himself with the prospect of our miscarriage, went away, and left us to manage it as we should think proper. Accordingly, having sawed off part of the splinter that stuck through the skin, we reduced the fracture, dressed the wound, applied the eighteen-tailed bandage, and put the leg in a box, *secundum artem*. Everything succeeded according to our wish, and we had the satisfaction of not only preserving the poor fellow's leg, but likewise of rendering the doctor contemptible among the ship's company, who had all their eyes on us during the course of this cure, which was completed in six weeks.

Skye Boat Song

SIR HAROLD BOULTON (1859–1935)

Speed bonnie boat, like a bird on the wing,
Onward, the sailors cry
Carry the lad that's born to be king
Over the sea to Skye

Loud the winds howl, loud the waves roar,
Thunder clouds rend the air;
Baffled our foes stand on the shore
Follow they will not dare

Though the waves leap, soft shall ye sleep
Ocean's a royal bed
Rocked in the deep, Flora will keep
Watch by your weary head

Many's the lad fought on that day
Well the claymore could wield
When the night came, silently lay
Dead on Culloden's field

Burned are our homes, exile and death
Scatter the loyal men
Yet, e'er the sword cool in the sheath,
Charlie will come again.

'John Paul Jones's Cruise in Home Waters'

from The Scots Magazine April 1778

When the American Revolution broke out in 1775 John Paul Jones, born at Arbigland, Kirkcudbrightshire, but by then a resident of Virginia, enlisted in the navy of the Continental Congress. Promoted Captain the next year he commanded the Providence *on a cruise against British shipping off Nova Scotia. In 1777 he was appointed to the sloop* Ranger, *which he took to France and then on a cruise around the coasts of Britain. The three news reports from* The Scots Magazine *show something of the impact of Jones's cruise.*

All these reports speak of the Ranger *as a privateer, that is, a privately owned armed ship licensed by a belligerent power to carry out warlike acts. This description is not accurate, as the* Ranger *was a commissioned vessel of the United States government – however the British government and the correspondents of* The Scots Magazine *did not recognise the United States, or its military and naval forces, and would not be prepared to grant the* Ranger *the status of a government ship.*

The attacks on Whitehaven and Kirkcudbright were on areas very familiar to Jones from his childhood by the Solway and early trading voyages from Whitehaven, then one of the most important English ports.

The raid on Lord Selkirk's house, described in our second extract, was to have an interesting and somewhat quixotic sequel. Jones was distressed to find that his crew had seized the Selkirks' silver plate but felt unable to deprive his men of the spoils of war. However when the booty was later sold he personally purchased it and had it returned to Lady Selkirk. A long correspondence between Jones and the Selkirks intervened, with Lord Selkirk writing:

Your genteel offer, sir, of returning the plate is very polite, but at the same time neither Lady Selkirk nor I can think of accepting of it, as you must purchase it you say for that purpose, but if your delicacy makes you unwilling to keep that share of its value which as Captain you are entitled to, without purchasing, I would in that case wish that part to be given to those private men who were on the party, as an encouragement for their good behaviour.

Six years later the sensibilities of both parties were assuaged and Jones effected the return of the Selkirks' silver plate, with, so tradition insists, the tea leaves still untouched in the kettle.

Jones's capture of HMS Drake, *like his famous victory in 1779 over HMS* Serapis, *proved a serious blow to the morale of the Royal Navy. The loss of the* Drake *overturned the British tradition of consistent victories in single ship action against opponents of similar force. Jones's contribution to the US Navy – of which he is rightly seen as the father – is well summed up by the monument in the US Naval Academy at Annapolis which bears the words 'He gave our Navy its earliest traditions of heroism and victory.'*

'Whitehaven, April 23

A little before three o'clock this morning a man rapped at several doors in Marlborough Street (adjoining one of the piers) and informed the people, that fire had been set to one of the ships in the harbour, matches were laid in several others; the whole would soon be in a blaze, and the town also destroyed; that he was one belonging to the privateer, but had escaped for the purpose of saving, if possible, the town and shipping from destruction. The alarm was immediately spread, and his account proved too true. The *Thompson*, Capt. Rich. Johnson, a new vessel, and one of the finest ever built here, was in a flame. It was low water, consequently all the shipping in the port was in the most imminent danger, and the vessel on which they had begun the diabolical work, lying close to one of the steaths, there was the greatest reason to fear that the flames would from it be communicated to the town. But by an uncommon exertion the fire was extinguished before it reached the rigging of the ship; and this, in a providential manner, prevented all the dreadful consequences which might have ensued. The incendiaries had spiked most of guns of both our batteries, several matches were found on board different vessels, and other combustible matter in different parts of the harbour.

Freeman (the deserter), on his examination, declared, that the party landed consisted of thirty men; that they had belonged to the *Ranger* privateer, fitted out at Piscataqua in New England, Capt. Jones commander; that she mounted eighteen guns besides swivels, and had on board between 140 and 150 men; that she had taken two prizes, and had sent them into France; and that the Captain declared, that the destruction of Whitehaven was his first object, seizing the person of Lord Selkirk was the next thing he wished, after which he would sail for Brest, and on his passage sink, burn, and destroy whatever fell in his way, belonging to Great Britain.'

'*Dumfries, April 24*
Yesterday afternoon an express arrived from Kirkcudbright, with accounts, that an American privateer of twenty guns had landed near the Isle (St Mary's), and that a party from her had plundered Lord Selkirk's house. Mrs Wood, lady of the late Governor of the Isle of Man, at present residing here, had gone, two or three days ago, on a visit to Lady Selkirk, and returned here last night. She informs, that they were all well, and in good spirits; and says, that yesterday morning, between ten and eleven, a servant brought word, that a press-gang had landed near the house. This the party from the privateer had given out, in order, as was supposed, to get out of the way all the servants and others who might oppose them. Presently between thirty and forty armed men came up; all of whom planted themselves round the house, except three, who entered, each with two horse-pistols at his side; and, with bayonets fixed, they demanded to see the lady of the house; and, upon her appearance, told her, with a mixture of rudeness and civility, who they were, and that all the plate must be delivered to them. Lady Selkirk behaved with great composure and presence of mind. She soon directed her plate to be delivered; with which, without doing any other damage, or asking for watches, jewels, or anything else (which is odd), the gentlemen made off. There is reason to think that there were some people among them acquainted with persons and places, and in particular one fellow, supposed to have been once a waiter at an inn in Kirkcudbright. The leader of the party, who was not the captain of the vessel, told, that their intention was to seize Lord Selkirk, who is now in London; that two other privateers were at hand; and that they had been at Whitehaven, where they had burnt some small vessels, but did not get done what they intended. When the affair was ended, Lady Selkirk, with her family and visitors, left the house.'

'*Port-Glasgow, April 27*
Last night Capt. Crawford, of the *Cambraes* wherry, arrived in town express from a cruise, confirms all the news-paper intelligence concerning the privateer on the coast, and further adds, that on Friday last, the privateer, intending some mischief in Belfast Loch, went in; but finding the *Drake* sloop of war there, stood out again. The *Drake*, not knowing what she was, sent her boat and gang to press her hands; which the *Ranger* took, and carried along with them, and the *Drake* followed

her, and on that evening engaged; but, night coming on, nothing was done till Saturday morning, when they again engaged; and, after a very hot engagement for an hour and five minutes, the *Drake* was obliged to strike; the captain and first lieutenant killed, twenty two men killed and wounded, she had also one of her topmasts carried away. They were so close on Galloway coast, that Capt. Crawford, lying in Lochgair, heard the firing, made loose, and stood out; but before she got in fight, the *Drake* was going away with the privateer. She had taken some fishing-boats on the coast of Ireland, whose crews were all put in irons during the engagement; but when it was over, they were all put in boats again and sent away; and, on their passage to the shore, Capt. Crawford intercepted them, and got all the intelligence: the fishermen also told Capt. Crawford, that the privateer was wishing much to fall in with him and Campbell's cutter. Capt. Crawford made all the sail he could for Clyde; and on Sunday morning fell in with the *Thetis* frigate off Plada, went on board, and gave Capt. Gillies all the intelligence, pointed out the course; and he, after giving Capt. Crawford an express for the admiralty, crowded all sail away for them.'

But it would seem the Thetis *never came up with the privateer.*

Various Doings in the West

from Mr Standfast

JOHN BUCHAN (1875–1946)

Mr Standfast, set in 1917, was Buchan's third thriller featuring Richard Hannay, who we find in this extract travelling up the west coast of Scotland in the character of Cornelius Brand, a South African mining engineer and pacifist. Hannay, the hero of The Thirty-nine Steps, *is now a Brigadier who has been recalled from the Western Front by British Intelligence to help search for a German master-spy. Hannay's ally, the Glasgow shop-steward Andrew Amos, has arranged a passage for Hannay/Brand on the* Tobermory, *a coastal cargo steamer, so that Hannay can watch Abel Gresson, an American suspected of being part of the German spy-ring, who has signed-on as purser on the* Tobermory. *As in all the best Buchan tales, every man's hand is against Hannay – the police have been set on his trail by the master-spy and he cannot reveal his identity to them without danger of exposing his true identity to the enemy.*

Apart from the description of the West Highland wanderings of the Tobermory *(a fictitious vessel but probably based on MacBrayne's cargo boats) the extract reminds us that travel over a large part of the west coast was controlled for security reasons during both world wars and travellers to the security zone required a passport. As the skipper tells Hannay: 'They'll no let ye go north o' Fort William without one.'*

The novel's title is taken from John Bunyan's seventeenth-century spiritual classic Pilgrim's Progress *– a work which Hannay and his fellow agents of British intelligence use as a type of code-book.*

❦

The *Tobermory* was no ship for passengers. Its decks were littered with a hundred oddments, so that a man could barely walk a step without tacking, and my bunk was simply a shelf in the frowsty little saloon, where the odour of ham and eggs hung like a fog. I joined her at Greenock and took a turn on deck with the captain after tea, when he told me the names of the big blue hills to the north. He had a fine old copper-coloured face and side-whiskers like an archbishop, and having spent all his days beating up the western seas, had as many yarns in his head as Peter himself.

'On this boat,' he announced, 'we don't ken what a day may bring forth. I may pit into Colonsay for twa hours and bide there three days. I get a telegram at Oban and the next thing I'm awa ayont Barra. Sheep's the difficult business. They maun be fetched for the sales, and they're dooms slow to lift. So ye see it's not what ye call a pleasure trip, Maister Brand.'

Indeed it wasn't, for the confounded tub wallowed like a fat sow as soon as we rounded a headland and got the weight of the south-western wind. When asked my purpose, I explained that I was a colonial of Scots extraction, who was paying his first visit to his fatherland and wanted to explore the beauties of the West Highlands. I let him gather that I was not rich in this world's goods.

'Ye'll have a passport?' he asked. 'They'll no let ye go north o' Fort William without one.'

Amos had said nothing about passports, so I looked blank.

'I could keep ye on board for the whole voyage,' he went on, 'but ye wouldna be permitted to land. If ye're seekin' enjoyment, it would be a poor job sittin' on this deck and admirin' the works o' God and no allowed to step on the pierhead. Ye should have applied to the military gentlemen in Glesca. But ye've plenty o' time to make up your mind afore we get to Oban. We've a heap o' calls to make Mull and Islay way.'

The purser came up to inquire about my ticket, and greeted me with a grin.

'Ye're acquaint with Mr Gresson, then?' said the captain. 'Weel, we're a cheery wee ship's company, and that's the great thing on this kind o' job.'

I made but a poor supper, for the wind had risen to half a gale, and I saw hours of wretchedness approaching. The trouble with me is that I cannot be honestly sick and get it over. Queasiness and headache beset me and there is no refuge but bed. I turned into my bunk, leaving the captain and the mate smoking shag not six feet from my head, and fell into a restless sleep. When I woke the place was empty, and smelt vilely of stale tobacco and cheese. My throbbing brows made sleep impossible, and I tried to ease them by staggering up on deck. I saw a clear windy sky, with every star as bright as a live coal, and a heaving waste of dark waters running to ink-black hills. Then a douche of spray caught me and sent me down the companion to my bunk again, where I lay for hours trying to make a plan of campaign.

I argued that if Amos had wanted me to have a passport he would have provided one, so I needn't bother my head about that. But it was my business to keep alongside Gresson, and if the boat stayed a week in some port and he went off ashore, I must follow him. Having no passport I would have to be always dodging trouble, which would handicap my movements and in all likelihood make me more conspicuous than I wanted. I guessed that Amos had denied me the passport for the very reason that he wanted Gresson to think me harmless. The area of danger would, therefore, be the passport country, somewhere north of Fort William.

But to follow Gresson I must run risks and enter that country. His suspicions, if he had any, would be lulled if I left the boat at Oban, but it was up to me to follow overland to the north and hit the place where the *Tobermory* made a long stay. The confounded tub had no plans; she wandered about the West Highlands looking for sheep and things; and the captain himself could give me no time-table of her voyage. It was incredible that Gresson should take all this trouble if he did not know that at some place – and the right place – he would have time to get a spell ashore. But I could scarcely ask Gresson for that information, though I determined to cast a wary fly over him. I knew roughly the *Tobermory*'s course – through the Sound of Islay to Colonsay; then up the east side of Mull to Oban; then through the Sound of Mull to the islands with names like cocktails, Rum and Eigg and Coll; then to Skye; and then for the outer Hebrides. I thought the last would be the place, and it seemed madness to leave the boat, for the Lord knew how I should get across the Minch. This consideration upset all my plans again, and I fell into a troubled sleep without coming to any conclusion.

Morning found us nosing between Jura and Islay, and about midday we touched at a little port, where we unloaded some cargo and took on a couple of shepherds who were going to Colonsay. The mellow afternoon and the good smell of salt and heather got rid of the dregs of my queasiness, and I spent a profitable hour on the pierhead with a guide-book called *Baddeley's Scotland*, and one of Bartholomew's maps. I was beginning to think that Amos might be able to tell me something, for a talk with the captain had suggested that the *Tobermory* would not dally long in the neighbourhood of Rum and Eigg. The big droving season was scarcely on yet, and sheep for the Oban market would be lifted on the return journey. In that case Skye was the first place to watch, and if I could get wind of any big cargo waiting there I would be able to make a plan. Amos was somewhere near the Kyle, and that was across the narrows from Skye. Looking at the map it seemed to me that, in spite of being passportless, I might be able somehow to make my way up through Morvern and Arisaig to the latitude of Skye. The difficulty would be to get across the strip of sea, but there must be boats to beg, borrow, or steal.

I was poring over *Baddeley* when Gresson sat down beside me. He was in good temper, and disposed to talk, and to my surprise his talk was all about the beauties of the countryside. There was a kind of apple-green light over everything; the steep heather hills cut into the sky like purple amethysts, while beyond the straits the western ocean stretched its pale molten gold to the sunset. Gresson waxed lyrical over the scene. 'This just about puts me right inside, Mr Brand. I've got to get away from that little old town pretty frequent or I begin to moult like a canary. A man feels a man when he gets to a place that smells as good as this. Why in hell do we ever get messed up in those stone and lime cages? I reckon some day I'll pull my freight for a clean location and settle down there and make little poems. This place would about content me. And there's a spot out in California in the Coast ranges that I've been keeping my eye on.' The odd thing was that I believe he meant it. His ugly face was lit up with a serious delight.

He told me he had taken this voyage before, so I got out *Baddeley* and asked for advice. 'I can't spend too much time on holidaying,' I told him, 'and I want to see all the beauty spots. But the best of them seem to be in the area that this fool British Government won't let you into without a passport. I suppose I shall have to leave you at Oban.'

'Too bad,' he said sympathetically. 'Well, they tell me there's some pretty sights round Oban.' And he thumbed the guide-book and began to read about Glencoe.

I said that was not my purpose, and pitched him a yarn about Prince Charlie and how my mother's great-great-grandfather had played some kind of part in that show. I told him I wanted to see the place where the Prince landed and where he left for France. 'So far as I can make out that won't take me into the passport country, but I'll have to do a bit of footslogging. Well, I'm used to padding the hoof. I must get the captain to put me off in Morvern, and then I can foot it round the top of Lochiel and get back to Oban through Appin. How's that for a holiday trek?'

He gave the scheme his approval. 'But if it was me, Mr Brand, I would have a shot at puzzling your gallant policemen. You and I don't take much stock in Governments and their two-cent laws, and it would be a good game to see just how far you could get into the forbidden land. A man like you could put up a good bluff on those hayseeds. I don't mind having a bet . . .'

'No,' I said, 'I'm out for a rest, and not for sport. If there was anything to be gained I'd undertake to bluff my way to the Orkney Islands. But it's a wearing job and I've better things to think about.'

'So? Well, enjoy yourself your own way. I'll be sorry when you leave us, for I owe you something for that rough-house, and beside there's darned little company in the old moss-back captain.'

That evening Gresson and I swopped yarns after supper to the accompaniment of the 'Ma Goad!' and 'Is't possible?' of captain and mate. I went to bed after a glass or two of weak grog, and made up for the last night's vigil by falling sound asleep. I had very little kit with me, beyond what I stood up in and could carry in my waterproof pockets, but on Amos's advice I had brought my little nickel-plated revolver. This lived by day in my hip-pocket, and at night I put it behind my pillow. But when I woke next morning to find us casting anchor in a bay below rough low hills, which I knew to be the island of Colonsay, I could find no trace of the revolver. I searched every inch of the bunk and only shook out feathers from the mouldy ticking. I remembered perfectly putting the thing behind my head before I went to sleep, and now it had vanished utterly. Of course I could not advertise my loss, and I didn't greatly mind it, for this was not a job where I could do much shooting. But it made me think a good deal about Mr Gresson. He simply could not suspect me; if he had bagged my gun, as I was pretty certain he had, it must be because he wanted it for himself and not that he might disarm me. Every way I argued it I reached the same conclusion. In Gresson's eyes I must seem as harmless as a child.

We spent the better part of a day at Colonsay, and Gresson, so far as his duties allowed, stuck to me like a limpet. Before I went ashore I wrote out a telegram for Amos. I devoted a hectic hour to the *Pilgrim's Progress*, but I could not compose any kind of intelligible message with reference to its text. We had all the same edition – the one in the *Golden Treasury* series – so I could have made up a sort of cipher by referring to lines and pages, but that would have taken up a dozen telegraph forms and seemed to me too elaborate for the purpose. So I sent this message:

Ochterlony, Post office, Kyle.
    I hope to spend part of holiday near you and to see you if boat's programme permits. Are any good cargoes waiting in your neighbourhood? Reply Post office, Oban.

It was highly important that Gresson should not see this, but it was the deuce of a business to shake him off. I went for a walk in the afternoon along the shore and passed the telegraph office, but the confounded fellow was with me all the time. My only chance was just before we sailed, when he had to go on board to check some cargo. As the telegraph office stood full in view of the ship's deck I did not go near it. But in the back-end of the clachan I found the schoolmaster, and got him to promise to send the wire. I also bought off him a couple of well-worn sevenpenny novels.

The result was that I delayed our departure for ten minutes, and when I came on board faced a wrathful Gresson. 'Where the hell have you been?' he asked. 'The weather's blowing up dirty and the old man's mad to get off. Didn't you get your legs stretched enough this afternoon?'

I explained humbly that I had been to the schoolmaster to get something to read, and produced my dingy red volumes. At that his brow cleared. I could see that his suspicions were set at rest.

We left Colonsay about six in the evening with the sky behind us banking for a storm, and the hills of Jura to starboard an angry purple. Colonsay was too low an island to be any kind of breakwater against a western gale, so the weather was bad from the start. Our course was north by east, and when we had passed the butt-end of the island we nosed about in the trough of big seas, shipping tons of water and rolling like a buffalo. I know as much about boats as about Egyptian hieroglyphics, but even my landsman's eyes could tell that we were in for a rough night. I was determined not to get queasy again, but when I went below the smell of tripe and onions promised to be my undoing; so I dined on a slab of chocolate and a cabin biscuit, put on my waterproof, and resolved to stick it out on deck.

I took up position near the bows, where I was out of reach of the oily steamer smells. It was as fresh as the top of a mountain, but mighty cold and wet, for a gusty drizzle had set in, and I got the spindrift of the big waves. There I balanced myself, as we lurched into the twilight, hanging on with one hand to a rope which descended from the stumpy mast. I noticed that there was only an indifferent rail between me and the edge, but that interested me and helped to keep off sickness. I swung to the movement of the vessel, and though I was mortally cold it was rather pleasant than otherwise. My notion was to get the nausea whipped out of me by the weather, and, when I was properly tired, to go down and turn in.

I stood there till the dark had fallen. By that time I was an automaton, the way a man gets on sentry-go, and I could have easily hung on till morning. My thoughts ranged about the earth, beginning with the business I had set out on, and presently – by way of recollections of Blenkiron and Peter – reaching the German forest where, in the Christmas of 1915, I had been nearly done in by fever and old Stumm. I remembered the bitter cold of that wild race, and the way the snow seemed to burn like fire when I stumbled and got my face into it. I reflected that sea-sickness was kitten's play to a good bout of malaria.

The weather was growing worse, and I was getting more than spindrift from the seas. I hooked my arm round the rope, for my fingers were numbing. Then I fell to dreaming again, principally about Fosse Manor and Mary Lamington. This so ravished me that I was as good as asleep. I was trying to reconstruct the picture as I had last seen her at Biggleswick station . . .

A heavy body collided with me and shook my arm from the rope. I slithered across the yard of deck, engulfed in a whirl of water. One foot caught a stanchion of the rail, and it gave with me, so that for an instant I was more than half overboard. But my fingers clawed wildly and caught in the links of what must have been the anchor chain. They held, though a ton's weight seemed to be tugging at my feet . . . Then the old tub rolled back, the waters slipped off, and I was sprawling on a wet deck with no breath in me and a gallon of brine in my windpipe.

I heard a voice cry out sharply, and a hand helped me to my feet. It was Gresson, and he seemed excited.

'God, Mr Brand, that was a close call! I was coming up to find you, when this damned ship took to lying on her side. I guess I must have cannoned into you, and I was calling myself bad names when I saw you rolling into the Atlantic. If I hadn't got a grip on the rope I would have been down beside you. Say, you're not hurt? I reckon you'd better come below and get a glass of rum under your belt. You're about as wet as mother's dish-clouts.'

There's one advantage about campaigning. You take your luck when it comes and don't worry about what might have been. I didn't think any more of the business, except that it had cured me of wanting to be sea-sick. I went down to the reeking cabin without one qualm in my stomach, and ate a good meal of welsh-rabbit and bottled Bass, with a tot of rum to follow up. Then I shed my wet garments, and slept in my bunk till we anchored off a village in Mull in a clear blue morning.

It took us four days to crawl up that coast and make Oban, for we seemed to be a floating general store for every hamlet in those parts. Gresson made himself very pleasant, as if he wanted to atone for nearly doing me in. We played some poker, and I read the little books I had got in Colonsay, and then rigged up a fishing-line, and caught saithe and lythe and an occasional big haddock. But I found the time pass slowly, and I was glad when about noon one day we came into a bay blocked with islands and saw a clean little town sitting on the hills, and the smoke of a railway engine.

I went ashore and purchased a better brand of hat in a tweed store. Then I made a bee-line for the post office, and asked for telegrams. One was given to me, and as I opened it I saw Gresson at my elbow.

It ran thus:

Brand, Post office, Oban. Page 117, paragraph 3. Ochterlony.

I passed it to Gresson with a rueful face.

'There's a piece of foolishness,' I said. 'I've got a cousin who's a Presbyterian minister up in Ross-shire, and before I knew about this passport humbug I wrote to him and offered to pay him a visit. I told him to wire me here if it was convenient, and the old idiot has sent me the wrong telegram. This was likely as not meant for some brother parson, who's got my message instead.'

'What's the guy's name?' Gresson asked curiously, peering at the signature.

'Ochterlony. David Ochterlony. He's a great swell at writing books, but he's no earthly use at handling the telegraph. However, it don't signify, seeing I'm not going near him.' I crumpled up the pink form and tossed it on the floor. Gresson and I walked back to the *Tobermory* together.

That afternoon, when I got a chance, I had out my *Pilgrim's Progress*. Page 117, paragraph 3, read:

Then I saw in my dream, that a little of the road, over against the Silver-mine, stood, Demas (gentlemanlike) to call to passengers to come and see: who said to Christian and his fellow, Ho, turn aside hither and I will show you a thing.

At tea I led the talk to my own past life. I yarned about my experiences as a mining engineer, and said I could never get out of the trick of looking at country with the eye of the prospector. 'For instance,' I said, 'if this had been Rhodesia, I would have said there was a good chance of copper in these little kopjes above the town. They're not unlike the hills round the Messina mine.' I told the captain that after the war I was thinking of turning my attention to the West Highlands and looking out for minerals.

'Ye'll make nothing of it,' said the captain. 'The costs are ower big, even if ye found the minerals, for ye'd have to import a' your labour. The West Hielandman is no fond o' hard work. Ye ken the psalm o' the crofter?

"O that the peats would cut themselves
The fish chump on the shore
And that I in my bed might lie
Henceforth for evermore!"'

'Has it ever been tried?' I asked.

'Often. There's marble and slate quarries, and there was word o' coal in Benbecula. And there's the iron mines at Ranna.'

'Where's that?' I asked.

'Up forenent Skye. We call in there, and generally bide a bit. There's a heap of cargo for Ranna, and we usually get a good load back. But as I tell ye, there's few Hielanders working there. Mostly Irish and lads frae Fife and Falkirk way.'

I didn't pursue the subject, for I had found Demas's silver-mine. If the *Tobermory* lay at Ranna for a week, Gresson would have time to do his own private business. Ranna would not be the spot, for the island was bare to the world in the middle of a much-frequented channel. But Skye was just across the way, and when I looked in my map at its big, wandering peninsulas I concluded that my guess had been right, and that Skye was the place to make for.

That night I sat on deck with Gresson, and in a wonderful starry silence we watched the lights die out of the houses in the town, and talked of a thousand things. I noticed – what I had had a hint of before – that my companion was no common man. There were moments when he forgot himself and talked like an educated gentleman: then he would remember, and relapse into the lingo of Leadville, Colorado. In my character of the ingenuous inquirer I set him posers about politics and economics, the kind of thing I might have been supposed to pick up from unintelligent browsing among little books. Generally he answered with some slangy catchword, but occasionally he was interested beyond his discretion, and treated me to a harangue like an equal. I discovered another thing, that he had a craze for poetry, and a capacious memory for it. I forget how we drifted into the subject, but I remember he quoted some queer haunting stuff which he said was Swinburne, and verses by people I had heard of from Letchford at Biggleswick. Then he saw by my silence that he had gone too far, and fell back into the jargon of the West. He wanted to know about my plans, and we went down into the cabin and had a look at the map. I explained my route, up Morvern and round the head of Lochiel, and back to Oban by the east side of Loch Linnhe.

'Got you,' he said. 'You've a hell of a walk before you. That bug never bit me, and I guess I'm not envying you any. And after that, Mr Brand?'

'Back to Glasgow to do some work for the cause,' I said lightly.

'Just so,' he said, with a grin. 'It's a great life if you don't weaken.'

We steamed out of the bay next morning at dawn, and about nine o'clock I got on shore at a little place called Lochaline. My kit was all

on my person, and my waterproof's pockets were stuffed with chocolates
and biscuits I had bought in Oban. The captain was discouraging. 'Ye'll
get your bellyful o' Hieland hills, Mr Brand, afore ye win round the Loch
head. Ye'll be wishin' yourself back on the *Tobermory*.' But Gresson
speeded me joyfully on my way, and said he wished he were coming
with me. He even accompanied me the first hundred yards, and waved
his hat after me till I was round the turn of the road.

The first stage in that journey was pure delight. I was thankful to be
rid of the infernal boat, and the hot summer scents coming down the glen
were comforting after the cold, salt smell of the sea. The road lay up the
side of a small bay, at the top of which a big white house stood among
gardens. Presently I had left the coast and was in a glen where a brown
salmon-river swirled through acres of bog-myrtle. It had its source in
a loch, from which the mountain rose steeply – a place so glassy in
that August forenoon that every scaur and wrinkle of the hillside was
faithfully reflected. After that I crossed a low pass to the head of another
sea-loch, and, following the map, struck over the shoulder of a great hill
and ate my luncheon far up on its side, with a wonderful vista of wood
and water below me.

All that morning I was very happy, not thinking about Gresson or
Ivery, but getting my mind clear in those wide spaces, and my lungs
filled with the brisk hill air. But I noticed one curious thing. On my
last visit to Scotland, when I covered more moorland miles a day than
any man since Claverhouse, I had been fascinated by the land, and had
pleased myself with plans for settling down in it. But now, after three
years of war and general racketing, I felt less drawn to that kind of
landscape. I wanted something more green and peaceful and habitable,
and it was to the Cotswolds that my memory turned with longing.

I puzzled over this till I realized that in all my Cotswold pictures a
figure kept going and coming – a young girl with a cloud of gold hair
and the strong, slim grace of a boy, who had sung 'Cherry Ripe' in a
moonlit garden. Up on that hillside I understood very clearly that I,
who had been as careless of women as any monk, had fallen wildly in
love with a child of half my age. I was loath to admit it, though for
weeks the conclusion had been forcing itself on me. Not that I didn't
revel in my madness, but that it seemed too hopeless a business, and
I had no use for barren philandering. But, seated on a rock munching
chocolate and biscuits, I faced up to the fact and resolved to trust my
luck. After all we were comrades in a big job, and it was up to me to
be man enough to win her. The thought seemed to brace any courage
that was in me. No task seemed too hard, with her approval to gain and

her companionship somewhere at the back of it. I sat for a long time in a happy dream, remembering all the glimpses I had had of her, and humming her song to an audience of one blackfaced sheep.

On the highroad half a mile below me, I saw a figure on a bicycle mounting the hill, and then getting off to mop its face at the summit. I turned my Zeiss glasses on to it, and observed that it was a country policeman. It caught sight of me, stared for a bit, tucked its machine into the side of the road, and then very slowly began to climb the hillside. Once it stopped, waved its hand and shouted something which I could not hear. I sat finishing my luncheon, till the features were revealed to me of a fat, oldish man, blowing like a grampus, his cap well on the back of a bald head, and his trousers tied about the shins with string.

There was a spring beside me, and I had out my flask to round off my meal.

'Have a drink,' I said.

His eye brightened, and a smile overran his moist face.

'Thank you, sir. It will be very warm coming up the brae.'

'You oughtn't to,' I said. 'You really oughtn't, you know. Scorching up hills and then doubling up a mountain are not good for your time of life.'

He raised the cap of my flask in solemn salutation. 'Your very good health.' Then he smacked his lips, and had several cupfuls of water from the spring.

'You will haf come from Achranich way, maybe?' he said in his soft sing-song, having at last found his breath.

'Just so. Fine weather for the birds, if there was anybody to shoot them.'

'Ach, no. There will be few shots fired today, for there are no gentlemen left in Morvern. But I wass asking you, if you come from Achranich, if you haf seen anybody on the road.'

From his pocket he extricated a brown envelope and a bulky telegraph form. 'Will you read it, sir, for I haf forgot my spectacles?'

It contained a description of one Brand, a South African and a suspected character, whom the police were warned to stop and return to Oban. The description wasn't bad, but it lacked any one good distinctive detail. Clearly the policeman, took me for an innocent pedestrian, probably the guest of some moorland shooting-box, with my brown face and rough tweeds and hobnailed shoes.

I frowned and puzzled a little. 'I did see a fellow about three miles back on the hillside. There's a public-house just where the burn comes in, and I think he was making for it. Maybe that was your man. This wire says "South African"; and now I remember the fellow had the look of a colonial.'

The policeman sighed. 'No doubt it will be the man. Perhaps he will haf a pistol and will shoot.'

'Not him,' I laughed. 'He looked a mangy sort of chap, and he'll be scared out of his senses at the sight of you. But take my advice and get somebody with you before you tackle him. You're always the better of a witness.'

'That is so,' he said, brightening. 'Ach, these are the bad times! In old days there wass nothing to do but watch the doors at the flowershows and keep the yachts from poaching the sea-trout. But now it is spies, spies, and "Donald, get out of your bed, and go off twenty mile to find a German." I wass wishing the war wass by, and the Germans all dead.'

'Hear, hear!' I cried, and on the strength of it gave him another dram.

I accompanied him to the road, and saw him mount his bicycle and zigzag like a snipe down the hill towards Achranich. Then I set off briskly northward. It was clear that the faster I moved the better.

As I went I paid disgusted tribute to the efficiency of the Scottish police. I wondered how on earth they had marked me down. Perhaps it was the Glasgow meeting, or perhaps my association with Ivery at Biggleswick. Anyhow there was somebody somewhere mighty quick at compiling a *dossier*. Unless I wanted to be bundled back to Oban I must make good speed to the Arisaig coast.

Presently the road fell to a gleaming sea-loch which lay like the blue blade of a sword among the purple of the hills. At the head there was a tiny clachan, nestled among birches and rowans, where a tawny burn wound to the sea. When I entered the place it was about four o'clock in the afternoon, and peace lay on it like a garment. In the wide, sunny street there was no sign of life, and no sound except of hens clucking and of bees busy among the roses. There was a little grey box of a kirk, and close to the bridge a thatched cottage which bore the sign of a post and telegraph office.

For the past hour I had been considering that I had better prepare for mishaps. If the police of these parts had been warned they might prove too much for me, and Gresson would be allowed to make his journey unwatched. The only thing to do was to send a wire to Amos and leave the matter in his hands. Whether that was possible or not depended upon this remote postal authority.

I entered the little shop, and passed from bright sunshine to a twilight smelling of paraffin and black-striped peppermint balls. An old woman with a mutch sat in an arm-chair behind the counter. She looked up at me over her spectacles and smiled, and I took to her on the instant. She had the kind of old wise face that God loves.

Beside her I noticed a little pile of books, one of which was a Bible. Open on her lap was a paper, the *United Free Church Monthly*. I noticed these details greedily, for I had to make up my mind on the part to play.

'It's a warm day, mistress,' I said, my voice falling into the broad Lowland speech, for I had an instinct that she was not of the Highlands.

She laid aside her paper. 'It is that, sir. It is grand weather for the hairst, but here that's no till the hinner end o' September, and at the best it's a bit scart o' aits.'

'Ay. It's a different thing down Annandale way,' I said.

Her face lit up. 'Are ye from Dumfries, sir?'

'Not just from Dumfries, but I know the Borders fine.'

'Ye'll no beat them,' she cried. 'Not that this is no a guid place and I've muckle to be thankfu' for since John Sanderson – that was ma man – brocht me here forty-seeven year syne come Martinmas. But the aulder I get the mair I think o' the bit whaur I was born. It was twae miles from Wamphray on the Lockerbie road, but they tell me the place is noo just a rickle o' stanes.'

'I was wondering, mistress, if I could get a cup of tea in the village.'

'Ye'll hae a cup wi' me,' she said. 'It's no often we see onybody frae the Borders hereaways. The kettle's just on the boil.'

She gave me tea and scones and butter, and black-currant jam, and treacle biscuits that melted in the mouth. And as we ate we talked of many things – chiefly of the war and of the wickedness of the world.

'There's nae lads left here,' she said. 'They a' joined the Camerons, and the feck o' them fell at an awfu' place called Lowse. John and me never had no boys, jist the one lassie that's married on Donald Frew, the Strontian carrier. I used to vex mysel' about it, but now I thank the Lord that in His mercy He spared me sorrow. But I wad hae liked to have had one laddie fechtin' for his country. I whiles wish I was a Catholic and could pit up prayers for the sodgers that are deid. It maun be a great consolation.'

I whipped out the *Pilgrim's Progress* from my pocket. 'That is the grand book for a time like this.'

'Fine I ken it,' she said. 'I got it for a prize in the Sabbath School when I was a lassie.'

I turned the pages. I read out a passage or two, and then I seemed struck with a sudden memory.

'This is a telegraph office, mistress. Could I trouble you to send a telegram? You see I've a cousin that's a minister in Ross-shire at the Kyle, and him and me are great correspondents. He was writing about something in the *Pilgrim's Progress*, and I think I'll send him a telegram in answer.'

'A letter would be cheaper,' she said.

'Ay, but I'm on holiday, and I've no time for writing.'

She gave me a form, and I wrote:

Ochterlony. Post Office, Kyle. – Demas will be at his mine within the week. Strive with him, lest I faint by the way.

'Ye're unco lavish wi' the words, sir,' was her only comment.

We parted with regret, and there was nearly a row when I tried to pay for the tea. I was bidden remember her to one Davie Tudhope, farmer in Nether Mirecleuch, the next time I passed by Wamphray.

The village was as quiet when I left it as when I had entered. I took my way up the hill with an easier mind, for I had got off the telegram, and I hoped I had covered my tracks. My friend the post-mistress would, if questioned, be unlikely to recognize any South African suspect in the frank and homely traveller who had spoken with her of Annandale and the *Pilgrim's Progress*.

The soft mulberry gloaming of the west coast was beginning to fall on the hills. I hoped to put in a dozen miles before dark to the next village on the map, where I might find quarters. But ere I had gone far I heard the sound of a motor behind me, and a car slipped past bearing three men. The driver favoured me with a sharp glance, and clapped on the brakes. I noted that the two men in the tonneau were carrying sporting rifles.

'Hi, you, sir,' he cried. 'Come here.' The two rifle-bearers – solemn gillies – brought their weapons to attention.

'By God,' he said, 'it's the man. What's your name? Keep him covered, Angus.' The gillies duly covered me, and I did not like the look of their wavering barrels. They were obviously as surprised as myself.

I had about half a second to make my plans. I advanced with a very stiff air, and asked him what the devil he meant. No Lowland Scots for me now. My tone was that of an adjutant of a Guards battalion.

My inquisitor was a tall man in an ulster, with a green felt hat on his small head. He had a lean, well-bred face and very choleric blue eyes. I set him down as a soldier, retired, Highland regiment or cavalry, old style.

He produced a telegraph form, like the policeman.

'Middle height – strongly built – grey tweeds – brown hat – speaks with a colonial accent – much sunburnt. What's your name, sir?'

I did not reply in a colonial accent, but with the *hauteur* of the British officer when stopped by a French sentry. I asked him again what the devil he had to do with my business. This made him angry, and he began to stammer.

'I'll teach you what I have to do with it. I'm a deputy-lieutenant of this county, and I have Admiralty instructions to watch the coast. Damn it, sir, I've a wire here from the Chief Constable describing you. You're Brand, a very dangerous fellow, and we want to know what the devil you're doing here.'

As I looked at his wrathful eye and lean head, which could not have held much brains, I saw that I must change my tone. If I irritated him he would get nasty and refuse to listen and hang me up for hours. So my voice became respectful.

'I beg your pardon, sir, but I've not been accustomed to be pulled up suddenly and asked for my credentials. My name is Blaikie – Captain Robert Blaikie, of the Scots Fusiliers. I'm home on three weeks' leave, to get a little peace after Hooge. We were only hauled out five days ago.' I hoped my old friend in the shell-shock hospital at Isham would pardon my borrowing his identity.

The man looked puzzled. 'How the devil am I to be satisfied about that? Have you any papers to prove it?'

'Why, no. I don't carry passports about with me on a walking tour. But you can wire to the depot, or to my London address.'

He pulled at his yellow moustache. 'I'm hanged if I know what to do. I want to get home for dinner. I tell you what, sir, I'll take you on with me and put you up for the night. My boy's at home convalescing, and if he says you're *pukka* I'll ask your pardon and give you a dashed good bottle of port. I'll trust him, and I warn you he's a keen hand.'

There was nothing to do but consent, and I got in beside him with an uneasy conscience. Supposing the son knew the real Blaikie! I asked the name of the boy's battalion, and was told the 10th Seaforths. That wasn't pleasant hearing, for they had been brigaded with us on the Somme. But Colonel Broadbury – for he told me his name – volunteered another piece of news which set my mind at rest. The boy was not yet twenty, and had only been out seven months. At Arras he had got a bit of shrapnel in his thigh, which had played the deuce with the sciatic nerve, and he was still on crutches.

We spun over ridges of moorland, always keeping northward, and brought up at a pleasant whitewashed house close to the sea. Colonel Broadbury ushered me into a hall where a small fire of peats was burning, and on a couch beside it lay a slim, pale-faced young man. He had dropped his policeman's manner, and behaved like a gentleman. 'Ted,' he said, 'I've brought a friend home for the night. I went out to look for a suspect and found a British officer. This is Captain Blaikie, of the Scots Fusiliers.'

The boy looked at me pleasantly. 'I'm very glad to meet you, sir. You'll excuse me not getting up, but I've got a game leg.' He was the copy of his father in features, but dark and sallow where the other was blond. He had just the same narrow head, and stubborn mouth, and honest, quick-tempered eyes. It is the type that makes dashing regimental officers, and earns V.C.'s, and gets done in wholesale. I was never that kind. I belonged to the school of the cunning cowards.

In the half-hour before dinner the last wisp of suspicion fled from my host's mind. For Ted Broadbury and I were immediately deep in 'shop'. I had met most of his senior officers, and I knew all about their doings at Arras, for his brigade had been across the river on my left. We fought the great fight over again, and yarned about technicalities and slanged the Staff in the way young officers have, the father throwing in questions that showed how mighty proud he was of his son. I had a bath before dinner, and as he led me to the bathroom he apologized very handsomely for his bad manners. 'Your coming's been a godsend for Ted. He was moping a bit in this place. And, though I say it that shouldn't, he's a dashed good boy.'

I had my promised bottle of port, and after dinner I took on the father at billiards. Then we settled in the smoking-room, and I laid myself out to entertain the pair. The result was that they would have had me stay a week, but I spoke of the shortness of my leave, and said I must get on to the railway and then back to Fort William for my luggage.

So I spent that night between clean sheets, and ate a Christian breakfast, and was given my host's car to set me a bit on the road. I dismissed it after half a dozen miles, and, following the map, struck over the hills to the west. About midday I topped a ridge, and beheld the Sound of Sleat shining beneath me. There were other things in the landscape. In the valley on the right a long goods train was crawling on the Mallaig railway. And across the strip of sea, like some fortress of the old gods, rose the dark bastions and turrets of the hills of Skye.

Terrible New-Year's Day Disaster

from Daily Record, Thursday 2nd January 1919

DISASTER AT STORNOWAY
LEAVE SHIP WITH LEWIS MEN RUNS ASHORE
FEARED LOSS OF 300 LIVES

A telegram from Stornoway, Isle of Lewis, reports that HM steam yacht *Amalthea* (the re-named *Iolaire*), the parent ship of the Stornoway Naval Base, went aground while entering the harbour there early yesterday morning.

The vessel was on the passage from Kyle of Lochalsh, and had on board Naval ratings, all Lewis men going home on New Year leave.

It is feared there has been loss of 300 lives, but according to official information received in London late yesterday afternoon, the chances appear to be that there have been fewer casualties. Several members of the crew succeeded in swimming ashore.

NEW-YEAR TRAGEDY
SAD HOME-COMING FOR THE GALLANT LEWISMEN
(From Our Own Correspondent)

Stornoway, Wednesday

The greatest disaster that has ever occurred off the Lewis coast took place early this morning when the steam yacht *Iolaire*, on Admiralty service, struck a reef of bad jagged rock known as the Beasts of Holm, eastward of about 300 yards from the harbour entrance and in a short time sunk in deep water.

The survivors report that in their opinion the navigating officer miscalculated his position, and, before those on board, who knew the locality thoroughly, became aware of the danger in time to warn him, the steamer struck the rocks.

Some of the villages which have suffered most seriously by this sad disaster are:

Lives Lost

Knock and Swoodle	17
Lurebost Lochs	13
Shawbost	40
Ness	40
Carloway	28
Back District	40
Point District	40
	218

There were 18 men from Knock and Swoodle, only one of them being saved. Three out of sixteen from Lurebost Lochs saved were Alexander Mackenzie, seriously injured, N. Mackenzie, and Archibald Ross; while the other losses affect nearly every other village in Lewis.

The estimated loss of life is 300.

SURVIVOR'S NARRATIVE
LIFEBOATS WITH 40 MEN ABOARD SWAMPED

Mr Lewis Alexander Maciver, son of Mr Murdo Maciver, bootmaker, and who was on the Bank of Scotland staff, Stornoway, when he joined the Navy in 1916, gives a very graphic description of the shipwreck and the loss of life.

He says the *Iolaire* left the Kyle about seven o'clock on Tuesday evening with 300 Navy men on New-Year's holiday leave. When leaving Kyle the yacht got damaged by striking against the pier.

Mr Maciver, who was the first ashore, was in the deck saloon with a Mr More when the steamer struck. They all rushed out and found that the steamer had heeled over to the starboard side to forty degrees. They went along the port side and remained there for some time. During a lull they scrambled down to the deck and got two lifeboats launched, in each of which 40 men found spaces; but when they reached the water the boats swamped and they were nearly all drowned.

The steamer moved from her position, her stern being inward towards the shore. Nearly a hundred men rushed aft, but it proved their undoing, as when they dropped into the sea the rollers coming round the stern, swept them against the rocks, where they were nearly all drowned.

When Mr Maciver, with others, rushed out from the deck saloon he saw about sixty men jump into the sea on the starboard side, but he fears that most of them were drowned.

Latterly he dropped overboard himself abreast the funnel, and, after swimming, and with the help of some wreckage, he was able to reach the shore after being over half an hour in the water, which was bitterly cold.

A FARMER'S HOSPITALITY

Taking his idea of his whereabouts from Stornoway Lighthouse, he walked westward until he came to a farmhouse. He roused the inmates, Mr Anderson Young and his family, who bade him welcome.

They soon had a blazing fire and hot drinks prepared. He told them what had occurred, and having changed his wet clothes, Mr Maciver was able to direct about 20 more survivors, some of those injured being helped along by their comrades.

Previous to their arrival their Stoneyfield hosts had in readiness hot tea and beds prepared, to which the injured were put.

Mr Maciver and the other survivors are full of gratitude to Mr & Mrs Young for their great attention and kindness. Mr Maciver remained at Stoneyfield until six o'clock, when he was able to walk home to his father's house in Church Street, to the amazement of his parents, as he had not advised them of his coming.

Mr Maciver says that when he dropped overboard the navigation officer and master were on the bridge, and they and the crew, about 12 in number, were all drowned.

One man, John Macdonald, Holm, a brother of Lieutenant Macdonald, who was drowned while in command of a mine sweeper which was mined some time ago, had a remarkable escape. He climbed one of the masts, which are still to be seen above water, and tied himself securely to it. He was discovered at daybreak this morning and was rescued with much difficulty by the boat from the Naval Barracks. He was benumbed and completely exhausted, but he speedily recovered.

The *Iolaire* was a steam yacht of 999 tons Thames measurement, built in 1902 by Messrs William Beardmore and Co., Dalmuir, for Sir Donald Currie, and handed over to the Admiralty early in the war for national purposes.

Iolaire

from Collected Poems

IAIN CRICHTON SMITH (1928–)

On New Year's Eve 1918 a ship called the *Iolaire* left Kyle of Lochalsh
to bring three hundred men home to Lewis after the war was over.
On New Year's morning 1919 the ship went on the rocks as a result
of a navigational error at the Beasts of Holm, a short distance from
Stornoway, the main town on the island. About two hundred sailors
were drowned. In the following poem I imagine an elder of the church
speaking as he is confronted with this mind-breaking event.

> The green washed over them. I saw them when
> the New Year brought them home. It was a day
> that orbed the horizon with an enigma.
> It seemed that there were masts. It seemed that men
> buzzed in the water round them. It seemed that fire
> shone in the water which was thin and white
> unravelling towards the shore. It seemed that I
> touched my fixed hat which seemed to float and then
> the sun illumined fish with naval caps,
> names of the vanished ships. In sloppy waves,
> in the fat of water, they came floating home
> bruising against their island. It is true,
> a minor error can inflict this death.
> That star is not responsible. It shone
> over the puffy blouse, the flapping blue
> trousers, the black boots. The seagull swam
> bonded to the water. Why not man?
> The lights were lit last night, the tables creaked
> with hoarded food. They willed the ship to port
> in the New Year which would erase the old,
> its errant voices, its unpractised tones.
> Have we done ill, I ask, my fixed body
> a simulacrum of the transient waste,
> for everything was mobile, plants that swayed,
> the keeling ship exploding and the splayed

cold insect bodies. I have seen your church
solid. This is not. The water pours
into the parting timbers where I ache
above the globular eyes. The slack heads turn
ringing the horizon without sound,
with mortal bells, a strange exuberant flower
unknown to our dry churchyards. I look up.
The sky begins to brighten as before,
remorseless amber, and the bruised blue grows
at the erupting edges. I have known you, God,
not as the playful one but as the black
thunderer from hills. I kneel
and touch this dumb blond head. My hand is scorched.
Its human quality confuses me.
I have not felt such hair so dear before
nor seen such real eyes. I kneel from you.
This water soaks me. I am running with
its tart sharp joy. I am floating here
in my black uniform. I am embraced
by these green ignorant waters. I am calm.

3
A LIVING FROM THE SEA

Almost all coastal nations have developed a fishing industry at one time or another and it is that way of earning a living from the sea which figures largely among the extracts in this section. It begins with the anonymous paean to the daring and virility of the whaling men from the east coast, 'The Bonny Ship the Diamond'. This rousing shanty stands in a way for all those who over centuries carved out a dangerous livelihood from distant waters, in this case from the Davis Strait between Greenland and Baffin Island. European whaling had begun in the Bay of Biscay, moved to Spitzbergen and then, when the stocks were depleted there, the whalers began to make the long, hazardous voyage to the northwest Atlantic. The *Diamond* like others of the Peterhead fleet celebrated in this song, could be many months, or indeed years, at sea – the record was the eleven-year trip of an American whaler.

The effect of the song is of a painting, a study of a quayside with the figures of the whaling men in their bonny blue jackets, with a frieze of weeping lasses. The men rejoice in their skill and manhood and it is clear that the lasses are weeping for their absence from them, not solely because of any dangers of the whaling grounds. The welcome the lasses will give them when they at last return will be long and energetic and the town will be 'bricht both day and nicht', but this time for reasons of celebration, unlike Greenland and the Davis Strait, 'where the sun it never sets, my lads, no darkness dims the sky'.

An emphatically macho tone can also be detected in the extract from *The Pirate*, but typically with Sir Walter Scott, in a much more buttoned-down manner. The pirate, Clement Cleveland, and his rival, the novel's hero, Mordaunt Mertoun, strive with each other to display their mettle against a whale stranded in a Shetland voe. Scott had only slight knowledge of the Northern Isles but in his seeming determination to write about all areas of Scotland he had absorbed local colour on his voyage of 1814 with the Lighthouse Commissioners (see *Pleasures of the Sea*), sufficient to complete *The Pirate* in 1821.

The struggle of the Shetlanders against the sea-monster forms one of Sir Walter's best set-pieces, with most of the characters of the novel displayed to advantage against its background, and with some fine description of character, mixed with flashes of humour. As a strenuous and exciting account of man against leviathan, it anticipates and arguably provides some inspiration for *Moby-Dick* (1851). The episode ends in the failure of the hunters and the whale escapes over the sand-bar, 'carrying with him a whole grove of the implements which had been planted in his body, and leaving behind him, on the waters, a dark red trace of his course'.

Curiously, there is a similar type of ending to the next piece, although in this case non-fiction, which is an extract from *Harpoon at a Venture*, by Gavin Maxwell. On this occasion it is a basking shark which escapes from the bloody attentions of its hunters and provides an inauspicious beginning to Maxwell's attempts to establish a viable commercial shark-fishing venture on the island of Soay at the end of the Second World War.

The quintessential Scottish fish is undoubtedly the herring. 'Of all the fish that swim in the sea, the herring is the fish for me,' sings Cilla Fisher, and probably only the Dutch have traditionally held the silver darlings in higher esteem, while the subtle combination of oatmeal and herring has a fair claim to be *the* taste of Scotland. A creel-full of five pieces of writing about the herring fishing begins with the observations of Thomas Pennant on the present and potential role of the industry in the political economy of the Hebrides in the 1770s. This is followed by three sets of verses about the vital part played by women in the fishing life at different times and in different parts of Scotland, and finally the first chapter of *The Silver Darlings*, Neil Gunn's late (1941) historical novel, set at the time of the Napoleonic Wars and the great herring boom of these years.

Many generations of Scots earned their living by going to sea, and until recently it could be said that most ships' engine rooms would feature a Glasgow accent or two and most families claim a relative who spends years at sea. Tom Gallacher, in his evocative collection of memories of Dumbarton, *Hunting Shadows*, remembers, as a boy watching the big ships passing downriver: 'They towered above us. The sand under our bare feet trembled to the vibration of their engines. Yelling and waving we pranced about. They were OUR ships. Their engine rooms were manned by OUR uncles and brothers and cousins.' Another writer with Dumbartonshire connections was Robert Bontine Cunninghame Graham and in his story *Christie Christison* he blends elements of his beloved Argentina with the Scots seafaring life: 'Christie Christison, a weather-beaten sailor, who still spoke his native dialect of Peterhead, despite his thirty years out in the [River] Plate.'

The said Peterhead vernacular is well known for being impenetrable to outsiders, but the piece which concludes this section of the anthology is written in a dialect to rival it – although repaying the effort to understand it in full measure. The Shetland fishermen in T.A. Robertson's poem, *Da Sang o da Papa Men*, have an almost epic quality, reminiscent of Odysseus and his crew, as they catch a wind-blown scent of flowers which turns their course in the direction of their native isle of Papa:

> Dan apo da wilsom water
> Comes da scent o flooers.

The Bonny Ship the Diamond

ANONYMOUS

The *Diamond* is a ship, my lads, for the Davis Strait she's bound,
And the quay it is all garnished with bonny lasses 'round;
Captain Thompson gives the order to sail the ocean wide,
Where the sun it never sets, my lads, no darkness dims the sky,

Chorus
So it's cheer up my lads, let your hearts never fail,
While the bonny ship, the *Diamond*, goes a-fishing for the whale.

Along the quay at Peterhead, the lasses stand aroon,
Wi' their shawls all pulled around them and the saut tears runnin'
doon;
Don't you weep, my bonny lass, though you be left behind,
For the rose will grow on Greenland's ice before we change our mind.

chorus

Here's a health to the *Resolution*, likewise the *Eliza Swan*,
Here's a health to the *Battler of Montrose* and the *Diamond*, ship
of fame;
We wear the trouser o' the white and the jackets o' the blue,
When we return to Peterhead, we'll hae sweethearts anoo,

chorus

It'll be bricht both day and nicht when the Greenland lads come hame,
Wi' a ship that's fu' of oil, my lads, and money to our name;
We'll make the cradles for to rock and the blankets for to tear,
And every lass in Peterhead sing 'Hushabye, my dear'.

'The Whale-hunt'

from The Pirate

SIR WALTER SCOTT (1771–1832)

Having absorbed the atmosphere of the Northern Isles on his voyage with the Lighthouse Commissioners, Scott published this novel in 1821 as part of the Waverley *sequence. There are two 'leading men' in this fine passage taken from Chapter 17: Clement Cleveland, the eponymous pirate and his rival, Mordaunt Mertun, who are vying for the hands of the two daughters of Magnus Troil, a rich Shetlander – or Zetlander, as Scott terms him.*

Other assorted characters are also displayed to fine advantage in this set-piece scene of the hunting down of a whale which has blundered into a Shetland voe, or inlet. It turns out to be an unsuccessful hunt, because as we read in one of Sir Walter's knockabout passages, they succeed only in getting in each other's way, with, for example, the bard, Claud Halcro, in the thick of the action, declaiming passages from his favourite poet, Dryden. Other light relief is provided by Triptolemus Yellowley, a farmer in the Mearns sent out to 'improve' agriculture among the islanders, and one in the long line of Scott's characters with fine, comic and rich Scots dialogue. Here is his sister, Mistress Baby's exhortation to Triptolemus to get some of the whale-oil, or 'ulzie' for the 'cruise', or lamp:

> They say that a' men share and share equals-aquals in the creature's ulzie and a pint o't wad be worth siller, to light the cruise in the lang dark nights that they speak of. Pit yourself forward man – there's a graip to ye – faint heart never wan fair lady; wha kens but what, when it's fresh, it may eat weel eneugh, and spare butter?

The morning which succeeds such a feast as that of Magnus Troil usually lacks a little of the zest which seasoned the revels of the preceding day, as the fashionable reader may have observed at a public breakfast during the race-week in a country town; for, in what is called the best society, these lingering moments are usually spent by the company each apart in their own dressing-rooms. At Burgh-Westra, it will readily be believed, no such space for retirement was afforded; and the lasses, with their paler cheeks, the elder dames, with many a wink and yawn, were compelled to meet with their male companions, headaches and all, just three hours after they had parted from each other.

Eric Scambester had done all that man could do to supply the full means of diverting the *ennui* of the morning meal. The board groaned with rounds of hung beef, made after the fashion of Zetland – with pasties – with baked meats – with fish, dressed and cured in every possible manner; nay, with the foreign delicacies of tea, coffee, and chocolate; for, as we have already had occasion to remark, the situation of these islands made them early acquainted with various articles of foreign luxury, which were, as yet, but little known in Scotland, where, at a much later period than that we write of, one pound of green tea was dressed like cabbage, and another converted into a vegetable sauce for salt beef, by the ignorance of the good housewives to whom they had been sent as rare presents.

Besides these preparations, the table exhibited whatever mighty potions are resorted to by *bons vivants* under the facetious name of a 'hair of the dog that bit you'. There was the potent Irish usquebaugh – right Nantz – genuine Schiedam – aquavitae from Caithness – and Golden Wasser from Hamburgh; there was rum of formidable antiquity, and cordials, from the Leeward Islands. After these details, it were needless to mention the stout home-brewed ale, the German mum and schwartz beer; and still more would it be beneath our dignity to dwell upon the innumerable sorts of pottage and flummery, together with the bland and various preparations of milk, for those who preferred thinner potations.

No wonder that the sight of so much good cheer awakened the appetite and raised the spirits of the fatigued revellers. The young men began immediately to seek out their partners of the preceding evening, and to renew the small talk which had driven the night so merrily away; while Magnus, with his stout old Norse kindred, encouraged, by precept and example, those of elder days and graver mood to a substantial flirtation with the good things before them. Still, however, there was a long period to be filled up before dinner; for the most protracted breakfast cannot well last above an hour; and it was to be feared that Claud Halcro meditated the occupation of this vacant morning with a formidable recitation of his own verses, besides telling, at its full length, the whole history of his introduction to glorious John Dryden. But fortune relieved the guests of Burgh-Westra from this threatened infliction, by sending them means of amusement peculiarly suited to their taste and habits.

Most of the guests were using their toothpicks, some were beginning to talk of what was to be done next, when, with haste in his step, fire in his eye, and a harpoon in his hand, Eric Scambester came to announce to the company that there was a whale on shore, or nearly so, at the throat of the voe! Then you might have seen such a joyous, boisterous, and universal bustle as only the love of sport, so deeply implanted in our nature, can possibly inspire. A set of country squires, about to beat for the first woodcocks of the season, were a comparison as petty in respect to the glee as in regard to the importance of the object. The battue upon a strong cover in Ettrick Forest, for the destruction of the foxes; the insurrection of the sportsmen of the Lennox, when one of the duke's deer gets out from Inch-Mirran; nay, the joyous rally of the fox-chase itself, with all its blythe accompaniments of hound and horn, fall infinitely short of the animation with which the gallant sons of Thule set off to encounter the monster whom the sea had sent for their amusement at so opportune a conjuncture.

The multifarious stores of Burgh-Westra were rummaged hastily for all sorts of arms which could be used on such an occasion. Harpoons, swords, pikes, and halberds fell to the lot of some; others contented themselves with hay-forks, spits, and whatever else could be found, that was at once long and sharp. Thus hastily equipped, one division, under the command of Captain Cleveland, hastened to man the boats which lay in the little haven, while the rest of the party hurried by land to the scene of action.

Poor Triptolemus was interrupted in a plan which he, too, had formed against the patience of the Zetlanders, and which was to have consisted in a lecture upon the agriculture and the capabilities of the country, by this sudden hubbub, which put an end at once to Halcro's poetry and to his no less formidable prose. It may be easily imagined that he took very little interest in the sport which was so suddenly substituted for his lucubrations, and he would not even have deigned to have looked upon the active scene which was about to take place, had he not been stimulated thereunto by the exhortations of Mistress Baby. 'Pit yoursell forward, man,' said that provident person – 'pit yoursell forward; wha kens whare a blessing may light? They say that a' men share and share equals-aquals in the creature's ulzie, and a pint o't wad be worth siller, to light the cruise in the lang dark nights that they speak of. Pit yourself forward, man – there's a graip to ye – faint heart never wan fair lady; wha kens but what, when it's fresh, it may eat weel eneugh, and spare butter?'

What zeal was added to Triptolemus's motions by the prospect of eating fresh train-oil instead of butter, we know not; but, as better might not be, he brandished the rural implement (a stable-fork) with which he was armed, and went down to wage battle with the whale.

The situation in which the enemy's ill fate had placed him was particularly favourable to the enterprise of the islanders. A tide of unusual height had carried the animal over a large bar of sand, into the voe or creek in which he was now lying. So soon as he found the water ebbing, he became sensible of his danger, and had made desperate efforts to get over the shallow water, where the waves broke on the bar; but hitherto he had rather injured than mended his condition, having got himself partly aground, and lying therefore particularly exposed to the meditated attack. At this moment the enemy came down upon him. The front ranks consisted of the young and hardy, armed in the miscellaneous manner we have described; while, to witness and animate their efforts, the young women, and the elderly persons of both sexes, took their place among the rocks which overhung the scene of action.

As the boats had to double a little headland ere they opened the mouth of the voe, those who came by land to the shores of the inlet had time to make the necessary reconnaissances upon the force and situation of the enemy, on whom they were about to commence a simultaneous attack by land and sea.

This duty the stout-hearted and experienced general, for so the Udaller might be termed, would entrust to no eyes but his own; and, indeed, his external appearance and his sage conduct rendered him alike qualified for the command which he enjoyed. His gold-laced hat was exchanged for a bearskin cap, his suit of blue broadcloth, with its scarlet lining, and loops, and frogs of bullion, had given place to a red flannel jacket, with buttons of black horn, over which he wore a seal-skin shirt curiously seamed and plaited on the bosom, such as are used by the Esquimaux, and sometimes by the Greenland whale-fishers. Sea-boots of a formidable size completed his dress, and in his hand he held a large whaling-knife, which he brandished, as if impatient to employ it in the operation of 'flinching' the huge animal which lay before them – that is, the act of separating its flesh from its bones. Upon closer examination, however, he was obliged to confess that the sport to which he had conducted his friends, however much it corresponded with the magnificent scale of his hospitality, was likely to be attended with its own peculiar dangers and difficulties.

The animal, upwards of sixty feet in length, was lying perfectly still, in a deep part of the voe into which it had weltered, and where it seemed to await the return of tide, of which it was probably assured by instinct. A council of experienced harpooners was instantly called, and it was agreed that an effort should be made to noose the tail of this torpid leviathan, by casting a cable around it, to be made fast by anchors to the shore, and thus to secure against his escape, in case the tide should make before they were able to despatch him. Three boats were destined to this delicate piece of service, one of which the Udaller himself proposed to command, while Cleveland and Mertoun were to direct the two others. This being decided, they sat down on the strand, waiting with impatience until the naval part of the force should arrive in the voe. It was during this interval that Triptolemus Yellowley, after measuring with his eyes the extraordinary size of the whale, observed that, in his poor mind, 'A wain with six owsen, or with sixty owsen either, if they were the owsen of the country, could not drag siccan a huge creature from the water, where it was now lying, to the sea-beach.'

Trifling as this remark may seem to the reader, it was connected with a subject which always fired the blood of the old Udaller, who, glancing upon Triptolemus a quick and stern look, asked him what the devil it signified, supposing a hundred oxen could not drag the whale upon the beach? Mr Yellowley, though not much liking the tone with which the question was put, felt that his dignity and his profit compelled him to answer as follows: 'Nay, sir, you know yoursell, Master Magnus Troil, and every one knows that knows anything, that whales of siccan size as may not be masterfully dragged on shore by the instrumentality of one wain with six owsen are the right and property of the admiral, who is at this time the same noble lord who is, moreover, chamberlain of these isles.'

'And I tell you, Mr Triptolemus Yellowley,' said the Udaller, 'as I would tell your master if he were here, that every man who risks his life to bring that fish ashore shall have an equal share and partition, according to our ancient and loveable Norse custom and wont; nay, if there is so much as a woman looking on, that will but touch the cable, she will be partner with us; ay, and more than all that, if she will but say there is a reason for it, we will assign a portion to the babe that is unborn.'

The strict principle of equity which dictated this last arrangement occasioned laughter among the men, and some slight confusion among the women. The factor, however, thought it shame to be so easily daunted. '*Suum cuique tribuito*,' said he: 'I will stand for my lord's right and my own.'

'Will you?' replied Magnus; 'then, by the Martyr's bones, you shall have no law of partition but that of God and St Olave, which we had before either factor, or treasurer, or chamberlain were heard of! All shall share that lend a hand, and never a one else. So you, Master Factor, shall be busy as well as other folk, and think yourself lucky to share like other folk. Jump into that boat (for the boats had by this time pulled round the headland), and you, my lads, make way for the factor in the stern-sheets: he shall be the first man this blessed day that shall strike the fish.'

The loud, authoritative voice, and the habit of absolute command inferred in the Udaller's whole manner, together with the conscious want of favourers and backers amongst the rest of the company, rendered it difficult for Triptolemus to evade compliance, although he was thus about to be placed in a situation equally novel and perilous. He was still, however, hesitating, and attempting an explanation, with a voice in which anger was qualified by fear, and both thinly disguised under an attempt to be jocular, and to represent the whole as a jest, when he heard the voice of Baby maundering in his ear, 'Wad he lose his share of the ulzie, and the lang Zetland winter coming on, when the lightest day in December is not so clear as a moonless night in the Mearns?'

This domestic instigation, in addition to those of fear of the Udaller and shame to seem less courageous than others, so inflamed the agriculturist's spirits that he shook his 'graip' aloft, and entered the boat with the air of Neptune himself, carrying on high his trident.

The three boats destined for this perilous service now approached the dark mass, which lay like an islet in the deepest part of the voe, and suffered them to approach without showing any sign of animation. Silently, and with such precaution as the extreme delicacy of the operation required, the intrepid adventurers, after the failure of their first attempt, and the expenditure of considerable time, succeeded in casting a cable around the body of the torpid monster, and in carrying the ends of it ashore, when an hundred hands were instantly employed in securing them. But, ere this was accomplished, the tide began to make fast, and the Udaller informed his assistants that either the fish must be killed, or at least greatly wounded, ere the depth of water on the bar was sufficient to float him, or that he was not unlikely to escape from their joint prowess.

'Wherefore,' said he, 'we must set to work, and the factor shall have the honour to make the first throw.'

The valiant Triptolemus caught the word; and it is necessary to say that the patience of the whale, in suffering himself to be noosed without resistance, had abated his terrors, and very much lowered the creature in his opinion. He protested the fish had no more wit, and scarcely more activity, than a black snail; and, influenced by this undue contempt of the adversary, he waited neither for a further signal, nor a better weapon,

nor a more suitable position, but, rising in his energy, hurled his graip
with all his force against the unfortunate monster. The boats had not yet
retreated from him to the distance necessary to ensure safety when this
injudicious commencement of the war took place.

Magnus Troil, who had only jested with the factor, and had reserved
the launching the first spear against the whale to some much more skilful
hand, had just time to exclaim, 'Mind yourselves, lads, or we are all
swamped!' when the monster, roused at once from inactivity by the
blow of the factor's missile, blew, with a noise resembling the explosion
of a steam-engine, a huge shower of water into the air, and at the same
time began to lash the waves with his tail in every direction. The boat in
which Magnus presided received the shower of brine which the animal
spouted aloft; and the adventurous Triptolemus, who had a full share of
the immersion, was so much astonished and terrified by the consequences
of his own valorous deed that he tumbled backwards amongst the feet
of the people, who, too busy to attend to him, were actively engaged
in getting the boat into shoal water, out of the whale's reach. Here he
lay for some minutes, trampled on by the feet of the boatmen, until
they lay on their oars to bale, when the Udaller ordered them to pull
to shore and land this spare hand, who had commenced the fishing so
inauspiciously.

While this was doing, the other boats had also pulled off to safer
distance, and now, from these as well as from the shore, the unfortunate
native of the deep was overwhelmed by all kinds of missiles: harpoons
and spears flew against him on all sides, guns were fired, and each
various means of annoyance plied which could excite him to exhaust
his strength in useless rage. When the animal found that he was locked
in by shallows on all sides, and became sensible, at the same time, of the
strain of the cable on his body, the convulsive efforts which he made
to escape, accompanied with sounds resembling deep and loud groans,
would have moved the compassion of all but a practised whale-fisher.
The repeated showers which he spouted into the air began now to be
mingled with blood, and the waves which surrounded him assumed
the same crimson appearance. Meantime, the attempts of the assailants
were redoubled; but Mordaunt Mertoun and Cleveland, in particular,
exerted themselves to the uttermost, contending who should display most
courage in approaching the monster, so tremendous in its agonies, and
should inflict the most deep and deadly wounds upon its huge bulk.

The contest seemed at last pretty well over; for, although the animal
continued from time to time to make frantic exertions for liberty, yet
its strength appeared so much exhausted, that, even with the assistance

of the tide, which had now risen considerably, it was thought it could scarcely extricate itself.

Magnus gave the signal to venture nearer to the whale, calling out at the same time, 'Close in, lads, he is not half so mad now. The factor may look for a winter's oil for the two lamps at Harfra. Pull close in, lads.'

Ere his orders could be obeyed, the other two boats had anticipated his purpose; and Mordaunt Mertoun, eager to distinguish himself above Cleveland, had, with the whole strength he possessed, plunged a half-pike into the body of the animal. But the leviathan, like a nation whose resources appear totally exhausted by previous losses and calamities, collected his whole remaining force for an effort which proved at once desperate and successful. The wound last received had probably reached through his external defences of blubber, and attained some very sensitive part of the system; for he roared aloud, as he sent to the sky a mingled sheet of brine and blood, and snapping the strong cable like a twig, overset Mertoun's boat with a blow of his tail, shot himself, by a mighty effort, over the bar, upon which the tide had now risen considerably, and made out to sea, carrying with him a whole grove of the implements which had been planted in his body, and leaving behind him, on the waters, a dark red trace of his course.

'Shark-fishing in Soay'

from Harpoon at a Venture

GAVIN MAXWELL (1914–69)

Harpoon at a Venture, *published in 1952, was writer and naturalist Gavin Maxwell's first book. Taken from early in the book, this extract shows something of the clarity and ease of his descriptions of land and seascape, and describes how a chance encounter with a basking shark gave him the enthusiasm to embark upon the enterprise which forms the matter of the book – having had an eventful war in the Special Forces he found himself in the Hebrides in 1944 and impetuously acquired Soay, a small island off the coast of Skye. As with a number of Maxwell's ventures, the shark-fishery proved to be a commercial flop, perhaps because he thought of it as 'the beginning of the long adventure of which this book is the story' rather than an enterprise to be built upon a secure financial base.*

The description of the machine-gunning of the shark is a trifle bloody for modern tastes, but this particular leviathan does gain the upper hand. In any case, the book is worth reading for its prose style, for Maxwell's ability to communicate passion, and his sense of excitement for the living world:

> The triangle grew until I was looking at a huge fin, a yard high and as long at the base. It seemed monstrous, this great black sail, the only visible thing upon limitless miles of pallid water. A few seconds later the notched tip of a second fin appeared some twenty feet astern of the first, moving in a leisurely way from side to side.

I decided to buy Soay if I could do so at a figure that would show me the small rate of interest from rentals and feu-duties that I received from my invested capital. I entered almost immediately into prolonged negotiations with the owner, Flora Macleod of Macleod, and the island became my property about a year later.

But during the latter part of those months of negotiation I began to feel a growing uneasiness. My medical category made it probable that I should survive the war, and the spirit in which at Blackwall I had first thought of a Hebridean island, a mood in which rest and remoteness from struggle seemed all that was desirable when the war was over, had left me. The years of hard work and organisation had become habit, breeding, as with so many others, a restlessness, an impatience with former interests and ambitions, and a desire for application and achievement. There was no clear way to the satisfaction of these cravings on Soay.

With the island were sold to me the salmon-fishing rights of its coast, a commercial bag-net fishing which had for some years been leased to Robert Powrie, owner or lessee of commercial salmon fisheries on both coasts of Scotland. But by an oversight his lease had been renewed for a further eight years during my negotiations, and the door to the only obvious work on Soay had been slammed in my face. Without the introduction of a new industry, it was difficult to see how the island could be developed or improved.

In the spring of 1944 I had bought a thirty-foot lobster-fishing boat, in which I spent the whole of my free time. By this date the routine of my department was no longer six and a half days' hard work and a free Sunday afternoon. Instead, it had become spasmodic and a little feverish; we would be asked the impossible, and for weeks on end would work all day and most of the night – then, without warning, we would find ourselves virtually unoccupied for an equal period. After D-day the work of our back-room was practically finished, and there was little to do but to clear away the mess. But our department could not be closed until the trend of events on the Continent made it certain that we could be of no further use, and during the latter part of that summer we had to stay where we were, waiting and often idle. It was as though all the week-end leaves that we had forfeited for three years were restored suddenly and in aggregate; we could not spend a night away, but our days were for the most part our own. The weather was brilliant, hot and still, and whilst many were bitter not to be able to spend this unexpected idleness with wives and families, I wanted nothing but to be where I was.

Those brazen days I spent in my boat, exploring the coast and the islands from Mull to the narrows of Skye, slipping imperceptibly back into a world I had almost forgotten, dream-like and shining. I used to visit the seal-rocks and spend hours watching the seals; sit among the burrows of a puffin colony and see the birds come and go, unafraid, from their nests; fish for conger eels by moonlight; catch mackerel and lobsters; and for the first time saw a Basking Shark at close quarters. It was the beginning of the long adventure of which this book is the story.

I had with me a Morar man, who looked after the boat for me; 'Foxy' he was called, both by his friends and his enemies. He was a little over thirty then, fat yet enormously strong – I have seen him lift

the back of a medium-sized saloon car clear of a ditch onto the road
– arms reaching almost to his knees, a massive boil-pitted neck, and
a foul mouth as fluent in English as in Gaelic. His requirements were
those of all mankind; though all, perhaps, a little magnified. He would
have made a good guerilla fighter in the Chouan tradition; not a leader,
because it was difficult to keep his attention focused on any one thing
for long. When Foxy started working he would do as much in an hour
as three other men, but how many such hours there would be was always
unpredictable.

We were returning from Glenelg; it was late afternoon, the sky paling
and the hills turning to deep plum, their edges sharp and hard, as though
cut from cardboard. We were about a mile off Isle Ornsay Lighthouse,
heading southward over a still, pale sea, when I noticed something
breaking the surface thirty yards from the boat. At first it was no more
than a ripple with a dark centre. The centre became a small triangle, black
and shiny, with a slight forward movement, leaving a light wake in the
still water. The triangle grew until I was looking at a huge fin, a yard
high and as long at the base. It seemed monstrous, this great black sail,
the only visible thing upon limitless miles of pallid water. A few seconds
later the notched tip of a second fin appeared some twenty feet astern of
the first, moving in a leisurely way from side to side.

It was some seconds before my brain would acknowledge that these
two fins must belong to the same creature. The impact of this realisation
was tremendous and indescribable: a muddle of excitement in which fear
and a sort of exultation were uppermost, as though this were a moment
for which I had been unconsciously waiting for a long time.

I could only guess at what was beneath the surface. In common with
the great majority whose lives have not been lived in fishing-boats, I had
no idea what Basking Sharks looked like. Once, years before, I had seen
them from the road bordering Loch Fyne, three great black sails cruising
in line ahead – heavy with the menace of boys' adventure stories and
shipwrecked sailors adrift in the Caribbean. I knew nothing of them,
their size or their habits; to me all sharks were man-eaters. That was
my state of knowledge as I looked at those two fins and guessed wildly
at what must lie below them.

Foxy's knowledge, though not encyclopaedic, was less sketchy than
my own. He knew the names by which the fishermen called them –
'muldoan', 'sailfish', 'sunfish', and the Gaelic name *cearbhan*; he knew
that they played havoc with the herring-nets; that their livers contained
large quantities of valuable oil; that they were immensely powerful and
could damage small boats; that long ago the people of the Islands used to

harpoon them from massed formations of small boats, to get a winter's supply of lamp-oil. He assumed that they fed upon the herring-shoals, because they were usually to be found where the herring were.

All this he told me as we closed in to the fish. I scrambled up on to the foredeck and stood in the bows, hoping to see clearly what lay below the surface.

The first Basking Shark of which one has a clear and entire view is terrifying. One may speak glibly of fish twenty, thirty, forty feet long, but until one looks down upon a living adult Basking Shark in clear water, the figures are meaningless and without implication. The bulk appears simply unbelievable. It is not possible to think of what one is looking at as a fish. It is longer than a London bus; it does not have scales like an ordinary fish; its movements are gigantic, ponderous, and unfamiliar; it seems a creature from a pre-historic world, of which the first sight is as unexpected, and in some way as shocking, as that of a dinosaur or iguanodon would be.

At ten yards I could make out a shadow below the surface; at five, as Foxy slipped the engine into neutral, I could see the whole form clear in transparent water. The body was brown, with irregular python markings upon it, a vast barrel that seemed to get steadily wider towards the incredibly distant head. The head was perhaps the most unexpected thing of all. The gills were by far the widest part, frill-like and gigantically distended, like a salamander's or a Komodo Dragon's. The upper jaw was a snout, the tip of which was now breaking the surface; the mouth was held wide open, and a child could have walked upright into that whitish cavern. As we began to sheer off, our wash slapped across the dorsal fin, and the shark submerged with a slight flurry of water about his tail.

Mounted in the bows of the *Gannet* was a Breda light machine-gun, which I carried to shoot up drifting mines, and also in the rather ridiculous hope of engaging a U-boat, since they had been sighted as near as Eigg. A Danish seaman had told me that a small launch, accurately handling a light machine-gun, could permanently damage the periscope and also command the conning-tower if a U-boat surfaced, since it would be unlikely to waste a torpedo on so insignificant a target.

Foxy said, 'Try him with the gun, Major.'

When I had finished loading two extra magazines, the fin had reappeared, apparently stationary, and within a stone's throw.

We circled it widely and approached from astern – the technique we later used for harpooning. I waited until the fin was abreast of me and not much more than a yard away; the boat was almost scraping the shark's side. I fired thirty rounds in a single burst, straight into the huge expanse of his flank, and saw a mass of small white marks spring out on the brown surface. A great undulating movement seemed to surge through him, and near the stern of the boat his tail shot clear of the water. Its width was a man's height; it lashed outward away from the boat and returned, missing Foxy's head by inches, to land with a tremendous slam upon the gunwale of the stern cockpit. It swung backward and hit the sea, flinging up a fountain of water that drenched us to the skin.

He was back on the surface in less than a minute. Six times we closed in; I had fired three hundred rounds into what was now a broad white target on his side. At the last burst he sank in a great turmoil of water, and it was ten minutes before the fin surfaced again. Now it seemed to me as though he was wallowing and out of control, the fin lying at an acute angle. I thought that he was mortally wounded, if not actually dead.

Foxy suggested that we should try to make fast to the fin with the *Gannet*'s boat-hook. He stood up on the foredeck, and I steered him as close to the fish as I could. I felt the bows bump against the shark's body; then Foxy took a tremendous swipe with the full force of eighteen stone. I could see the hook bite deep into the base of the apparently helplessly rolling fin. There was just time for Foxy's triumphant shout of 'Got the b—,' then the boat-hook was torn from his hands, and those gorilla-like arms were waving wildly in a frantic effort to keep balance, as shark and boat-hook disappeared in a boil of white water.

It was some time before the boat-hook came to the surface; then, several hundred yards away, it shot ten feet out of the sea, as though scornfully hurled back from below. We did not see the shark again.

Basking Shark

from Collected Poems

NORMAN MACCAIG (1910–1996)

To stub an oar on a rock where none should be,
To have it rise with a slounge out of the sea
Is a thing that happened once (too often) to me.

But not too often – though enough. I count as gain
That once I met, on a sea tin-tacked with rain,
That roomsized monster with a matchbox brain.

He displaced more than water. He shoggled me
Centuries back – this decadent townee
Shook on a wrong branch of his family tree.

Swish up the dirt and, when it settles, a spring
Is all the clearer. I saw me, in one fling,
Emerging from the slime of everything.

So who's the monster? The thought made me grow pale
For twenty seconds while, sail after sail,
The tall fin slid away and then the tail.

'The Herring Fishery'

from A Tour in Scotland and Voyage to the Hebrides, 1772

THOMAS PENNANT (1726–98)

Thomas Pennant was one of the founding fathers of British natural history and travel writing. Born in Flintshire and educated at Oxford, he first came to public notice by the publication of British Zoology *in 1766. In 1769 he performed an extensive and pioneering tour in Scotland, covering 1200 miles through Lowland and Highland Scotland. In 1771 he published his observations in a highly successful and influential volume – Dr Johnson said of his writing, '. . . he's the best traveller I ever read; he observes more things than any one else does.' Such was the success of his first tour that he returned in 1772 for a journey which would take him up the western seaboard and among the then little-visited Hebridean islands. Our extract on the Scottish Herring Fishery comes from this second tour.*

To reach the islands of the West Coast in the 1770s was not an easy undertaking and Pennant chartered a 90-ton cutter Lady Frederic Campbell, *under the command of Captain Archibald Thomson, at Greenock. He boarded her on 12th June and sailed in her for two months exploring the islands of the Clyde, the inner Hebrides and the sea-lochs of the north-west. Pennant's enquiring mind embraced investigations into natural history, archaeological remains, scenic beauty and the economy of the area. His comments on herring, a fish that a later sailor in these waters, Neil Munro's Para Handy, described as 'a great, great mystery', display Pennant's curiosity, taste for precise information and concern for the welfare of those he travelled among.*

Found in our harbour some busses, just anchored, in expectation of finding the shoals of herring usually here at this season; but at present were disappointed: a few were taken, sufficient to convince us of their superiority in goodness over those of the South: they were not larger, but as they had not wasted themselves by being in roe, their backs and the part next to the tail were double the thickness of the others, and the meat rich beyond expression.

Mr Anderson gives to the Scotch a knowledge of great antiquity in the herring fishery: he says that the Netherlanders resorted to these coasts as early as AD 836, to purchase salted fish of the natives; but imposing on the strangers, they learned the art, and took up the trade, in after-times of such immense emolument to the Dutch.

Sir Walter Raleigh's observations on that head, extracted from the same author, are extremely worthy of the attention of the curious, and excite reflections on the vast strength resulting from the wisdom of well-applied industry.

In 1603, remarks that great man, the Dutch sold to different nations as many herrings as amounted to 1,759,000 pounds sterling. In the year 1615 they at once sent out 2000 busses and employed in them 37,000 fishermen. In the year 1618 they sent out 3000 ships, with 5000 men to take the herring, and 9000 more ships to transport and sell the fish, which by sea and land employed 150,000 men besides those first mentioned. All this wealth was gotten on our coasts while our attention was taken up in a distant whale fishery.

The Scottish monarchs for a long time seemed to direct all their attention to the preservation of the salmon fishery; probably because their subjects were such novices in sea affairs. At length James III endeavoured to stimulate his great men to these patriotic undertakings; for by an act of his third parliament, he compelled certain lords spiritual and temporal, and burghs 'to make ships and boats with nets and other pertinents for fishing'. That the same should be made in each burgh 'in number according to the substance of each burgh and the least of them to be of twenty tunn and that all idle men be compelled by the sheriffs in the country to go on board the same'.

But his successors, by a very false policy, rendered this wise institution of little effect; for they in a manner prevented their subjects from becoming a maritime people, by directing that no white fish should be sent out of the realm, but that strangers may come and buy them; that freeports be first served, the cargoes sold to the freemen who are to come and transport the same. The Dutch at this very time having an open trade.

It is well known that there have been many attempts made to secure this treasure to ourselves, but without success: in the late reign a very strong effort was made and bounties allowed for the encouragement of British adventurers: the first was of thirty shillings per tun to every buss of seventy tuns and upwards ...

To every tun are two hundred and eighty yards of nets; so a vessel of eighty tuns carries twenty thousand square yards: each net is twelve

yards long and ten deep; and every boat takes out from twenty to thirty
nets and puts them together so as to form a long train: they are sunk at
each end of the train by a stone, which weighs it down to the full extent.
The top is supported by buoys made of sheepskin, with a hollow stick
at the mouth, fastened tight; through this the skin is blown up and then
stopt with a peg to prevent the escape of the air. Sometimes these buoys
are placed at the top of the nets; at other time the nets are suffered to
sink deeper by the lengthening the cords fastened to them, every cord
being for that purpose ten or twelve fathoms long. But the best fisheries
are generally in more shallow water.

The nets are made at Greenock, in Knapdale, Bute and Arran; but
the best are procured from Ireland and, I think, from some parts of
Caernarvonshire.

The fishing is always performed in the night, unless by accident. The
busses remain at anchor, and send out their boats a little before sun-set,
which continue out in winter and summer till daylight; often taking up
and emptying their nets, which they do ten or twelve times in a night in
case of good success. During winter it is a most dangerous and fatiguing
employ, by reason of the greatness and frequency of the gales in these
seas, and in such gales are the most successful captures; but by the
providence of heaven the fishers are seldom lost; and, what is wonderful,
few are visited with illness. They go out well prepared, with a warm great
coat, boots and skin aprons and a good provision of beef and spirits. The
same good fortune attends the busses who, in the tempestuous season and
in the darkest nights, are continually shifting in these narrow seas from
harbour to harbour. Sometimes eighty barrels of herring are taken in a
night by the boats of a single vessel. It once happened in Loch-Slappan
in Skie that a buss of eighty tuns might have taken two hundred barrels
in one night, with ten thousand square yards of net; but the master was
obliged to desist, for want of a sufficient number of hands to preserve
the capture.

The herrings are preserved by salting after the entrails are taken out;
an operation performed by the country people, who get three-halfpence
per barrel for their trouble; and sometimes, even in the winter, can gain
fifteen-pence a day. This employs both women and children, but the
salting is only entrusted to the crew of the busses. The fish are laid on
their backs in the barrels, and layers of salt between them. The entrails
are not lost, for they are boiled into an oil: eight thousand fish will yield
ten gallons, valued at one shilling the gallon.

A vessel of eighty tuns takes out a hundred and forty barrels of salt:
a drawback of two shillings and eight-pence is allowed for each barrel

used for the foreign or Irish exportation of the fish; but there is a duty of one shilling per barrel for the home consumption, and the same for those sent to Ireland.

The barrels are made of oak staves, chiefly from Virginia: the hoops from several parts of our own island, and are made either of oak, birch, hazel or willow: the last from Holland, liable to a duty. The barrels cost about three shillings each; they hold from five to eight hundred fish, according to the size of the fish; are made to contain thirty-two gallons. The barrels are inspected by proper officers: a cooper examines them if they are statutable and good; if faulty he destroys them, and obliges the maker to stand to the loss.

The herrings in general are exported to the West-Indies, to feed the negroes, or to Ireland, for the Irish are not allowed to fish in these seas. By having a drawback of five-pence a barrel, and by re-packing the fish in new barrels of twenty-eight gallons, they are enabled to export them to our colonies at a cheaper rate than the Scots can do. The trade declines apace; the bounty, which was well paid originally kept up the spirits of the fishery; but for the last six years the arrears have been very injurious to several adventurers, who have sold out at thirty per cent loss, besides that of their interest.

The migration of the herrings has been very fully treated of in the 3d vol. of the *British Zoology*: it is superfluous to load this work with a repetition; I shall therefore only mention the observations that occur to me in this voyage, as pertinent to the present place.

Loch-Broom has been celebrated for three or four centuries as the resort of herrings. They generally appear here in July: those that turn into this bay are part of the brigade that detaches itself from the Western column of that great army that annually deserts the vast depths of the arctic circle, and come, heaven-directed, to the seats of population, offered as a cheap food to millions, whom wasteful luxury or iron-hearted avarice hath deprived, by enhancing the price, of the wonted supports of the poor.

The migration of these fish from their Northern retreat is regular: their visits to the Western isles and coasts certain: but their attachment to one particular loch, extremely precarious. All have their turns; that which swarmed with fish one year, is totally deserted the following; yet the next loch to it be crowded with the shoals. These changes of place give often full employ to the busses, who are continually shifting their harbour in quest of news concerning these important wanderers.

They commonly appear here in July; the latter end of August they go into deep water, and continue there for some time, without any apparent cause: in November they return to the shallows, when a new fishery commences, which continues till January; at that time the herrings become full of roe, and are useless as articles of commerce. Some doubt whether these herrings that appear in November are not part of a new migration; for they are as fat, and make the same appearance, as those that composed the first.

The signs of the arrival of the herrings are flocks of gulls, who catch up the fish while they skim on the surface; and of gannets, who plunge and bring them up from considerable depths. Both these birds are closely attended to by the fishers.

Cod-fish, haddocks and dog-fish follow the herrings in vast multitudes; these voracious fish keep on the outsides of the columns, and may be a concurrent reason of driving the shoals into bays and creeks. In Summer they come into the bays generally with the warmest weather, and with easy gales. During Winter the hard gales from N. West are supposed to assist in forcing them into shelter. East winds are very unfavourable to the fishery.

In a fine day, when the fish appear near the surface, they exhibit an amazing brilliancy of colours; all the various coruscations that dart from the diamond, sapphire and emerald, enrich their tract: but during night, if they 'break', i.e. play on the surface, the sea appears on fire, luminous as the brightest phosphorus. During a gale, that part of the ocean which is occupied by the great shoals, appears as if covered with the oil that is emitted from them. They appear to be greatly affected by lightening: during that phenomenon they sink towards the bottom, and move regularly in parallel shoals one above the other.

The enemies that assail these fish in the Winter season are varied, not diminished: of the birds, the gannets disappear: the gulls still continue their persecutions; whales, polacks and porpesses are added to their number of foes: these follow in droves; the whales deliberately, opening their vast mouths, taking them by hundreds. These monsters keep on the outside, for the body of the phalanx of herrings is so thick as to be impenetrable by these unwieldy animals.

The herring-fishers never observe the remains of any kind of food in the stomachs of that fish, as long as they are in good condition: as soon as they become foul or poor, they will greedily rise to the fly, and be taken like the whiting-pollack.

They do not deposit their spawn in sand or mud or weeds like other fish, but leave it in the water, suspended in a gelatinous matter, of such a gravity as prevents it from floating to the surface, or sinking to the bottom. The fishermen discover this by finding the slimy matter adhering to the hay ropes sometimes in use to hold the stone that sinks the nets, the middle part being slimed over, the top and bottom clear.

Before I leave this bay it must be observed that there are here, as in most of the lochs, a few, a very few of the natives who possess a boat and nets; and fish in order to sell the capture fresh to the busses: the utmost these poor people can attain to are the boat and nets; they are too indigent to become masters of barrels, or of salt, to the great loss of the public as well theirselves. Were magazines of salt established in these distant parts; was encouragement given to these distant Britons, so that they might be enabled by degrees to furnish themselves with the requisites for fishing, they would soon form themselves into seamen, by the course of life they must apply themselves to; the busses would be certain of finding a ready market of fish, ready cured; the natives taught industry, which would be quickened by the profits made by the commodity, which they might afford cheaper, as taken at their very doors, without the wear and tear of distant voyages, as in the present case. Half of the hands employed now in fishing and curing generally come out as raw seamen as the inhabitants of these parts: they do not return with much greater experience in the working of a ship, being employed entirely in the boats, or in salting of the herrings, and seem on board as aukward as marines in comparison of able seamen. A bounty on these home captures would stimulate the people to industry; would drive from their minds the thoughts of emigrations and would never lessen the number of seamen, as it would be an incitement for more adventurers to fit out vessels, because they would have a double chance of freight, from their own captures, and from those of the residents, who might form a stock from shoals of fish, which often escape while the former are wind-bound, or wandering from loch to loch.

The Fisher Lass

ANONYMOUS

Twas in the month of August one morning by the sea
When violets and primroses were strewed on every lea
I met a pretty damsel for an empress she would pass
My heart was captivated by a bonny fisher lass.

The petticoats she wore were short and tight above her knee
Her handsome legs and ankles, how they delighted me
Her rosy cheeks and yellow hair so neatly they compared
With her creel she trudges daily, doth the bonny fisher lass.

'Good morning to you fair maid' I unto her did say
Oh why are you so early or where are you going this way?
I am going to the rockland, sir, oh pray now let me pass
For to get my lines in order, said the bonny fisher lass.

I am going the rocks behind, sir, some mussels for to pick
No matter whether it be snow or rain the bait we have to get
But I will lend a helping hand, for your pardon I will ask
So I'll go along my journey said the bonny fisher lass.

My father's out on the ocean wide there toiling in his boat
And for to make a livelihood he often goes afloat
And when he doth return again so lovingly he will grasp
In his bosom, his charming fisher lass.

When the storm arises I out upon the pier
I stand and watch sincerely for I must dread and fear
Lest he should meet with a watery grave and be smashed
                                        from my grasp
So I would wander broken-hearted said the bonny fisher lass.

Song of the Fish-gutters

ANONYMOUS

Come, a' ye fisher lassies, aye, it's come awa' wi' me
Fae Cairnbulg and Gamrie and fae Inverallochie;
Fae Buckie and fae Aberdeen an' a' the country roon
We're awa' tae gut the herrin', we're awa' tae Yarmouth toon.

Rise up in the morning wi' your bundles in your hand
Be at the station early or you'll surely hae to stand,
Tak' plenty to eat and a kettle for your tea,
Or you'll mebbe die of hunger on the way to Yarmouth quay.

The journey it's a lang ane and it tak's a day or twa,
And when you reach your lodgin', sure it's soond asleep you fa'
But ye rise at five wi' the sleep still in your e'e
You're awa' tae find the gutting yards along the Yarmouth quay.

It's early in the morning and it's late into the nicht,
Your hands a' cut and chappit and they look an unco sicht;
And you greet like a wean when you put them in the bree
And you wish you were a thoosand mile awa' fae Yarmouth quay.

There's coopers there and curers there and buyers, canny chiels
And lassies at the pickling and others at the creels,
And you'll wish the fish had been a' left in the sea
By the time you finish guttin' herrin' on the Yarmouth quay.

We've gutted fish in Lerwick and in Stornoway and Shields
Warked along the Humber 'mongst the barrels and the creels
Whitby, Grimsby, we've traivelled up and doon,
But the place to see the herrin' is the quay at Yarmouth toon.

Clann Nighean an Sgadain

RUARAIDH MACTHOMAIS
(Derick S. Thomson) (1921–)
Translation by the author

An gàire mar chraiteachan salainn
ga fhroiseadh bho 'm bial,
an sàl 's am picil air an teanga,
's na meuran cruinne, goirid a dheanadh giullachd,
no a thogadh leanabh gu socair, cuimir,
seasgair, fallain,
gun mhearachd,
's na sùilean cho domhainn ri fèath.

B'e bun-os-cionn na h-eachdraidh a dh'fhàg iad
'nan tràillean aig ciùrairean cutach,
thall 's a-bhos air Galldachd 's an Sasuinn.
Bu shaillte an duais a thàrr iad
ás na mìltean bharaillean ud,
gaoth na mara geur air an craiceann,
is eallach a' bhochdainn 'nan ciste,
is mara b'e an gàire
shaoileadh tu gu robh an teud briste.

Ach bha craiteachan uaille air an cridhe,
ga chumail fallain,
is bheireadh cutag an teanga
slisinn á fanaid nan Gall –
agus bha obair rompa fhathast
nuair gheibheadh iad dhachaidh,
ged nach biodh maoin ac':
air oidhche robach gheamhraidh,
ma bha sud an dàn dhaibh,
dheanadh iad daoine.

The Herring Girls

Their laughter like a sprinkling of salt
showered from their lips,
brine and pickle on their tongues,
and the stubby short fingers that could handle fish,
or lift a child gently, neatly,
safely, wholesomely,
unerringly,
and the eyes that were as deep as a calm.

The topsy-turvy of history had made them
slaves to short-arsed curers,
here and there in the Lowlands, in England.
Salt the reward they won
from those thousands of barrels,
the sea-wind sharp on their skins,
and the burden of poverty in their kists,
and were it not for their laughter
you might think the harp-string was broken.

But there was a sprinkling of pride in their hearts,
keeping them sound,
and their tongues' gutting-knife
would tear a strip from the Lowlanders' mockery
and there was work awaiting them
when they got home,
though they had no wealth:
on a wild winter's night,
if that were their lot,
they would make men.

The Derelict Boat

from The Silver Darlings

NEIL GUNN (1891–1973)

The Caithness village of Dunbeath between Helmsdale and Wick had a history not unlike the unnamed settlement of The Silver Darlings *(1941); to that strath also people came in the early years of the nineteenth century from an interior which was being devastated. Dunbeath was the novelist Neil Gunn's birthplace – his father had been a fisherman there – and there was a folk memory which surfaced when he wrote passages like these:*

> They had come from beyond the mountain which rose up behind them, from inland valleys and swelling pastures, where they and their people before them had lived from time immemorial. The landlord had driven them from these valleys and pastures, and burned their houses, and set them here against the sea-shore to live if they could and, if not, to die.

And the novel goes on to mention the old themes of starvation and exile, but also records the note of hope – for the time being – which sounded from the arrival of the 'Silver Darlings', which brought the prosperous herring fisheries to Scotland's coasts in the years following the Napoleonic wars, as recorded in songs and poems previously in this chapter.

This, the first chapter of the novel, is a splendid example of Gunn's grasp of history in setting time and place, while rapidly moving forward characterisation and incident. The first sign of the menacing presence on this coastline of the Royal Navy sloop and its sinister press-gang, is a case in point:

> They all sat up, with little shudders of cold, and looked at the ship. Canvas was now breaking out both behind and in front of her high mast. 'She'll be a merchant ship,' said Tormad, and turned to see what the herring boats were doing. He was surprised to find that already they were beginning to leave the ground.

As Tormad tried to flick a limpet out of the boiling pot, he burnt his fingers, upset the pot, and spilt the whole contents over the fire, so that there was a sudden hissing with a cloud of ashes and steam. Fortunately the fire was outside, round the back of the cottage, where Catrine boiled clothes on her washing day.

'Did you ever see the beat of that?' he asked, hissing through his teeth and flailing his hand in the air.

It was so like him, and she so loved him, that she turned away.

He kicked the smouldering peats apart and began retrieving the limpets, which, being hot, stung him frequently. Holding one in the corner of his jacket, he gouged out its flesh easily with his thumb-nail. Whole and clean it came, and he cried: 'They're ready!' delighted after all with his judgement. 'I'll put the fire on for you,' he said, 'in a whip,' as he scraped limpets and yellow ash together into a small rush basket.

'I don't need it,' she answered. 'Never mind. And what's the good of blowing the ashes off that, you great fool?'

'Because I always like,' said Tormad, 'to leave things neat and tidy.'

As he had probably never left anything neat and tidy in his life, Catrine turned from him towards the house. His lids lowered and his eyes glimmered in a dark humour, as, following, he looked at her back and the carry of her fair head. She was very light on the foot always, and could break into a run as quickly as she could laugh. When laughter beset her it doubled her up, but if anyone tried to catch her in the helpless middle of it, she would arch her waist and whirl off with a little abrupt yelp. He knew by the way she walked with her head up exactly how she was feeling. She did not want to break down, to discourage him, but the tears would beat her if they got half a chance. By keeping very busy and leaving the house at once, he would not give them the chance. In his twenty-four years he felt full of a great competence. Catrine was only nineteen.

'Yonder's Ronnie,' he said, pausing for a moment at the door. 'They'll be waiting for me. Let me see, now. You have the scone and the drop of milk. There's the net. And here's the limpets.' He stood looking around their simple living-room, with its fire in the middle of the floor, and added, 'Yes, that's everything. I'll be going.'

'All right, then,' she said calmly, standing quite straight, her shoulder to him.

He looked at her side face, his eyes going black. If a fly touched his sympathy, he might half-kill a man, to save it. 'Very well,' he said, 'that's fine.' He slung the net on to his left shoulder and balanced it, then lifted the limpets and the food. 'You needn't come down,' he said. 'Don't you come. There's no need. Everything's fine.'

'All right,' she answered.

He should have gone then, but the sympathy in him was his greatest weakness. He stood looking at her.

'Why don't you go?' she asked sharply, without turning her head.

'Catrine,' he said gently, 'why won't you give me your blessing?'

'Why don't you go?' she cried.

'Catrine—'

'Go!' she screamed. 'Go!'

He took the step between them. 'Catrine—'

'Oh, why don't you go?' He felt her teeth biting at his chest and her fingers digging into his back like little iron claws. The net fell from him and the small rush basket and the pocket of food. Her tears had won against her and were making her savage. Her sobs were tearing gulps.

He soothed her as best he could, and the Gaelic tongue helped him for it is full of the tenderest endearments. 'You see,' he whispered in her hair, 'it's all for you – and himself. There's nothing here, Catrine; nothing in this barren strip of land for us. And the men who are going to the sea are making money. Could I do less than them, when I have the strength in me not to see them in my way? Be reasonable now, Catrine, love of my heart, my little one, my wild pigeon. Listen now. It's your help I need . . .'

Under his talk she was quietening – indeed his words had brought a soft emotion into his own throat – and he thought they had never come so near to a grown-up understanding of life together, when suddenly, her fingers gripping his flesh, she threw her head back and looked right into his eyes. 'I'll never let you go,' she said. 'I've got you. I'll never let you go.' He knew her wayward moods. But this was something far beyond. It was hard and challenging, without any warmth. Her eyes were suddenly those of an enemy, deliberately calculating, cold as greed.

He looked away, not wanting to believe it, and said, 'Don't be foolish, Catrine.' Her fingers were hurting him. 'Come, now, I'll have to go.' He tried gently to free himself from her grasp; but she held on the more firmly. Her strength was astonishing. He made to take a step away. She twisted her legs round his legs, so that he staggered and they nearly fell. He appealed to her again, but she only increased her fighting hold, her teeth deep in his clothes. The strangling pressure on his neck was irking him. Impatience beset him. This was too much. He finally set his strength against her and tore her arms from his neck. 'Why are you behaving like this?' he cried, crossing her writhing arms against her body. But she struggled like one possessed, in a wild fury, and he was panting when finally he disentangled himself and left her on the clay floor choking with sobs, her face hidden.

Easing his neck, he looked about him and then down at the gathered heap she made. The anger in his mind was baffled and weary. After all he had done; selling his second beast to help buy the old boat and net; tearing the rocks out of the barren land; striving – striving . . . it was hard on a fellow. He bent down and heaved the net to his shoulder; lifted the limpets; stood for a moment looking at her; then, without a word, turned and walked out.

The ground sloped down to a narrow flatness before it tumbled over a steep face of earth and broken rock to the sea-beach. All that primeval hill-side of heath and whin and moss was slowly being broken-in to thin strips of cultivated land by those who lived in the little cabins of stone and turf dotted here and there with rounded backs like earth-mounds. They had come from beyond the mountain which rose up behind them, from inland valleys and swelling pastures, where they and their people before them had lived from time immemorial. The landlord had driven them from these valleys and pastures, and burned their houses, and set them here against the sea-shore to live if they could and, if not, to die.

The first year had been the worst. Many had died. Many had been carried away in empty lime ships. A great number had perished on the sea. But a greater number, it was believed, were alive in Nova Scotia and elsewhere in Canada and other lands, though fighting against dreadful tribulations and adversities. It had been a bitter and terrible time. Some said it had been brought upon them for their sins, and some said it had been a visitation of the Lord upon the world because of the wicked doings of the anti-Christ, Napoleon. But with Napoleon at last in St Helena, the burnings and evictions went on; and as for their sins, to many of them, if not to all, it seemed that their lives had been pleasant and inoffensive in their loved inland valleys; and even in an odd year, when harvests had been bad and cattle lean, even now the memory of it seemed lapped around with an increased kindliness of one to another.

Tormad's heels sank into the earth. He was a heavy broad fellow, a little above the average in height, with black hair that sometimes glistened. His eyes were a very dark blue and had an expression in them exasperated and sad. He knew why his wife hated the sea, but she needn't have gone to such lengths to show it. That first winter had been a terror. For one long spell, they had had little or nothing to live on but shell-fish and seaweed. Often they ate the wrong thing and colic and dysentery were everywhere. Old men, trying to live on nothing to give the young the better chance, had become unbelievably gaunt, so that children would sometimes run from them, frightened. What had preyed on Catrine's mind more than anything was the death of her uncle. He had been one of the most heartening men in their little colony – for there were many such colonies along that wild coast – with the gaiety in him that was natural to Catrine herself. He had got nimble at hunting the waves and was daring anyhow. They had cleaned the shore to the lowest edge of the ebb, and one day, following the suction of the receding wave, he slipped, and, before he could get up, the next wave had him and sucked him over a shallow ledge. His arms lathered the water for a moment while horrified eyes watched. Then he sank and did not come up.

Yet it was out of that very sea that hope was now coming to them. The landlord who had burned them out in order to have a suitable desolation for sheep, had set about making a harbour at the mouth of the river, the same river that, with its tributaries, had threaded their inland valleys. Money had been advanced by him (at 6½ per cent. interest) to erect buildings for dealing with fish. All along these coasts – the coasts of the Moray Firth – there was a new stirring of sea life. The people would yet live, the people themselves; for no landlord owned the sea, and what the people caught there would be their own – or very nearly (for landlords over a long period continued to levy tribute on the fish landed). It was the end of the Napoleonic era. For the Moray Firth it was the beginning of the herring fisheries, of a busy, fabulous time among the common people of that weathered northern land.

A foretaste of the adventurous happy years to come was upon Tormad. Round the corner, at the mouth of the river, Helmsdale was getting under way. It was near the end of July and the height of the herring season. Yesterday a boat from the south side of the Firth had had a shot of herring that must have brought in nearly sixteen pounds. Sixteen golden sovereigns for one night's work. It was a terrible amount of money. Four in the crew made it four pounds a man. Four pounds for one night – out of nothing! It so stirred the imaginations of the people that it seemed to them uncanny; seemed to them at times hardly right, as if some evil chance must be lurking somewhere, ready to pounce.

Old men and women from the gable-ends of their wretched cabins saw Tormad going by with the net on his shoulder. They stood still, silent, but others not so old began to come from their little holdings, and already a group of boys were trotting behind Tormad. His young brother, Norman, who was fifteen, strode by his side with pride. He had secretly made up his mind that next year he was going to sea himself.

When he came to the crest, Tormad saw the three members of his crew round the bow of the boat, keeping her stern in the water. They were learning! Others were on the beach, waiting. He went down the short steep slanting path, and out over the stones to the boat, into which he let the net fall with a thud. 'I see you have the two lines,' he said, and laid the basket of bait beside them. 'I think that's everything. Are you ready?'

'Yes,' said Ronnie, a quiet lean fellow, with a sallow face, two years older than Tormad. Ian was a year younger than Tormad; but Torquil was only eighteen, and though he had been able to contribute nothing to the purchase of the boat and gear, he was going with them because they couldn't keep him back. Tormad was full of business. Bending down he took one or two steps forward to see that no boulder might damage the planking as they pushed off. A small wave splashed over his feet and he pulled them out smartly as if he had been stung, just saving himself from falling on his face by gripping the gunnel. The boys laughed, for this had often happened to themselves and they liked Tormad. His eyes brightened in his flushed face. 'That's the baptism,' he cried back to them comically. They were delighted, and came and put their hands on the boat, touching it as if it were a strange horse. Norman gripped it firmly. Looking up, Tormad saw the people in a line along the edge of the crest. The whole colony was seeing them off. He felt the pressure of eyes and decided it was high time they were away. But suddenly voices cried from the crest. All on the shore looked up, and presently Tormad saw Catrine coming over the crest and down the steep path. His whole face went dark and congested as he moved up the stones to meet her.

'You forgot your food,' she cried, holding the satchel in front of her and stepping lightly on her toes.

'Did I?' He smiled. He did not know what more to say so he pulled open the satchel's mouth and gazed into it. 'That's fine,' he said, glancing up at her. For one moment her brown eyes – they were her loveliest feature – looked at him, and then they looked away, wild and shy. Altogether she was like something that might fly away, her large mouth smiling and blood-red. There was at times a gay lightness about her, like blown leaves. They could not say anything, because of the eyes around them. And the lids of Catrine's own eyes were fired a little with the recent weeping. 'Well, so long,' he said, with a laugh, raising a hand in homely salute and farewell. As he came back to the boat, the small stones roared from his heels. 'Out with her, boys!' As the three clambered aboard, Tormad gave the final push and landed neatly in the bows.

'Hold your oar in, Ian,' he whispered and began to pull with all his strength. They had had some practice with the oars, bringing the boat up from Golspie, and Tormad soon had the bow swinging round to sea. But he kept pulling so strongly that, before Ian could get a proper start, the bow was almost in-shore again. Tormad now held water, exasperated that they were not making a good start before the people. When the bow went seaward, he dug in fiercely. 'Keep her like that!' he cried, giving way with all his force.

On the pull of the oar, Ian's slim body was levered off the seat and writhed like an eel. He had not Tormad's bull-shoulders, but he had all Tormad's pride and would sooner that his sinews cracked than that his tongue should cry halt. But the boat was now gathering way, and Ronnie at the tiller began to feel the kick of Tormad's oar, the excitement in him making his face sallower than usual. His eyes gleamed with the knowledge that he was guiding Tormad's wild strength and sending the boat straight on her course. 'You're doing fine,' he said quietly. The two oars described a high half-circle, hit the water, and dug in. 'Boys, we're making a good show.'

The exultance in Ronnie's voice was a great encouragement. Not that Tormad needed any spur, for he could see Catrine standing on the beach where he had left her. His love for her came over him in half-blinding spasms. He could have cracked the oar and the boat and the world. Indeed, if the oar broke in his hands it would be with relief. His mind was mazed with exultation and sorrow, but singing underneath was the song of what he would yet do for her, and knew he would do for her, if God spared him.

That wildness in the house – it was her own wildness, her own mad wildness, to protect him and herself and him to come. He could see her still standing all alone. Extraordinary how out of a man's greatest strength could mount a softness near to tears.

'Careful, Tormad, or you'll burst your thole pin,' said Ronnie. 'Careful, boy.'

'Not yet,' said Tormad. 'Keep her going, Ian.'

'I'll keep her going till I burst,' said Ian.

The shore receded from them, and soon the folk were moving up the beach, and Tormad lost sight of Catrine. The folk were like small animals, like little dark calves. After a while, Ronnie called a halt. 'It's our turn now.'

They changed places in the boat so warily that she scarcely rocked. Tormad wiped the sweat from his eyes and Ian leaned forward, drawing his shoulders from his sticky vest. Not until that moment did they fully realise that they were by themselves, cut off, on the breast of the ocean.

They had never before been so far from land, and the slow movement of the sea became a living motion under them. It brimmed up against the boat and choked its own mouth, then moved away; and came again and moved away, without end, slow, heedless, and terrible, its power restrained, like the power in some great invisible bull. Fear, feather light, kept them wary, like the expectancy of a blow in a dark place.

'There's no hurry, boys,' said Tormad quietly. 'I'll be keeping my eyes open now for the signs.'

The old Golspie man, who had been white-fishing half a century before herring-fishing started at Helmsdale, had given Tormad certain land-marks by which he might direct himself to the best grounds. Tormad had tried to memorize these marks as well as he could, but, inclined to be over-sanguine and the whole business of buying the boat exciting him, he had not grasped fully the need for the double bearing to give him his angle. Not that he showed any indecision now. 'There's Brora yonder,' he said. 'And that point away far off is Tarbat Ness. Now on this side – will you look? – that's Berriedale Head. You wouldn't think it's six miles off! We have to go three miles out and I shouldn't think we're far off that now. Pull away gently for a little yet, boys, and then we'll try it.' No-one spoke, and after they had pulled out, for what seemed a long time, over a sea that must be getting deeper and deeper, Tormad stopped them. 'We'll try her at that,' he said. Then he gazed around him with what was meant to be a seaman's eye.

They all gazed around, but what they saw was the land, and with a little cry of surprise Torquil pointed to the ridge of a hill going far inland, over the valley of Kildonan. They knew it like the back of a hand, and their minds filled with pictures, with memories of boyhood and familiar scenes. This was the time of year when they would be away from home at the summer shielings with the cattle, the happiest time in all the year, living in turf bothies, with the young girls there and many of the old. 'Hand me up that line, Ian,' said Tormad, who had the limpéts at his feet.

From the basket he took four limpets and gouged out their flesh with his thumb. The tackle consisted of a short cross-spar of slim hazel with the line tied to the middle of it and a hook on a short horse-hair snood dangling from each end. To the end of the line, which hung a foot or more below the middle of the spar, was tied a heavy sinker. Upon each hook Tormad fixed two limpets, the hard, leathery surfaces to the inside. 'That's the way it's done,' he explained, and dropped hooks and sinker overboard. They had half a dozen herring with them which might have been better bait, but the Golspie man had been used to mussels and limpets, and Tormad had taken a fancy to the limpets.

As yard after yard of line was unwound from the fork-shaped hazel stick, they had a new way of realising the sea's depth. 'It's got no bottom to it, I do believe,' said Tormad humorously. Still the line went out; and out. 'It's not feeling so heavy, I think,' said Tormad, as if listening through his fingers. Clearly he was in doubt. He looked at the amount still wound on the stick, and let out more, and then more. Down went the line, coil after coil, and they were beginning to believe that maybe the sea had, in fact, no bottom, when suddenly the pull ceased and the line went slack. 'I've got it!' cried Tormad, heaving a breath. They were all relieved, and Tormad went on cheerfully to demonstrate how one must lift the sinker a yard or more off the bottom and then work the line up and down, waiting all the time for the feel of the bite.

They watched him until his mouth fell open. 'I think I've got something.' He gulped, then pulled – but the line refused to come. It came a little way and then pulled back. 'It feels like a whale,' he said, his eyes round, his head cocked. 'O God, it's something heavy indeed!' Excitement got hold of them all strongly. What if it *was* a whale?

The forked stick was very nearly jerked out of Tormad's hands. He had to let out more line quickly. Then a little more. Leviathan was moving away from under them!

Their hearts went across them. The boat rose on the heave of the sea. Now that they were clear of the land, a gentle wind darkened the surface of the waters. A small ripple suddenly slapped the clinched planking like a hand slapping a face. The sound startled them. Ronnie looked at the sea. 'We're drifting,' he said. 'The oars, boys – quick!' cried Tormad. 'Quick, or all the line will be out!' Ronnie and Ian each shoved an oar out, and Ronnie pulled the bow round so smartly towards the wind that Tormad, on his feet, lurched and fell sideways, clutching at the line, which all at once went slack in his hands. On his knees he began hauling in rapidly. The line came to a clean end. Sinker and hooks and cross-spar were gone.

Tormad stared at the frayed end against his palm. No-one spoke. Tormad stared at the sea. It came under the boat in a slow heave and passed on.

'When one place is no good, you try another,' he said quietly. 'Let us go farther out.'

Ian and Ronnie swung the oars. Torquil was looking a bit grey. He had been underfed for a long time, but the blue of his eyes held an intolerant green.

'I wonder were you stuck in the bottom?' Ronnie asked.

'Himself knows,' said Tormad.

When they stopped, they did not know quite what to do, for they were frightened now to use the second line. There was no sign of gulls about to signify herring. Nothing but this heaving immensity, treacherous and deep as death. That time he had fallen, Tormad remembered the joke against him in Helmsdale: 'Between her two skins of tar, she's rotten.' The old Golspie man was supposed to have fooled them – to his humorous credit, because a boat is there to be examined before it is bought. But Tormad had been shy of asking a Helmsdale man to go with him, not merely because of the long distance in the short busy season but also because he could hardly appear as a real fisherman with only the one old net. So the idea he had put about was that they were going to try for white-fish with the hand-line – to begin with, anyway. Accordingly and naturally they had come to sea before the other boats, which would not put out from the harbour for two or three hours yet, as nets were never shot until the evening. There was also the instinctive desire to keep to themselves until they knew enough not to be laughed at, for the folk from the glens were sensitive and had their own hidden pride.

And now the first hand-line was gone.

'We're drifting,' said Tormad, who had been staring at the land. Then he noticed Torquil on his knees in the bow, his back to them, his head down.

'What's wrong with you, Torquil?'

'Nothing!' snapped Torquil.

Ronnie looked over his shoulder. 'Feeling sick?' he asked gently.

Torquil's body gave a convulsive spasm. He retched, but there was nothing in his stomach. 'What's this?' asked Ian, who was next to him, putting his hand on his shoulder.

'Shut up!' said Torquil. He had tied a single hook to the end of the broken line, and a foot or so above the hook had knotted the line about one of the slim stones that were to be used for sinking the net. 'Give me the bait!'

His fingers shook as he handled the hook, and the smell and look of the pulpy yellow bait made him retch again. But he baited the hook as Tormad had done and dropped it over the side.

They watched him, fascinated, until Ronnie noticed the increasing slant on the line and put out his oar. Already experience was teaching them that they must 'hold up' a boat against the wind-drift. Ian and Ronnie pulled gently as if to make no noise, for they now had a premonition that something strange was going to happen.

As Torquil worked the line up and down they waited. It was the odd thing always that did happen! Then Torquil's grey face quickened and his eyes flashed. Swiftly he began hauling in the line. In his haste, his hands and arms got meshed in the coils. The rowers forgot their oars. Tormad's lips came apart.

When Torquil stopped hauling, as if something had hit him, they craned over the edge of the boat and saw a great grey back that frightened them. 'Stand away!' screamed Torquil, and catching the line low down he heaved. The hook and line parted company as a huge cod fell thrashing on the bottom boards. Tormad lunged at it as if it were a dangerous beast and tried to throttle it. Finally, he lifted it in his arms and bashed its head against the edge of Ronnie's seat. From the stretched-out, dead, but still quivering fish, they lifted their eyes and looked at one another.

'Torquil, my hero,' said Tormad softly. He began laughing huskily. They all began to laugh. They swayed and hit one another great friendly thumps.

'We'll do it yet, boys!' said Ronnie.

They would do it. They would do it, by the sign beneath them. The great slippery belly of the sign made them rock with laughter.

But Torquil had now discovered his hook was gone. When they found it inside the cod's mouth they could hardly retrieve it for the weakness that mirth had put in their fingers.

But now Tormad was busy with the second line. When, after a shout and much fierce hauling, he produced a single little whiting, he could do no more than nod at the dangling fish with helpless good humour.

They got going in earnest. Whether they caught anything in the net or not, here was enough success already to justify a first venture. And presently when a good-sized haddock appeared, and shortly after that a flat fish with beautiful red spots, and then – of all things – a crab, the excitement in that fourteen-foot boat rose very high. But Ronnie failed to land the crab. Just as he was swinging it into the boat, it let go its hold of the bait, fell on the flat of its back on the narrow gunnel, balanced for an instant and tumbled back into the sea. Tormad dived to the shoulder after it, badly rocking the boat, but fortunately for him did no more than touch one of the great claws as it sank beyond reach. Then he caught his oar just as it was slipping from between the pins. What next? They were all laughing and Torquil's sickness seemed completely cured. Their eyes were bright and very quick. They cautioned one another not to take liberties with the boat, but whenever two hands began hauling rapidly, four heads tried to see what was coming up. Each passed a line on after a short spell of fishing. Tormad had a dramatic moment when he struck what he felt was a heavy fish. He swore by Donan's Seat that it was a monster, the biggest yet. His hooks came up as they had gone down, the baits whole. 'I don't care what you say,' declared Tormad, 'that fish was three bushes if he was an ounce.' 'Do you think perhaps it may have been the bottom?' asked Ian. 'No, nor your own bottom,' said Tormad shortly. 'Bottom indeed! Didn't I feel the jag-jag of his mouth to each side? Man, do you think I don't know the difference between the bottom and a fish's mouth?' 'No, it's not the bottom,' said Ronnie. 'How do you know?' asked Ian. 'Because,' said Ronnie, 'the bottom here is hard and clean. I let my sinker lie for a little while on it. That's how I got the crab. Pull just a little more strongly – just a very little. We don't want to drift off this spot.'

By the time they saw the boats coming out from the harbour mouth they didn't mind who would inspect their catch. It was a fine evening, with the wind, from the land, inclined to fall. They watched the small fleet with an increase of excitement and a certain self-consciousness, expecting them to pass close by and in a friendly way call a few sarcastic greetings. 'We'll just answer, off-hand, "Oh, about a cran or two." Like that,' said Tormad. 'Leave it to me.'

But the herring boats did not come near them. They watched the oars rising and falling like the legs of great beetles as the small fleet headed south. They were all open boats, one or two of the largest some twenty feet in length. The use of sail on this northern coast was as yet little understood and on this fair evening not one was to be seen.

Tormad began wondering if he had come to the wrong place. They discussed this. 'We're doing fine here,' said Ronnie. 'And it's as well we should have the first night by ourselves.' They all agreed with this in their hearts, but Tormad said he wasn't so sure. He didn't see why they shouldn't go where anyone else went. Success had given a fillip to his adventurous mood. Tormad could be put up or down, and when he was up he could be very high. But in the end he smiled. 'Ach well, it's fine here, boys, by ourselves and we're doing grand.' Often enough the herring boats caught little or nothing. Perhaps they themselves in this spot might be lucky. It would be a joke if theirs would be the only boat to go into Helmsdale with herring in the morning! They laughed. They had made up their minds to distribute all the white fish they caught among their own folk as a first offering to good luck, and now Ian began to mimic old Morag's astonishment when he went up and presented her with the cod. He did it very well, hanging to high-pitched vowels and flapping his hands. Life was good, too!

'They're shooting their nets now,' said Tormad. Some two miles to the south the boats were scattered over the sea. Blue shadows came down the hills. Tormad blew up his big buoy until his eyes disappeared. He had got it from the man in Golspie, and though its skin crackled with age it seemed tight enough. He could hardly blow up the second one for laughing, because it was the bag of an old set of pipes to which they had danced many a time as boys. It had a legendary history, for the old piper, its owner, had been a wild enough lad in his day. When he was driven from his home, he cursed the landlord-woman (who had inherited all that land), her sassenach husband, her factors, in tongues of fire. Then he had broken his pipes, tearing them apart. It had been an impressive, a terrifying scene, and shortly after it he had died.

Well, here was the bag, and perhaps it marked not an end but a beginning! They had had a little superstitious fear about using it. But they couldn't afford to buy another buoy, and, anyway, they argued, if it brought them luck it would be a revenge over the powers that be. The dead piper wouldn't be disappointed at that!

The net was made of hemp and, being old, was coarse and stiff, but quite strong. The large buoy, tied to the outer end by a fathom of rope, was first slung overboard; then as Ronnie and Torquil let out the net, with its back-rope and corks, Tormad slipped a flat stone into each noose as it came along on the foot-rope, Ian meantime keeping the boat going ahead for the wind had all but dropped. It took them a long time, for Tormad would insist on hauling at the part of the net already in the sea to make sure that it was going down as straight as a fence. He got wet from hand to neck doing this, without being aware of it. At last he dropped the piper's bag upon the sea with his blessing, adding, 'Now play you the tune of your life, my hero, and let himself smile on us from the green glens of Paradise.' Ian rowed away the three fathoms of rope – all they had – by which they would swing to the net as to an anchor. Tormad made fast. The oars were shipped. And now it was food.

Everything was going better than they had expected. They could easily make hand-line tackle – so long as they had the line. They talked away, full of hope, as they munched their dark-brown bere scones and drank their milk. When they had finished eating, they started at the lines again, and there was a short spell in the half-light when they caught large-sized haddock as quickly as they could haul them in. Then everything went very quiet and the darkness came down – or as much darkness as they would have on that northern summer night. They were tired now, for they hadn't had much sleep the last two nights, what with going to Golspie and bringing the boat back along the shore and the excitement of the whole strange venture. They would stretch themselves out between the timbers as best they could. This they did, and above them they saw the stars, and under them they felt the sea rise and fall.

'Does it never go quiet at all?' asked Ian.

'Never,' said Tormad.

'A strange thing, that,' said Ronnie. 'Never.'

Their voices grew quiet and full of wonder and a warm friendliness. They told one another all the queer things they ever heard about the sea. After a time Ronnie murmured, 'I think Torquil has fallen asleep.' Torquil muttered vaguely. They all closed their eyes. It seemed to them that they never really fell asleep, though their thoughts were like dreams going their own way. Every now and again one of them stirred; but for long spells they breathed heavily. The stars were gone, when Ronnie opened his eyes wide, looked about him and sat up. It was chilly and the surface of the water dark in an air of wind, but to the north-east, beyond the distant rim of the sea, was the white light of morning. And then, out from Berriedale Head, he saw a ship with a light, like a small star, over her. The star disappeared as he gazed. He wakened Tormad with his hand.

They all sat up, with little shudders of cold, and looked at the ship. Canvas was now breaking out both behind and in front of her high mast. 'She'll be a merchant ship,' said Tormad, and turned to see what the herring boats were doing. He was surprised to find that already they were beginning to leave the ground. They couldn't have much herring, surely. Then his face opened in dismay. 'The piper's bag is gone!' he cried. There was no sign of the corks. He stumbled aft and caught the swing-rope. They leaned over the sides. As Tormad hauled strongly, the piper's bag appeared, bobbing and breaking the surface. And then their eyes widened and their breath stopped. Tormad began appealing softly to the God of their fathers. Then his voice cleared and rose. 'It's herring, boys! Herring! Herring!' The net was so full of herring that it had pulled the floats under the surface, all except the end buoy, which was half submerged.

They forgot all about the ship; they forgot everything, except the herrings, the lithe silver fish, the swift flashing ones, hundreds and thousands of them, the silver darlings. No moment like this had ever come to them in their lives. They were drunk with the excitement and staggered freely about the boat. Tormad took to shouting orders. The wind had changed and, growing steady, was throwing them a little on the net. 'Keep her off,' shouted Tormad. 'Take the oars, Ian. The foot-rope, Ronnie.' Tormad was now pulling on the back-rope with all his strength, but could only lift the net inch by inch. But already herring were tumbling into the boat, for Torquil was nimble and Ronnie persuasive. 'Take it easy,' said Ronnie, seeing the congestion in Tormad's neck. 'Take it easy, or the whole net may tear away. We've plenty of time, boys.' 'Don't be losing them,' grunted Tormad, his heel against the stern post. 'Take them all. Alie the piper is watching us.' They laughed at that. The piper had done his part, full to overflowing. It was always the way he had done things whatever. No half-measures with Alie.

'The ship is coming this way,' said Ian.

'Let her come,' said Tormad, not even turning his head.

But Ronnie looked over his shoulder. His face brightened. 'She'll be a big schooner come to take the barrels of herring away maybe.'

'Of course,' said Tormad. 'What else would she be?' And the vague fear that had touched them at first sight of the ship almost vanished.

'Perhaps she'll offer to buy our herrings,' suggested Torquil.

'She might easily do that,' Tormad grunted out, the sweat now running. 'But if she does – she'll pay – the full price.'

More than half the net was in and Torquil glittered with scales in the rising sun, when Ian said, 'She's coming very close.'

She crossed their bow at a cable length, and then, slowly running up into the wind until her great sails shook, she came to a standstill so close that they could see the men moving about her decks.

Fear touched them once more, because they had learned that everything that spoke of power and wealth had to be feared.

'Pay no attention,' muttered Tormad. 'The sea at least is free.'

A voice as loud as a horn called to them, but they were not sure of the words, for what English they had was strange to them even in their own mouths. So they doggedly hauled away at the net.

'There's a boat coming,' said Ian.

'Let it come,' said Tormad, giving it a quick glance.

Four oars rose and fell smartly and the ship's boat drew abreast. Two men sat in the stern, with long-nosed pistols. One man, standing, asked them in a loud voice if they heard the ship's hail.

'Careful, Torquil,' said Tormad softly. 'Don't lose the darlings.'

Then the man with the loud voice expressed his anger in a terse oath which the four lads didn't understand, though they gathered its intent. But they did not look at the man; they looked at the net whose back-rope Tormad contrived to haul steadily.

Whereupon in the King's name the man commanded them to drop the net and come alongside His Majesty's ship of war and present themselves to the commander, and if they didn't do this quietly and at once, things would happen to them of a bloody and astonishing nature.

'There's three crans in this net,' said Tormad to Ronnie, 'if there's a herring.'

An order was whipped out. Smartly the visiting boat closed on Tormad's bow and in no time a stout rope was passed through the ring-bolt in the stem. 'Give way!' The four oars dug in, rose and dug in ... But Tormad, on the back-rope, held both boats stationary. 'Let go there!' shouted the voice in stentorian wrath.

Tormad, his face swelling with blood and anger, looked over his shoulder. 'Let go yourself!' he cried in his best English.

'Ease away!' As they stood down on the fishing-boat, the two near oars were smartly shipped and direct contact was made by Tormad's feet. The man who was giving orders held a cutlass. He raised it above his head with intent to sever the back-rope of the net. Tormad dropped the rope and in a twinkling whipped his right fist to the jaw with such force that the man overbalanced against his own gunnel and went head first into the sea. With the lunge of the blow, Tormad's boat had gone from under his feet and he, too, would have pitched into the sea if he had not grasped the gunnel of the other boat. In this straddled, helpless position, a pistol-stock hit him on the head with so solid a crack that the sound of it touched Torquil's stomach.

Tormad was pulled into the ship's boat like a sack. From the sea they hauled a gasping, hawking, purple-faced man who doubled over his own knees in a writhing effort at vomit. In his surprise he had taken the water down both channels. Presently he lifted his head and glared with mouth askew and made the men jump with an ordering sweep of his fist.

But Torquil now had hold of the back-rope.

There was to be no more nonsense, however. When the pistol-point had no power over Torquil, a swipe from it numbed his arms so that he could not even hit the man who, grabbing him by the neck, thrust him against both gunnels, which were grappled.

Ronnie and Ian immediately tried to haul him away, and there was a scuffle in which both of them were belaboured and finally forced back. Threatened by pistol and steel, they were ordered to throw their net overboard; but the voice of authority behind croaked, 'Heave the bloody thing over yourselves!'

Two men remained guard over Ronnie and Ian as their boat was taken in tow.

Alongside the sloop, a rope was passed under Tormad's arms and he was hauled upward, hands dangling, head lolling, with dark blood running down past one ear and under the chin. Torquil was made to climb the rope-ladder, then Ronnie, then Ian.

The commander of the sloop looked over the rail. 'Take all the fish and cast her off.'

The little incident had provided an amusing diversion for the ship's company. Tormad's senseless body was regarded here and there with a wink and a smile of private satisfaction. He hadn't done badly, he hadn't. The leader of the press-gang was not a favourite.

Men jumped to their stations. The bows fell off. The great area of canvas above a fixed bowsprit stayed to the masthead, took the light morning breeze. The boom of the mainsail clacked over. The square topsail was set, and the royal sloop, white ensign over her stern, set a southerly course.

The long suave lines of the hills by Kildonan caught a mist of rose as the sun came up. The little cabins were still as sleep in the chill of the silver morning. The sea glittered from Berriedale Head to Loth, vacant in all that space save for one small derelict boat.

Christie Christison

ROBERT BONTINE CUNNINGHAME GRAHAM
(1852–1936)

Politician, travel writer and essayist, Cunninghame Graham, or Don Roberto, as his wide circle of friends in many parts of the world called him, was a man of irrepressible energies and interests – at one time or another he was president, indeed the inaugural president, of the Scottish Labour Party, of the National Party of Scotland, and finally in 1934, of the Scottish National Party. From the distinguished family of the Grahams, and often thought of as simply what we would now call a celebrity, he wrote many fine things about Scotland – such as Beattock for Moffat *– and equally about South America, the setting for many of his adventures in a long and eventful life, and source of his nickname.*

The short story here has just such a Latin-American background, in an Argentina which Graham knew well, and where he died. Christie Christison is an old expatriate Scot from the north-east – a sea-captain turned merchant – who meets with his cronies in the bar of Claraz's Hotel to yarn away the hours. Then one day, unexpectedly, he 'launched into the story of his life, to the amazement of his friends, who never thought he either had a story to impart, or if he had that it would ever issue from his lips'. The story – really two stories – is how he lost his ship and, before that, found his wife again.

Of all the guests that used to come to Claraz's Hotel, there was none stranger or more interesting than Christie Christison, a weather-beaten sailor, who still spoke his native dialect of Peterhead, despite his thirty years out in the Plate. He used to bring an air into the room with him of old salt fish and rum, and of cold wintry nights in the low latitudes down by the Horn. This, too, though it was years since he had been at sea.

Although the world had gone so well with him, and by degrees he had become one of the biggest merchants in the place, he yet preserved the speech and manners of a Greenland whaler, which calling he had followed in his youth.

The Arctic cold and tropic suns, during the years that he had traded up and down the coast, had turned his naturally fair complexion to a mottled hue, and whisky, or the sun, had touched his nose so fiercely that it furnished a great fund of witticism amongst the other guests.

Mansel said that the skipper's nose reminded him of the port light of an old sugar droger, and Cossart had it that no chemist's window in Montmartre had any *flacon*, bottle you call him, eh? of such resplendent hue. Most of them knew he had a history, but no one ever heard him tell it, although it was well known he had come out from Peterhead in the dark ages, when Rosas terrorised the Plate, in his own schooner, the *Rosebud*, and piled her up at last, somewhere on the Patagonian coast, upon a trip down to the Falkland Islands. He used to talk about his schooner as if she had been one of the finest craft afloat; but an old Yankee skipper, who had known her, swore she was a bull-nosed, round-sterned sort of oyster-mouching vessel, with an old deck-house like a town hall, straight-sided, and with a lime-juice look about her that made him tired.

Whatever were her merits or her faults, she certainly had made her skipper's fortune, or at least laid the foundation of it; for, having started as a trader, he gradually began to act, half as a carrier, half as a mail-boat, going to Stanley every three months or so with mails and letters, and coming back with wool.

Little by little, aided by his wife, a stout, hard-featured woman from his native town, he got a little capital into his hands.

When he was on a voyage, Jean used to search about to get a cargo for his next trip, so that when the inevitable came and the old *Rosebud* ran upon the reef down at San Julian, Christie was what he called 'weel-daein', and forsook the sea for good.

He settled down in Buenos Aires as a wool-broker, and by degrees altered his clothes to the full-skirted coat of Melton cloth, with ample side-pockets, the heather mixture trousers, and tall white hat with a black band, that formed his uniform up to his dying day. He wore a Newgate frill of beard and a blue necktie, which made a striking contrast with his face, browned by the sun and wind, and skin like a dried piece of mare's hide, through which the colour of his northern blood shone darkly, like the red in an old-fashioned cooking apple after a touch of frost.

Except a few objurgatory phrases, he had learned no Spanish, and his own speech remained the purest dialect of Aberdeenshire – coarse, rough and racy, and double-shotted with an infinity of oaths, relics of his old whaling days, when, as he used to say, he started life, like a young rook, up in the crow's-nest of a bluff-bowed and broad-beamed five-hundred barrel boat, sailing from Peterhead.

Things had gone well with him, and he had taken to himself as partner a fellow-countryman, one Andrew Nicholson, who had passed all his youth in Edinburgh in an insurance office. Quiet, unassuming, and yet not without traces of that pawky humour which few Scots are born entirely lacking in, he had fallen by degrees into a sort of worship of his chief, whose sallies, rough and indecent as they often were, fairly convulsed him, making him laugh until the tears ran down his face, as he exclaimed, 'Hear to him, man, he's awfu' rich, I'm tellin' ye.'

Christie took little notice of his adoration except to say, 'Andra man, dinna expose yourself,' or something of the kind.

In fact, no one could understand how two such ill-assorted men came to be friends, except perhaps because they both were Scotchmen, or because Andrew's superior education and well-brushed black clothes appealed to Christison.

He himself could not write, but knew enough to sign his name, which feat he executed with many puffings, blowings, and an occasional oath.

Still he was shrewd in business, which he executed almost entirely by telegram, refusing to avail himself of any code, saying, 'he couldna stand them; some day ye lads will get a cargo of dolls' eyes, when ye have sent for maize. Language is gude enough for me, I hae no secrets. Damn yer monkey talk.'

His house at Flores was the place of call of all the ship captains who visited the port. There they would sit and drink, talking about the want of lights on such and such a coast, of skippers who had lost their ships twenty or thirty years ago, the price of whale oil, and of things that interest their kind; whilst Mrs Christison sat knitting, looking as if she never in her life had moved from Peterhead, in her grey gown and woollen shawl, fastened across her breast by a brooch, with a picture of her man, 'in natural colouring'. Their life was homely, and differed little from what it had been in the old days when they were poor, except that now and then they took the air in an old battered carriage – which Christison had taken for a debt – looking uncomfortable and stiff, dressed in their Sunday clothes. Their want of knowledge of the language of the place kept them apart from others of their class, and Christison, although he swore by Buenos Aires, which he had seen emerge from a provincial town to a great city, yet cursed the people, calling them a 'damned set of natives', which term he generally applied to all but Englishmen.

Certainly nothing was more unlike a 'native' than the ex-skipper now turned merchant, in his ways, speech, and dress. Courtesy, which was innate in natives of the place, was to him not only quite superfluous, but a thing to be avoided, whilst his strange habit of devouring bread fresh from the oven, washed down with sweet champagne, gained him the nickname of the 'Scotch Ostrich', which nickname he accepted in good part as a just tribute to his digestive powers, remarking that 'the Baptist, John, ye mind, aye fed on locusts and wild honey, and a strong man aye liked strong meat, all the worrld o'er.'

In the lives of the elderly Aberdeenshire couple, few would have looked for a romantic story, for the hard-featured merchant and his quiet home-keeping wife appeared so happy and contented in their snug villa on the Flores road. No one in Buenos Aires suspected anything, and most likely Christison would have died, remembered only by his tall white hat, had he not one day chosen to tell his tale.

A fierce *pampero* had sprung up in an hour, the sky had turned that vivid green that marks storms from the south in Buenos Aires. Whirlfire kept the sky lighted till an arch had formed in the south-east, and then the storm broke, blinding and terrible, with a strange, seething noise. The wind, tearing along the narrow streets, forced everyone to fly for refuge.

People on foot darted into the nearest house, and horsemen, flying like birds before the storm, sought refuge anywhere they could, their horses, slipping and sliding on the rough, paved streets, sending out showers of sparks as they stopped suddenly, just as a skater sends out a spray of ice. The deep-cut streets, with their raised pavements, soon turned to watercourses, from three to four feet deep, through which the current ran so fiercely that it was quite impossible to pass on foot. The horsemen, galloping for shelter, passed through them with the water banking up against their horses on the stream side, though they plied whip and spurs.

After the first hour of the tempest, when a little light began to dawn towards the south, and the peals of thunder slacken a little in intensity, men's nerves became relaxed from the over-tension that a *pampero* brings with it, just as if nature had been overwound, and by degrees was paying out the chain.

Storm-stayed at Claraz's sat several men, Cossart, George Mansel, one Don José Hernández and Christie Christison. Perhaps the *pampero* had strung up his nerves, or perhaps the desire that all men feel at times to tell what is expedient they should keep concealed, impelled him, but any rate he launched into the story of his life, to the amazement of his friends, who never thought he either had a story to impart, or if he had that it would ever issue from his lips.

'Ye mind the *Rosebud?*' he remarked.

None of the assembled men had ever seen her, although she still was well remembered on the coast.

'Weel, weel, I mind the time she was well kent, a bonny craft. Old Andrew Reid o' Buckieside, he built her, back in the fifties. When he went under, he had to sell his house of Buckieside. I bought her cheap.

'It's fifteen years and mair, come Martinmas, since I piled her up ... I canna think how I managed it, knowing the bay, San Julian, ye ken, sae weel.

'It was a wee bit hazy, but still I thought I could get in wi' the blue pigeon going.

'I mind it yet, ye see you hae to keep the rocks where they say they ganakers all congregate before they die, right in a line with yon bit island.

'I heard the water shoaling as the leadsman sung out in the chains, but still kept on, feeling quite sure I knew the channel, when, bang she touches, grates a little, and sticks dead fast, wi' a long shiver o' her keel. Yon rocks must have been sharp as razors, for she began to fill at once.

'No chance for any help down in San Julian Bay in those days, nothing but ane o' they *pulperías* kept by a Basque, a wee bit place, wi' a ditch and bank, and a small brass cannon stuck above the gate. I got what gear I could into the boat, and started for the beach.

'Jean, myself, three o' the men, and an old Dago I carried with me as an interpreter.

'The other sailormen, and a big dog we had aboard, got into the other boat, and we all came ashore. Luckily it was calm, and the old *Rosebud* had struck not above two or three hundred yards from land. Man, San Julian was a dreich place in they days, naething but the bit fortified *pulpería* I was tellin' ye aboot. The owner, old Don Augusty, a Basque, ye ken, just ca'ed his place the "Rose of the South". He micht as well have called it the "Rose of Sharon". Deil a rose for miles, or any sort of flower.

'Well, men, next day it just began to blow, and in a day or two knockit the old *Rosebud* fair to matchwood. Jean, she grat sair to see her gae to bits, and I cursit a while, though I felt like greetin' too, I'm tellin' ye. There we were sort o' marooned, a' the lot of us, without a chance of getting off maybe for months; for in these days devil a ship but an odd whaler now and then ever came nigh the place. By a special mercy Yanquetruz's band of they Pehuelches happened to come to trade.

'Quiet enough folk yon Indians, and Yanquetruz himself had been brocht up in Buenos Aires in a mission school.

'Man, a braw fellow! Six foot six at least, and sat his horse just like a picture. We bought horses from him, and got a man to guide us up to the Welsh settlement at Chubut, a hundred leagues away.

'Richt gude beasts they gave us, and we got through fine, though I almost thocht I had lost Jean.

'Yanquetruz spoke English pretty well, Spanish of course, and as I tellt ye, he was a bonny man.

'Weel, he sort o' fell in love wi' Jean, and one day he came up to the *pulpería*, and getting off his horse, a braw black piebald wi' an eye like fire intil him, he asked to speak to me. First we had *caña*, and then *carlón*, then some more *caña*, and yon *vino seco*, and syne some more *carlón*. I couldna richtly see what he was driving at. However, all of a sudden he says, "Wife very pretty, Indian he like buy."

'I told him Christians didna sell their wives, and we had some more *caña*, and then he says, "Indian like Christian woman, she more big, more white than Indian girl."

'To make a long tale short, he offered me his horse and fifty dollars, then several ganaker skins, they ca' them *guillapices*, and finally in addition a mare and foal. Man, they were bonny beasts, both red roan piebalds, and to pick any Indian girl I liked. Not a bad price down there at San Julian, where the chief could hae cut all our throats had he been minded to.

'. . . Na, na, we werna' fou, just a wee miraculous. Don Augusty was sort o' scared when he heard what Yanquetruz was saying, and got his pistol handy and a bit axe he keepit for emergencies behind the counter. Losh me, yon Yanquetruz was that ceevil, a body couldna tak fuff at him.

'At last I told him I wasna on to trade, and we both had a tot of square-faced gin to clean our mouths a bit, and oot to the *palenque*, where the chief's horse was tied.

'A bonny beastie, his mane hogged and cut into castles, like a clipped yew hedge, his tail plated and tied with a piece of white mare's hide, and everything upon him solid silver, just like a dinner-service.

'The chief took his spear in his hand – it had been stuck into the ground – and leaning on it, loupit on his horse. Ye ken they deevils mount frae the offside. He gied a yell that fetched his Indians racing. They had killed a cow, and some of them were daubed with blood; for they folk dinna wait for cooking when they are sharp set. Others were three-parts drunk, and came stottering along, with square-faced gin bottles in their hands.

'Their horses werna tied, nor even hobbled. Na, na, they just stood waiting with the reins upon the ground. Soon as they saw the chief – I canna tell ye how the thing was done – they didna mount, they didna loup, they just melted on their beasts, catching the spears out of the ground as they got up.

'Sirs me, they Indians just took flight like birds, raising sich yellochs, running their horses up against each other, twisting and turning and carrying on in sich a way, just like fishing-boats running for harbour at Buckie or Montrose.

'Our guide turned out a richt yin, and brocht us through, up to Chubut wi'out a scratch upon the paint.

'A pairfect pilot, though he had naething in the wide world to guide him through they wild stony plains.

'That's how I lost the *Rosebud*, and noo, ma freens, I'll tell you how it was I got Jean, but that was years ago.

'In my youth up in Peterhead I was a sailorman. I went to sea in they North Sea whaling craft, Duff and McAlister's, ye ken. As time went on, I got rated as a harpooner . . . mony's the richt whale I hae fastened into. That was the time when everything was dune by hand. Nane of your harpoon guns, nane of your dynamite, naething but muscle and a keen eye. First strike yer whale, and then pull after him. Talk of yer fox hunts . . . set them up, indeed.

'Jean's father keepit a bit shop in Aberdeen, and we had got acquaint. I cannot richtly mind the way o' it. Her father and her mother were aye against our marryin', for ye ken I had naething but my pay, and that only when I could get a ship. Whiles, too, I drinkit a wee bit. Naething to signify, but then Jean's father was an elder of the kirk, and maist particular.

'Jean was a bonny lassie then, awfu' high-spirited. I used to wonder whiles, if some day when her father had been oot at the kirk, someone hadna slippit in to tak tea with her mither . . . I ken I'm haverin'.

'Well, we were married, and though we lo'ed each other, we were aye bickerin'. Maistly aboot naething, but ye see, we were both young and spirited. Jean liket admiration, which was natural enough at her age, and I liket speerits, so that ane night, after a word or two, I gied her bit daud or two, maybe it was the speerits, for in the morning, when I wakit, I felt about for Jean, intending to ask pardon, and feelin' a bit shamed. There was no Jean, and I thocht that she was hidin' just to frichten me.

'I called, but naething, and pittin' on ma clothes, searchit the hoose, but there was naebody. She left no message for me, and nane of the neighbours kent anything aboot her.

'She hadna' gone to Aberdeen, and though her father and me searchit up and doon, we got no tidings of her. Sort o' unchancy, just for a day or two. However, there was naething to be done, and in a month or so I sold my furniture and shipped for a long cruise.

'Man, a long cruise it was, three months or more blocked in the ice, and then a month in Greenland trying to get the scurvy out of the ship's company, and so one way or another, about seven months slipped past before we sighted Peterhead. Seven months without a sight of any woman; for men, they Esquimaux aye gied me a skunner wi' their fur clothes and oily faces, they lookit to be baboons.

'We got in on a Sabbath, and I am just tellin' ye, as soon as I was free, maybe about three o' the afternoon, I fairly ran all the way richt up to Maggie Bauchop's.

'I see the place the noo, up a bit wynd. The town was awfu' quiet, and no one cared to pass too close to the wynd foot in daylight, for fear o' the clash o' tongues. I didna care a rap for that, if there had been a lion in the path, same as once happened to ane o' the prophets – Balaam, I think it was, in the Old Book. I wouldna hae stood back a minute if there had been a woman on the other side.

'Weel, I went up to the door, and rappit on it. Maggie came to it, and says she, "Eh, Christie, is that you?" for she aye kent a customer. A braw, fat woman, Maggie Bauchop was. For years she had followed the old trade, till she had pit awa' a little siller, and started business for hersel'.

'Weel she kent a' the tricks o' it, and still she was a sort of God-fearin' kind o' bitch . . . treated her lassies weel, and didna cheat them about their victuals and their claithes. "Come in," she says, "Christie, my man. Where hae ye come from?"

'I tellt her, and says I, "Maggie, gie us yer best, I've been seven months at sea."

'"Hoot, man," she says, "the lassies arena up. We had a fearfu' spate o' drink yestreen, an awfu' lot of ships is in the port. Sit ye doon, Christie. Here's the Old Book to ye. Na, na, ye needna look at it like that. There's bonny pictures in it, o' the prophets . . . each wi' his lass, ye ken."

'When she went out, I looked a little at the book – man, a fine hot one, and then as the time passed I started whistlin' a tune, something I had heard up aboot Hammerfest. The door flees open, and in walks Maggie, looking awfu' mad.

'"Christie," she skirls, "I'll hae na whistlin' in ma hoose, upon the Sabbath day. I canna hae my lassies learned sich ways, so stop it, or get out."

'Man, I just lauch at her, and I says, "The lassies, woman. Whistlin' can hardly hurt them, considerin' how they live."

'Maggie just glowered at me, and "Christie," she says, "you and men like ye may defile their bodies; but whilst I live na one shall harm their souls, puir lambies, wi' whistlin' on His day. No, not in my hoose, that's what I'm tellin' ye."

'I laughed, and said, "Weel, send us in ane o' your lambies!" and turned to look at a picture of Queen Victoria's Prince Albert picnickin' at Balmoral. When I looked round a girl had come into the room. She was dressed in a striped sort of petticoat and a white jacket, a blouse I think ye ca' the thing, and stood wi' her back to me as she was speaking to Maggie at the door.

'I drew her to me, and was pulling her towards the bed – seven months at sea, ye ken – when we passed by a looking-glass. I saw her face in it, just for a minute, as we were sort o' strugglin'. Ma God, I lowsed her quick enough, and stotterin' backwards sat down upon a chair. 'Twas Jean, who had run off after the bit quarrel that we had more than a year ago. I didna speak, nor did Jean say a word.

'What's that you say?

'Na, na, ma ain wife in sichlike a place, hae ye no delicacy, man? I settled up wi' Maggie, tellin' her Jean was an old friend o' mine, and took her by the hand. We gaed away to Edinburgh, and there I married her again. Sort of haversome job, but Jean just wanted it, ye ken. How she came there I never asked her.

'Judge not, the Ould Book says, and after all 'twas me gien' her the daud. Weel, weel, things sort of prospered after that. I bought the *Rosebud*, and as ye know piled her up and down at San Julian, some fifteen years ago.

'I never raised ma hand on Jean again. Na, na, I had suffered for it, and Jean, if so be she needed ony sort of purification, man, she got it, standing at the wheel o' nichts on the old schooner wi' the spray flyin', on the passage out.

'Not a drop, thanky, Don Hosey. Good nicht, Mr Mansel. Bongsoir, Cossart, I'm just off hame. Jean will be waiting for me.'

Da Sang o Da Papa Men

'VAGALAND' (T.A. ROBERTSON) (1909–73)

T.A. Robertson, a Shetland poet who wrote under the name of 'Vagaland', was born in 1909, educated at the Anderson Institute, Lerwick and at Edinburgh University and worked as a teacher in Shetland until his retirement in 1970. He was associated with The New Shetlander *magazine and many of the 'Vagaland' poems first appeared in its columns.*

The evocative 'Da Sang o Da Papa Men' tells of the fishermen of Papa and their ability to navigate back to their island from the fishing grounds of Foula by the scent of flowers borne over the waves. The Horn of Papa referred to in the chorus was a natural rock arch which collapsed in a gale in 1953.

Two specific references may require explanation. 'Fishy-knots' in verse one refers to a traditional belief that certain knots in a ship's planking brought good luck – as opposed to a 'misforen' or unlucky knot. In the last verse 'Skrime da moder-dy' means to make out a movement of the sea by which the fishermen could find their way home.

Chorus:
Oot bewast da Horn o Papa,
  Rowin Foula doon!
Ower a hidden piece o water,
  Rowin Foula doon!
Round da boat da tide-lumps makkin
Sunlicht trowe da cloods is brakkin;
We maan geng whaar fish is takkin,
  Rowin Foula doon!

Fishy-knots wir boat haes, truly,
  Nae misforen knot
We hae towes and bowes an cappies,
  Ballast ida shott,
Paets, fir fire ita da kyettle,
  Taaties fir da pot.

chorus

Laek a lass at's hoidin, laachin,
   Coortit be her voeers,
Papa sometimes lies in Simmer
   Veiled wi ask an shooers;
Dan apo da wilsom water
   Comes da scent o flooers.

chorus

We can bide ashore nae langer –
   We maan geng and try.
We'll win back, boys, if we soodna
   Skrime da moder-dy,
Fir da scent o flooers in Papa
   Leds wis aa da wye.

chorus

4
VOYAGES

We begin with the poem, *The Birlinn of Clanranald*, by Alasdair MacMhaighstir Alasdair, written in the years after the '45 but telling a lyrical story of a voyage – from South Uist to Carrick Fergus in Ireland – which could stand for any of the voyages on the Hebridean seaways over a thousand years or more. This Birlinn or galley is in a way emblematic – it is a splendid example of fitness for purpose, both in terms of the crew and the technological 'rightness' of their vessel. Every crew-member is worthy of his place in the boat because – like the look-out man, the 'ocean cloud-seer', who can

> Catch and note the landmarks
> With keen vision,
> Since they and the God of weather
> Are our lode-star

– each has a special task to perform. Similarly, the ship itself displays a kind of perfection which has evolved from a line of vessels like the Galley of Lorne, the Scoto-Norse Nyvaigs of Somerled and the pure Norse longships themselves. We do not know the purpose of the voyage; the vessel is presumably a war-galley, but at journey's end the voyagers do not use the arms they have brought with them, they simply take 'meat and drink in plenty'. They are called heroes but they are heroic only in the way that they function together to drive the Birlinn on, to test it and all its living parts – like crew and 'gear and tackle' – against the elements. So much so that there is

> No mast left unbent,
> Sail untorn,
> Yard unsplit, or hoop unhurt,
> Oar uninjured.

The voyage of the crew of the Birlinn was like that which had been taken in the other direction by Columba in the sixth century – an epic crossing of the sea lanes which bound together Celtic Scotland and Ireland, part of the tradition of voyager-saints like Brendan. Like the voyage more than a century later which took the great illuminated book from Iona to the safety of the monastery of Kells. The Irish Sea and North Channel and the Minches were the highways of Scotland's west coast which had carried the first Scots from Ulster to Argyll and also threw the coasts open to Norse invaders and settlers who were to be another dynamic influence on the language and culture of Scotland, particularly in the Hebrides and in the Northern Isles.

By the eighteenth century the ignorance of the Gaelic language in the Lowlands and beyond was such that *The Birlinn of Clanranald* was inaccessible to travellers like Johnson and Boswell. The Englishman's *A Journey to the Western Islands of Scotland*, a description of their astounding 1773 journey, which was undertaken when he was in his sixties, and in contrast to Boswell's more chatty and personal reminiscence is a shrewd but sometimes moving account of a society in disintegration after Culloden. The song, *I Was Young in Strathglass*, was carried over to Nova Scotia soon after, but by the time of the collection which included the version of the *Mingulay Boat Song*, Gaelic song is being presented in a bowdlerised English for an audience outside the Gaeltacht, but carrying with it remnants of haunting beauty.

In the other non-Gaelic-speaking areas of Scotland the hundred years preceding the visit of Johnson and Boswell had been an only marginally less bloody experience. However in 1695 when the 'Company of Scotland Trading to Africa and the Indies' was established there were many in the Lowlands who saw the prospect of worldwide trade to the Darien Isthmus as a fast route to prosperity. Indeed, the Highlands played a part here too, because William III was among those encouraging the venture, with the intention of distracting attention from the Massacre of Glencoe the previous year. So it was that the most ambitious and most tragic Scottish sea-borne adventure came about. The Darien expeditions of 1698 and 1699 to the 'Door of the Seas, the Key of the Universe' were abject failures, the King proved a fair-weather friend, and the consequence was severe damage to the Scottish psyche as a whole.

PETITION FROM THE COUNCIL GENERAL OF THE COMPANY
OF SCOTLAND TO THE KING

4th December 1699

We cannot but reckon it a hardship from our neighbouring nation [England], that we who are His Majesties subjects should be denyed the benefite of having our Colony supplied with provisions from the English Plantations by English vessels in the ordinary way of commerce ... while at the same time neither the Dutch at Curacao, the Danes at St Thomas nor the French at St Christophers ... were ever denied the benefite thereof, except in case of declared warr.

The Darien fiasco began the long and hurtful process of emigration very inauspiciously. It got little better – as Doctor Johnson observed, 'To hinder insurrection, by driving away the people, and to govern peaceably, by having no subjects, is an expedient that argues no great profundity of politics.' Nevertheless there were many in the following centuries who embarked on that watery highway with strong elements of hope and optimism mixed with a natural trepidation. The names of some emigrant ships became symbols for this often traumatic process – ships like the *Hector* which took 200 people from Ullapool to Nova Scotia in 1773, or in this century the *Metagama*, a Canadian Pacific Railways liner which carried some 300 emigrants, mostly young men, from Stornoway to John Galt's Ontario.

The *Metagama* sailing was not the largest movement of emigrants, nor indeed was she the first Canadian liner to call at a Hebridean port. She was, however, the largest liner to carry out such a mission and indeed was the largest ship to have anchored in the Minch. Because of the significance of the emigration of so many young people from small communities of Lewis and elsewhere in the Highlands, the *Metagama*'s voyage became something of a media event, with thirty journalists and photographers descending on Stornoway. The popular Glasgow daily *The Bulletin* covered the story over two days, with its front page devoted to photographs of the harbour and on-board scenes. On Monday 23rd April, its correspondent had written under the headline 'Brighter Life Promise':

Stornoway bade farewell on Saturday to 300 young Lewismen, the salt of the island, who sailed away in the good ship *Metagama*, the CPR liner, for Canada. They are going out to the Province of Ontario to serve as hired hands on farms there ... The men went away in cheerful spirit. Doubtless they and their families felt the parting but they contrived to hide their most intimate feelings under an exterior which suggested that they were thinking only of a promise of a brighter life in the Dominion out West.

The inhabitants flocked to Stornoway from all parts, and the piers were thronged with a multitude of friends to wish them God-speed ... On board the liner the lightsomeness was maintained by the emigrants. They danced reels to the tune of the pipes with a fervour that showed up the insipidity of the fox-trotting of the city ballroom. But a few casual observers on the *Metagama* caught a glimpse of the serious side of these young men, one that suggested the influence of their Presbyterian upbringing.

Just before the second batch of emigrants were brought aboard the liner I saw them in a brief service of religious devotion. Two ministers had come out with them from Stornoway, and as they were marshalled on one of the lower decks of the liner one of the ministers offered prayer in Gaelic. It was an impressive spectacle to watch these boys, who a moment before had been so flippant of mood, and became so again immediately afterwards, standing cap in hand in reverential mien while their minister prayed for blessing and strength to them in their future career.

That and the final scene when the liner weighed anchor and steamed slowly out from the anchorage were the most memorable features of a stirring day.

Now to a slightly more relaxed approach, from forty-odd years earlier. Robert Louis Stevenson wrote *The Amateur Emigrant* as an account of the voyage he took in 1879 on an emigrant ship to California. He was in search of the seductive American Fanny Osbourne, later his wife, as much as he was after 'colour' as a writer; in a way Stevenson's fictional voyages, as in *Treasure Island*, or if you prefer through his imagination, seem more memorable than his real journeys.

The revolution in sea transport brought about by the invention of steam propulsion, which led to the drastic shortening of many voyages and a shrinking of the great oceans, was presaged in fictional terms by John Galt's *The Steamboat* (1821). Galt was to spend some time in Canada – he founded the city of Guelph in Ontario and arranged for the settlement by Scots of parts of Ontario. However, this novel is one of his *Tales of the West* and is set in the area around the Clyde and its firth. It was published the year after this comment had actually appeared in the *Greenock Advertiser*:

The great facilities now afforded for visiting many parts of this country, by means of the cheap and safe conveyance of these vessels, continues to be everywhere on the increase. At present it must afford much satisfaction to all those interested in the Northern parts of our Island to learn that a communication is now to be opened, by this admirable invention, to many parts of the Highlands, which were lately and are yet comparatively inaccessible by roads. It is now intended that a Steam-boat shall begin to ply from the Clyde to the Lewes, through the Crinan Canal and Sound

of Mull – to call at Tobermory – from thence to the Sound of Skye –
call at Isle-Ornsay, Lochalsh, Castlemoil, Portree and afterward go
on to Stornoway. The Steam-boat *Highland Chieftain*, has already
gone as far as the Sound of Skye on this route, for a trial, and
performed the passage in the remarkably short space of 35 hours
from Glasgow – a distance of 235 miles, notwithstanding she had
to stem currents which run so violently in the Sounds of Skye and
Mull. She returned in nearly the same time, and encountered, with
great intrepidity, very severe weather. The track now proposed that
this Steam-boat shall run, will be highly gratifying in the summer
months, for an excursion.

However the Age of Sail was not quite at an end and a century later
Edward Gaitens wrote a story about one of the last of the windjammers.
The Sailing Ship first appeared in *The Scots Magazine* in 1939 and
the extract included here shows a gritty realism in the description of
manual dock labour which contrasts with the romantic symbolism of
the three-master. A sharp wind of realism also blows through the thinly
disguised autobiographical account of A.J. Cronin's first voyage as a
ship's doctor given in *Adventures in Two Worlds* (1952).

Finally we draw together some of the previous threads with a chapter
from *Mardi*, by Herman Melville. Melville is included here because he
was a descendant of a Scots emigrant from Fife and was an enthusiastic
Scotophile who came here as a tourist in 1856. Moreover, his sailor in
Mardi 'hailed from the isle of Skye, one of the constellated Hebrides' and
his voice was 'hoarse as a storm roaring round the old peak of Mull'. 'The
Skyeman' might in fact be viewed as a descendant of those Hebridean
seafarers we first met bending their backs in the *Birlinn of Clanranald*.

The Birlinn of Clanranald

ALASDAIR MACMHAIGHSTIR ALASDAIR, CAPTAIN
ALASDAIR MACDONALD (c. 1695–1770)
Translation by Alexander Nicolson (1827–93)

*This, probably the greatest sea-poem in any language from the British
Isles, was written by a schoolmaster turned soldier at the time of the
'45. Probably first recited to the Chief of Clanranald himself in the
aftermath of the rebellion, it evokes the heroic days of the seaborne
Gaels and proclaims their ancient values, culture and language. The form
is extremely dramatic and with its* Blessing of the Ship *is part of an
uninterrupted tradition stretching from the* Sea Prayer of the Columban
past. *In* The Lyon in Mourning, *a collection of Jacobite material, Bishop
Robert Forbes reported that 'several of the Captain's acquaintances have
informed me that he is by far the best Erse poet in Scotland, and that he
has written many songs in pure Irish'. Modern opinion would agree at
any rate that this poem is probably the greatest long poem in the Gaelic
language.*

The Birlinn *has been translated in recent years by Hugh MacDiarmid
and, less surprisingly, by Ian Crichton Smith. The translation used here,
however, is by Alexander or Alasdair Nicolson, a lawyer and Gaelic
scholar, who revised the Gaelic Bible. He is also remembered for being a
member of the Napier [Crofting] Commission and a lover of the outdoors
– he had the distinction of having a peak, Sgurr Alasdair, in the Cuillins
named after him.*

I *The Blessing of the Ship*

> MAY God bless the bark of Clan-Ranald,
>   The first day she floats on the brine!
> Himself and his strong men to man her,
>   The heroes whom none can outshine!
>
> May the Holy Trinity's blessing
>   Rule the hurricane breath of the air,
> And swept be the rough wild waters,
>   To draw us to haven fair.
>
> Father, Creator of Ocean,
>   Of each wind that blows on the deep,
> Bless our slim bark and our gallants,
>   Herself and her crew safe keep.
> And Thou, O Son, bless our anchor,
>   Our sails, shrouds, and helm do thou bless,
> Each tackle that hangs from our masts,
>   And guide us to port in peace.
>
> Our mast-hoops and yards do thou bless,
>   Our masts and our ropes one and all,
> Our stays and our haulyards preserve,
>   And let no mischance befall.
> The Holy Ghost be at the helm,
>   And show the right track to go,
> He knoweth each port 'neath the sun,
>   On His care ourselves we throw.

II *The Blessing of the Arms*

> God's blessing be upon our swords,
>   Our keen grey brands of Spain,
> Our heavy coats of mail, on which
>   The sword-sweep falls in vain.
>
> Our gauntlets and our corselets,
>   Our deftly-figured shields,
> Whate'er our belts do carry,
>   Whatever warrior wields.

Our polished bows of yew-tree,
   That bend in battle's din,
Our birchen shafts that split not,
   Cased in grim badger's skin.

Bless thou our dirks and pistols,
   Our good kilts in their folds,
And every kind of warlike gear
   McDonell's bark now holds!

Be ye not soft nor mild of mood
   To face the war of weather,
While four planks of our bark remain,
   Or two sticks cling together.

While 'neath your feet she swims, while one
   Thole-pin hold up its head,
Yield ye not to the ocean's frown,
   Whate'er ye see of dread.

If ye fight well, nor let the sea
   Aught weakly in you find,
To your stout striving she will yield,
   And bow her haughty mind.

Thus to thy foe upon the land
   If thou give in no inch,
Look not to see his courage rise,
   But rather that it flinch.

And even so with the great sea
   When thou hast bravely striven,
She will submit to thee at length,
   As wills the King of Heaven.

III *Incitement for Rowing to the Sailing-place*

To bring the galley, so black and shapely,
   To the sailing-point,
Shove ye out from her the tough blades,
   Level, bare, and grey.

The smooth-handled oars, well-fashioned,
    Light and easy,
That will do the rowing stout and sturdy,
    Quick-palmed, blazing,
That will send the surge in sparkles,
    Up to skyward,
All in flying spindrift flashing,
    Like a fire-shower!
With the fierce and pithy pelting
    Of the oar-bank,
That will wound the swelling billows,
    With their bending.
With the knife-blades of the white thin oars
    Smiting bodies,
On the crest of the blue hills and glens,
    Rough and heaving.
O! stretch ye, and pull, and bend ye,
    In the rowlocks,
The broad-bladed pinewood saplings,
    With white palm force!
The heavy and the stalwart strong men,
    Leaning on to her,
With their sinewy arms so brawny,
    Knotted, hairy,
That will raise and drop together,
    With one motion,
Her grey glistening shafts all even,
    'Neath the wave-tops!
A stout champion at the fore-oar,
    Crying 'Onward!'
A chant that wakens the spirit,
    In the shoulders,
That will thrust the galley hissing
    Through each cold glen,
Cleaving the roaring billows
    With the hard prow,
Driving the mountain monsters
    On before her.
'Hùgan!' on sea, a shrill slogan,
    Whack on thole-pins!

Crash go the rolling wave-tops
  'Gainst the timbers.
Oars complaining, bloody blisters
  On each strong palm
Of the heroes stout whose rowing,
  White froth churning,
Sends a quiver through each oak plank,
  Wood and iron;
Blades are tossed about, and clanking
  On her sides rap.
There's the manly crew to rock her,
  Stiff and stately,
And drive on the slender galley
  In face of ocean,
Fronting the bristling blue-black waves
  With strong arm pith!
That's the powerful and the lively crew,
  Behind an oar-bank,
That will pound the grey-backed eddies
  With choice rowing,
Unwearied, unbroken, unbending,
  Breasting danger!

IV *Then when the men were seated at the oars, for rowing under the wind to the sailing point, stout Malcolm, son of Ranald of the Ocean, being on the fore oar, called on them for a boat-song, and this was it:*

Now since you're all chosen,
And ranked in good order,
With a bold stately plunge send her forward!
  With a bold stately plunge send her forward!

A plunge quick and handy,
Not reckless nor languid,
Keeping watch on the grey briny storm-hills,
  Keeping watch on the grey briny storm-hills.

With a plunge of full vigour,
That will strain bone and sinew,
Let her track gleam behind her in glory!
  Let her track gleam behind her in glory!

And to stir up your neighbour,
Raise a song light and cheery,
This good chant from the mouth of your fore-oar,
   This good chant from the mouth of your fore-oar.

While rowlocks are grinding,
Palms blistered and shining,
Oars twisting in curls of the billows,
   Oars twisting in curls of the billows.

Let your cheeks be all glowing,
Hands peeled skin all showing,
Great drops from your brows quickly falling,
   Great drops from your brows quickly falling.

Bend, stretch ye, and strain ye
Your fir-shafts of grey hue,
And watch well the salt currents swirling,
   And watch well the salt currents swirling.

The oar-bank on each side
Churns with labour the brine,
Dashing swift in the face of the surges,
   Dashing swift in the face of the surges.

Pull clean, as one man,
Cleaving waves at each span,
With hearty good will, and not tardy,
   With hearty good will, and not tardy.

Strike even and steady,
Looking oft to each other,
Wake the life in your sinews and arms,
   Wake the life in your sinews and arms.

Let her good sides of oak
Meet with resolute stroke
The wild bulging glens piled before her,
   The wild bulging glens piled before her.

Let the sea grey and surging
Swell with rough angry murmur,
And the high rolling waters go moaning,
   And the high rolling waters go moaning.

The wan waters washing
O'er the bows ever dashing,
While streams sigh and welter behind her,
   While streams sigh and welter behind her.

Stretch, pull ye, and bend ye
The smooth shafts so slender,
With the pith in your strong arms abiding,
   With the pith in your strong arms abiding.

Clear the point there before you,
With brow-sweat fast pouring,
Then hoist sail from Uist of wild geese!
   Then hoist sail from Uist of wild geese!

V *They then rowed to the sailing-point*

When they now had smartly brought her
   To the sailing-point,
They set free the sixteen oars
   From the rowlocks,
Laid them quickly at the sides,
   Clear of rope pins.
Clanranald then ordered his vassals
That choice ocean hands be provided,
Men whom no terror could frighten,
Or any mischance that could happen.

VI *It was ordered, after they had been chosen, that every man should
go to his own special charge, and accordingly the helmsman was called
to sit at the helm in these words:*

Let there sit to steer a weighty champion,
   Powerful, free of limb;
Neither rise nor fall of sea must ever
   From his place move him;
A good sturdy fellow, full of pith,
   Thick-set, broad-based,
Quick and nice of hand, and careful,
   Watchful, wary,
Dexterous, patient, and unflurried
   In face of danger.
When he hears the rough sea coming,
   With a bellow,

He will keep her head up trimly
    To the surges,
He will keep her going steady,
    Without waver,
Guiding sheet and tack with looking,
    Eye to windward.
A thumbnail's breadth from his right course
    He won't diverge,
Spite of crested rollers coming,
    That bounding surge,
He will sail to wind so close,
    If need he see,
That every bolt, and plank, and timber,
    Will creaking be;
He will not flinch, nor yield to panic,
    Whate'er the terror,
Even were the hoary-headed sea
    To his ears upswelling;
That will not make the hero shudder,
    Nor move his place in,
Where safe he sitteth in the stern,
    The helm embracing,
Keeping watch on the grey-headed sea,
    Old and hoary,
That rolls on in hill and valley,
    Fiercely roaring;
The bolt-rope of the sail with luffing
    He will not shake,
But with full canvas, he will let her
    Run on and take,
Keeping her on her way so tightly
    O'er billows' crest,
Running on like smoking spindrift,
    Straight to her rest.

VII *A man to have charge of the rigging was ordered out:*

Let this stout big-fisted man sit
    At the rigging,
He must be sedate and careful,
    Strong-grasped, grippy,

Who will lower down a yard-arm
    When squalls frown,
And relieve the mast and rigging,
    Slackening down,
Knowing how the wind is coming,
    For sailing meet,
Answering watchfully his motions
    Who holds the sheet,
Ever helpful to the tackle,
    Lest a rope fail of the rigging,
    Stout and hairy.

VIII *A man was set apart for the sheet:*

Let a sheet-man on the thwart sit,
    Stout and bony,
Hairy, sinewy, and strong
    Is his fore-arm,
Broad and thick his hands and fingers,
    Hard and horny,
To let out the sheet or haul it
    With force of scrambling;
Who will draw it to him in rough weather,
    When the squall blows,
But let it out when the wind falls,
    Slackening slowly.

IX *A man was set apart for the fore-sheet:*

Let a lusty trim man take his seat,
    Smart and handy,
That will work the fore-hoist deftly,
    On the wind side;
That will raise the sail or lower it
    To belaying-pin,
According as the breeze may come,
    Or crested billow;
And if he see the tempest rising,
    Hear it sighing,
Let him fix down with a tight strong grasp
    To the bottom.

X *A look-out man was ordered to the bow:*

> Let an ocean cloud-seer rise and stand
>   At the bow,
> And let him sure knowledge give us
>   Of our harbour,
> Let him look to the four quarters
>   Of the heavens,
> And let him tell the steersman,
>   'Right she goeth';
> Let him catch and note the landmarks
>   With keen vision,
> Since they and the God of weather
>   Are our lode-star.

XI *A man was set apart for the haulyards:*

> At the main haulyards let there sit
>   A man of mettle,
> A well-knit, free-limbed, able fellow,
>   Handsome, comely,
> A man careful and not fussy,
>   Quick and stern,
> Who will shorten sail as need is,
>   Skilful, restless,
> Leaning on with heavy pull
>   To the haulyard,
> Bending on his weighty fists
>   To the timber.
> He won't fix the chafing rope
>   With a tight knot,
> But belay it firm and cunning
>   With a slip-knot;
> Lest when the cry comes to slacken,
>   It should stop him,
> And that it may glide with humming
>   Off the pin.

XII *A teller of the waters was set apart, the sea having grown very rough, and the helmsman said to him:*

> Let a teller of the waters
>   Sit beside me,

That will sharply on the wind's heart
  Keep his eye.
Choose a man that's somewhat timid,
  Shrewd and cautious,
But I ask not a complete,
  Thorough coward.
Let him watch well to perceive
  Showers to windward,
Whether the squall come at first,
  Or come after,
That he may give warning duly,
  Up to rouse me,
And if he see any danger,
  Not be silent.
If he see a drowning sea
  Coming roaring,
He must shout out, 'Keep her fine edge
  Swiftly to it.'
He must be prudent and cry out
  Loudly, 'Breaker!'
Must not from the helmsman hide
  Any danger.
Let there be no water-herald
  But him only,
Fear and babbling wordy tumult
  Cause a panic.

XIII *A baler was ordered out, as the sea was breaking over them fore and aft:*

Set ye to bale out the brine
  An active hero,
Who will never faint nor fear
  For sea roaring,
Who will not get numb or weak
  For cold of brine or hail,
Dashing on his breast and neck
  In chill splashes;
With a great round wooden vessel
  In his brown fist,
Ever pouring out the water
  In that rushes.

Who won't straighten his strong back
   From firm stiffness,
Till he leave not on her floor
   One drop running,
And though all her boards were leaking
   Like a riddle,
Will keep every bit as dry
   As a cask-stave.

XIV *Two were ordered for hauling the back-stays, in case the sails might be carried away by the exceeding roughness of the weather.*

Set a pair of stout-boned strong men,
   Big-limbed, hairy,
To watch with vigour and keep safe
   The back sail ropes,
With the marrow and the might
   Of their strong arms;
Who will heave them in or slacken,
   As the need is,
Keep them always straight and trim
   In the middle.
These be Duncan, son of Cormac,
   And John Mac Ian,
Thickset, skilful, and bold fellows,
   Both from Canna.

XV *Six were chosen as a reserve, in case any of those named should fail or be carried overboard by a sea, so that one of these might take his place:*

Let six rise now, quick and ready,
   Handy, lively,
Who will go, and come, and leap
   Up and down her,
Like a hare on mountain top,
   Dogs pursuing,
Who can climb the tight hard shrouds
   Of slender hemp,
Nimbly as the May-time squirrel
   Up a tree-trunk,

Who'll be ready, agile, brave,
    Active, knowing,
To take off her and take down,
    In good order,
Working with good will and spirit
    McDonell's galley.

XVI *Everything appertaining to the voyage having now been set in order,*
each hero went smartly, without fear or reluctance, to the exact place
appointed him; and they hoisted sail about sunrise on the day of the Feast
of St Bride, bearing out from the mouth of Loch Eynort in South Uist:

The sun bursting golden yellow
    From his cloud-husk;
Then the sky grew tawny, smoky,
    Full of gloom;
It waxed wave-blue, thick, buff-speckled,
    Dun and troubled;
Every colour of the tartan
    Marked the heavens.
A rainbow 'dog' is seen to westward—
    Stormy presage;
Flying clouds by strong winds riven,
    Squally showers.
They lifted up the speckled sails,
    Towering, tight,
And they stretched the rigid shrouds up
    Tense and stiff,
To the tall and stately masts,
    Red and resiny:
They were tied so taut and knotty,
    Without blunder,
Through the iron eyelet holes
    And the round blocks.
They fixed every rope of rigging
    Quick in order,
And each man at his place sat down,
    To watch smartly.
Opened then the windows of the sky,
    Spotted, grey-blue,
For blowing of the gurly wind
    And the storm bands,

And the dark-grey ocean all around him
 Drew his mantle—
His rough woolly robe of dun-black,
 Horrid, flowing:
It swelled up in mountains and in glens,
 Rough and shaggy,
Till the tumbling sea was roaring
 All in hills up.
The blue deep opened up its jaws
 Wide and threatening,
Pouring up against each other
 In deadly struggle;
A man's deed it was to look at
 The fiery mountains,
Flashes of wild-fire sparkling
 On each summit.
In front the high hoary surges
 Came fiercely raving,
And the hind seas onward swelling,
 Hoarsely bellowed.
Every time we rose up grandly
 On the wave-tops,
Need was then to lower sail
 Quick and smartly;
When we sank into the glens,
 With a gulp down,
Every stitch of sail she had
 Was hauled to mast top.
The high, broad-skirted, heaving waves
 Came on raging,
Before ever they were near us
 We heard them roaring,
Sweeping bare the smaller waves
 As with scourges,
Making one great deadly sea,
 Dire for steering.
When we fell down from the crest
 Of shaggy billows,
Almost did our keel then smite
 The shelly bottom,

The sea churning and swishing,
   All through other.
Then were seals and great sea monsters
   Sorely troubled,
The swell and surges of the sea,
   And ship's going,
Spattered their white brains about
   Through the water,
While they howled aloud in terror,
   Bitter moaning,
Crying to us, 'We are subjects,
   Drag us on board.'
All the small fish of the sea
   Turned up, speckled,
Dead in myriads with the roll
   Of the ocean.
The stones and shell-fish from below
   Floated upward,
Torn up by the rattling swell
   Of the proud sea.
The whole deep, like mess of gruel,
   Foul and turbid,
With blood and filth of helpless monsters,
   Of bad red colour,
The great, horny, clawy creatures,
   Broad-pawed, clumsy,
All strange head from mouth to gills,
   Throats a-gaping.
The whole deep was full of spectres,
   All a-crawling,
With the paws and tails of monsters,
   All a-sprawling,
Horrid was the screeching, groaning,
   To give ear to,
That would drive to sheer distraction
   Fifty warriors.
The crew lost all sense of hearing,
   With the listening
To the screeching chant of demons,
   And beast uproar,

The under-noise of the sea dashing
  'Gainst the galley,
The upper noise of the bow plashing
  Among sea-pigs;
While the wind renewed its blowing
  From the westward.
With every kind of trying torment
  We were troubled,
Blinded with the spray of surges,
  Dashing o'er us,
All the night long, awful thunder
  And fierce lightning,
Fire-balls burning in the rigging
  And the tackle,
With a brimstone smoke and smell,
  Fairly choking;
The upper and the under powers
  Warring with us,
Earth and fire, and wind and water,
  Raised against us.
But when it defied the sea
  To subdue us,
She took pity with a smile,
  And made peace.
Yet was no mast left unbent,
  Sail untorn,
Yard unsplit, or hoop unhurt,
  Oar uninjured;
Not a stay was left unsprung,
  Shroud unstrained,
Nail or coupling left unbroken,
  Fishy! Fashy!
Not a thwart or bit of gunwale
  But bore token,
Everything of gear or tackle
  In her weakened,
Not a knee or timber in her
  But was loosened;
All her bends and timber couplings
  Were quite shaken,

Not a tiller was unsplit,
  Helm unbroken,
Every stick in her was creaking
  And disordered,
Every treenail in her drawn,
  And plank damaged,
Every nail without a rivet
  Could be lifted:
Not a rope there was unloosened,
  Nor spike unbent,
Not a thing pertaining to her
  But was worsened!
The sea cried peace with us at length
  At Islay Sound Cross,
And the harsh-voiced wind was bidden
  To give over.
She lifted from us to high regions
  Of the heavens,
And the sea, a smooth white table,
  Ceased from barking.
Thanks we gave to the High King
  Of the elements,
Good Clan-Ranald who preserved
  From death horrid;
Then we took down the thin sails,
  Speckled canvas,
Let down the fine smooth red masts
  Along her floor,
Shoved out the slim, shining oars,
  Smooth and coloured,
Of the far McBarras cut
  In Finnan Island;
And we rowed with steady swinging,
  Without failing,
To good harbour 'neath the heights
  Of Carrick Fergus.
We cast anchor at our leisure
  In the roads there,
And took meat and drink in plenty,
  And abode there.

'Raasay'

from A Journey to the Western Islands of Scotland
SAMUEL JOHNSON (1709–84)

James Boswell, Doctor Johnson's biographer and companion on the 'Highland Jaunt' of 1773 appears elsewhere in this book. Johnson's perspective, in this extract taken from the Raasay section of the Journey, *is interesting in that he is always alert to the social nuances of the strange people – or so they must have seemed to the Lichfield schoolmaster – among whom he was travelling. Of special note is his reference to the song of farewell to Scotland, composed by one of the 'Islanders that was going . . . to seek his fortune in America', which was sung at the laird's house on the evening of their landing on Raasay. This was indeed a song about what he calls 'this epidemical fury of emigration'. Boswell echoed the phrase in describing it as 'the rage for emigration'. In fact, Johnson was the first writer in English to mention the subject of emigration.*

Perhaps significantly, Johnson says that the lady next to him – perhaps moved to tears by the song – 'thought herself not equal to the work of translating'. In an attempt to make good this omission, the Johnson extract is followed by a song I Was Young in Strathglass *which may not be dissimilar to that heard by Johnson. It was composed by an emigrant, Dòmhnall Gobha (Donald the Blacksmith) not many years later. Collected and translated by Margaret Macdonell in* The Emigrant Experience: Songs of Highland Emigrants in North America, *this sad little song leaves us in no doubt of the guilt of some landlords in bringing about depopulation:*

> *The coward who now rules us*
> *evicted his own, few remain;*
> *he prefers sheep in the hills*
> *to a kilted retinue.*

At the first intermission of the stormy weather we were informed, that the boat, which was to convey us to *Raasay*, attended us on the coast. We had from this time our intelligence facilitated, and our conversation enlarged, by the company of Mr Macqueen, minister of a parish in *Sky*, whose knowledge and politeness give him a title equally to kindness and respect, and who, from this time, never forsook us till we were preparing to leave Sky, and the adjacent places.

The boat was under the direction of Mr *Malcolm Macleod*, a gentleman of *Raasay*. The water was calm, and the rowers were vigorous; so that our passage was quick and pleasant. When we came near the island, we saw the laird's house, a neat modern fabrick, and found Mr *Macleod*, the proprietor of the Island, with many gentlemen, expecting us on the beach. We had, as at all other places, some difficulty in landing. The craggs were irregularly broken, and a false step would have been very mischievous.

It seemed that the rocks might, with no great labour, have been hewn almost into a regular flight of steps; and as there are no other landing places, I considered this rugged ascent as the consequence of a form of life inured to hardships, and therefore not studious of nice accommodations. But I know not whether, for many ages, it was not considered as a part of military policy, to keep the country not easily accessible. The rocks are natural fortifications, and an enemy climbing with difficulty, was easily destroyed by those who stood high above him.

Our reception exceeded our expectations. We found nothing but civility, elegance, and plenty. After the usual refreshments, and the usual conversation, the evening came upon us. The carpet was then rolled off the floor; the musician was called, and the whole company was invited to dance, nor did ever fairies trip with greater alacrity. The general air of festivity, which predominated in this place, so far remote from all those regions which the mind has been used to contemplate as the mansions of pleasure, struck the imagination with a delightful surprise, analogous to that which is felt at an unexpected emersion from darkness into light.

When it was time to sup, the dance ceased, and six and thirty persons sat down to two tables in the same room. After supper the ladies sung *Erse* songs, to which I listened as an *English* audience to an *Italian* opera, delighted with the sound of words which I did not understand.

I inquired the subjects of the songs, and was told of one, that it was a love song, and of another, that it was a farewell composed by one of the Islanders that was going, in this epidemical fury of emigration, to seek his fortune in *America*. What sentiments would rise, on such an occasion, in the heart of one who had not been taught to lament by precedent, I should gladly have known; but the lady, by whom I sat, thought herself not equal to the work of translating.

Bha Mi òg ann a' Strathghlais

DÒMHNALL GOBHA (DONALD CHISHOLM)
Translation by Margaret Macdonell

Bha mi òg ann a' Strathghlais,
'S bha mi 'n dùil nach rachainn as,
Ach bho'n chaidh na suinn fo lic
Nis gabhaidh mi 'n ratreuta.
  Tha mo cheann-sa niste liath,
  'N déidh na chunnacas leam riamh;
  'S ged is éiginn dhomh bhith triall,
  A shiorrachd, 's beag mo spéis dha.

Ged a tha mo choiseachd trom,
Togaidh mi m'aigneadh le fonn;
'S 'n uair a theid mi air an long,
Có chuireas rium geall-réise?

'N tacharan seo th'air ar ceann
Sgiot e dhaoine 's tha iad gann;
'S fheàrr leis caoraich chuir am fang
No fir an camp fo fhéileadh.

Comunn càirdeil chan 'eil ann,
Chan 'eil éisdeachd aig fear fann;
Mur cuir thu caoraich ri gleann
Bidh tu air cheann na déirce.

'N uair a bha mi làidir, òg,
Dheanainn cosnadh air gach dòigh;
Ach an nis bho'n dh'fhalbh mo threòir,
Tha mi air stòras feumach.

Gheibh sinn acraichean bho'n rìgh,
Tighearnan gu'n dean e dhinn;
Cha b'ionnan 's a bhith mar bha 'n linn
Bha pàidheadh cìs do Cheusar.

Na biodh eagal oirbh mu'n chuan;
Faicibh mar sgoilt a' Mhuir Ruadh.
Tha cumhachdan an Tì tha shuas
An diugh cho buan 's an ceud là.

I was Young in Strathglass

[When] I was young in Strathglass
I had no thought of leaving there;
now that the gallant men have gone
I, too, shall leave.
  My hair is now grey
  after all I have seen;
  although I must set forth,
  I have little zest for doing so.

Though my step is heavy
I will stir my spirit with song.
When I embark on the ship,
who will challenge me?

The coward who now rules us
evicted his own, few remain;
he prefers sheep in the hills
to a kilted retinue.

There is no cordial agreement,
no hearing for the poor man;
if one does not raise sheep in the glens
he brings himself to penury.

When I was young and strong
I could earn my living in many ways;
now that my vigour is spent
I am in want.

We shall get grants from the king;
he will make us proprietors.
We shall not be like the generations
who paid tribute to Caesar.

Do not fear the sea;
mind how the Red Sea was divided.
The powers of God above
are as strong today as on the very first day.

Mingulay Boat Song

HUGH S. ROBERTON (1874–1952)

Heel yo ho, boys; let her go, boys;
Bring her head round, into the weather,
Hill you ho, boys, let her go, boys
Sailing homeward to Mingulay

What care we though, white the Minch is?
What care we for wind or weather?
Let her go boys; every inch is
Sailing homeward to Mingulay.

Wives are waiting, by the pier head,
Or looking seaward, from the heather;
Pull her round, boys, then you'll anchor
'Ere the sun sets on Mingulay.

Ships return now, heavy laden
Mothers holdin' bairns a-cryin'
They'll return, though, when the sun sets
They'll return to Mingulay.

Early Impressions

from The Amateur Emigrant

ROBERT LOUIS STEVENSON (1850–94)

In 1879 Fanny Osbourne sent a telegram to Robert Louis Stevenson from California – its exact contents were never known, but they were sufficient to cause the infatuated young Scot to buy a steerage ticket on the emigrant ship, Devonia, *sailing from the Tail of the Bank to New York, en route to Oakland in California. In the second chapter of* The Amateur Emigrant, Early Impressions, *RLS gives us an essay on the subject of emigration – 'nothing more agreeable to picture and nothing more pathetic to behold' – discusses the motives of and comments on how his fellow passengers adjust to life aboard this 'one small iron country on the deep'. With his usual astonishing facility, Stevenson paints a picture of those from whom he at first distances himself – he does not consider himself an emigrant, having boarded the* Devonia *only because of his shortage of funds – and then comes to identify with, so that he writes of 'the first fusion of our little nationality together'. The description of the children on board is delightful: 'It was odd to hear them, throughout the voyage, employ shore words to designate portions of the vessel. "Co' 'way doon to yon dyke," I heard one say, probably meaning the bulwark.'*

Stevenson catches the note of yearning that is so dominant in all writing about 'Home' and about 'The New World'. He says of 'Auld Lang Syne', which they sing on board, even in foul weather: 'Had not Burns contemplated emigration, I scarce believe he would have found that note.'

❧

We steamed out of the Clyde on Thursday night, and early on the Friday forenoon we took in our last batch of emigrants at Lough Foyle, in Ireland, and said farewell to Europe. The company was now complete, and began to draw together, by inscrutable magnetisms, upon the deck. There were Scots and Irish in plenty, a few English, a few Americans, a good handful of Scandinavians, a German or two, and one Russian; all now belonging for ten days to one small iron country on the deep.

As I walked the deck and looked round upon my fellow-passengers, thus curiously assorted from all northern Europe, I began for the first time to understand the nature of emigration. Day by day throughout the passage, and thenceforward across all the States, and on to the shores of the Pacific, this knowledge grew more clear and melancholy. Emigration, from a word of the most cheerful import, came to sound most dismally in my ear. There is nothing more agreeable to picture and nothing more pathetic to behold. The abstract idea, as conceived at home, is hopeful and adventurous. A young man, you fancy, scorning restraints and helpers, issues forth into life, that great battle, to fight for his own hand. The most pleasant stories of ambition, of difficulties overcome, and of ultimate success, are but as episodes to this great epic of self-help. The epic is composed of individual heroisms; it stands to them as the victorious war which subdued an empire stands to the personal act of bravery which spiked a single cannon and was adequately rewarded with a medal. For in emigration the young men enter direct and by the shipload on their heritage of work; empty continents swarm, as at the bo'sun's whistle, with industrious hands, and whole new empires are domesticated to the service of man.

This is the closet picture, and is found, on trial, to consist mostly of embellishments. The more I saw of my fellow-passengers, the less I was tempted to the lyric note. Comparatively few of the men were below thirty; many were married and encumbered with families; not a few were already up in years; and this itself was out of tune with my imaginations, for the ideal emigrant should certainly be young. Again, I thought he should offer to the eye some bold type of humanity, with bluff or hawk-like features, and the stamp of an eager and pushing disposition. Now those around me were for the most part quiet, orderly, obedient citizens, family men broken by adversity, elderly youths who had failed to place themselves in life, and people who had seen better days. Mildness was the prevailing character; mild mirth and mild endurance. In a word I was not taking part in an impetuous and conquering sally, such as swept over Mexico or Siberia, but found myself, like Marmion, 'in the lost battle, borne down by the flying.'

Labouring mankind had in the last years, and throughout Great Britain, sustained a prolonged and crushing series of defeats. I had heard vaguely of these reverses; of whole streets of houses standing deserted by the Tyne, the cellar-doors broken and removed for firewood; of homeless men loitering at the street-corners of Glasgow with their chests beside them; of closed factories, useless strikes, and starving girls. But I had never taken them home to me or represented these distresses livingly to my imagination. A turn of the market may be a calamity as disastrous as the French retreat from Moscow; but it hardly lends itself to lively treatment, and makes a trifling figure in the morning papers. We may struggle as we please, we are not born economists. The individual is more affecting than the mass. It is by the scenic accidents, and the appeal to the carnal eye, that for the most part we grasp the significance of tragedies. Thus it was only now, when I found myself involved in the rout, that I began to appreciate how sharp had been the battle. We were a company of the rejected; the drunken, the incompetent, the weak, the prodigal, all who had been unable to prevail against circumstances in the one land, were now fleeing pitifully to another; and though one or two might still succeed, all had already failed. We were a shipful of failures, the broken men of England. Yet it must not be supposed that these people exhibited depression. The scene, on the contrary, was cheerful. Not a tear was shed on board the vessel. All were full of hope for the future, and showed an inclination to innocent gaiety. Some were heard to sing, and all began to scrape acquaintance with small jests and ready laughter.

The children found each other out like dogs, and ran about the decks scraping acquaintance after their fashion also. 'What do you call your mither?' I heard one ask. 'Mawmaw,' was the reply, indicating, I fancy, a shade of difference in the social scale. When people pass each other on the high seas of life at so early an age, the contact is but slight, and the relation more like what we may imagine to be the friendship of flies than that of men; it is so quickly joined, so easily dissolved, so open in its communications and so devoid of deeper human qualities. The children, I observed, were all in a band, and as thick as thieves at a fair, while their elders were still ceremoniously manoeuvring on the outskirts of acquaintance. The sea, the ship, and the seamen were soon as familiar as home to these half-conscious little ones. It was odd to hear them, throughout the voyage, employ shore words to designate portions of the vessel. 'Co' 'way doon to yon dyke,' I heard one say, probably meaning the bulwark. I often had my heart in my mouth, watching them climb into the shrouds or on the rails while the ship went swinging through the waves; and I admired and envied the courage of their mothers, who sat by in the sun and looked on with composure at these perilous feats. 'He'll maybe be a sailor,' I heard one remark; 'now's the time to learn.' I had been on the point of running forward to interfere, but stood back at that, reproved. Very few in the more delicate classes have the nerve to look upon the peril of one dear to them; but the life of poorer folk, where necessity is so much more immediate and imperious, braces even a mother to this extreme of endurance. And perhaps, after all, it is better that the lad should break his neck than that you should break his spirit.

And since I am here on the chapter of the children, I must mention one little fellow, whose family belonged to Steerage No. 4 and 5, and who, wherever he went, was like a strain of music round the ship. He was an ugly, merry, unbreeched child of three, his lint-white hair in a tangle, his face smeared with suet and treacle; but he ran to and fro with so natural a step, and fell and picked himself up again with such grace and good-humour, that he might fairly be called beautiful when he was in motion. To meet him, crowing with laughter and beating an accompaniment to his own mirth with a tin spoon upon a tin cup, was to meet a little triumph of the human species. Even when his mother and the rest of his family lay sick and prostrate around him, he sat upright in their midst and sang aloud in the pleasant heartlessness of infancy.

Throughout the Friday, intimacy among us men made but few advances. We discussed the probable duration of the voyage, we exchanged pieces of information, naming our trades, what we hoped to find in the new world, or what we were fleeing from in the old; and, above all, we condoled together over the food and the vileness of the steerage. One or two had been so near famine that you may say they had run into the ship with the devil at their heels; and to these all seemed for the best in the best of possible steamers. But the majority were hugely discontented. Coming as they did from a country in so low a state as Great Britain, many of them from Glasgow, which commercially speaking was as good as dead, and many having long been out of work, I was surprised to find them so dainty in their notions. I myself lived almost exclusively on bread, porridge, and soup, precisely as it was supplied to them, and found it, if not luxurious, at least sufficient. But these working men were loud in their outcries. It was not 'food for human beings', it was 'only fit for pigs', it was 'a disgrace'. Many of them lived almost entirely upon biscuit, others on their own private supplies, and some paid extra for better rations from the ship. This marvellously changed my notion of the degree of luxury habitual to the artisan. I was prepared to hear him grumble, for grumbling is the traveller's pastime; but I was not prepared to find him turn away from a diet which was palatable to myself. Words I should have disregarded, or taken with a liberal allowance; but when a man prefers dry biscuit there can be no question of the sincerity of his disgust.

With one of their complaints I could most heartily sympathise. A single night of the steerage had filled them with horror. I had myself suffered, even in my decent second-cabin berth, from the lack of air; and as the night promised to be fine and quiet, I determined to sleep on deck, and advised all who complained of their quarters to follow my example. I daresay a dozen of others agreed to do so, and I thought we should have been quite a party. Yet when I brought up my rug about seven bells, there was no one to be seen but the watch. That chimerical terror of good night-air, which makes men close their windows, list their doors, and seal themselves up with their own poisonous exhalations, had sent all these healthy workmen down below. One would think we had been brought up in a fever country; yet in England the most malarious districts are in the bedchambers.

I felt saddened at this defection, and yet half-pleased to have the night so quietly to myself. The wind had hauled a little ahead on the starboard bow, and was dry but chilly. I found a shelter near the fire-hole, and made myself snug for the night. The ship moved over the uneven sea with a gentle and cradling movement. The ponderous, organic labours of the engine in her bowels occupied the mind, and prepared it for slumber. From time to time a heavier lurch would disturb me as I lay, and recall me to the obscure borders of consciousness; or I heard, as it were through a veil, the clear note of the clapper on the brass and the beautiful sea-cry, 'All's well!' I know nothing, whether for poetry or music, that can surpass the effect of these two syllables in the darkness of a night at sea.

The day dawned fairly enough, and during the early part we had some pleasant hours to improve acquaintance in the open air; but towards nightfall the wind freshened, the rain began to fall, and the sea rose so high that it was difficult to keep one's footing on the deck. I have spoken of our concerts. We were indeed a musical ship's company, and cheered our way into exile with the fiddle, the accordion, and the songs of all nations. (Night after night we gathered at the aftermost limit of our domain, where it bordered on that of the saloon. Performers were called up with acclamation, some shame-faced and hanging the head, others willing and as bold as brass.) Good, bad, or indifferent – Scottish, English, Irish, Russian, German or Norse, – the songs were received with generous applause. Once or twice, a recitation, very spiritedly rendered in a powerful Scottish accent, varied the proceedings; and once we sought in vain to dance a quadrille, eight men of us together, to the music of the violin. The performers were all humorous, frisky fellows, who loved to cut capers in private life; but as soon as they were arranged for the dance, they conducted themselves like so many mutes at a funeral. I have never seen decorum pushed so far; and as this was not expected, the quadrille was soon whistled down, and the dancers departed under a cloud. Eight Frenchmen, even eight Englishmen from another rank of society, would have dared to make some fun for themselves and the spectators; but the working man, when sober, takes an extreme and even melancholy view of personal deportment. A fifth-form schoolboy is not more careful of dignity. He dares not be comical; his fun must escape from him unprepared, and above all, it must be unaccompanied by any physical demonstration. I like his society under most circumstances, but let me never again join with him in public gambols.

But the impulse to sing was strong, and triumphed over modesty and even the inclemencies of sea and sky. On this rough Saturday night, we got together by the main deck-house, in a place sheltered from the wind and rain. Some clinging to a ladder which led to the hurricane deck, and the rest knitting arms or taking hands, we made a ring to support the women in the violent lurching of the ship; and when we were thus disposed, sang to our hearts' content. Some of the songs were appropriate to the scene; others strikingly the reverse. Bastard doggerel of the music-hall, such as, 'Around her splendid form, I weaved the magic circle,' sounded bald, bleak, and pitifully silly. 'We don't want to fight, but, by Jingo, if we do,' was in some measure saved by the vigour and unanimity with which the chorus was thrown forth into the night. I observed a Platt-Deutsch mason, entirely innocent of English, adding heartily to the general effect. And perhaps the German mason is but a fair example of the sincerity with which the song was rendered; for nearly all with whom I conversed upon the subject were bitterly opposed to war, and attributed their own misfortunes, and frequently their own taste for whisky, to the campaigns in Zululand and Afghanistan.

Every now and again, however, some song that touched the pathos of our situation was given forth; and you could hear by the voices that took up the burden how the sentiment came home to each. 'The Anchor's Weighed' was true for us. We were indeed 'Rocked on the bosom of the stormy deep.' How many of us could say with the singer, 'I'm lonely to-night, love, without you,' or 'Go, some one, and tell them from me, to write me a letter from home!' And when was there a more appropriate moment for 'Auld Lang Syne' than now, when the land, the friends, and the affections of that mingled but beloved time were fading and fleeing behind us in the vessel's wake? It pointed forward to the hour when these labours should be overpast, to the return voyage, and to many a meeting in the sanded inn, when those who had parted in the spring of youth should again drink a cup of kindness in their age. Had not Burns contemplated emigration, I scarce believe he would have found that note.

(This was the first fusion of our little nationality together. The wind sang shrill in the rigging; the rain fell small and thick; the whole group, linked together as it was, was shaken and swung to and fro as the swift steamer shore into the waves. It was a general embrace, both friendly and helpful, like what one imagines of old Christian Agapes. I turned many times to look behind me on the moving desert of seas, now cloud-canopied and lit with but a low nocturnal glimmer along the line of the horizon. It hemmed us in and cut us off on our swift-travelling oasis. And yet this waste was part a playground for the stormy petrel; and on the least tooth of reef, outcropping in a thousand miles of unfathomable ocean, the gull makes its home and dwells in a busy polity. And small as was our iron world, it made yet a large and habitable place in the Atlantic, compared with our globe upon the seas of space.)

All Sunday the weather remained wild and cloudy; many were prostrated by sickness; only five sat down to tea in the second cabin, and two of these departed abruptly ere the meal was at an end. The Sabbath was observed strictly by the majority of the emigrants. I heard an old woman express her surprise that 'the ship didna gae doon', as she saw some one pass her with a chess-board on the holy day. Some sang Scottish psalms. Many went to service, and in true Scottish fashion came back ill pleased with their divine. 'I didna think he was an experienced preacher,' said one girl to me.

It was a bleak, uncomfortable day; but at night, by six bells, although the wind had not yet moderated, the clouds were all wrecked and blown away behind the rim of the horizon, and the stars came out thickly overhead. I saw Venus burning as steadily and sweetly across this hurly-burly of the winds and waters as ever at home upon the summer woods. The engine pounded, the screw tossed out of the water with a roar, and shook the ship from end to end; the bows battled with loud reports against the billows; and as I stood in the lee-scuppers and looked up to where the funnel leaned out over my head, vomiting smoke, and the black and monstrous topsails blotted, at each lurch, a different crop of stars, it seemed as if all this trouble were a thing of small account, and that just above the mast reigned peace unbroken and eternal.

The Voyage

from Treasure Island

ROBERT LOUIS STEVENSON

Chapter 4, The Voyage, *of Stevenson's most famous story, is included as contrast to his previous account of a real voyage. In a way, however, it can be shown to have certain links with his destination in* The Amateur Emigrant. *At the time of publication of* Treasure Island *in 1883, only four years after his voyage to the USA, RLS suggested in a letter to a friend that 'The scenery [of Captain Flint's island] is Californian in part, and in part* chic'. *Others have commented on a number of ways in which the fictitious landscape of Treasure Island can be said to resemble the scenery of Monterey and Silverado, the latter a place noted for its treasure of silver. The novel, or romance, is also a first-person narrative, in the same way as the autobiographical accounts of Stevenson in America.*

This chapter is a marvel of compression in that it forms a bridge between the prologue material, dealing with Jim Hawkins's acquisition of the map, and the mutiny and the arrival at the island. There is no overtly Scottish feature in the book – although the skipper of the Hispaniola, *Captain Smollett, could be an arch reference to another Scot who wrote about the sea, Tobias Smollett.* Treasure Island *was written during a family holiday at Braemar in 1881, partly to amuse his thirteen-year-old stepson Lloyd Osbourne.*

All that night we were in a great bustle getting things stowed in their place, and boatfuls of the squire's friends, Mr Blandly and the like, coming off to wish him a good voyage and a safe return. We never had a night at the 'Admiral Benbow' when I had half the work; and I was dog-tired when, a little before dawn, the boatswain sounded his pipe, and the crew began to man the capstan-bars. I might have been twice as weary, yet I would not have left the deck; all was so new and interesting to me – the brief commands, the shrill note of the whistle, the men bustling to their places in the glimmer of the ship's lanterns.

'Now, Barbecue, tip us a stave,' cried one voice.

'The old one,' cried another.

'Ay, ay, mates,' said Long John, who was standing by, with his crutch under his arm, and at once broke out in the air and words I knew so well:

'Fifteen men on the dead man's chest—'

And then the whole crew bore chorus:

'Yo-ho-ho, and a bottle of rum!'

And at the third 'ho!' drove the bars before them with a will.

Even at that exciting moment it carried me back to the old 'Admiral Benbow' in a second; and I seemed to hear the voice of the captain piping in the chorus. But soon the anchor was short up; soon it was hanging dripping at the bows; soon the sails began to draw, and the land and shipping to flit by on either side; and before I could lie down to snatch an hour of slumber the *Hispaniola* had begun her voyage to the Isle of Treasure.

I am not going to relate that voyage in detail. It was fairly prosperous. The ship proved to be a good ship, the crew were capable seamen, and the captain thoroughly understood his business. But before we came the length of Treasure Island, two or three things had happened which require to be known.

Mr Arrow, first of all, turned out even worse than the captain had feared. He had no command among the men, and people did what they pleased with him. But that was by no means the worst of it; for after a day or two at sea he began to appear on deck with hazy eye, red cheeks, stuttering tongue, and other marks of drunkenness. Time after time he was ordered below in disgrace. Sometimes he fell and cut himself; sometimes he lay all day long in his little bunk at one side of the companion; sometimes for a day or two he would be almost sober and attend to his work at least passably.

In the meantime, we could never make out where he got the drink. That was the ship's mystery. Watch him as we pleased, we could do nothing to solve it; and when we asked him to his face, he would only laugh, if he were drunk, and if he were sober, deny solemnly that he ever tasted anything but water.

He was not only useless as an officer, and a bad influence amongst the men, but it was plain that at this rate he must soon kill himself outright; so nobody was much surprised nor very sorry when one dark night, with a head sea, he disappeared entirely and was seen no more.

'Overboard!' said the captain. 'Well, gentlemen, that saves the trouble of putting him in irons.'

But there we were, without a mate; and it was necessary, of course, to advance one of the men. The boatswain, Job Anderson, was the likeliest man aboard, and, though he kept his old title, he served in a way as mate. Mr Trelawney had followed the sea, and his knowledge made him very useful, for he often took a watch himself in easy weather. And the coxswain, Israel Hands, was a careful, wily, old, experienced seaman, who could be trusted at a pinch with almost anything.

He was a great confidant of Long John Silver, and so the mention of his name leads me on to speak of our ship's cook, Barbecue, as the men called him.

Aboard ship he carried his crutch by a lanyard round his neck, to have both hands as free as possible. It was something to see him wedge the foot of the crutch against a bulkhead, and, propped against it, yielding to every movement of the ship, get on with his cooking like someone safe ashore. Still more strange was it to see him in the heaviest of weather cross the deck. He had a line or two rigged up to help him across the widest spaces – Long John's earrings, they were called; and he would hand himself from one place to another, now using the crutch, now trailing it alongside by the lanyard, as quickly as another man could walk. Yet some of the men who had sailed with him before expressed their pity to see him so reduced.

'He's no common man, Barbecue,' said the coxswain to me. 'He had good schooling in his young days, and can speak like a book when so minded; and brave – a lion's nothing alongside of Long John! I seen him grapple four, and knock their heads together – him unarmed.'

All the crew respected and even obeyed him. He had a way of talking to each, and doing everybody some particular service. To me he was unweariedly kind; and always glad to see me in the galley, which he kept as clean as a new pin; the dishes hanging up burnished, and his parrot in a cage in one corner.

'Come away, Hawkins,' he would say; 'come and have a yarn with John. Nobody more welcome than yourself, my son. Sit you down, and hear the news. Here's Cap'n Flint – I calls my parrot Cap'n Flint, after the famous buccaneer – here's Cap'n Flint predicting success to our v'yage. Wasn't you, Cap'n?'

And the parrot would say, with great rapidity: 'Pieces of eight! pieces of eight! pieces of eight!' till you wondered that it was not out of breath, or till John threw his handkerchief over the cage.

'Now, that bird,' he would say, 'is, may be, two hundred years old, Hawkins – they lives for ever mostly; and if anybody's seen more wickedness, it must be the devil himself. She's sailed with England, the great Cap'n England, the pirate. She's been at Madagascar, and at Malabar, and Surinam, and Providence, and Portobello. She was at the fishing up of the wrecked Plate ships. It's there she learned "Pieces of eight," and little wonder; three hundred and fifty thousand of 'em, Hawkins! She was at the boarding of the *Viceroy of the Indies* out of Goa, she was; and to look at her you would think she was a babby. But you smelt powder – didn't you, Cap'n?'

'Stand by to go about,' the parrot would scream.

'Ah, she's a handsome craft, she is,' the cook would say, and give her sugar from his pocket, and then the bird would peck at the bars and swear straight on, passing belief for wickedness. 'There,' John would add, 'you can't touch pitch and not be mucked, lad. Here's this poor old innocent bird o' mine swearing blue fire, and none the wiser, you may lay to that. She would swear the same, in a manner of speaking, before chaplain.' And John would touch his forelock with a solemn way he had, that made me think he was the best of men.

In the meantime, squire and Captain Smollett were still on pretty distant terms with one another. The squire made no bones about the matter; he despised the captain. The captain, on his part, never spoke but when he was spoken to, and then sharp and short and dry, and not a word wasted. He owned, when driven into a corner, that he seemed to have been wrong about the crew, that some of them were as brisk as he wanted to see, and all had behaved fairly well. As for the ship, he had taken a downright fancy to her. 'She'll lie a point nearer the wind than a man has a right to expect of his own married wife, sir. But,' he would add, 'all I say is we're not home again, and I don't like the cruise.'

The squire, at this, would turn away and march up and down the deck, chin in air.

'A trifle more of that man,' he would say, 'and I should explode.'

We had some heavy weather, which only proved the qualities of the *Hispaniola*. Every man on board seemed well content, and they must have been hard to please if they had been otherwise; for it is my belief there was never a ship's company so spoiled since Noah put to sea. Double grog was going on the least excuse; there was duff on odd days, as, for instance, if the squire heard it was any man's birthday; and always a barrel of apples standing broached in the waist, for any one to help himself that had a fancy.

'Never knew good come of it, yet,' the captain said to Dr Livesey. 'Spoil foc's'le hands, make devils. That's my belief.'

But good did come of the apple barrel, as you shall hear; for if it had not been for that, we should have had no note of warning, and might all have perished by the hand of treachery.

This was how it came about.

We had run up the trades to get the wind of the island we were after – I am not allowed to be more plain – and now we were running down for it with a bright look-out day and night. It was about the last day of our outward voyage, by the largest computation; some time that night, or, at latest, before noon of the morrow, we should sight the Treasure Island. We were heading S.S.W., and had a steady breeze abeam and a quiet sea. The *Hispaniola* rolled steadily, dipping her bowsprit now and then with a whiff of spray. All was drawing alow and aloft; every one was in the bravest spirits; because we were now so near an end of the first part of our adventure.

Now, just after sundown, when all my work was over, and I was on my way to my berth, it occurred to me that I should like an apple. I ran on deck. The watch was all forward looking out for the island. The man at the helm was watching the luff of the sail, and whistling away gently to himself; and that was the only sound excepting the swish of the sea against the bows and around the sides of the ship.

In I got bodily into the apple barrel, and found there was scarce an apple left; but sitting down there in the dark, what with the sound of the waters and the rocking movement of the ship, I had either fallen asleep, or was on the point of doing so, when a heavy man sat down with rather a clash close by. The barrel shook as he leaned his shoulder against it, and I was just about to jump up when the man began to speak. It was Silver's voice, and, before I had heard a dozen words, I would not have shown myself for all the world, but lay there, trembling and listening, in the extreme of fear and curiosity; for from these dozen words I understood that the lives of all the honest men aboard depended upon me alone.

'In the Firth'

from The Steamboat

JOHN GALT (1779–1839)

The extract from The Steamboat, *published in 1822, provides an enter-taining example of the curious combination of a pioneer of the Scottish novel writing about a pioneering steam vessel, on the very Firth of Clyde which was the birthplace of both novelist and shipbuilding industry. Galt was born at Irvine and lived for a time in Greenock and* The Steamboat *is one of those* Tales of the West, *as he called them, which described contemporary life and manners, although in this extract he does not use the marvellous flexible Scots which is a feature of the writing of this prolific novelist – a man incidentally who also found time to act as an immigration officer in Ontario and to found the city of Guelph in that Province.*

Typical of novels of the period, the narrative is capable of accommodat-ing a number of tales told by characters within the main storyline, and here there is an account of a West Indian hurricane given by a 'sailor lad' from 'Rue, on the Gairloch'. Galt cleverly uses this device, however, to point an ironic contrast between the twin 'disasters' of the Caribbean hurricane and the stranding of the Waterloo, *'that had come all the way from Glasgow like a swan before the wind, stuck fast in the mud' off Greenock. When at last the passengers are freed from their perilous situation, they take refreshments 'at the pleasant hotel of Helensburgh' – the Baths Hotel in fact, which was owned by one Henry Bell, the man who had built the earlier pioneering steamboat, the* Comet.

Chapter III

After landing, as I have noticed, our cargo of Greenockians, the steam was again set to work, and the vessel, with all that orderliness and activity which belongs to the enginery, moved round, and, turning her latter end to Greenock, walked over the waters straight to Helensburgh. This is not a long voyage naturally, being no more than four miles, if so much; but it is not without dangers; and we had a lively taste and type of the perils of shipwreck in crossing the bank – a great shoal that lies midway in the sea; for it happened that we were later for the tide than the captain had thought, so that, when we were in what the jack-tars call the mid-channel, the gallant Waterloo, that had come all the way from Glasgow like a swan before the wind, stuck fast in the mud. Never shall I forget the dunt that dirled on my heart when she stopped, and the engines would go no further. Fortunately, as I was told, this came to pass just at the turn of the tide, or otherwise there is no saying what the consequences might have been; it being certain, that if the accident had happened an hour before, we should have been obligated to wait more than two hours, instead of half an hour; and if, in the course of that time, a tempest had arisen, it is morally certain, the vessel lying high and dry, that the waves would have beaten over her, and, in all human probability, dashed her to pieces, by which every soul on board would to a certainty have perished; for we were so far from land, both on the Greenock and the Helensburgh coast, that no help by boat or tackle could have been afforded. It was a dreadful situation, indeed, that we were in; and when I reflected on the fickleness of the winds, and the treachery of the seas, my anxieties found but a small comfort in the calm that was then in the air, and the glassy face of the sunny waters around us. However, I kept up my spirits, and waited for the flowing of the tide with as much composure as could reasonably be called for, from a man who had never been a venture at sea before, but had spent his days in a shop in the Saltmarket, as quietly as an hour-glass ebbing its sands in a corner.

While we were in this state, I fell into discourse with a sailor lad who had come home from Jamaica in the West Indies, and was going over from Greenock to see his friends, who lived at the Rue, on the Gairloch side; and falling into discourse, we naturally conversed about what might be the consequence of our lying on the bank, and if the vessel should chance to spring a leak, and such other concerns as, from less to more, led us on to talk of ships sinking in the great ocean, or taking fire thousands of miles from any land, and all those other storms and perils among which the lot of the mariner is cast. And I was expressing to him my amazement that ever any man who had been cast away, could afterwards think of going again to sea. 'Ah!' said he; 'for all that, the sailor's life is a heartsome life. If we risk limb and life, we are spared from the sneaking anxieties that make other men so shamefaced. Besides, sir, there is a pleasure in our dangers, and common suffering opens the generosity of the heart; so that, when we have little wherewith to help one another, we make up for it in kindness.' I could not but wonder how this sailor lad had learned to speak in this style of language, and he satisfied me by telling me that his father had been a dominie, and that he had received a good education, to qualify him, please God, to take the command of a vessel. I then spoke to him very particularly about what he might have seen and met with in the course of his seafaring life, and so led him on to relate, as follows, an account of a hurricane, by which the ship that he was in was lost, and every soul on board, save himself, a dog, and a black fellow, perished.

The Hurricane

We were going up (said he) from Trinidad to St Kitts, in as fine weather as ever was seen in the heavens, and we expected to make a brisk passage; but, in the third night after our departure, about the middle of the second watch, the wind fell on a sudden dead calm – I was on deck at the time – every one was surprised – for it had been blowing a steady breeze till that moment. It had, however, been noticed the night before, that the cat was freaking about, and climbing the rigging with a storm in her tail – a sign which is never known to fail.

Towards morning, the air in the West Indies becomes lighter and fresher; but in that night, we observed, it grew close and sultry, and about sunrise the heat was very heavy – yet the sky was clear, not a speck of cloud to be seen – the sea, however, was discoloured, as at the mouth of a river. An old man-of-war's man whom we had on board, one Thomas Buoy, who had been in the Ramilies when the Ville de Paris went down, was very uneasy at these signs, and said they reminded him of the weather before that hurricane.

All day the dead calm and the oppressive heat continued, but still over-head the heavens were bright. About noon, however, just as we had taken an observation, Thomas bade me notice a sort of smoky haze spreading round the horizon. 'I don't like that,' said he; nor did I either, although I had no reason on my part. At sunset, this vapour had thickened in the west into two or three strips of black cloud – some of the men thought they betokened rain and thunder. 'And wind too,' said Thomas Buoy, as he walked the deck thoughtfully. However, the night set in as beautiful as ever. Every star in the firmament was out, beaming like the lamp in the binnacle; but, for all that, the dead calm and the sultry air lay heavy on the spirits of all on board, and the ship was a log on the water.

About half a glass before midnight, the man at the helm saw a fire-ball at the mainmast head, and in a short time another on the foremast. When the watch was changed, there was one at each mast-head. Some of the sailors had seen such lights before, without harm following, but nobody liked them.

During the watch, the men were not so cheerful as usual, as I heard in the morning, and Thomas Buoy kept himself aloof, and was frequently heard to say, 'God help us!' The mate had that night come suddenly on deck, terrified out of his sleep by a dream, in which he thought he saw a large black Newfoundland dog come down into the captain's state-room, and run off with him in his teeth. But the daylight came round, and the weather for a time was finer than ever; a breeze sprang up, and the ship went at a brave rate, but Thomas Buoy remarked that the skies were streaked with flakes of goat's-hair, and said the wind was not yet come. At noon, he pointed out to the captain a small round black cloud in the north-west, which he solemnly said was the eye of a hurricane. Every other vapour changed its shape and hue but that cloud – It was fixed; and, as Thomas said, looked at us with vengeance. Towards the evening it began to alter, and gradually to spread, until the whole heaven, from the south-west to the north, was filled with the dark and rolling omens of a thunder-storm and tempest. The wind frequently veered from one point to another, and every now and then came out with a sudden puff, as if the devil had been fetching his breath. We prepared for the worst – took in sail, and struck the topgallant masts. About an hour after sunset, it began to lighten fiercely along the horizon, but we heard no thunder.

This confirmed the fears of Thomas Buoy. 'It is now gathering,' said he; 'these flashes are Beelzebub's rockets, thrown up as signals for action.' Surely the old man felt the hand of fate upon him, for all his apprehensions were confirmed.

The wind, as the night darkened, came on gusty and rougher – now it blew a steady breeze from the north; but in a moment there was a pause, and then a squall came roaring from the west, as if all the trade-winds that were blowing from the east since the last hurricane had been furiously driven back. Still the hand of mercy struggled with the tempest; and it was not till midnight that it came flapping forth with all its wings, in the dreadful license of full liberty.

As we were all snug aloft, the captain, who was a steady seaman – poor fellow, a better never trode on oak – ordered the watch to be kept as usual, that, in case of accidents, the men might come fresh to their duty, but few of us turned in. The mate sat with Thomas, listening to what he had suffered on board the Ramilies, and hearing the howls of the hurricane above. While he was in one of the wildest passages of his old stories, a sheet of lightning struck the mizzen, and the whole party declared, that in the same moment they saw something in the likeness of a large black Newfoundland dog, such as the mate had seen in his dream, run past them, as it were from the hold, and escape upon deck. The mizzen topmast was rent into splinters, and the captain was so wounded in the head by one of the pieces, that I assisted to carry him to his cot.

We were now driving along at the mercy of the wind, which was blowing so strong, sweeping round the compass like a whirlpool, that the ocean was flying all spindrift. In this state we continued three hours, till, in a sudden checking round of a squall, a sea broke on board, which carried away the boats, the binnacle, two men at the helm, and every thing on deck that was not a part of the ship. She was almost upset by the shock; and we found, when we expected that she would have righted from the lurch, the cargo had shifted, by which the rudder was rendered useless – and still the hurricane was increasing.

The daylight began at last to dawn, but the air was so thick, that we could not see across the deck; and, but that we knew from the force of the wind, that the vessel must be going, and that, too, at a great rate, no one on board could say she was in motion.

About two hours after sunrise, we saw, on the larboard side, something vast and dark, through the spindrift; at first we took it for a line-of-battle ship lying to, but in a moment Thomas Buoy clapped his hands in despair, and cried, 'The land! the land!'

The words were scarcely out of his mouth, when the ship struck with such force, that all her masts were started. The cry was then, 'Cut away!' but in an instant she struck again, and the masts were thrown overboard. The third shock did her business; – she gave, as it were, a deep groan, and, hogging up in midships, yawned asunder by the main hatchway, her stern sinking into the water with the poor captain in his cot, and all the brave fellows who were at the moment at the mizzen chains, cutting away the rigging.

I happened at the time to be on the forecastle; and, looking a-head, saw that the bowsprit reached to the rocks. I called on all to follow me; and, running out at once, got safe to the cliff; but in the same moment, the wreck lurched over, and filling, went down with all the crew, except a black fellow, whom the captain had brought as steward from Trinidad, and a little dog that he was taking as a present to a lady at St Thomas's. – How the dog escaped I cannot tell, for he was on the land before me; but the black fellow was like a sea-gull, and saved himself by swimming.

It seemed to me, that at the very time when we reached the shore, the gale slackened; for the air soon after became lighter, and I saw we were not far from a sugar plantation, all the mills and houses belonging to which were scattered like shingles and splinters.

* * *

Just as the sailor had got to this crisis of his story, the steamboat began to move, and in the course of a minute or two she was paddling her way towards Helensburgh; and her motion made every body again so jocose and lively, that I could not but marvel at the depths of the mysteries of the heart of man. As we drew near to the shore, the sailor had forgotten all the earnest solemnity of his tale, and was the blithest in the boat. Fain would I have questioned him about the particulars of what ensued when he found himself in the plantation; but he was no longer in a humour to attend to me, his heart being taken up with the thought of getting to his friends – just like a young dog that has broken loose from a confinement, so that I was left in a kind of an unsatisfied state, with the image of the broken ship in my mind, with her riven planks and timbers, grinning like the jaws of death amidst the raging waters; the which haunted me till I got a chack of dinner at the hotel, and a comfortable tumbler of excellent old double-rum toddy. But I should mention, that till the dinner was gotten ready, I had a pleasant walk along the shore, as far as the Cairn-dhue, and saw on the right hand, among its verdant plantations, the lordly castle of Ardincaple, and on the left, ayont the loch, the modern mansion which the Duke of Argyle is building there among the groves of Roseneath; with which, it's my opinion, no situation in this country-side can compare, for hill and dale, and wood and water, and other comely and romantic incidents of Highland mountains, all rocky and fantastical, like a painted picture by some famous o'er-sea limner.

Chapter IV

When I had ate my dinner and drunk my toddy at the pleasant hotel of Helensburgh, in which there are both hot and cold baths for invalid persons, and others afflicted with the rheumatics, and suchlike incomes, I went out again to take another walk, for I had plenty of time on my hands, as the steam-boat was not to sail for Glasgow till six o'clock. At first, it was my intent to take a survey of the country and agriculture, and to see what promise there was on the ground of a harvest; but in sauntering along the road towards the hill of Ardmore, I foregathered with Mr and Mrs McWaft, and four of their childer. They had been for some time at Helensburgh for the salt water, the gudeman having been troubled with some inward complaint that sat upon his spirits, and turned all to sour that he ate or drank.

Nobody could be more glad to see an old acquaintance than they were to see me, and Mrs McWaft was just in a perplexity to think that I could ever have ventured to leave my shop so long, and come such a voyage by myself; but I told her that I had been constrained by the want of health, and that maybe before the summer was done she might see me again; for that I had got a vast of entertainment, and was, moreover, appetised to such a degree, that I had made a better dinner that day, and with a relish, than I had done for years past; which she was very happy to hear, hoping the like in time would be the lot of her gudeman, who was still in a declining way, though he took the salt water inwardly every morning, and the warm bath outwardly every other day. Thus, as we were standing in the road, holding a free-and-easy talking about our ails and concerns, and the childer were diverting themselves pu'ing the gowans and chasing the bees and butterflies, Mr McWaft said that I could do no less than go back with them and take a glass of wine, and, insisting kindly thereon, I found myself obligated to do so; accordingly, I turned with them, and went into the house where they had their salt-water quarters.

It was one of the thackit houses near the burn – a very sweet place, to be sure, of its kind; but I could not help wondering to hear how Mr McWaft ever expected to grow better in it, which, compared with his own bein house on the second flat of Paterson's lan', was both damp and vastly inconvenient. The floor of the best room was clay, and to cover the naked walls they had brought carpets from home, which they hung round them like curtains, behind which carpets all sorts of foul clothes, shoes, and things to be kept out of sight, I could observe, were huddled.

Meanwhile, Mrs McWaft had got out the wine and the glasses, and a loaf of bread that was blue moulded from the damp of the house; and I said to her, 'that surely the cause which had such an effect on the bread, must be of some consequence to the body.' 'But the sea and country air,' replied Mr McWaft, 'makes up for more than all such sort of inconveniences.' So we drank our wine and conversed on divers subjects, rehearsing. in the way of a sketch, the stories related in my foregoing pages, which both the mistress and gudeman declared were as full of the extraordinaries as any thing they had ever heard of.

The Sailing Ship

EDWARD GAITENS (1897–1966)

The Scots Magazine of May 1939 carried this short story which takes the old three-masted sailing ship as a highly coloured metaphor for freedom (or escapism?): 'He was sailing on, away from unemployment and slums and wretchedness, far from the ignorance and misunderstanding of his parents, to the infinite nobility of the sea!' Gaitens, a largely self-taught product of the Gorbals, contrasts the fine sailing ship that he sees in the docks with the harsh reality of life in the city of Glasgow. Encouraged to write by such as James Bridie, he has left work which is probably among the least sentimental of accounts of working class life in Scotland in the thirties and forties. In a way reminiscent of Sean O'Casey, he came closer than most to fully describing the nature of manual labour and its impact on men.

Edward Gaitens only wrote one novel, The Dance of the Apprentices *(1946), but* The Sailing Ship *covers some of the same ground as the longer work – he includes as one of his themes the treatment of conscientious objectors during and after the Great War, having been one himself and having spent two years in prison.*

Mrs Regan yelled at her son: 'Get up, ye lazy pig! Rise up an' look for work an' don't shame me before the neebors!' She stopped sweeping the floor and approached the set-in bed, brandishing the brush over him with insane gestures. The veins bulged in her scrawny neck, her eyes were crazy, she was red from her brow to the top of her breast, like a person in the throes of suffocation. 'Get up, d'ye hear? Get out o' this house an' never come back, ye lazy coward! Ye'll not be lyin' there day-in day-out an' neebors whisperin'.' She came closer, sneering: 'D'ye ken whit they call ye? "Johnny Regan, the dirty Conshy, the wee gentleman that's too good for work!"'

He stared in silent misery at the wall, holding in his rage, conquering the inherited violence in his blood. How he hated her! He would always hate her. Always! When she was long dead and gone, her memory would be nauseous! His hands gripped the undersheet in the vehemence of restraint. She screamed down at him: 'A conshense objaictor! My, ye're a rare son! A conshense objaictor an' socialish! Ma braw Terence is lyin' deid in France, while you're lyin' here safe an' weel!'

Why must she taunt him so horribly; making him itch to inflict the brutality he had witnessed so often since childhood? He had gone to prison, driven by wild idealism, believing his action would end life like this! He turned on the pillow and said quietly: 'Ach, shut up, will ye? Don't make yourself uglier than you are!' He could have plucked out his tongue. He had not meant to say that. But her nagging would enrage a saint! She became speechless and struck him with the broom handle, hard, vicious blows. Any reference to her disfigurement always infuriated her.

One of her aimless blows hit his elbow and he felt sick with sudden pain. He must stop this! He leapt from bed, as he was, in pants and semmit, and seized the broom handle. 'Stop it now, Mother! Stop it, for God's sake! D'ye hear me!' he shouted, pleading, at her crazed face. 'Have you gone mad? You'll hurt yourself!' But he could not wrest the brush from her, and he regarded, with horrified interest, her thin, red arms, amazed at her strength. Then rage gusted through him like a furnace blast. One good blow would settle her! He trembled, blinded by emotion, and let go his hold. She began receding from him as though from a ghost, walking slowly backwards holding the broom straight in front of her, terrified by the burning fixity of his gaze. He followed, slowly, ominously, with clenched fists. As she got round the lop-sided table, she darted from the room, slamming the door after her.

For several minutes he stood trembling and staring as if she was still there; then, aware that his bare feet were wet with the sodden tea-leaves she always threw down to lay the summer dust, he exclaimed: 'Ach, hell!' and stepped uncomfortably to the shallow window-bay, where his socks and trousers lay heaped on a chair. He pulled them and his boots on and sat regarding the street. Inflamed by a base desire to rush into the kitchen after her, he clapped his hands to his eyes. 'No! For Christ's sake! Not that!' His own mother! He ought to pity her and all warped people. A sense of the waste of life deeply affected him. One set of people embarrassed or bored by possessing much more than they needed, while others were continually distressed and dismayed by the lack of common human needs. Five years after the appalling waste of beautiful human energy and lives in war, he saw it still around him in slums, unemployment, preventable ignorance and disease.

Waste!

No one could call him a coward. He would have shouldered a rifle in a revolution. Let them whisper 'Coward' behind his back: none of them had the courage to step up and say it. But returned soldiers had said: 'Ah wish Ah'd had the pluck tae be a Conshy, like you, Johnny. It was four years of hell.' And those same men were unemployed, their lives as aimless and empty as his own. How gladly he would man any gun used to batter these tenements to the ground!

Why did he linger on here anyway? Some queer loyalty was keeping him, some faint hope of a return of the humble prosperity and friendliness and cheer that once had brightened this sad house. If only that recurring sickness did not afflict him. He would have adventured from here long ago. That two years' imprisonment, with underfeeding on bad food, had left him with some mysterious weakness. For days it disabled him; and these nights, crushed with three others in that bed it was impossible to sleep for the heat and the bugs.

He stood up vigorously and hustled into his waistcoat and jacket, trying, by activity, to divert his thoughts from their dark channel. What was the matter with him? He was only twenty-six and Life, fascinating, beautiful, waited for him to turn his youth to account.

He thought of going into the kitchen for a wash, but he knew she would set her tongue on him, and once more his feelings darkened. He looked at his collar and tie on the back of the chair. Why worry? Why bother putting them on! Why worry about anything? He strode into the lobby and met her waiting there, sullenly contrite. 'D'ye want ony breakfast, son?' she asked. He opened the door and passed out. 'I'm not hungry!' he cast back at her.

Ay, sure she would give him breakfast! he reflected as he turned out of the dark close into the main road. With his father and two brothers out of work like himself, bread and margarine and stewed tea was all the poor soul had to offer him this morning. And she would have nagged him like one of the Furies while he ate it. His heart turned back to her; he should never forget that she wasn't responsible for those mad fits; her nerves were fretted raw by worry and care; he believed she loved him, but he was aware that affection is a delicate thing, driven deep into people and lost behind the tough exterior they develop to face a sordid life.

Ach, if only he had a Woodbine! He raked his pockets for a stub. Across the street he saw a man stoop and pick a fag-end from the gutter, wipe it on his sleeve and stuff it into his clay pipe. His ache for a smoke tempted him to do the same, but with no food in him the idea made him squeamish. Never mind! He might get a few hours' casual work. Then his pockets would jingle!

The sky was sprinkled with gay clouds that sailed and shone as if there were no unemployment and slums in the world. At least he could smile at the sky! Perhaps the sea was like that today, limitless, deep azure, with ships roving about it like those clouds. He saw a cloud shaped like a swimming man with arms stretched in the breast-stroke. It sailed to a good wind, and he watched it awhile, wondering how long it would keep its form, till the wind tore it and bundled it into another shape. He laughed, and his heart stood up in him cheerful and fearless, his shoulders squared and he walked with manlier step.

From every by-street the sounds of the hordes of tenement children, on holiday these times, came to him; laughing and calling, each day they marvellously discovered happiness, like some lovely jewel, in the gutters and back courts of the big city. His soul joined with them as they sported and ran, and he was lightened with belief that war and poverty would sometime vanish away like an evil dream and that wakened Man would stand amazed at his blundering and turn to find happiness as simply and innocently as those ragged children were finding it now.

So exalted, he realised he had walked, without tiring, the four miles from his home to the docks. He entered the wide gates and strolled through crowds of idle dockers, vigorously discussing football, religion or politics in the assertive Scottish manner. Small chance of his getting work here! And even if he did, he would have to quit if the union delegate demanded to see his membership badge and card. But he was not saddened. The dazzled waters of the harbour immediately foiled his disappointment, and he inhaled the breath of travel and the smell of merchandise from the abounding light and heat. Flashing pinions curved in the blaze; he sensed them like a wreath around his head and smiled at the pigeons crooning their passion and quarrelling on the warehouse roofs, or seeking spilled grain and indian corn among the very feet of the men.

He watched a big tramp steamship manoeuvring into the first great basin. It was the only vessel there, and he recalled the prosperous days of the port, when every basin was so crowded with masts and funnels that it was hardly possible to row a dinghy between the herded ships. He sauntered around and, lifting his head to watch a wheeling gull, saw the towering masts and cross-trees of a sailing ship peering over the stern of a steamship. It was ten years since he had beheld a sailing ship and one of such a size as the height of those masts hinted she must be, and he almost ran towards her in delighted excitement.

He stood close and contemplated her with amazement as though she was a phantom which had sailed out of the past of buccaneers and pirates and which might at any moment fade from sight. She was a long, slim three-master, newly painted a pale blue, with the name *France* glittering in solid brass letters on her prow that pointed proudly at the bluff stern of the steamship like an upheld spear. She looked all too slender for her great calling; her spars were crowded white with resting gulls, still as sculptured birds, and as Regan gazed past them at the sky he was taken by desire to get a job on her.

He walked smartly up the gangway. There was apparently no one aboard, and he was elated by his solitary experience as he looked along the clean, bare decks where every hatch was battened down and everything stowed away. If only he might get work on her! That would be a manly break with the mean life of the tenements. Once he had faced the seas with her, he could never return to that life again. There was hardly a part of the ship he could have named, but he placed his hand fondly on her hot rail as though he had sailed with her for many years and knew her intimately. He leant over the side and saw hundreds of monkey-nuts floating, bright in the narrow space between the quay and ship. He had not noticed them when he hurried forward, with all his eyes for her, but now he saw them plentifully scattered about the dock and on the travelling crane, under which they shone like nuggets of gold on the coal-dust lying where a vessel had been coaled.

Monkey-nuts! They must have fallen from the hoisted sacks; they must have been her cargo; she had come from the tropics! His fancy wandered into passionate depths of tropical forests, he heard the chattering scream of monkeys, saw small bodies swing and little eyes flash in the green gloom; and he felt convinced that the tropic heat, soaked deep in her planks, was mounting from her decks through the soles of his feet into his body.

He turned to see an immensely tall, broad man in sea-going uniform stepping from a cabin away forrard. His heart bounded. Here was his chance! He walked towards him, summoning all his spirit to ask for a job, without the vaguest idea what to say, regretting his ignorance and inexperience of sea-life. The sailor, tanned and handsome, with blond hair gleaming under his officer's cap, stopped and looked dumbly at Regan, who felt most painfully at that moment the complete absence of breakfast in his belly. Trembling, he removed his cap and said shakily: 'Good-morning, sir! Do you need any sailors?' while he felt his blood scald his cheeks and seemed to himself the utterest fool alive. The officer stared a moment, then took a long, twisted black cheroot from his mouth and waved it vaguely about, as if taking in the whole harbour. 'All my grew iss 'ere!' he said. It was a Scandinavian voice. 'I haf no yobs! You haf been a sailor? Ya? No?' He replaced his cigar and stared stonily, then removed it and burst out with an uproarious laugh, pointing it at the dizzy masts: 'You could yoomp up there, ya? No, I sink you are yoost too schmall!'

Regan wanted to run off the ship. What a bloody fool he was! Fancy the likes of him expecting to get a berth, with hundreds of seasoned seamen unemployed! He felt mortified by the officer's scorn of his physique. He was the last and slightest of eight strong brothers, but he had never been regarded as a weakling.

'Hi!' The officer was calling him back, and hope flared up in him again. As he approached, the officer took a cheroot from his outside breast pocket and offered it silently, with a vast grin on his face. Regan accepted it and descended to the dock where he stuffed his pockets with monkey-nuts and sat on the big iron wheel of the crane eating them and flicking the shells over the quayside. He shrugged his shoulders. Ach, well! At least, he could admire the beauty of the ship if he couldn't sail with her! He loved the way her slim bows curved, like the flanks of a fawn. *France*: that was a light little name that suited her beautiful poise. He had heard it said that the Clyde would never see a windjammer again; that they had all been requisitioned, dismasted and turned into steamships for war service. And here was a lovely one whose decks he had walked!

When he was sick of monkey-nuts, he begged for a match from a passing docker and lit the black cheroot. It was pure tobacco leaf and he thought he had burned his throat out with the first inhalation, while his head swam and he coughed violently. He stubbed the cheroot out against the crane and put it in his pocket as a souvenir.

In this great basin, where there were only three ships, all the light of day appeared to be concentrated, and in the intense path of the sun floating seagulls vanished as if they were burned away, like the phoenix bird consumed by its own fire, and Regan blessed his luck for coming upon this ship in such glad weather.

The steamship was unloading a cargo of Canadian wheat, through an elevator projecting from her hold on to the warehouse roof. He went and leant against the sliding door of the shed and watched the wheat pour an aureate stream to the ground in a rising, golden hill. Then he saw a big, red-headed man descending the gangway of the wheat boat. It was 'Big' Willie McBride, the stevedore, who lived in his neighbourhood and picked up a living as a street bookmaker, when there was no work at the docks. 'Hi, young Regan, come 'ere!' he called. 'D'ye want a job?' he asked as Regan came over. 'It's light

work, shovellin' wheat for a couple o' days, an' worth thirty bob
tae ye?'

What luck! Regan smiled eagerly. 'You bet, Mac! Glad to get anything!
I'm skinned!'

McBride took him aboard the steamship and sent him down the hold,
where he was handed a light, flat-bedded wooden shovel and joined nine
other men, five of whom fed the endless belt of the elevator with wheat
while four others poured it into huge sacks which were tied, roped
together in fours and hoisted above by a steam-winch on deck.

Regan set-to shovelling the grain into the cups on the revolving belt.
It was stifling down here; very soon he breathed with great difficulty,
and his head was throbbing painfully when the ganger shouted: 'Come
on, boays! Up on deck for yer blow!' They climbed up and were replaced
by ten others. They could only work in shifts of half an hour, with
fifteen-minute spells on deck, as the wheat-dust clogged their throats
and nostrils, turning to paste in the moisture of breath.

At every turn on deck, Regan leant on the stern-rail and gazed down on
the *France*. One time, in the evening, the other men joined him, curious at
his quietness; and Paddy, a six-foot, handsome young Irishman, in dirty
flannels and a blue guernsey, said loudly: 'Take a good look at the old
hooker, me buckos, for she'll mebbe never come up the Clyde again!'
Someone said: 'Ay, it's three years sin' she was last here. D'ye ken her,
Paddy?' Paddy replied: 'Dew Oi know her! Shure Oi sailed wid that
same win'-jammer three years ago. Her skipper was a darlin' sailor an'
a dirthy slave-driver. A big, yella-haired Dane, he was, wid a wallop on
him like a steam-hammer. Shure Oi seen 'im knock a dago clean across
the deck wid a little flick uv the back uv his han'! She was a hell-ship,
I'm tellin' ye, an' her grub wasn't fit for pigs, so Oi left her at Ryo dee
Janeeraw an' sailed home to Belfast in a cattle-boat!' Regan, listening to
him, knew proudly that he would have sailed with her had he got the
chance, no matter how hard might be the life she gave him.

After midnight, when they all sat up on deck again, gratefully breathing
the sweet air, Regan blessed the *France* for his luck. Her holystoned
decks and every detail of her shone clear in the glow of the moon, as he
whispered down: 'Thanks, lovely ship, for getting me this day's work!'
Behind him, Paddy, who was tipsy, produced a bottle of whisky and
sat swigging and humming by himself. Someone said: 'Give us a song,
Paddy!' The Irishman stood up proudly, swaying, and passed the bottle
round. 'Shure, Oi'll give ye'se a song!' he shouted. 'Oi'll lift yer hearts
to the mouths of ye! Sing up, ye sods! Sing up!' They all laughed and
joined him, singing:

'Oh, whisky is the life of man,
Whisky, Johnny!
Oh, whisky murdered my old man,
So it's whisky for my Johnny!'

Regan turned and joined them. 'Shut up, everybody!' he cried. 'Let Paddy sing by himself! Give us a solo, Paddy,' he said. 'Do you know "Shenandoah"?' He realised that the Irishman had a fine voice, but he was spoiling it with the drink. He wanted to hear a song that would honour the sailing ship, a sad old song of the sea. Paddy stared at him in drunken amazement and cried thickly: 'Dew Oi know "Shenandjo"! Will ye'se listen to him? Dew Oi know "Shenandjo"! Shure Oi lisped it at me ole man's knee!' He began singing. The lovely old shanty gripped him, and he sang it seriously, with romantic sweetness:

'Oh Shenandoah, I long to see you,
Away, you rolling river!
Away! We're bound away,
Across the wide Missouri!'

Someone produced a mouth-organ and played it softly and well, and it sparkled in the moonlight.

'"Tis ten long years since last I saw thee,
Away, you rolling river! . . .'

From the ship across the basin a cook cast a pail of slop-water over the side. It flashed an instant tongue of silver and vanished in the dappled iridescence below, and the cook let the bucket dangle while he listened to the song quavering tenderly about the harbour. Regan was deeply moved. Ay, this was the song for a sailing ship! 'Shenandoah'. It was a poem in a name, and it sang of simple men who had travelled far, who carried pictures of relatives or sweethearts and were always promising to write home and always failing, men who had died abroad and never saw their homes again – the forgotten legions of wanderers in the long history of the sea. Ach, he must escape from the prison of the slums!

'Oh, Shenandoah, I love your daughter,
Away, you rolling river! . . .'

The big form of McBride suddenly loomed before them, and his mighty roar burst amid them like a thunderclap: 'Heh! Whit's this? A bloody tea-party? Get doon below, ye shower o' bastards! Yer spell's up ten meenits ago! Jump to it, ye lousy bunch o' scrimshankers!' They all scuttled down the hold, except Regan and Paddy, who, gleefully swinging his bottle, lurched into the stevedore, and the two big men faced each other. Highlander and Irishman, they were of a size and breadth, and they measured each other's splendid build with admiring, mocking eyes. Paddy offered McBride the bottle and the stevedore thrust it away. 'Tae hell wi' yer whisky, man! Ah've goat tae get the wheat oot o' this ship. Ah'll hiv a dram wi' ye efter that's done, no before!'

In spite of his hatred of the violence in himself, Regan sat watching, thrilled, expecting a fight. Paddy suddenly vented a great laugh and stumbled down the hold, shouting: 'Ach, we're buddies, Mac!' McBride shouted after him: 'Sure, we're buddies, but you buckle intae that wheat, sod ye!' Then he turned. 'Whit's the matter wi' you, Regan?' Regan jumped out of his trance. 'Okay, Mac! I thought there was going to be a scrap!' McBride laughed good-naturedly. 'Ach, Ah wouldnae scrap wi' Paddy. He's okay! Noo beat it doon below!'

All night the wheat hissed down the elevator chute and the steam-winch rattled, hoisting up the sacks. Then the flanges of the bulk-heads showed clear and the many tons of wheat sifted surely down till the floor of the hold was visible. Late in the next afternoon the elevator stopped, the last few hundredweights of wheat were hoisted up in sacks and run down the gangplank in trucks on to the dock, and the whole gang left the wheat-boat to be paid off in the warehouse. 'It's me for the boozer an' a bloody guid wet!' Regan heard some of them say as they went away with their money. For two days' and a night's work he had earned over thirty shillings. He thrust it into his pocket and went and sat on the wheel of the crane. He was very tired, his head ached, and he coughed up wheat-dust from his throat, while he gazed longingly at the sailing ship till dusk descended. He had decided what he would do. He would give his mother half of his earnings, buy himself a second-hand pair of strong boots and tramp to London with his few shillings. But not before he had watched the *France* sailing down the Clyde. When he had bade her farewell he would never return. She would speed to the ocean, he would take to the road, and with every mile that he walked his thoughts would follow her.

After supper he picked up the newspaper which his father had just laid down and his eye fell on the 'List of Sailings'. Only a dozen ships were listed, but with excitement he read that the *France* was sailing next day on the afternoon tide. He threw the paper aside and hunched by the fire, staring at the invisible, voyaging with a sailing ship, till his mother, fretted by his immobility, said: 'Whit are ye starin' at, Johnny? Ye look daft, glarin' like that! Ye should go oot tae the pictures or doon tae the chapel for an hoor. Ye hivnae been tae Mass since ye came hame fae London' – she was always ashamed to mention the word 'prison'. He rose and thrust past her. 'Ach, I'm tired!' he said and went into the parlour, undressed and lay down, wakeful a long while, thinking of the *France*.

At her hour of departure next day he was by her side, waiting while ropes were cast aboard her from the pilot-tug, watching every pause and turn she made in the great basin till her prow pointed away from the city. At last she set out, very slowly, in the wake of the tug, with that tall blond man prominent on her deck, shouting instructions, the man who had given him the cheroot. Regan took that out and looked at it, and the keepsake seemed to bind him to her more as he followed along the dockside till his way was barred. Then he hurried out to the road and jumped on a tram and rode till he came to another free part of the river, and stood on the shore waiting till she came up. This way, riding on trams and buses, he followed her slow progress, while his heart grew sadder with every mile that she sailed beyond Glasgow. The flood was opening wider for her, the shores receding; she was leaving the grand little river, with its long and plucky history of shipmaking, maybe for ever. He recalled the Irishman's words. He would never see her again!

At the end he took a bus out to Dumbarton and stood on the shore nearby the great Rock. He saw the tug leave her and turn towards home with a hoot of farewell from its siren, like the cry of a timid friend deserting a gay adventurer. Then, like a gallant gesture, she unfurled all her sails and made her beauty terrible for his eyes. She was lovelier far than he had seen her yet as she came slowly on like a floating bird unfolding its wings for flight. She had a dream-like loveliness, and as she came opposite where he stood alone, he impulsively tore off his cap and waved it, then threw it on the ground and stood with his head proudly up, ennobled by her grace.

Sunset met her like a song of praise and his heart went after her as she rippled past. Ach, if he could only have served her on her last few voyages, before she was dismasted and broken up! She dipped slowly into the dying sun and the waters fanned out from her bows like flowing blood. Then the sun went swiftly down and her beauty was buried in the darkness. 'Goodbye, lovely ship!' he called after her. 'Goodbye! Goodbye, *France*!'

So ecstatic was his concentration upon that vanishing ship that he felt her decks quiver under his feet, saw her high spars tremble, heard the flap of her sails, as he gazed with uplifted head. He was sailing on, away from unemployment and slums and wretchedness, far from the ignorance and misunderstanding of his parents, to the infinite nobility of the sea! His eyes were moist, his hands in his pockets painfully clenched, his limbs shook like a saint's in the ardour of prayer. And for a long time he stood there bareheaded, unaware that darkness, with small rain and a cold wind, had enveloped his transported body.

'Maiden Voyage'

from Adventures in Two Worlds

A.J. CRONIN (1896–1981)

Archibald Joseph Cronin had a career as a novelist which we now see as a foretaste, or perhaps an omen, of the best-sellers of our part of the century. He perfected a kind of 'middlebrow fiction' which attracted a multitude of readers and which presented storylines in dramatic settings that lent themselves readily to adaptation by a string of movie-makers – in just such a way as his often inferior successors today produce the raw material for television 'mini-series'. In The Citadel, *for example, he highlighted issues about public health and private medicine in a dramatic fashion which led to important debate and action. Even the Doctor Finlay stories were not without a strand of social comment at the time.*

This chapter from Adventures in Two Worlds *is similar in that he brings in the racist remarks of the 'first class passengers' as a startling beginning to his almost Conrad-like description of a young doctor's first voyage on 'the* Ranaganji', *sailing from Liverpool to Calcutta. Cronin had taken a similar voyage after graduating from Glasgow University; here, as in much of his work, the veneer of fiction is thin, with only names like Winton, for Glasgow, to distinguish the story from reality. Curiously, another more distinguished Scots novelist, Tobias Smollett, was born in Dumbartonshire, became a doctor and made a reputation from writing about a sea journey.*

'Look, my dear! Did you ever in your life see such an absurdly comic creature!'

A smartly dressed woman, first-class passenger on the *Ranaganji*, about to sail from Liverpool on the long voyage to Calcutta, made this remark, in a high, 'well-bred' voice, to her companion, a young man with a military yet foppish air, as they stood before me on the liner's upper deck. Following their amused gaze, my eyes came to rest upon a squat, very ugly native seaman, with short legs and a large disproportionate head, scarred by a cicatrice which ran from ear to temple, whom I recognized as the Indian *serang*, or quartermaster of the ship. He was quietly superintending the crew of lascars now completing the loading of baggage into the hold from the Mersey lighter alongside.

'Looks hardly human,' agreed the man of Mars, twisting his embryo moustache, with a superior smile. 'Inclines a chap to believe, don't you know, that dear old Darwin was not altogether wrong . . . what?'

I turned away silently and went below to my cabin. Three weeks before, to my inexpressible joy, I had taken my medical degree. Never shall I forget that breathless moment when, in a fever of anxiety and suspense, scanning the list pinned upon the University notice board, knowing that my small store of money was finally exhausted, that I had neither the funds nor the energy to repeat that culminating effort – sitting up night after night over my textbooks with a wet towel round my forehead till the crack of dawn – I discovered, not only that I had passed, but that the examining board had given me honours as well. Nor am I ashamed to confess to the moisture that rushed into my eyes, almost blinding me, although 'Doggy' Chisholm, who stood beside me and who had also passed, commented ironically as he gripped my hand.

'Slight lachrymal-gland activity this morning, Doctor. May I prescribe a hundredth of atropine? Or a good glass of beer?'

He could afford to be lighthearted. His father, provost of Winton, owned the Laughlan steelworks.

And then, as if this were not enough, I had been fortunate enough, through the good offices of my old chief, Professor Stockman, to be appointed temporary ship's doctor on the S.S. *Ranaganji*. While he was putting me through my medical 'oral' Stockman had decided that I was extremely run down, that the trip to India and back would set me up again.

The voyage began favourably in calm, clear weather. We crossed the Bay of Biscay without suffering unduly from the turbulent waters of that shallow sea and soon were through the Strait of Gibraltar, traversing the tranquil Mediterranean under azure skies. The *Ranaganji* was a stout old tub, manned by white officers, with an entirely native Indian crew. She had done fine work in the war, but since her coal-burning engines had not been lately reconditioned, she was exceedingly slow – capable, indeed, of a bare ten knots. This, however, was no defect to the young physician, for whom every day of balmy breezes, of brilliant sunshine and entrancing novelty – swift visions of foam-girt islands, the mysterious African coastline, distant white-walled villages, porpoises gambolling in the creamy wake – was an added source of sheer delight.

The ship was crowded, packed with passengers from stem to stern. Transportation had been impossible for the four years of hostilities, and with the restoration of peace everyone wanted to travel, not only the usual tourists and pleasure seekers, but businessmen tied up at home for many months by D.O.R.A. regulations, cotton and jute merchants bound for Calcutta and Bhagalpur, Ceylon tea planters and Cawnpore mill owners, together with a large number of Anglo-Indian army officers, many of whom were accompanied by their wives and families.

From the first night out there was tremendous gaiety on board. This was the beginning of that postwar era when, after the murderous holocaust of the trenches, the years of slaughter, mud, and misery, of anxiety, frustration, and fear, the world suddenly went mad and, like a revivified corpse, embarked on a wild and frantic spree. Lunch and cocktail parties, sweepstakes on the ship's run, 'horse racing' and deck sports of every kind, impromptu concerts and fancy-dress galas – these were but a few of the diversions afforded by these halcyon days and feverish nights. For such junkets the ship's doctor is always in demand, and although my inclination lay to more meditative ways, I was usually drawn into the festivities.

Chief among the social promoters – those people who on shipboard excel at 'getting things up' – was Miss Jope-Smith, the woman whom I had overheard on the boat deck the morning of our departure and who, with her brother, Ronald, a cavalry subaltern posted to Bengal, sat, unfortunately, at my table in the dining saloon. Madge Jope-Smith was a thrusting person, handsome in a hard sort of way, obviously over thirty, though got up in a dashing style to look younger. She was not only a snob but a bore, an assertive bore, who talked incessantly of her 'place' in Cheltenham, her titled friends, her 'personal maid', her horses, dogs, and exploits in the field of fox-hunting – though I suspected that her quarry in the chase, whom, to her infinite chagrin, she had not so far brought to bay, was man. Never at any meal did she fail to inform us of how welcome she would be in the best society of Peshawar and Darjeeling. Arising from the prospect of her sojourn in India, the leitmotif of her conversation, reduced to its elemental note, was the superiority of the English upper classes and the need for impressing this upon the subject native races. She constantly abused the table steward, a nice Parsee boy who was well-meaning but slow, and having scolded him into complete confusion, she would cast her bold glance around the table.

'These people have to be kept down, you know. Don't you agree, Ronnie?'

'By Jove, yes.' Her brother, quite innocuous, was a dependable echo. 'You're absolutely right.'

'If you let them get away with it, there's no knowing what ideas they'd get in their heads.'

'Yes, by Jove. I mean, well, after all . . ., remember how we had to shoot them down in the Mutiny.'

'Exactly. Now I'm a liberal-minded woman. But they're such a poor lot at best. Not an ounce of stamina. No loyalty. And treacherous, too . . . Why, I remember Colonel Bentley once told me . . .'

We reached Port Said. Everyone went ashore, excitedly, came back loaded with purchases from Simon Artz, with silks, shawls, cigarettes, scent, and jewellery. That night, as the anchor was weighed and we glided past the De Lesseps statue into the snaky waters of the Suez Canal, the orchestra played louder than ever, the dance waxed faster and more furious. The desert reached away on either hand, camels and Bedouin encampments were silhouetted against the purple sunset. Then we were through the Red Sea, past the barren rocks of Aden, and out upon the wide Arabian Sea.

On the following morning, as I held my consultations in the surgery adjoining my cabin, the *serang*, Hasan, appeared, bringing with him two of his lascar deck hands. Waiting in the doorway until I bade him enter, he inclined his head in a respectful salaam and addressed me. His voice, as if broken long ago in its conflict with the roar of wind and water, was hoarse, yet it had a steady undertone.

'Doctor Sahib, I fear these men are sick.'

The seamen certainly did not look well; they complained of general malaise, of intense headache and racking bone pains. They looked frightened, too, as though suspecting something serious to be amiss, rolling the whites of their eyes as I asked them to strip and began my examination. Both were fevered, with thickly furred tongues and that dry skin, burning to the touch, which is nature's gravest warning. As yet there was no sign of lung involvement. No inflammation of the throat. Nothing abnormal in the abdomen. Instinctively I thought of malaria. And then, to my horror, as I once again took the pulse, my palpitating fingers became aware of a scattering of hard little nodules, exactly like lead shot, under the wrist skin of each man. It was an unmistakable symptom, and immediately, inspecting more closely the areas behind the knees and beneath the armpits, I found in each case a definite papular eruption.

Young and inexperienced in my profession, I had not learned to control my feelings, nor had I yet acquired that dissimulation which masks the sentence of death with a comforting smile. My expression must have altered visibly, for although the *serang* said nothing, his lined and battered face assumed a look of deeper gravity. For a moment I looked into his eyes, and even then, while realising that he knew as well as I the nature of the malady before us, I could not but experience, as a kind of shock, the resolution, the intrepid calmness of his gaze. Still he said nothing. When I told him in a low voice to wait in the surgery with the men, he again simply inclined his head.

Hurriedly, with beating heart, I made my way to the bridge. Captain Hamble was not there, but in the chartroom below. He looked up sharply as I burst in.

'Sir' – my voice broke – 'I have to report smallpox on board. Two of the deck hands.'

I saw his lips draw tightly together. He was a thickset man of fifty-five, with close-cropped hair and sandy, bushy eyebrows, known as a strict disciplinarian, something of a martinet, but also as a just and fair-minded officer. Now his brick-dust complexion assumed a deeper tinge.

'Smallpox.' He repeated the word under his breath. 'You're sure?'

'Quite, sir.' And I added, 'We have no lymph in our medical supplies.'

'Would we carry enough for fifteen hundred passengers? Don't be a fool!'

He bit his lip angrily and, frowning deeply, began to pace up and down the narrow chartroom.

'Doctor,' he said, drawing up at last and coming close to me, his words unmistakably grim, 'forget that remark of mine . . . I was upset and didn't mean it. Now, listen, you are in charge of the health of the ship. It's entirely up to you. I can't give you any of my officers; I'm overloaded and understaffed. But I am going to give you the *serang*. He understands these fellows. And believe me, he's the finest man I have. Between you, you've got to keep this thing from spreading. And what's more, don't let a whisper of it get out, or with this fancy lot we have on board we'll have a bloody panic, as sure as God's my Maker.'

I left the chartroom, realising, with a weakness in my stomach, the desperate responsibility of my position. Gone now was the carefree ease I had enjoyed, reclining in a deck chair reading Pierre Loti and dreaming romantically into the sunset of my own secret desire to write, treating nothing more serious than a cut finger or a case of mild seasickness. Here we were, in the middle of the Arabian Sea, fifteen hundred passengers aboard, no means whatever of vaccinating them, and smallpox. . . . The most deadly contagion in the whole dictionary of disease.

Back in the surgery one of the lascars was in the grip of a violent rigor.
I turned from the shivering man to the *serang*, whose incalculable eyes
remained fixed upon me.

'You know?' I asked him.

'Yes, Sahib. I have seen this before.'

'We've got to isolate these men . . ., check on the contacts. . . .' As
I spoke, trying to assume a cheerfulness and confidence I did not feel,
Hasan quietly acquiesced.

'Yes, Sahib . . . I shall do what I can to help you.'

There was no sick bay on board, not an inch of available cabin
space. One look at the crowded forecastle showed the impossibility of
sergregating the infected men anywhere in the crew's quarters. Baffled,
I looked at the *serang*, who, undismayed, again turned upon me the full
force of his eyes.

'We will make a shelter on the afterdeck, Doctor Sahib. Very cool
there. With plenty of fresh air.'

In the stern of the ship, admirably protected from view by a battery
of derricks and donkey engines, he set to work, moving about, squat
and noiseless, his powerful head and long pliant arms conveying the
same impression of strength and composure that was reflected upon his
flattened and misshapen face. Within an hour, he had erected, with silent
efficiency, a large canvas shelter, tautly secured, and roped off from the
surrounding deck. Mattresses and sheets were then brought up and the
two patients comfortably installed.

Our next step was to muster the crew for a thorough medical inspection. One of the stokers, who complained of fever and headache, showed
the prodromal nodules with the beginnings of the typical rash. He was
isolated with the other cases.

'And now . . . who is going to help me attend to these men?'

Hasan glanced at me in surprise.

'Why, naturally it is I.'

'You must be careful. This disease is most contagious.'

The *serang*, had he known me better, might perhaps have smiled. As
it was, the austerity of his expression did not relax.

'I am not afraid, Doctor Sahib.'

Together, Hasan and I sponged the patients with permanganate solution, administered to each man a strong antipyretic, hung sheets soaked
in disinfectant round the shelter, and set up within this little secret area
of quarantine a cooking stove where liquids could be heated and simple
meals prepared. Finally, while the passengers were at lunch, we cleared
the night watch from the forecastle and, with some sulphur candles which

Hasan disinterred from the ship's stores, thoroughly fumigated the crew's quarters. With this accomplished, I felt somewhat easier in my mind.

Next morning, however, brought fresh cause for concern. At the muster which I held at daybreak, I found three fresh cases among the deck hands. The men already segregated were much worse, covered from head to toe by that foul purulent eruption which is the most horrible symptom of the disease. And that same afternoon, four more of the crew sickened. We now had ten cases in our makeshift lazaretto. It was a situation to test the strongest nerves. But the *serang*, calm and unperturbed, his eyes steadfast beneath the misshapen frontal bones of his dark, cicatrised face, gave me fresh heart. Merely to be beside him made it difficult to despair. In tending the patients he was indefatigable; giving them water, relieving their intolerable skin irritation with the lotion I had made up, cooking for them in the makeshift galley, always on hand when I needed him to help me lift and sponge a semi-conscious man – and all this carried out with complete and contemptuous disregard for his own safety.

'Be careful of yourself,' I had to beg him. 'Do not go quite so close.'

Now indeed, he showed his strong teeth, stained pink with betel nut, in a sudden, fleeting smile . . . yet a smile so faint, so transitory and, above all, tinged with such native sadness that it broke only for an instant his deep and natural tranquillity.

'Are you careful of yourself, Doctor Sahib?'

'Indeed I am. Besides, this is my work.'

'Do not worry, Doctor Sahib. I am strong. And it is my work too.'

By this time, except for emergency calls, I had placed myself more or less in quarantine. At the captain's suggestion, to allay suspicion, it was given out that I had caught a chill and was indisposed. I ceased to go to the dining saloon, and all my meals were brought on a tray to my cabin. In the evening, as I sat at my solitary dinner, hearing the music of the string band and the sway and shuffle of the dancers on the deck above, it was difficult to restrain a mood of bitterness. In that frenetic whirl, how little they guessed their danger! There came to my mind Barbey d'Aurevilly's tale of the *bal masqué* held by the French king at Avignon, whither the court had retired to escape the pestilence prevailing in Paris, and where, at the height of the gaiety, when all unmasked themselves, a gaunt stranger stood revealed in their midst, bearing on his hectic features the fatal stigmata of the Black Death. With equal morbidness I watched my own person for the first sign of the disease, not from fear – oddly, I was so weighed down by responsibility that I had slight concern for myself – but with a queer detachment and the conviction that I would contract the malady; fatally, no doubt, since I had not been vaccinated since I was a child. And in this state of heightening tension I cursed the slowness of the ship, that lack of speed which had previously given me cause for satisfaction. Although we were moving full steam ahead, Colombo, the nearest port of call, was still eight days away.

Twice a day I reported to the captain. His anxiety, without doubt, far exceeded mine, but his years and the habit of command helped him to control it. When he heard what I had to tell him he nodded once or twice, considering me with harassed, irascible eyes, seeming almost to look beyond me to his board of company directors in distant Liverpool. Then, dismissing me, he forced out a word of encouragement:

'Good. You're doing all right. See you keep it up.'

But could we keep it up? In the course of the next forty-eight hours first one, then three more of the stokers, who had been suspect overnight, went to join the others on the afterdeck. A total of fourteen now. And one of the earlier victims had lapsed into coma, seemed likely to die at any hour. Under this added load, I could not sleep, and though I spent most of the daylight hours in the lazaretto, even at night I could not keep away from the stern of the ship. And there, where I knew I should find him, watchful and mute under the stars, was the *serang*.

How shall I describe the solace which flowed toward me from him as he stood there, in meditation, brooding rather, silhouetted against the taffrail, with his long arms folded on his bare chest, motionless as a statue? A silver whistle, symbol of his office, hung by a lanyard from his muscular neck. The tropic moon, rolling in the velvet sky, brought out the deep lines on his face which, despite its latent energy, had the immobility of carved ebony. When a sick man groaned faintly with the pain of his tormented universe, he would step forward, without sound, to succour him. And then, returning, he would fold his arms, while the ship, an atom detached from earth and lost upon the ocean, surged slowly forward.

He had no fondness for speech. But despite the silences of our long night vigils I gathered, gradually, some fragments of his history. He was from the Punjab, whence his parents, sturdy and nomadic Pathans, had wandered to southern India. There, like so many in that coastal area, he had, as a boy, taken to a seafaring life. For nearly forty years he had given himself to the oceans of the world, and fifteen of these years had been spent in the *Ranaganji*. Small wonder he regarded the old ship as his home. Indeed, he had no other, no place on shore, neither family nor friends in the great land mass of India. He had never married. The tackle block which, falling from the masthead, had so frightfully broken and disfigured his features had turned his thoughts from women.

By religion he was a Jain, yet there was in him something far beyond the teaching of the sects, a faith inculcated by the purifying eternal wind, the beauty and the desolation of great waters, by waves pounding on grey rocks, on palm-fringed beaches, by blue-white snow upon distant mountain peaks, lush jungles steaming in the tropic sunset, by the united mysteries of a thousand landfalls and departures.

In all his life he had acquired nothing, neither property nor money – his few possessions, contained in his ship chest, might be worth a few rupees. The thought hurt me, and in an access of mistaken sympathy, I exclaimed:

'Hasan, you are doing so much in this emergency, the company must give you extra pay.'

His forehead creased perplexedly. He was silent for a long moment, a disconcerting silence broken only by the slow thud of the propeller shaft and the wheezing rattle of the sick. Then he answered:

'What use is money, Doctor Sahib, to one who has all he needs? I am well enough the way I am.'

He was unmistakably sincere, completely detached from the usual hope of reward, austerely contemptuous of all personal advantage. Money had no interest for him, he had always despised it. He knew none of those feverish desires with which it is inseparably linked. Instead he had courage, self-control, and faith. The men he worked among lived poor and died poor. It had become the habit of his mind to disregard tomorrow.

Standing with him, in the liquid moonlight, I was stung by a strange pang. Beside his clear simplicity the world's values suddenly seemed dross. A great party had started in the saloon, brilliantly illuminated by coloured electric globes. The raised voices and bursts of laughter, the popping of champagne corks, the incessant backward drift of jazz intensified in me the feeling that mankind had sacrificed the spirit for the flesh, had become sapped of virtue, dreading any prospect not insulated by ease, by the smug protection that can be bought with gold.

Indeed, as I viewed my own outlook toward the future, my passionate desire for success and wealth, I was conscious of a secret shame. I turned my back upon the tumult and from the milky white sea beyond, from the sighing emptiness of the night, there came to me the echo of those immortal words: 'O ye of little faith! Take no thought, saying, What shall we eat? or, What shall we drink? or, Where withal shall we be clothed?'

On the following day we lost two of our patients. It was Hasan himself who sewed their shrouds, who in his hoarse and hollow voice read aloud a short passage from the Ramayana before their bodies, wrapped in sailcloth, with a weight at their feet, were cast overboard at midnight.

No fresh cases developed. And a week later, in the sulphurous light of early dawn, we anchored off Colombo, the Cingalese port doctor and officials came aboard, all formalities were completed. Before the first of the passengers was awake, the yellow flag had been lowered and the sick men taken off to hospital. Several of the patients showed signs of having passed the crisis, but three, helpless and delirious, a mass of running sores, were carried to the lighter, like children, in the arms of Hasan. As we stood together, watching the flat launch bobbing towards the shore, I saw that the *serang*'s dark cheeks were wet with tears.

Our passage through the Bay of Bengal was brief and uneventful. I had barely time to recover myself, or to realise that the epidemic had been confined, before we had navigated the mud flats of the Hoogli and were anchored alongside the quay at Calcutta. A general celebration marked our arrival – sirens blowing, favours floating in the breeze, final rounds of drinks, the decks crowded with people waving and shouting greetings to friends meeting them on the dock. Suddenly, at my elbow, I heard the familiar shrilling of Miss Jope-Smith.

'Oh, look, look, Ronnie. There's that absurd creature again.'

Once more I followed their united gaze. And there, again, down in the afterhold, knocking out the hatch battens to unload the baggage, his squat figure foreshortened from above, with long arms swinging, more ungainly than ever, was the object of their mirth – Hasan.

The huntress from Cheltenham swung round, bent her wit, her fascinations upon me.

'Where did you keep him all the voyage, Doctor dear? In a special cage?'

Silence – a vision of the *serang*'s nobility rising before me.

'Yes. . . , in a way. . . it was a cage. . . But isn't it queer, Miss Jope-Smith – the animals were all outside.'

Though I kept my voice even, I thought that I should suffocate. Abruptly I turned away, went below to my cabin, and beat my clenched fists hard against the wooden bulkhead.

'The Skyeman'

from Mardi

HERMAN MELVILLE (1819–91)

At the time I now write of, we must have been something more than sixty degrees to the west of the Gallipagos. And having attained a desirable longitude, we were standing northward for our arctic destination: around us one wide sea.

But due west, though distant a thousand miles, stretched north and south an almost endless Archipelago, here and there inhabited, but little known; and mostly unfrequented, even by whalemen, who go almost everywhere. Beginning at the southerly termination of this great chain, it comprises the islands loosely known as Ellice's Group; then, the Kingsmill Isles; then, the Radack and Mulgrave clusters. These islands had been represented to me as mostly of coral formation, low and fertile, and abounding in a variety of fruits. The language of the people was said to be very similar to that of the Navigator Islands, from which their ancestors are supposed to have emigrated.

And thus much being said, all has been related that I then knew of the islands in question. Enough, however, that they existed at all; and that our path thereto lay over a pleasant sea, and before a reliable Trade wind. The distance, though great, was merely an extension of water; so much blankness to be sailed over; and in a craft, too, that properly managed has been known to outlive great ships in a gale. For this much is true of a whale-boat, the cunningest thing in its way ever fabricated by man.

Upon one of the Kingsmill Islands, then, I determined to plant my foot, come what come would. And I was equally determined that one of the ship's boats should float me thither. But I had no idea of being without a companion. It would be a weary watch to keep all by myself, with naught but the horizon in sight.

Now, among the crew was a fine old seaman, one Jarl; how old, no one could tell, not even himself. Forecastle chronology is ever vague and defective. 'Man and boy,' said honest Jarl, 'I have lived ever since I can remember.' And truly, who may call to mind when he was not? To ourselves, we all seem coeval with creation. Whence it comes, that it is so hard to die, ere the world itself is departed.

Jarl hailed from the isle of Skye, one of the constellated Hebrides. Hence, they often called him the Skyeman. And though he was far from being piratical of soul, he was yet an old Norseman to behold. His hands were brawny as the paws of a bear; his voice hoarse as a storm roaring round the old peak of Mull; and his long yellow hair waved round his head like a sunset. My life for it, Jarl, thy ancestors were Vikings, who many a time sailed over the salt German sea and the Baltic; who wedded their Brynhildas in Jutland; and are now quaffing mead in the halls of Valhalla, and beating time with their cans to the hymns of the Scalds. Ah! how the old Sagas run through me!

Yet Jarl, the descendant of heroes and kings, was a lone, friendless mariner on the main, only true to his origin in the sea-life that he led. But so it had been, and forever will be. What yeoman shall swear that he is not descended from Alfred? what dunce, that he is not sprung of old Homer? King Noah, God bless him! fathered us all. Then hold up your heads, oh ye Helots, blood potential flows through your veins. All of us have monarchs and sages for kinsmen; nay, angels and archangels for cousins; since in antediluvian days, the sons of God did verily wed with our mothers, the irresistible daughters of Eve. Thus all generations are blended: and heaven and earth of one kin: the hierarchies of seraphs in the uttermost skies; the thrones and principalities in the zodiac; the shades that roam throughout space; the nations and families, flocks and folds of the earth; one and all, brothers in essence – oh, be we then brothers indeed! All things form but one whole; the universe a Judea, and God Jehovah its head. Then no more let us start with affright. In a theocracy, what is to fear? Let us compose ourselves to death as fagged horsemen sleep in the saddle. Let us welcome even ghosts when they rise. Away with our stares and grimaces. The New Zealander's tattooing is not a prodigy; nor the Chinaman's ways an enigma. No custom is strange; no creed is absurd; no foe, but who will in the end prove a friend. In heaven, at last, our good, old, white-haired father Adam will greet all alike, and sociality forever prevail. Christian shall join hands between Gentile and Jew; grim Dante forget his Infernos, and shake sides with fat Rabelais; and monk Luther, over a flagon of old nectar, talk over old times with Pope Leo. Then shall we sit by the sages, who of yore gave laws to the Medes and Persians in the sun; by the cavalry captains in Perseus, who cried, 'To horse!' when waked by their Last Trump sounding to the charge; by the old hunters, who, eternities ago, hunted the moose in Orion; by the minstrels, who sang in the Milky Way when Jesus our Saviour was born. Then shall we list to no shallow gossip of Magellans and Drakes; but give ear to the voyagers who have circumnavigated the Ecliptic; who rounded the Polar Star as Cape Horn. Then shall the Stagirite and Kant be forgotten, and another folio than theirs be turned over for wisdom; even the folio now spread with horoscopes as yet undeciphered, the heaven of heavens on high.

Now, in old Jarl's lingo there was never an idiom. Your aboriginal tar is too much of a cosmopolitan for that. Long companionship with seamen of all tribes: Manillamen, Anglo-Saxons, Cholos, Lascars, and Danes, wear away in good time all mother-tongue stammerings. You sink your clan; down goes your nation; you speak a world's language, jovially jabbering in the Lingua-Franca of the forecastle.

True to his calling, the Skyeman was very illiterate; witless of Salamanca, Heidelberg, or Brazen-Nose; in Delhi, had never turned over the books of the Brahmins. For geography, in which sailors should be adepts, since they are forever turning over and over the great globe of globes, poor Jarl was deplorably lacking. According to his view of the matter, this terraqueous world had been formed in the manner of a tart; the land being a mere marginal crust, within which rolled the watery world proper. Such seemed my good Viking's theory of cosmography. As for other worlds, he weened not of them; yet full as much as Chrysostom.

Ah, Jarl! an honest, earnest wight; so true and simple, that the secret operations of thy soul were more inscrutable than the subtle workings of Spinoza's.

Thus much be said of the Skyeman; for he was exceedingly taciturn, and but seldom will speak for himself.

Now, higher sympathies apart, for Jarl I had a wonderful liking; for he loved me; from the first had cleaved to me.

It is sometimes the case, that an old mariner like him will conceive a very strong attachment for some young sailor, his shipmate; an attachment so devoted, as to be wholly inexplicable, unless originating in that heart-loneliness which overtakes most seamen as they grow aged; impelling them to fasten upon some chance object of regard. But however it was, my Viking, thy unbidden affection was the noblest homage ever paid me. And frankly, I am more inclined to think well of myself, as in some way deserving thy devotion, than from the rounded compliments of more cultivated minds.

Now, at sea, and in the fellowship of sailors, all men appear as they are. No school like a ship for studying human nature. The contact of one man with another is too near and constant to favour deceit. You wear your character as loosely as your flowing trowsers. Vain all endeavours to assume qualities not yours; or to conceal those you possess. Incognitos, however desirable, are out of the question. And thus aboard of all ships in which I have sailed, I have invariably been known by a sort of drawing-room title. Not – let me hurry to say – that I put hand in tar bucket with a squeamish air, or ascended the rigging with a Chesterfieldian mince. No, no, I was never better than my vocation; and mine have been many. I showed as brown a chest, and as hard a hand, as the tarriest tar of them all. And never did shipmate of mine upbraid me with a genteel disinclination to duty, though it carried me to truck of mainmast, or jib-boom-end, in the most wolfish blast that ever howled.

Whence, then, this annoying appellation? for annoying it most assuredly was. It was because of something in me that could not be hidden; stealing out in an occasional polysyllable; an otherwise incomprehensible deliberation in dining; remote, unguarded allusions to Belles-Lettres affairs; and other trifles superfluous to mention.

But suffice it to say, that it had gone abroad among the *Arcturion*'s crew, that at some indefinite period of my career I had been a 'nob'. But Jarl seemed to go further. He must have taken me for one of the House of Hanover in disguise; or, haply, for bonneted Charles Edward the Pretender, who, like the Wandering Jew, may yet be a vagrant. At any rate, his loyalty was extreme. Unsolicited, he was my laundress and tailor; a most expert one, too; and when at meal-times my turn came round to look out at the mast-head, or stand at the wheel, he catered for me among the 'kids' in the forecastle with unwearied assiduity. Many's the good lump of 'duff' for which I was indebted to my good Viking's good care of me. And like Sesostris I was served by a monarch. Yet in some degree the obligation was mutual. For be it known that, in sea-parlance, we were *chummies*.

Now this *chummying* among sailors is like the brotherhood subsisting between a brace of collegians (chums) rooming together. It is a Fides-Achates-ship, a league of offence and defence, a co-partnership of chests and toilets, a bond of love and good feeling, and a mutual championship of the absent one. True, my nautical reminiscences remind me of sundry lazy, ne'er-do-well, unprofitable, and abominable chummies; chummies, who at meal-times were last at the 'kids', when their unfortunate partners were high upon the spars; chummies, who affected awkwardness at the needle, and conscientious scruples about dabbling in the suds; so that chummy the simple was made to do all the work of the firm, while chummy the cunning played the sleeping partner in his hammock. Out upon such chummies!

But I appeal to thee, honest Jarl, if I was ever chummy the cunning. Never mind if thou didst fabricate my tarpaulins; and with Samaritan charity bind up the rents, and pour needle and thread into the frightful gashes that agonised my hapless nether integuments, which thou calledst 'ducks'; – didst thou not expressly declare that all these things, and more, thou wouldst do for me, despite my own quaint thimble, fashioned from the ivory tusk of a whale? Nay; could I even wrest from thy wilful hands my very shirt, when once thou hadst it steaming in an unsavoury pickle in thy capacious vat, a decapitated cask? Full well thou knowest, Jarl, that these things are true; and I am bound to say it, to disclaim any lurking desire to reap advantage from thy great good-nature.

Now my Viking for me, thought I, when I cast about for a comrade; and my Viking alone.

5

PERILS OF THE SEA

Scotland has had its share of maritime tragedy to temper her proud record of maritime innovation and adventurous seafaring. Some of these tragedies are etched on the national consciousness – the loss of 189 fishermen from Eyemouth and other east coast fishing ports in the great disaster of 1881, the sinking of the Clyde-built car-ferry *Princess Victoria* in the North Channel with the loss of 128 lives in 1953, the sinking of the newly launched *Daphne* on the Clyde in 1883 and more recently the Piper Alpha oil-rig disaster in 1988, with the loss of 167 lives.

Our extracts are, in general, less harrowing than these, although the anonymous ballad *The Lowlands of Holland* is a reminder of the price that the sea can extract, both from the seafarer and those who wait, on land, for their return. The lines in Carolina Oliphant, Lady Nairne's *Caller Herrin*':

> Wives and mithers, maist despairin',
> Ca' them lives o' men

movingly remind us of the price paid for even this 'vulgar fairin''.

The dangers of war at sea are dealt with elsewhere – in this section we look at storms, shipwrecks and marooning. Marooning, as we are told by Robert Louis Stevenson in *Treasure Island*, was a

> . . . horrible kind of punishment common enough among the buccaneers, in which the offender is put ashore with a little powder and shot, and left behind on some desolate and distant island.

Marooning was a dread fate – Ben Gunn tells Jim Hawkins he had

> . . . lived on goats since then, and berries, and oysters. Wherever a man is, says I, a man can do for himself. But, mate, my heart is sore for Christian diet. You mightn't happen to have a piece of cheese about you, now? No? Well, many's the long night I've dreamed of cheese – toasted, mostly – and woke up again, and here I were.

Reflecting the world-wide influence of the Scottish seaman the locales range from pirate water and the coral atolls of the Pacific to the more familiar perils to be found in home waters.

Some reports of maritime accidents and sinkings bring home in a very special way the sense of personal loss and individual tragedy – few more poignantly than the report of the recovery of bodies from the collision of the *Ayr* and *Comet II* steamboats off Greenock in 1825. One of the unidentified bodies recovered from the Clyde was

A stout young woman, unknown; had on a brown bombazine gown, coarse grey worsted stockings, and shoes tied with white tape, supposed to have come on at Oban, and then to have had on a black bonnet and two black feathers.

The Lowlands of Holland

ANONYMOUS

My love has built a bonnie ship, and set her on the sea,
With seven score good mariners to bear her company.
There's three score is sunk, and three score dead at sea;
And the Lowlands of Holland has twined my love and me.

My love he built another ship, and set her on the main,
And nane but twenty mariners for to bring her hame;
But the weary wind began to rise, and the sea began to rout;
My love then, and his bonnie ship, turned withershins about.

There shall neither coif come on my head, nor comb come in my hair;
There shall neither coal nor candle-licht shine in my bower mair;
Nor will I love another one until the day I die,
For I never loved a love but ane, and he's drown'd in the sea.

'O haud your tongue, my daughter dear, be still and be content;
There are mair lads in Galloway, ye need nae sair lament.'
O! there is nane in Galloway, there's nane at a' for me;
For I never loved a love but ane, and he's drown'd in the sea.

'The Rescue of Alexander Selkirk'

from A Cruising Voyage Round the World

WOODES ROGERS (16??–1732)

In his A Cruising Voyage Round the World, *published in 1712, Woodes Rogers, a sea-captain and later Governor of the Bahamas, gave the first account of Alexander Selkirk, the Scottish seafarer whose life and adventures were to be the inspiration for Daniel Defoe's* Robinson Crusoe.

Selkirk, who was born in Largo, Fife, in 1676, ran away to sea to avoid answering a charge of indecent conduct in church. Evidently a difficult and contumacious character, Selkirk nevertheless showed ability in his chosen profession and was appointed sailing master on the Cinque-Ports *which formed part of William Dampier's privateering expedition to the South Seas in 1703. In September 1704 while at Juan Fernandez, 400 miles off the coast of present-day Chile, Selkirk quarrelled with the* Cinque-Ports' *captain and was put ashore, alone, on this uninhabited Pacific island. Here Selkirk lived alone for over four years until his rescue by Rogers and his entry into literary fame. In 1713 Richard Steele gave a wider circulation to Selkirk's story in an essay in* The Englishman. *Defoe in 1719 took the essence of Selkirk's story: the island, the isolation, living off the land and the goatskin clothes, but transferred the action to an island off the Orinoco River on the Atlantic coast of Venezuela and turned the Scot Selkirk into 'Robinson Crusoe, of York, Mariner' and the marooning into a shipwreck.*

After his rescue Selkirk continued his seagoing career, with a brief period living as a recluse at home in Largo, from where he eloped with a local woman, before deserting her. He settled in England, married a widow in 1720 and died in 1721 while serving as master's mate on HMS Weymouth.

Immediately our Pinnace return'd from the shore, and brought abundance of Crawfish, with a Man cloth'd in Goat-Skins, who look'd wilder than the first Owners of them. He had been on the Island four Years and four Months, being left there by Capt. *Stradling* in the *Cinque-Ports*; his

Name was *Alexander Selkirk* a *Scotch* Man, who had been Master of the
Cinque-Ports, a Ship that came here last with Capt. *Dampier*, who told
me that this was the best Man in her; so I immediately agreed with him to
be a Mate on board our Ship. 'Twas he that made the Fire last night when
he saw our Ships, which he judg'd to be *English*. During his stay here he
saw several Ships pass by, but only two came in to anchor. As he went
to view them, he found 'em to be *Spaniards*, and retir'd from 'em; upon
which they shot at him. Had they been *French*, he would have submitted;
but chose to risque his dying alone on the Island, rather than fall into the
hands of the *Spaniards* in these parts, because he apprehended they would
murder him, or make a Slave of him in the Mines, for he fear'd they would
spare no Stranger that might be capable of discovering the *South-Sea*. The
Spaniards had landed, before he knew what they were, and they came so
near him that he had much ado to escape; for they not only shot at him
but pursu'd him into the Woods, where he climb'd to the top of a Tree,
at the foot of which they made water, and kill'd several Goats just by,
but went off again without discovering him. He told us that he was born
at *Largo* in the Country of *Fife* in *Scotland*, and was bred a Sailor from
his Youth. The reason of his being left here was a difference betwixt him
and his Captain; which, together with the Ships being leaky, made him
willing rather to stay here than go along with him at first; and when he
was at last willing, the Captain would not receive him. He had been in the
Island before to wood and water, when two of the Ships Company were
left upon it for six Months till the Ship return'd, being chas'd thence by
two *French South-Sea* Ships.

He had with him his Clothes and Bedding, with a Fire-lock, some
Powder, Bullets, and Tobacco, a Hatchet, a Knife, a Kettle, a Bible,
some practical Pieces, and his Mathematical Instruments and Books.
He diverted and provided for himself as well as he could; but for the
first eight months had much ado to bear up against Melancholy, and the
Terror of being left alone in such a desolate place. He built two Hutts
with Piemento Trees, cover'd them with long Grass, and lin'd them with
the Skins of Goats, which he kill'd with his Gun as he wanted, so long
as his Powder lasted, which was but a pound; and that being near spent,
he got fire by rubbing two sticks of Piemento Wood together upon his
knee. In the lesser Hutt, at some distance from the other, he dress'd his
Victuals, and in the larger he slept, and employ'd himself in reading,
singing Psalms, and praying; so that he said he was a better Christian
while in this Solitude than ever he was before, or than, he was afraid, he
should ever be again. At first he never eat anything till Hunger constrain'd
him, partly for grief and partly for want of Bread and Salt; nor did he go to

bed till he could watch no longer: the Piemento Wood, which burnt very clear, serv'd him both for Firing and Candle, and refresh'd him with its fragrant Smell.

He might have had Fish enough, but could not eat 'em for want of Salt, because they occasion'd a Looseness; except Crawfish, which are there as large as our Lobsters, and very good: These he sometimes broil'd, and at other times boil'd, as he did his Goats Flesh, of which he made very good Broth, for they are not so rank as ours: he kept an Account of 500 that he kill'd while there, and caught as many more, which he mark'd on the Ear and let go. When his Powder fail'd, he took them by speed of foot; for his way of living and continual Exercise of walking and running, clear'd him of all gross Humours, so that he ran with wonderful Swiftness thro the Woods and up the Rocks and Hills, as we perceiv'd when we employ'd him to catch Goats for us. We had a Bull-Dog, which we sent with several of our nimblest Runners to help him in catching Goats; but he distanc'd and tir'd both the Dog and the Men, catch'd the Goats, and brought 'em to us on his back. He told us that his Agility in pursuing a Goat had once like to have cost him his Life; he pursu'd it with so much Eagerness that he catch'd hold of it on the brink of a Precipice, of which he was not aware, the Bushes having hid it from him; so that he fell with the Goat down the said Precipice a great height, and was so stunn'd and bruised with the Fall, that he narrowly escap'd with his Life, and when he came to his Senses, found the Goat dead under him. He lay there about 24 hours, and was scarce able to crawl to his Hutt, which was about a mile distant, or to stir abroad again in ten days.

He came at last to relish his Meat well enough without Salt or Bread, and in the Season had plenty of good Turnips, which had been sow'd there by Capt. *Dampier*'s Men, and have now overspread some Acres of Ground. He had enough of good Cabbage from the Cabbage-Trees, and season'd his Meat with the Fruit of the Piemento Trees, which is the same as the *Jamaica* Pepper, and smells deliciously. He found there also a black Pepper call'd *Malagita*, which was very good to expel Wind, and against Griping of the Guts.

He soon wore out all his Shoes and Clothes by running thro the Woods; and at last being forc'd to shift without them, his Feet became so hard, that he run everywhere without Annoyance: and it was some time before he could wear Shoes after we found him; for not being us'd to any so long, his Feet swell'd when he came first to wear 'em again.

After he had conquer'd his Melancholy, he diverted himself sometimes by cutting his Name on the Trees, and the Time of his being left and Continuance there. He was at first much pester'd with Cats and Rats, that had bred in great numbers from some of each Species which had got ashore from Ships that put in there to wood and water. The Rats gnaw'd his Feet and Clothes while asleep, which oblig'd him to cherish the Cats with his Goats-flesh; by which many of them became so tame, that they would lie about him in hundreds, and soon deliver'd him from the Rats. He likewise tamed some Kids, and to divert himself would now and then sing and dance with them and his Cats: so that by the Care of Providence and Vigour of his Youth, being now but about 30 years old, he came at last to conquer all the Inconveniences of his Solitude, and to be very easy. When his Clothes wore out, he made himself a Coat and Cap of Goat-Skins, which he stitch'd together with little Thongs of the same, that he cut with his Knife. He had no other Needle but a Nail; and when his Knife was wore to the back, he made others as well as he could of some Iron Hoops that were left ashore, which he beat thin and ground upon Stones. Having some Linen Cloth by him, he sow'd himself Shirts with a Nail, and stitch'd 'em with the Worsted of his old Stockings, which he pull'd out on purpose. He had his last Shirt on when we found him on the Island.

At his first coming on board with us, he had so much forgot his Language for want of Use, that we could scarce understand him, for he seem'd to speak his words by halves. We offer'd him a Dram, but he would not touch it, having drank nothing but Water since his being there, and 'twas some time before he could relish our Victuals.

He could give us an account of no other Product of the Island than what we have mention'd, except small black Plums, which are very good, but hard to come at, the Trees which bear 'em growing on high Mountains and Rocks. Piemento Trees are plenty here, and we saw some of 60 foot high, and about two yards thick; and Cotton Trees higher, and near four fathom round in the Stock.

The Climate is so good, that the Trees and Grass are verdant all the year. The Winter lasts no longer than *June* and *July*, and is not then severe, there being only a small Frost and a little Hail, but sometimes great Rains. The Heat of the Summer is equally moderate, and there's not much Thunder or tempestuous Weather of any sort. He saw no venomous or savage Creature on the Island, nor any other sort of Beast but Goats, *etc.*, as abovementioned; the first of which had been put ashore here on purpose for a Breed by *Juan Fernando*, a *Spaniard*, who settled there with some Families for a time, till the Continent of *Chili* began to submit to the *Spaniards*; which being more profitable, tempted them to quit this Island, which is capable of maintaining a good number of People, and of being made so strong that they could not be easily dislodg'd.

'The Wreck of the *Covenant*'

from Kidnapped

ROBERT LOUIS STEVENSON (1850–94)

Stevenson's most famous Scottish novel, Kidnapped, *was finished in 1886 while RLS was living quietly for the sake of his health in Bournemouth. However distant in miles and atmosphere this gem of the English Riviera might be from the Highlands of Scotland in the aftermath of the '45 Rising, Stevenson's links to his homeland remained strong. Symbolic of these links was the name of his Bournemouth villa – 'Skerryvore' – called after the great rock lighthouse built by his family in the wild seas off Tiree. In the days when his father still had hopes that Robert might follow in the family tradition of engineering and lighthouse construction the young Stevenson had travelled round Scotland's west coast and visited the tidal island of Earraid, off Mull, which was the Skerryvore supply base and, at the time of his visit, the construction base for the equally spectacular Dubh Heartach lighthouse. These travels furnished Stevenson with experience which he worked into* Kidnapped – *and inspired a dedicatory poem for his Bournemouth villa.*

SKERRYVORE

For love of lovely words, and for the sake
Of those, my kinsmen and my countrymen,
Who, early and late in the windy ocean toiled
To plant a star for seamen, where was then
The surfy haunt of seals and cormorants:
I, on the lintel of this cot, inscribe
The name of a strong tower.

In June 1751 the sixteen-year-old hero of Kidnapped, *David Balfour, whose father has just died, is sent off to his uncle Ebenezer Balfour at the House of Shaws, where he meets with a strangely hostile reception from his only living relative, a miser and a recluse. Ebenezer has David kidnapped and taken on board the brig* Covenant, *outward bound from the Forth for the Carolinas, where David is to be sold into slavery as an indentured servant.*

Off the west coast of Scotland the Covenant *inadvertently collides with a small boat but manages to rescue its passenger, Alan Breck Stewart, a Jacobite agent carrying messages and gold between the pro-Jacobite clans and their exiled leaders. The rascally captain of the* Covenant, *Hoseason, and his Mate Mr Riach resolve to seize Alan (and more importantly his belt of gold coins) but the lowland pro-Government Whiggish David strikes up an unlikely and uneasy alliance with the Highland Jacobite outlaw and the ill-matched pair defend themselves successfully against the crew's attacks.*

However, the overmastering threat of the sea, for the Covenant *has been running through the Sea of the Hebrides in a fierce gale, forces the two sides into a truce. Our extract tells of the loss of the* Covenant *and David's stranding on Earraid.*

Chapter 13 The loss of the brig

It was already late at night, and as dark as it ever would be at that season of the year (and that is to say, it was still pretty bright), when Hoseason clapped his head into the round-house door.

'Here,' said he, 'come out and see if ye can pilot.'

'Is this one of your tricks?' asked Alan.

'Do I look like tricks?' cries the captain. 'I have other things to think of – my brig's in danger!'

By the concerned look of his face, and, above all, by the sharp tones in which he spoke of his brig, it was plain to both of us he was in deadly earnest; and so Alan and I, with no great fear of treachery, stepped on deck.

The sky was clear; it blew hard, and was bitter cold; a great deal of daylight lingered; and the moon, which was nearly full, shone brightly. The brig was close hauled, so as to round the south-west corner of the Island of Mull; the hills of which (and Ben More above them all, with a wisp of mist upon the top of it) lay full upon the larboard bow. Though it was no good point of sailing for the *Covenant*, she tore through the seas at a great rate, pitching and straining, and pursued by the westerly swell.

Altogether it was no such ill night to keep the seas in; and I had begun to wonder what it was that sat so heavily upon the captain, when the brig rising suddenly on the top of a high swell, he pointed and cried to us to look. Away on the lee bow, a thing like a fountain rose out of the moonlit sea, and immediately after we heard a low sound of roaring.

'What do ye call that?' asked the captain, gloomily.

'The sea breaking on a reef,' said Alan. 'And now ye ken where it is; and what better would ye have?'

'Ay,' said Hoseason, 'if it was the only one.'

And sure enough just as he spoke there came a second fountain further to the south.

'There!' said Hoseason. 'Ye see for yourself. If I had kent of these reefs, if I had had a chart, or if Shuan had been spared, it's not sixty guineas, no, nor six hundred, would have made me risk my brig in sic a stoneyard! But you, sir, that was to pilot us, have ye never a word?'

'I'm thinking,' said Alan, 'these'll be what they call the Torran Rocks.'

'Are there many of them?' says the captain.

'Truly, sir, I am nae pilot,' said Alan; 'but it sticks in my mind there are ten miles of them.'

Mr Riach and the captain looked at each other.

'There's a way through them, I suppose?' said the captain.

'Doubtless,' said Alan; 'but where? But it somehow runs in my mind once more, that it is clearer under the land.'

'So?' said Hoseason. 'We'll have to haul our wind then, Mr Riach; we'll have to come as near in about the end of Mull as we can take her, sir; and even then we'll have the land to keep the wind off us, and that stoneyard on our lee. Well, we're in for it now, and may as well crack on.'

With that he gave an order to the steersman, and sent Riach to the foretop. There were only five men on deck, counting the officers; these were all that were fit (or, at least, both fit and willing) for their work; and two of these were hurt. So, as I say, it fell to Mr Riach to go aloft, and he sat there looking out and hailing the deck with news of all he saw.

'The sea to the south is thick,' he cried; and then, after a while, 'It does seem clearer in by the land.'

'Well, sir,' said Hoseason to Alan, 'we'll try your way of it. But I think I might as well trust to a blind fiddler. Pray God you're right.'

'Pray God I am!' says Alan to me. 'But where did I hear it? Well, well it will be as it must.'

As we got nearer to the turn of the land the reefs began to be sown here and there on our very path; and Mr Riach sometimes cried down to us to change the course. Sometimes, indeed, none too soon; for one reef was so close on the brig's weather board that when a sea burst upon it the lighter sprays fell upon her deck and wetted us like rain.

The brightness of the night showed us these perils as clearly as by day, which was, perhaps, the more alarming. It showed me, too, the face of the captain as he stood by the steersman, now on one foot, now on the other, and sometimes blowing in his hands, but still listening and looking and as steady as steel. Neither he nor Mr Riach had shown well in the fighting;

but I saw they were brave in their own trade, and admired them all the more because I found Alan very white.

'Ochone, David,' says he, 'this is no the kind of death I fancy.'

'What, Alan!' I cried, 'you're not afraid?'

'No,' said he, wetting his lips, 'but you'll allow yourself, it's a cold ending.'

By this time, now and then sheering to one side or the other to avoid a reef, but still hugging the wind and the land, we had got round Iona and begun to come alongside Mull. The tide at the tail of the land ran very strong, and threw the brig about. Two hands were put to the helm, and Hoseason himself would sometimes lend a help; and it was strange to see three strong men throw their weight upon the tiller, and it (like a living thing) struggle against and drive them back. This would have been the greater danger, had not the sea been for some while free of obstacles. Mr Riach, besides, announced from the top that he saw clear water ahead.

'Ye were right,' said Hoseason to Alan. 'Ye have saved the brig, sir; I'll mind that when we come to clear accounts.' And I believe he not only meant what he said, but would have done it; so high a place did the *Covenant* hold in his affections.

But this is matter only for conjecture, things having gone otherwise than he forecast.

'Keep her away a point,' sings out Mr Riach. 'Reef to windward!'

And just at the same time the tide caught the brig, and threw the wind out of her sails. She came round into the wind like a top, and the next moment struck the reef with such a dunch as threw us all flat upon the deck, and came near to shake Mr Riach from his place upon the mast.

I was on my feet in a minute. The reef on which we had struck was close in under the south-west end of Mull, off a little isle they call Earraid, which lay low and black upon the larboard. Sometimes the swell broke clean over us; sometimes it only ground the poor brig upon the reef, so that we could hear her beat herself to pieces; and what with the great noise of the sails, and the singing of the wind, and the flying of the spray in the moonlight, and the sense of danger, I think my head must have been partly turned, for I could scarcely understand the things I saw.

Presently I observed Mr Riach and the seamen busy round the skiff; and still in the same blank, ran over to assist them; and as soon as I set my hand to work, my mind came clear again. It was no very easy task, for the skiff lay amidships and was full of hamper, and the breaking of the heavier seas continually forced us to give over and hold on; but we all wrought like horses while we could.

Meanwhile such of the wounded as could move came clambering out of the fore-scuttle and began to help; while the rest that lay helpless in their bunks harrowed me with screaming and begging to be saved.

The captain took no part. It seemed he was struck stupid. He stood holding by the shrouds, talking to himself and groaning out aloud whenever the ship hammered on the rock. His brig was like wife and child to him; he had looked on, day by day, at the mishandling of poor Ransome; but when it came to the brig, he seemed to suffer along with her.

All the time of our working at the boat, I remember only one other thing: that I asked Alan, looking across at the shore, what country it was; and he answered, it was the worst possible for him, for it was a land of the Campbells.

We had one of the wounded men told off to keep a watch upon the seas and cry us warning. Well, we had the boat about ready to be launched, when this man sang out pretty shrill: 'For God's sake, hold on!' We knew by his tone that it was something more than ordinary; and sure enough, there followed a sea so huge that it lifted the brig right up and canted her over on her beam. Whether the cry came too late or my hold was too weak, I know not; but at the sudden tilting of the ship I was cast clean over the bulwarks into the sea.

I went down, and drank my fill; and then came up, and got a blink of the moon; and then down again. They say a man sinks the third time for good. I cannot be made like other folk, then; for I would not like to write how often I went down or how often I came up again. All the while, I was being hurled along, and beaten upon and choked, and then swallowed whole; and the thing was so distracting to my wits, that I was neither sorry nor afraid.

Presently, I found I was holding to a spar, which helped me somewhat. And then all of a sudden I was in quiet water, and began to come to myself.

It was the spare yard I had got hold of, and I was amazed to see how far I had travelled from the brig. I hailed her, indeed; but it was plain she was already out of cry. She was still holding together; but whether or not they had yet launched the boat, I was too far off and too low down to see.

While I was hailing the brig, I spied a tract of water lying between us, where no great waves came, but which yet boiled white all over and bristled in the moon with rings and bubbles. Sometimes the whole tract swung to one side, like the tail of a live serpent; sometimes, for a glimpse, it all would disappear and then boil up again. What it was I had no guess, which for the time increased my fear of it; but I now know it must have been the roost or tide race, which had carried me away so fast and tumbled me about so cruelly, and at last, as if tired of that play, had flung out me and the spare yard upon its landward margin.

I now lay quite becalmed, and began to feel that a man can die of cold as well as of drowning. The shores of Earraid were close in; I could see in the moonlight the dots of heather and the sparkling of the mica in the rocks.

'Well,' thought I to myself, 'if I cannot get as far as that, it's strange!'

I had no skill of swimming, Essen water being small in our neighbourhood; but when I laid hold upon the yard with both arms, and kicked out with both feet, I soon begun to find that I was moving. Hard work it was, and mortally slow; but in about an hour of kicking and splashing, I had got well in between the points of a sandy bay surrounded by low hills.

The sea was here quite quiet; there was no sound of any surf; the moon shone clear; and I thought in my heart I had never seen a place so desert and desolate. But it was dry land; and when at last it grew so shallow that I could leave the yard and wade ashore upon my feet, I cannot tell if I was more tired or more grateful. Both at least, I was: tired as I never was before that night; and grateful to God as I trust I have been often, though never with more cause.

Chapter 14 The islet

With my stepping ashore I began the most unhappy part of my adventures. It was half-past twelve in the morning, and though the wind was broken by the land, it was a cold night. I dared not sit down (for I thought I should have frozen), but took off my shoes and walked to and fro upon the sand, barefoot, and beating my breast, with infinite weariness. There was no sound of man or cattle; not a cock crew, though it was about the hour of their first waking; only the surf broke outside in the distance, which put me in mind of my perils and those of my friend. To walk by the sea at that hour of the morning, and in a place so desert-like and lonesome, struck me with a kind of fear.

As soon as the day began to break I put on my shoes and climbed a hill – the ruggedest scramble I ever undertook – falling, the whole way, between big blocks of granite or leaping from one to another. When I got to the top the dawn was come. There was no sign of the brig, which must have lifted from the reef and sunk. The boat, too, was nowhere to be seen. There was never a sail upon the ocean; and in what I could see of the land, was neither house nor man.

I was afraid to think what had befallen my shipmates, and afraid to look longer at so empty a scene. What with my wet clothes and weariness, and

my belly that now began to ache with hunger, I had enough to trouble
me without that. So I set off eastward along the south coast, hoping to
find a house where I might warm myself, and perhaps get news of those
I had lost. And at the worst, I considered the sun would soon rise and
dry my clothes.

After a little, my way was stopped by a creek or inlet of the sea, which
seemed to run pretty deep into the land; and as I had no means to get
across, I must needs change my direction to go about the end of it. It
was still the roughest kind of walking; indeed the whole, not only of
Earraid, but of the neighbouring part of Mull (which they call the Ross)
is nothing but a jumble of granite rocks with heather in among. At first
the creek kept narrowing as I had looked to see; but presently to my
surprise it began to widen out again. At this I scratched my head, but
had still no notion of the truth; until at last I came to a rising ground,
and it burst upon me all in a moment that I was cast upon a little, barren
isle, and cut off on every side by the salt seas.

Instead of the sun rising to dry me, it came on to rain, with a thick
mist; so that my case was lamentable.

I stood in the rain, and shivered, and wondered what to do, till it
occurred to me that perhaps the creek was fordable. Back I went to the
narrowest point and waded in. But not three yards from shore, I plumped
in head over ears; and if ever I was heard of more it was rather by God's
grace than my own prudence. I was no wetter (for that could hardly be)
but I was all the colder for this mishap; and having lost another hope,
was the more unhappy.

And now, all at once, the yard came in my head. What had carried
me through the roost, would surely serve me to cross this little quiet
creek in safety. With that I set off, undaunted, across the top of the
isle, to fetch and carry it back. It was a weary tramp in all ways, and
if hope had not buoyed me up, I must have cast myself down and given
up. Whether with the sea salt, or because I was growing fevered, I was
distressed with thirst, and had to stop, as I went, and drink the peaty
water out of the hags.

I came to the bay at last, more dead than alive; and at the first glance,
I thought the yard was something further out than when I left it. In I
went, for the third time, into the sea. The sand was smooth and firm
and shelved gradually down; so that I could wade out till the water
was almost to my neck and the little waves splashed into my face.
But at that depth my feet began to leave me and I durst venture in
no further. As for the yard, I saw it bobbing very quietly some twenty
feet in front of me.

I had borne up well until this last disappointment; but at that I came ashore, and flung myself down upon the sands and wept.

The time I spent upon the island is still so horrible a thought to me, that I must pass it lightly over. In all the books I have read of people cast away, they had either their pockets full of tools, or a chest of things would be thrown upon the beach along with them, as if on purpose. My case was very different. I had nothing in my pockets but money and Alan's silver button; and being inland bred, I was as much short of knowledge as of means.

I knew indeed that shell-fish were counted good to eat; and among the rocks of the isle I found a great plenty of limpets, which at first I could scarcely strike from their places, not knowing quickness to be needful. There were, besides, some of the little shells that we call buckies; I think periwinkle is the English name. Of these two I made my whole diet, devouring them cold and raw as I found them; and so hungry was I, that at first they seemed to me delicious.

Perhaps they were out of season, or perhaps there was something wrong in the sea about my island. But at least I had no sooner eaten my first meal than I was seized with giddiness and retching, and lay for a long time no better than dead. A second trial of the same food (indeed I had no other) did better with me and revived my strength. But as long as I was on the island, I never knew what to expect when I had eaten; sometimes all was well, and sometimes I was thrown into a miserable sickness; nor could I ever distinguish what particular fish it was that hurt me.

All day it streamed rain; the island ran like a sop; there was no dry spot to be found; and when I lay down that night, between two boulders that made a kind of roof, my feet were in a bog.

The second day I crossed the island to all sides. There was no one part of it better than another; it was all desolate and rocky; nothing living on it but game birds which I lacked the means to kill, and the gulls which haunted the outlying rocks in a prodigious number. But the creek, or straits, that cut off the isle from the main land of the Ross, opened out on the north into a bay, and the bay again opened into the sound of Iona; and it was the neighbourhood of this place that I chose to be my home; though if I had thought upon the very name of home in such a spot, I must have burst out weeping.

I had good reasons for my choice. There was in this part of the isle a little hut of a house like a pig's hut, where fishers used to sleep when they came there upon their business; but the turf roof of it had fallen entirely in; so that the hut was of no use to me, and gave me less shelter than my rocks. What was more important, the shell-fish on which I lived grew there in great plenty; when the tide was out I could gather a peck at a time: and this was doubtless a convenience. But the other reason went deeper. I had become in no way used to the horrid solitude of the isle, but still looked round me on all sides (like a man that was hunted) between fear and hope that I might see some human creature coming. Now, from a little up the hillside over the bay, I could catch a sight of the great, ancient church and the roofs of the people's houses in Iona. And on the other hand, over the low country of the Ross, I saw smoke go up, morning and evening, as if from a homestead in a hollow of the land.

I used to watch this smoke, when I was wet and cold, and had my head half turned with loneliness; and think of the fireside and the company, till my heart burned. It was the same with the roofs of Iona. Altogether, this sight I had of men's homes and comfortable lives, although it put a point on my own sufferings, yet it kept hope alive, and helped me to eat my raw shell-fish (which had soon grown to be a disgust) and saved me from the sense of horror I had whenever I was quite alone with dead rocks, and fowls, and the rain, and the cold sea.

I say it kept hope alive; and indeed it seemed impossible that I should be left to die on the shores of my own country, and within view of a church tower and the smoke of men's houses. But the second day passed; and though as long as the light lasted I kept a bright look-out for boats on the Sound or men passing on the Ross, no help came near me. It still rained; and I turned in to sleep, as wet as ever and with a cruel sore throat, but a little comforted, perhaps, by having said good night to my next neighbours, the people of Iona.

Charles the Second declared a man could stay out-doors more days in the year in the climate of England than in any other. This was very like a king with a palace at his back and changes of dry clothes. But he must have had better luck on his flight from Worcester than I had on that miserable isle. It was the height of the summer; yet it rained for more than twenty-four hours, and did not clear until the afternoon of the third day.

This was the day of incidents. In the morning I saw a red deer, a buck with a fine spread of antlers, standing in the rain on the top of the island; but he had scarce seen me rise from under my rock, before he trotted off upon the other side. I supposed he must have swum the straits; though what should bring any creature to Earraid, was more than I could fancy.

A little after, as I was jumping about after my limpets, I was startled by a guinea-piece, which fell upon a rock in front of me and glanced off into the sea. When the sailors gave me my money again, they kept back not only about a third of the whole sum, but my father's leather purse; so that from that day out, I carried my gold loose in a pocket with a button. I now saw there must be a hole, and clapped my hand to the place in a great hurry. But this was to lock the stable door after the steed was stolen. I had left the shore at Queensferry with near on fifty pounds; now I found no more than two guinea-pieces and a silver shilling.

It is true I picked up a third guinea a little after, where it lay shining on a piece of turf. That made a fortune of three pounds and four shillings, English money, for a lad, the rightful heir of an estate, and now starving on an isle at the extreme end of the wild Highlands.

This state of my affairs dashed me still further; and indeed my plight on that third morning was truly pitiful. My clothes were beginning to rot; my stockings in particular were quite worn through, so that my shanks went naked; my hands had grown quite soft with the continual soaking; my throat was very sore, my strength had much abated, and my heart so turned against the horrid stuff I was condemned to eat, that the very sight of it came near to sicken me.

And yet the worst was not yet come.

There is a pretty high rock on the north-west of Earraid, which (because it had a flat top and overlooked the Sound) I was much in the habit of frequenting; not that ever I stayed in one place, save when asleep, my misery giving me no rest. Indeed I wore myself down with continual and aimless goings and comings in the rain.

As soon, however, as the sun came out, I lay down on the top of that rock to dry myself. The comfort of the sunshine is a thing I cannot tell. It set me thinking hopefully of my deliverance, of which I had begun to despair; and I scanned the sea and the Ross with a fresh interest. On the south of my rock, a part of the island jutted out and hid the open ocean, so that a boat could thus come quite near me upon that side, and I be none the wiser.

Well, all of a sudden, a coble with a brown sail and a pair of fishers aboard of it, came flying round that corner of the isle, bound for Iona. I shouted out, and then fell on my knees on the rock and reached up my hands and prayed to them. They were near enough to hear – I could even see the colour of their hair; and there was no doubt but they observed me, for they cried out in the Gaelic tongue, and laughed. But the boat never turned aside, and flew on, right before my eyes, for Iona.

I could not believe such wickedness, and ran along the shore from rock to rock, crying on them piteously; even after they were out of reach of my voice, I still cried and waved to them; and when they were quite gone, I thought my heart would have burst. All the time of my troubles I wept only twice. Once, when I could not reach the yard; and now, the second time, when these fishers turned a deaf ear to my cries. But this time I wept and roared like a wicked child, tearing up the turf with my nails and grinding my face in the earth. If a wish would kill men, those two fishers would never have seen morning, and I should likely have died upon my island.

When I was a little over my anger, I must eat again, but with such loathing of the mess as I could now scarce control. Sure enough, I should have done as well to fast, for my fishes poisoned me again. I had all my first pains; my throat was so sore I could scarce swallow; I had a fit of strong shuddering, which clucked my teeth together; and there came on me that dreadful sense of illness, which we have no name for either in Scotch or English. I thought I should have died, and made my peace with God, forgiving all men, even my uncle and the fishers; and as soon as I had thus made up my mind to the worst, clearness came upon me: I observed the night was falling dry; my clothes were dried a good deal; truly, I was in a better case than ever before, since I had landed on the isle; and so I got to sleep at last, with a thought of gratitude.

The next day (which was the fourth of this horrible life of mine) I found my bodily strength run very low. But the sun shone, the air was sweet, and what I managed to eat of the shell-fish agreed well with me and revived my courage.

I was scarce back on my rock (where I went always the first thing after I had eaten) before I observed a boat coming down the Sound, and with her head, as I thought, in my direction.

I began at once to hope and fear exceedingly; for I thought these men might have thought better of their cruelty and be coming back to my assistance. But another disappointment, such as yesterday's, was more than I could bear. I turned my back, accordingly, upon the sea, and did not look again till I had counted many hundreds. The boat was still heading for the island. The next time I counted the full thousand, as slowly as I could, my heart beating so as to hurt me. And then it was out of all question. She was coming straight to Earraid!

I could no longer hold myself back, but ran to the sea side and out, from one rock to another, as far as I could go. It is a marvel I was not drowned; for when I was brought to a stand at last, my legs shook under me, and my mouth was so dry, I must wet it with the sea-water before I was able to shout.

All this time the boat was coming on; and now I was able to perceive it was the same boat and the same two men as yesterday. This I knew by their hair, which the one had of a bright yellow and the other black. But now there was a third man along with them, who looked to be of a better class.

As soon as they were come within easy speech, they let down their sail and lay quiet. In spite of my supplications, they drew no nearer in, and what frightened me most of all, the new man tee-hee'd with laughter as he talked and looked at me.

Then he stood up in the boat and addressed me a long while, speaking fast and with many wavings of his hand. I told him I had no Gaelic; and at this he became very angry, and I began to suspect he thought he was talking English. Listening very close, I caught the word 'whateffer' several times; but all the rest was Gaelic, and might have been Greek and Hebrew for me.

'Whatever,' said I, to show him I had caught a word.

'Yes, yes – yes, yes,' says he, and then he looked at the other men, as much as to say, 'I told you I spoke English,' and began again as hard as ever in the Gaelic.

This time I picked out another word, 'tide'. Then I had a flash of hope. I remembered he was always waving his hand towards the mainland of the Ross.

'Do you mean when the tide is out—?' I cried, and could not finish.

'Yes, yes,' said he. 'Tide.'

At that I turned tail upon their boat (where my adviser had once more begun to tee-hee with laughter), leaped back the way I had come, from one stone to another, and set off running across the isle as I had never run before. In about half an hour I came out upon the shores of the creek; and, sure enough, it was shrunk into a little trickle of water, through which I dashed, not above my knees, and landed with a shout on the main island.

A sea-bred boy would not have stayed a day on Earraid; which is only what they call a tidal islet, and except in the bottom of the neaps, can be entered and left twice in every twenty-four hours, either dry-shod, or at the most by wading. Even I, who had the tide going out and in before me in the bay, and even watched for the ebbs, the better to get my shell-fish – even I (I say) if I had sat down to think, instead of raging at my fate, must have soon guessed the secret, and got free. It was no wonder the fishers had not understood me. The wonder was rather that they had ever guessed my pitiful illusion, and taken the trouble to come back. I had starved with cold and hunger on that island for close upon one hundred hours. But for the fishers, I might have left my bones there, in pure folly. And even as it was, I had paid for it pretty dear, not only in past sufferings, but in my present case; being clothed like a beggarman, scarce able to walk, and in great pain of my sore throat.

I have seen wicked men and fools, a great many of both; and I believe they both get paid in the end; but the fools first.

'A Storm off Coll'

from Journal of a Tour to the Hebrides

JAMES BOSWELL (1740–95)

In the Autumn of 1773 James Boswell, Scottish advocate, traveller, writer and heir to an Ayrshire estate, set off on a tour of the Highlands and Islands of Scotland with his friend, hero and father-figure, Dr Samuel Johnson, poet, essayist, lexicographer and controversialist.

The relationship between the two men has often been reduced to the portrayal of Boswell as a toady and scalp-hunter who allowed Johnson to exercise his anti-Scottish sentiments at Boswell and his nation's expense. The reality is more complex. Boswell admired and respected Johnson, while noting of him and other English critics: '... when I humour any of them in an outrageous contempt of Scotland, I fairly own I treat them as children. And thus I have, at some moments, found myself obliged to treat even Dr Johnson.' For his part Johnson had a genuine affection and regard for Boswell – as he wrote in his account of their travels Boswell was: '... a companion, whose acuteness would help my inquiry, and whose gaiety of conversation and civility of manners are sufficient to counteract the inconveniencies of travel ...'

The two travellers had a variety of experiences and some rough quarters on their adventurous journey into these little-known and little-travelled regions of Scotland. In the less than thirty years since the collapse of the last Jacobite rising little had been done to open up the Highlands and only a few adventurous travellers like Thomas Pennant had gone before to write of the landscape and customs of Scotland beyond the Highland line. Boswell was in the prime of life, at thirty-three, while Johnson, who celebrated his sixty-fourth birthday on the tour and had suffered from ill health throughout his life, might have been thought a little old for adventuring by land and sea. They were accompanied on their 'Highland jaunt' by Joseph Ritter, Boswell's Bohemian manservant – whom Johnson characterised as '... a civil man, and a wise man'.

Many hardships and 'inconveniencies of travel' were to come their way – but the most dangerous episode was a sea-voyage from Armadale in Skye. This was undertaken in the company of Donald MacLean, the son of the Laird of Coll. The intended destination was Mull but the stress of the weather forced the ship to make for the Island of Coll, where the

young laird piloted them into the harbour. Boswell's gift for self-analysis
is well demonstrated in the passage where, frightened by the storm, he
asks MacLean (Boswell refers to him by the name of his property – which
he spells Col) if there was anything he could do. MacLean tells him to
hold on to a rope – and Boswell later reflects: '... his object was to keep
me out of the way of those who were busy working the vessel, and at the
same time to divert my fear, by employing me ...'

Sunday, 3rd October

Joseph reported that the wind was still against us. Dr Johnson said, 'A
wind, or not a wind? that is the question;' for he can amuse himself at
times with a little play of words, or rather of sentences. I remember when
he turned his cup at Aberbrothick, where we drank tea, he muttered,
Claudite jam rivos, pueri. I must again and again apologise to fastidious
readers, for recording such minute particulars. They prove the scrupulous
fidelity of my Journal. Dr Johnson said it was a very exact picture of a
portion of his life.

   While we were chatting in the indolent stile of men who were to stay
here all this day at least, we were suddenly roused by being told that the
wind was fair, that a little fleet of herring-busses was passing by for Mull,
and that Mr Simpson's vessel was about to sail. Hugh McDonald, the
skipper, came to us, and was impatient that we should get ready, which
we soon did. Dr Johnson, with composure and solemnity, repeated the
observation of Epictetus, that, 'as man has the voyage of death before
him – whatever may be his employment, he should be ready at the
master's call; and an old man should never be far from the shore, lest
he should not be able to get himself ready.' He rode, and I and the other
gentlemen walked, about an English mile to the shore, where the vessel
lay. Dr Johnson said, he should never forget Sky, and returned thanks
for all civilities. We were carried to the vessel in a small boat which she
had, and we set sail very briskly about one o'clock. I was much pleased
with the motion for many hours. Dr Johnson grew sick, and retired
under cover, as it rained a good deal. I kept above, that I might have
fresh air, and finding myself not affected by the motion of the vessel, I
exulted in being a stout seaman, while Dr Johnson was quite in a state
of annihilation. But I was soon humbled; for after imagining that I could
go with ease to America or the East-Indies, I became very sick, but kept
above board, though it rained hard.

   As we had been detained so long in Sky by bad weather, we gave up
the scheme that Col had planned for us of visiting several islands, and

contented ourselves with the prospect of seeing Mull, and Icolmkill and Inchkenneth, which lie near to it.

Mr Simpson was sanguine in his hopes for a while, the wind being fair for us. He said, he would land us at Icolmkill that night. But when the wind failed, it was resolved we should make for the sound of Mull, and land in the harbour of Tobermorie. We kept near the five herring vessels for some time; but afterwards four of them got before us, and one little wherry fell behind us. When we got in full view of the point of Ardnamurchan, the wind changed, and was directly against our getting into the sound. We were then obliged to tack, and get forward in that tedious manner. As we advanced, the storm grew greater, and the sea very rough. Col then began to talk of making for Egg, or Canna, or his own island. Our skipper said, he would get us into the Sound. Having struggled for this a good while in vain, he said, he would push forward till we were near the land of Mull, where we might cast anchor, and lie till the morning; for although, before this, there had been a good moon, and I had pretty distinctly seen not only the land of Mull, but up the Sound, and the country of Morven as at one end of it, the night was now grown very dark. Our crew consisted of one McDonald, our skipper, and two sailors, one of whom had but one eye; Mr Simpson himself, Col, and Hugh McDonald his servant, all helped. Simpson said, he would willingly go for Col, if young Col or his servant would undertake to pilot us to a harbour; but, as the island is low land, it was dangerous to run upon it in the dark. Col and his servant appeared a little dubious. The scheme of running for Canna seemed then to be embraced; but Canna was ten leagues off, all out of our way; and they were afraid to attempt the harbour of Egg. All these different plans were successively in agitation. The old skipper still tried to make for the land of Mull; but then it was considered that there was no place there where we could anchor in safety. Much time was lost in striving against the storm. At last it became so rough, and threatened to be so much worse, that Col and his servant took more courage, and said they would undertake to hit one of the harbours in Col. 'Then let us run for it in GOD's name,' said the skipper; and instantly we turned towards it. The little wherry, which had fallen behind us, had hard work. The master begged that, if we made for Col, we should put out a light to him. Accordingly one of the sailors waved a glowing peat for some time. The various difficulties that were started gave me a good deal of apprehension, from which I was relieved, when I found we were to run for a harbour before the wind. But my relief was but of short duration; for I soon heard that our sails were very bad, and were in danger of being torn in pieces, in which case we should be driven upon the rocky shore of Col. It was very dark, and there was a heavy and incessant rain. The sparks of the burning peat flew so much about, that I dreaded the vessel might take fire. Then, as Col was a sportsman, and had powder on board, I figured that we might be blown up. Simpson and he appeared a little frightened, which made me more so; and the perpetual talking, or rather shouting, which was carried on in Erse, alarmed me still more. A man is always suspicious of what is saying in an unknown tongue; and, if fear be his passion at the time, he grows more afraid. Our vessel often lay so much on one side, that I trembled lest she should be overset; and indeed they told me afterwards, that they had run her sometimes to within an inch of the water, so anxious were they to make what haste they could before the night should be worse. I now saw what I never saw before, a prodigious sea, with immense billows coming upon a vessel, so as that it seemed hardly possible to escape. There was something grandly horrible in the sight. I am glad I have seen it once. Amidst all these terrifying circumstances, I endeavoured to compose my mind. It was not easy to do it; for all the stories that I had heard of the dangerous sailing among the Hebrides, which is proverbial, came full upon my recollection. When I thought of those who were dearest to me, and would suffer severely, should I be lost, I upbraided myself, as not having a sufficient cause for putting myself in such danger. Piety afforded me comfort; yet I was disturbed by the objections that have been made against a particular providence, and by the arguments of those who maintain that it is in vain to hope that the petitions of an individual, or even of congregations, can have any influence with the Deity; objections which have been often made, and which Dr Hawkesworth has lately revived, in his Preface to the Voyages to the South Seas; but Dr Ogden's excellent doctrine on the efficacy of intercession prevailed.

It was half an hour after eleven before we set ourselves in the course for Col. As I saw them all busy doing something, I asked Col, with much earnestness, what I could do. He, with a happy readiness, put into my hand a rope, which was fixed to the top of one of the masts, and told me to hold it till he bade me pull. If I had considered the matter, I might have seen that this could not be of the least service; but his object was to keep me out of the way of those who were busy working the vessel, and at the same time to divert my fear, by employing me, and making me think that I was of use. Thus did I stand firm to my post, while the wind and rain beat upon me, always expecting a call to pull my rope.

The man with one eye steered; old McDonald, and Col and his servant, lay upon the fore-castle, looking sharp out for the harbour. It was necessary to carry much *cloth*, as they termed it, that is to say, much sail, in order to keep the vessel off the shore of Col. This made violent plunging in a rough sea. At last they spied the harbour of Lochiern, and Col cried, 'Thank God, we are safe!' We ran up till we were opposite to it, and soon afterwards we got into it, and cast anchor.

Dr Johnson had all this time been quiet and unconcerned. He had lain down on one of the beds, and having got free from sickness, was satisfied. The truth is, he knew nothing of the danger we were in: but, fearless and unconcerned, might have said, in the words which he has chosen for the motto to his *Rambler*,

Quo me cunque rapit tempestas, deferor hospes.[1]

Once, during the doubtful consultations, he asked whither we were going; and upon being told that it was not certain whether to Mull or Col, he cried, 'Col for my money!' I now went down, with Col and Mr Simpson, to visit him. He was lying in philosophick tranquillity, with a greyhound of Col's at his back, keeping him warm. Col is quite the *Juvenis qui gaudet canibus*. He had, when we left Talisker, two greyhounds, two terriers, a pointer, and a large Newfoundland water-dog. He lost one of his terriers by the road, but had still five dogs with him. I was very ill, and very desirous to get to shore. When I was told that we could not land that night, as the storm had now increased, I looked so miserably, as Col afterwards informed me, that what Shakespeare has made the Frenchman say of the English soldiers, when scantily dieted, '*Piteous they will look, like drowned mice!*' might, I believe, have been well applied to me. There was in the harbour, before us, a Campbell-town vessel, the *Betty*, Kenneth Morison master, taking in kelp, and bound for Ireland. We sent our boat to beg beds for two gentlemen, and that the master would send his boat, which was larger than ours. He accordingly did so, and Col and I were accommodated in his vessel till the morning.

[1]For as the tempest drives, I shape my way. FRANCIS.

'A Storm off Coll'

from A Journey to the Western Islands of Scotland

SAMUEL JOHNSON (1709–84)

By way of contrast to Boswell's extended description of the storm of 3rd October, and his reflections on his emotions, we have Dr Johnson's account. This, in contrast, is laconic in its brevity and detachment. The Doctor had after all been, in Boswell's phrase, 'in a state of annihilation' due to seasickness and had retired to the limited shelter the small craft provided.

Having waited some days at *Armidel*, we were flattered at last with a wind that promised to convey us to *Mull*. We went on board a boat that was taking in kelp, and left the Isle of *Sky* behind us. We were doomed to experience, like others, the danger of trusting to the wind, which blew against us, in a short time, with such violence, that we, being no seasoned sailors, were willing to call it a tempest. I was sea-sick and lay down. Mr *Boswell* kept the deck. The master knew not well whither to go; and our difficulties might perhaps have filled a very pathetick page, had not Mr *Maclean* of *Col*, who, with every other qualification which insular life requires, is a very active and skilful mariner, piloted us safe into his own harbour.

Caller Herrin'

CAROLINA OLIPHANT, LADY NAIRNE (1766–1845)

Wha'll buy my caller herrin'?
　　They're bonnie fish and halesome farin';
Wha'll buy my caller herrin',
　　New drawn frae the Forth?

When ye were sleepin' on your pillows,
　　Dream'd ye aught o' our puir fellows,
Darkling as they fac'd the billows,
　　A' to fill the woven willows?
　　　　Buy my caller herrin',
　　　　New drawn frae the Forth.

Wha'll buy my caller herrin'?
　　They're no brought here without brave darin';
Buy my caller herrin',
　　Haul'd through wind and rain.
　　　　Wha'll buy my caller herrin'? *etc.*

Wha'll buy my caller herrin'?　　ı
　　Oh, ye may ca' them vulgar farin'—
Wives and mithers, maist despairin',
　　Ca' them lives o' men.
　　　　Wha'll buy my caller herrin'? *etc.*

When the creel o' herrin' passes,
　　Ladies, clad in silks and laces,
Gather in their braw pelisses,
　　Cast their heads and screw their faces,
　　　　Wha'll buy my caller herrin'? *etc.*

Caller herrin's no got lightlie:—
　　Ye can trip the spring fu' tightlie;
Spite o' tauntin', flauntin', flingin',
　　Gow has set you a' a-singing
　　　　Wha'll buy my caller herrin'? *etc.*

Neebour wives, now tent my tellin';
　When the bonnie fish ye're sellin',
At ae word be in yere dealin'—
　Truth will stand when a' thing's failin',
Wha'll buy my caller herrin'?
　They're bonnie fish and halesome farin',
Wha'll buy my caller herrin',
　New drawn frae the Forth?

'The Wreck of the *Arrow*'

from The Coral Island

R.M. BALLANTYNE (1825–94)

Of all the Victorian authors of boys' adventure novels few were more successful than the Edinburgh-born Robert Michael Ballantyne. After an adventurous career with the Hudson's Bay Company Ballantyne turned to writing, with the semi-autobiographical The Young Fur-Traders, *his first publication in 1856. Two years later came his most famous book and the only one to remain continuously in print since then,* The Coral Island.

The exciting tale of three young shipmates cast away on a Pacific island is typical of Ballantyne's style – the young heroes struggle gallantly against the forces of nature and the threat of cannibals before being rescued. Ballantyne's style owes much to Victorian ideas of Empire and service – but at his best, and The Coral Island *is probably his best, his tales are still worth reading, and no Scottish anthology of sea stories could be complete without introducing its readers to Ralph, Peterkin and Jack.*

Chapter I

Roving has always been, and still is, my ruling passion, the joy of my heart, the very sunshine of my existence. In childhood, in boyhood, and in man's estate, I have been a rover; not a mere rambler among the woody glens and upon the hill-tops of my own native land, but an enthusiastic rover throughout the length and breadth of the wide, wide world.

It was a wild, black night of howling storm, the night in which I was born on the foaming bosom of the broad Atlantic Ocean. My father was a sea-captain; my grandfather was a sea-captain; my great-grandfather had been a marine. Nobody could tell positively what occupation *his* father had followed; but my dear mother used to assert that he had been a midshipman, whose grandfather, on the mother's side, had been an admiral in the royal navy. At any rate we knew that, as far back as our family could be traced, it had been intimately connected with the great watery waste. Indeed this was the case on both sides of the house; for my mother always went to sea with my father on his long voyages, and so spent the greater part of her life upon the water.

Thus it was, I suppose, that I came to inherit a roving disposition. Soon after I was born, my father, being old, retired from a seafaring life, purchased a small cottage in a fishing village on the west coast of England, and settled down to spend the evening of his life on the shores of the sea which had for so many years been his home. It was not long after this that I began to show the roving spirit that dwelt within me. For some time past my infant legs had been gaining strength, so that I came to be dissatisfied with rubbing the skin off my chubby knees by walking on them, and made many attempts to stand up and walk like a man; all of which attempts, however, resulted in my sitting down violently and in sudden surprise. One day I took advantage of my dear mother's absence to make another effort; and, to my joy, I actually succeeded in reaching the doorstep, over which I tumbled into a pool of muddy water that lay before my father's cottage door. Ah, how vividly I remember the horror of my poor mother when she found me sweltering in the mud amongst a group of cackling ducks, and the tenderness with which she stripped off my dripping clothes and washed my dirty little body! From this time forth my rambles became more frequent, and, as I grew older, more distant, until at last I had wandered far and near on the shore and in the woods around our humble dwelling, and did not rest content until my father bound me apprentice to a coasting vessel, and let me go to sea.

For some years I was happy in visiting the seaports, and in coasting along the shores of my native land. My Christian name was Ralph, and my comrades added to this the name of Rover, in consequence of the passion which I always evinced for travelling. Rover was not my real name, but as I never received any other I came at last to answer to it as naturally as to my proper name; and, as it is not a bad one, I see no good reason why I should not introduce myself to the reader as Ralph Rover. My shipmates were kind, good-natured fellows, and they and I got on very well together. They did, indeed, very frequently make game of and banter me, but not unkindly; and I overheard them sometimes saying that Ralph Rover was a 'queer, old-fashioned fellow'. This, I must confess, surprised me much, and I pondered the saying long, but could come at no satisfactory conclusion as to that wherein my old-fashionedness lay. It is true I was a quiet lad, and seldom spoke except when spoken to. Moreover, I never could understand the jokes of my companions even when they were explained to me, which dullness in apprehension occasioned me much grief; however, I tried to make up for it by smiling and looking pleased when I observed that they were laughing at some witticism which I had failed to detect. I was also very fond of inquiring into the nature of things and their causes, and often fell into fits of abstraction while thus engaged in my mind. But in all this I saw nothing that did not seem to be exceedingly natural, and could by no means understand why my comrades should call me 'an old-fashioned fellow'.

Now, while engaged in the coasting trade, I fell in with many seamen who had travelled to almost every quarter of the globe; and I freely confess that my heart glowed ardently within me as they recounted their wild adventures in foreign lands – the dreadful storms they had weathered, the appalling dangers they had escaped, the wonderful creatures they had seen both on the land and in the sea, and the interesting lands and strange people they had visited. But of all the places of which they told me, none captivated and charmed my imagination so much as the Coral Islands of the Southern Seas. They told me of thousands of beautiful fertile islands that had been formed by a small creature called the coral insect, where summer reigned nearly all the year round – where the trees were laden with a constant harvest of luxuriant fruit – where the climate was almost perpetually delightful – yet where, strange to say, men were wild, bloodthirsty savages, excepting in those favoured isles to which the gospel of our Saviour had been conveyed. These exciting accounts had so great an effect upon my mind, that, when I reached the age of fifteen, I resolved to make a voyage to the South Seas.

I had no little difficulty at first in prevailing on my dear parents to let me go; but when I urged on my father that he would never have become a great captain had he remained in the coasting trade, he saw the truth of what I said, and gave his consent. My dear mother, seeing that my father had made up his mind, no longer offered opposition to my wishes. 'But oh, Ralph,' she said, on the day I bade her adieu, 'come back soon to us, my dear boy, for we are getting old now, Ralph, and may not have many years to live.'

I will not take up my reader's time with a minute account of all that occurred before I took my final leave of my dear parents. Suffice it to say, that my father placed me under the charge of an old mess-mate of his own, a merchant captain, who was on the point of sailing to the South Seas in his own ship, the *Arrow*. My mother gave me her blessing and a small Bible; and her last request was, that I would never forget to read a chapter every day, and say my prayers; which I promised, with tears in my eyes, that I would certainly do.

Soon afterwards I went on board the *Arrow*, which was a fine large ship, and set sail for the islands of the Pacific Ocean.

Chapter II

It was a bright, beautiful, warm day when our ship spread her canvas to the breeze, and sailed for the regions of the south. Oh, how my heart bounded with delight as I listened to the merry chorus of the sailors, while they hauled at the ropes and got in the anchor! The captain shouted – the men ran to obey – the noble ship bent over to the breeze, and the shore gradually faded from my view, while I stood looking on with a kind of feeling that the whole was a delightful dream.

The first thing that struck me as being different from anything I had yet seen during my short career on the sea, was the hoisting of the anchor on deck, and lashing it firmly down with ropes, as if we had now bid adieu to the land for ever, and would require its services no more.

'There, lass,' cried a broad-shouldered jack-tar, giving the fluke of the anchor a hearty slap with his hand after the housing was completed, 'there, lass, take a good nap now, for we shan't ask you to kiss the mud again for many a long day to come!'

And so it was. That anchor did not 'kiss the mud' for many long days afterwards; and when at last it did, it was for the last time!

There were a number of boys in the ship, but two of them were my special favourites. Jack Martin was a tall, strapping, broad-shouldered youth of eighteen, with a handsome, good-humoured, firm face. He had had a good education, was clever and hearty and lion-like in his actions, but mild and quiet in disposition. Jack was a general favourite, and had a peculiar fondness for me. My other companion was Peterkin Gay. He was little, quick, funny, decidedly mischievous, and about fourteen years old. But Peterkin's mischief was almost always harmless, else he could not have been so much beloved as he was.

'Hallo! youngster,' said Jack Martin, giving me a slap on the shoulder, the day I joined the ship, 'come below and I'll show you your berth. You and I are to be mess-mates, and I think we shall be good friends, for I like the look o' you.'

Jack was right. He and I and Peterkin afterwards became the best and staunchest friends that ever tossed together on the stormy waves.

I shall say little about the first part of our voyage. We had the usual amount of rough weather and calm; also we saw many strange fish rolling in the sea, and I was greatly delighted one day by seeing a shoal of flying-fish dart out of the water and skim through the air about a foot above the surface. They were pursued by dolphins, which feed on them, and one flying-fish in its terror flew over the ship, struck on the rigging, and fell upon the deck. Its wings were just fins elongated, and we found that they could never fly far at a time, and never mounted into the air like birds, but skimmed along the surface of the sea. Jack and I had it for dinner, and found it remarkably good.

When we approached Cape Horn, at the southern extremity of America, the weather became very cold and stormy, and the sailors began to tell stories about the furious gales and the dangers of that terrible cape.

'Cape Horn,' said one, 'is the most horrible headland I ever doubled. I've sailed round it twice already, and both times the ship was a'most blow'd out o' the water.'

'An' I've been round it once,' said another, 'an' that time the sails were split, and the ropes frozen in the blocks, so that they wouldn't work, and we wos all but lost.'

'An' I've been round it five times,' cried a third, 'an' every time wos wuss than another, the gales wos so tree-mendous!'

'And I've been round it no times at all,' cried Peterkin, with an impudent wink of his eye, 'an' *that* time I wos blow'd inside out!'

Nevertheless, we passed the dreaded cape without much rough weather, and, in the course of a few weeks afterwards, were sailing gently, before a warm tropical breeze, over the Pacific Ocean. Thus we proceeded on our voyage, sometimes bounding merrily before a fair breeze, at other times floating calmly on the glassy wave and fishing for the curious inhabitants of the deep – all of which, although the sailors thought little of them, were strange, and interesting, and very wonderful to me.

At last we came among the Coral Islands of the Pacific, and I shall never forget the delight with which I gazed – when we chanced to pass one – at the pure, white, dazzling shores, and the verdant palm trees, which looked bright and beautiful in the sunshine. And often did we three long to be landed on one, imagining that we should certainly find perfect happiness there! Our wish was granted sooner than we expected.

One night, soon after we entered the tropics, an awful storm burst upon our ship. The first squall of wind carried away two of our masts, and left only the foremast standing. Even this, however, was more than enough, for we did not dare to hoist a rag of sail on it. For five days the tempest raged in all its fury. Everything was swept off the decks except one small boat. The steersman was lashed to the wheel, lest he should be washed away, and we all gave ourselves up for lost. The captain said that he had no idea where we were, as we had been blown far out of our course; and we feared much that we might get among the dangerous coral reefs which are so numerous in the Pacific. At daybreak on the sixth morning of the gale we saw land ahead. It was an island encircled by a reef of coral on which the waves broke in fury. There was calm water within this reef, but we could only see one narrow opening into it. For this opening we steered, but, ere we reached it, a tremendous wave broke on our stern, tore the rudder completely off, and left us at the mercy of the winds and waves.

'It's all over with us now, lads,' said the captain to the men; 'get the boat ready to launch; we shall be on the rocks in less than half an hour.'

The men obeyed in gloomy silence, for they felt that there was little hope of so small a boat living in such a sea.

'Come, boys,' said Jack Martin, in a grave tone, to me and Peterkin, as we stood on the quarterdeck awaiting our fate, 'come, boys, we three shall stick together. You see it is impossible that the little boat can reach the shore, crowded with men. It will be sure to upset, so I mean rather to trust myself to a large oar. I see through the telescope that the ship will strike at the tail of the reef, where the waves break into the quiet water inside; so, if we manage to cling to the oar till it is driven over the breakers, we may perhaps gain the shore. What say you; will you join me?'

We gladly agreed to follow Jack, for he inspired us with confidence, although I could perceive, by the sad tone of his voice, that he had little hope; and, indeed, when I looked at the white waves that lashed the reef and boiled against the rocks as if in fury, I felt that there was but a step between us and death. My heart sank within me; but at that moment my thoughts turned to my beloved mother, and I remembered those words, which were among the last that she said to me: 'Ralph, my dearest child, always remember in the hour of danger to look to your Lord and Saviour Jesus Christ. He alone is both able and willing to save your body and your soul.' So I felt much comforted when I thought thereon.

The ship was now very near the rocks. The men were ready with the boat, and the captain beside them giving orders, when a tremendous wave came towards us. We three ran towards the bow to lay hold of our oar, and had barely reached it when the wave fell on the deck with a crash like thunder. At the same moment the ship struck, the foremast broke off close to the deck and went over the side, carrying the boat and men along with it. Our oar got entangled with the wreck, and Jack seized an axe to cut it free, but, owing to the motion of the ship, he missed the cordage and struck the axe deep into the oar. Another wave, however, washed it clear of the wreck. We all seized hold of it, and the next instant we were struggling in the wild sea. The last thing I saw was the boat whirling in the surf, and all the sailors tossed into the foaming waves. Then I became insensible.

On recovering from my swoon, I found myself lying on a bank of soft grass, under the shelter of an overhanging rock, with Peterkin on his knees by my side, tenderly bathing my temples with water, and endeavouring to stop the blood that flowed from a wound in my forehead.

Chapter III

There is a strange and peculiar sensation experienced in recovering from a state of insensibility, which is almost indescribable; a sort of dreamy, confused consciousness; a half-waking half-sleeping condition, accompanied with a feeling of weariness, which, however, is by no means disagreeable. As I slowly recovered and heard the voice of Peterkin inquiring whether I felt better, I thought that I must have overslept myself, and should be sent to the mast-head for being lazy; but before I could leap up in haste, the thought seemed to vanish suddenly away, and I fancied that I must have been ill. Then a balmy breeze fanned my cheek, and I thought of home, and the garden at the back of my father's cottage, with its luxuriant flowers, and the sweet-scented honeysuckle that my dear mother trained so carefully upon the trellised porch. But the roaring of the surf put these delightful thoughts to flight, and I was back again at sea, watching the dolphins and the flying-fish, and reefing topsails off the wild and stormy Cape Horn. Gradually the roar of the surf became louder and more distinct. I thought of being wrecked far, far away from my native land, and slowly opened my eyes to meet those of my companion Jack, who, with a look of intense anxiety, was gazing into my face.

'Speak to us, my dear Ralph,' whispered Jack, tenderly, 'are you better now?'

I smiled and looked up, saying: 'Better; why, what do you mean, Jack? I'm quite well.'

'Then what are you shamming for, and frightening us in this way?' said Peterkin, smiling through his tears; for the poor boy had been really under the impression that I was dying.

I now raised myself on my elbow, and putting my hand to my forehead, found that it had been cut pretty severely, and that I had lost a good deal of blood.

'Come, come, Ralph,' said Jack, pressing me gently backward, 'lie down, my boy; you're not right yet. Wet your lips with this water, it's cool and clear as crystal. I got it from a spring close at hand. There now, don't say a word, hold your tongue,' said he, seeing me about to speak. 'I'll tell you all about it, but you must not utter a syllable till you have rested well.'

'Oh! don't stop him from speaking, Jack,' said Peterkin, who, now that his fears for my safety were removed, busied himself in erecting a shelter of broken branches in order to protect me from the wind; which, however, was almost unnecessary, for the rock beside which I had been laid completely broke the force of the gale. 'Let him speak, Jack; it's a comfort to hear that he's alive, after lying there stiff and white and sulky for a whole hour, just like an Egyptian mummy. Never saw such a fellow as you are, Ralph; always up to mischief. You've almost knocked out all my teeth and more than half choked me, and now you go shamming dead! It's very wicked of you, indeed it is.'

While Peterkin ran on in this style, my faculties became quite clear again, and I began to understand my position. 'What do you mean by saying I half choked you, Peterkin?' said I.

'What do I mean? Is English not your mother tongue, or do you want me to repeat it in French, by way of making it clearer? Don't you remember—'

'I remember nothing,' said I, interrupting him, 'after we were thrown into the sea.'

'Hush, Peterkin,' said Jack, 'you're exciting Ralph with your nonsense. I'll explain it to you. You recollect that after the ship struck, we three sprang over the bow into the sea; well, I noticed that the oar struck your head and gave you that cut on the brow, which nearly stunned you, so that you grasped Peterkin round the neck without knowing apparently what you were about. In doing so you pushed the telescope – which you clung to as if it had been your life – against Peterkin's mouth—'

'Pushed it against his mouth!' interrupted Peterkin, 'say crammed it down his throat. Why, there's a distinct mark of the brass rim on the back of my gullet at this moment!'

'Well, well, be that as it may,' continued Jack, 'you clung to him, Ralph, till I feared you really would choke him; but I saw that he had a good hold of the oar, so I exerted myself to the utmost to push you towards the shore, which we luckily reached without much trouble, for the water inside the reef is quite calm.'

'But the captain and crew, what of them?' I inquired, anxiously.

Jack shook his head.

'Are they lost?'

'No, they are not lost, I hope, but I fear there is not much chance of their being saved. The ship struck at the very tail of the island on which we were cast. When the boat was tossed into the sea it fortunately did not upset, although it shipped a good deal of water, and all the men managed to scramble into it; but before they could get the oars out the gale carried them past the point and away to leeward of the island. After we landed I saw them endeavouring to pull towards us, but as they had only one pair of oars out of the eight that belong to the boat, and as the wind was blowing right in their teeth, they gradually lost ground. Then I saw them put about and hoist some sort of sail, a blanket, I fancy, for it was too small for the boat – and in half an hour they were out of sight.'

'Poor fellows,' I murmured, sorrowfully.

'But the more I think about it, I've better hope of them,' continued Jack, in a more cheerful tone. 'You see, Ralph, I've read a great deal about these South Sea Islands, and I know that in many places they are scattered about in thousands over the sea, so they're almost sure to fall in with one of them before long.'

'I'm sure I hope so,' said Peterkin, earnestly. 'But what has become of the wreck, Jack? I saw you clambering up the rocks there while I was watching Ralph. Did you say she had gone to pieces?'

'No, she has not gone to pieces, but she has gone to the bottom,' replied Jack. 'As I said before, she struck on the tail of the island and stove in her bow, but the next breaker swung her clear, and she floated away to leeward. The poor fellows in the boat made a hard struggle to reach her, but long before they came near her she filled and went down. It was after she foundered that I saw them trying to pull to the island.'

There was a long silence after Jack ceased speaking, and I have no doubt that each was revolving in his mind our extraordinary position. For my part I cannot say that my reflections were very agreeable. I knew that we were on an island, for Jack had said so, but whether it was inhabited or not I did not know. If it should be inhabited, I felt certain, from all I had heard of South Sea islanders, that we should be roasted alive and eaten. If it should turn out to be uninhabited, I fancied that we should be starved to death. 'Oh!' thought I, 'if the ship had only struck on the rocks we might have done pretty well, for we could have obtained provisions from her, and tools to enable us to build a shelter, but now – alas! alas! we are lost!' These last words I uttered aloud in my distress.

'Lost! Ralph?' exclaimed Jack, while a smile overspread his hearty countenance. 'Saved, you should have said. Your cogitations seem to have taken a wrong road, and led you to a wrong conclusion.'

'Do you know what conclusion *I* have come to?' said Peterkin. 'I have made up my mind that it's capital – first rate – the best thing that ever happened to us, and the most splendid prospect that ever lay before three jolly young tars. We've got an island all to ourselves. We'll take possession in the name of the king; we'll go and enter the service of its black inhabitants. Of course we'll rise, naturally, to the top of affairs.

White men always do in savage countries. You shall be king, Jack; Ralph, prime minister, and I shall be—'

'The court jester,' interrupted Jack.

'No,' retorted Peterkin, 'I have no title at all. I shall merely accept a highly responsible situation under government, for you see, Jack, I'm fond of having an enormous salary and nothing to do.'

'But suppose there are no natives?'

'Then we'll build a charming villa, and plant a lovely garden round it, stuck all full of the most splendiferous tropical flowers, and we'll farm the land, plant, sow, reap, eat, sleep, and be merry.'

'But to be serious,' said Jack, assuming a grave expression of countenance, which I observed always had the effect of checking Peterkin's disposition to make fun of everything, 'we are really in rather an uncomfortable position. If this is a desert island, we shall have to live very much like the wild beasts, for we have not a tool of any kind, not even a knife.'

'Yes, we have *that*,' said Peterkin, fumbling in his trousers pocket, from which he drew forth a small penknife with only one blade, and that was broken.

'Well, that's better than nothing; but come,' said Jack, rising, 'we are wasting our time in *talking* instead of *doing*. You seem well enough to walk now, Ralph, let us see what we have got in our pockets, and then let us climb some hill and ascertain what sort of island we have been cast upon, for, whether good or bad, it seems likely to be our home for some time to come.'

The Canal Boatman

from Glasgow Evening News 24th November 1898

NEIL MUNRO (1863–1930)

Neil Munro, historical novelist, poet and creator of the immortal puffer skipper Para Handy, was also a journalist. In this role he contributed a regular literary feature to the Glasgow Evening News. *In his column for 24th November 1898 he provided a bravura display of his wit and skill as a literary impersonator in seven short stories imitating the styles of notable writers of the day – Conrad, Kipling, George Meredith, J.M. Barrie, Henry Newbolt, R.B. Cunninghame Graham. Munro's sense of humour is testified to by the seventh pastiche, which is a work entitled 'The Celtic Pilgrim' by N–l M–n–o and was inspired by his recent collection of short stories* The Lost Pibroch.

The pseudo-Conradian epic 'The Canal Boatman' is a stirring story of hurricanes, the heart of darkness and the lonely struggle of men against the sea – or actually a dirty night on the Forth and Clyde Canal. It is also an affectionate reminder of Munro's friendship with Conrad. They had met in September 1898 when Conrad, unhappy with his second career as a novelist, had come to Glasgow in the hope of returning to his earlier life at sea and finding employment as a ship's captain. The two writers had dined at a mutual friend's house and later walked around Glasgow until the small hours of the morning. Each greatly admired the other's writing and their friendship was to continue until Conrad's death.

'The Canal Boatman' by J–h C–n–r–d

A curious craft, surely, combining in her lines and utilities little of the speed of the felucca, galley, galleot, pram or dhow, yet in her vast, heavy illusion of beam recalling some of the *chasses-marées*, or corvets I have seen lurking off the little lost cays and lagoons between the Ladrones and the Salomon Islands. It had begun to blow immediately after leaving Lock 16. We hove to at Camelon, pumped, spliced the main-brace, pumped and spliced the main-brace again. It was terrible, and yet, somehow, I was proud of the ship and felt something – you know the feeling – one of exaltation, of zest, of triumph. We set out again, and near

Kirkintilloch the hurricane struck us, a cruel, unrelenting sou'wester, setting the waves mountain high, blinding our poor brutes of horses as they laboured incessantly on the towing path. That night had a quality of dark I have seen in no other time or place. Faint phosphorescent gleams in the far distance but accentuated it, and through the night there came the most wonderful and elusive odours. Something indescribable, a devil's impulse, a supernatural allurement in the night, seemed to call on us to quit the ship so fearfully weltering in the storm and risk all in the long boat. We felt we could make land somehow, for we were young, and all the poignances, the essence, the infatuation, of youth were ours. I think of it often under the most ludicrous circumstances – of the *Mary Jane* churning in a velvet-black night, the galley fire showing up MacTaggart's legs as he stood at the wheel, the horses breathing hard, bent over the cable tow, the impenetrable and vast and terrible darkness. Not a sound came from the land. We were the serfs of the sea, to be knocked about and get up, again, and fall again, and again stand up square to that old bully of the night.

For some inscrutable reason the skipper was anxious to get ahead and make an early landfall at Kirkintilloch. He was a man with a red nose and it was his first voyage on that route.

'We'll do it, we'll do it; it's only ten minutes past ten,' he cried, as we tied up at the pawls at Kirkintilloch. There was a strange exultation in his utterance. He hurried up to a house of refreshment and I shall never forget his look of surprise and pain to find it shut.

'Blind me!' said he, 'have they ten o'clock closing here too?' And he put his face in his hands and wept like a child.

Ah! old times, old times, will they ever come back again with the zest, the hope, the joy, the illusion?

'The Clyde Gale of 1911'

from Glasgow Evening News 6th November 1911

NEIL MUNRO (1863–1930)

'The Looker-On', his regular weekly column in the Glasgow Evening
News, *gave Neil Munro a platform to write about the things that
excited, interested and amused him. It was in 'The Looker-On' that
his fictional characters, Erchie, Jimmy Swan the Joy Traveller, and, of
course, Para Handy, first appeared, but the column was also used for
personal reflection, social comment and more conventional reportage.
Munro's description of the great Clyde Gale of November 1911 provides
an excellent example of his style and a fine description of the perils of
the sea. As an economical craftsman Munro also used his experience of
the gale and his description of the storm-tossed Firth of Clyde as the
point of departure for one of his classic Para Handy stories 'An Ocean
Tragedy'. This was published in his column on 20th November 1911 –
just a fortnight after the appearance of the following piece – and brought
his readers the news that the* Vital Spark *had been out in the Great Gale,
but had been brought safe to port by her intrepid skipper.*

With those who have been born and bred upon the coast there is nearly
always to be found a curious illusion that the greatest storms invariably
take place on Sundays. It is one of those impressions that originate
in youth, when things a little out of the ordinary bite deep into the
memory; when a familiar tree, blown down in a night of hurricane,
appears portentous as in later years will seem the upheaval of a dynasty;
when a wrecked gabbart on the beach below the garden wall hints, for
the first time, strangely, at the brutal power of nature, and creates an
epoch in the mind.

The official meteorologists, going by statistics, merely smile at the
notoriety which the popular superstition of the coast confers on Sunday,
but the notion will persist even among old sailors who have met
the storms of all the oceans. Sunday gales gain emphasis from the
circumstances under which they are observed. They appear a kind of
secular outrage upon that calm which we expect from Sabbath, that calm

which youth but rarely has appreciated, rather pleased, indeed, to have it broken by a dog-fight or the commotion created by a choked and flooded syver. Storms that take place in school-hours sacrifice no inconsiderable part of their importance for the young by not putting off till Sunday, when their impressiveness would gain enormously from the fact that they made venturing out to church impossible or gave a certain poignancy to the joy of standing for hours in the lee of a quay-head shipping-box, with sea-drenched Sunday suits, to be afterwards accounted for at home in circumstances which fixed the occasion even more deeply in the recollection.

A storm gains prominence from your having leisure to observe it, and it is probable that the typhoons described by Mr Joseph Conrad are more fierce (for the moment) to the reader in a snug armchair beside a jolly fire than to poor Jack cowering aft or fisting canvas out upon lashing yards in the actual experience. For adults as well as children, therefore, Sunday's storms are marked. They desolate the streets of cities; give the house unwonted charms of refuge. Bravo! good walls, tight roof; 'blow, winds, and crack your cheeks!' our shelter makes your fury impotent and renders it not quite unpleasing. The shop is shut. There is no business doing anywhere, and we are not losing anything – except we be shipowners and underwriters. 'Bithidh sgeul ri innse air so!' as they say in glens – there will be tales of this to tell, but that is for tomorrow. Today the visible casualties are minor; fallen slates, rhones, signboards, and chimney-cans in towns; flooded gardens and upturned trees at the coast and in the country.

November has already come up to its reputation – woods bare at last, fields cold and sodden, woods silent and songless; and the pent-up winds and rains of all summer and autumn let loose upon us now in one wild week-end. The glass dropped suddenly down on Friday afternoon, and before it had reached its lowest the gale was on, but only a second-rater as compared with Saturday night's and Sunday's. Delusively the barometer began to rise again from six o'clock on Friday evening till four in the following afternoon, when it swiftly dropped till midnight and, more deliberately, till noon on Sunday, when it started to mount rapidly again in the midst of a terrific storm.

The Firth of Clyde has never looked more vicious. The further shores invisible; what could be seen of water in the dull grey light of morning was up-tossed in creaming breakers, swept by incessant spindrift, not in patches, but in a single cloud, that blew all day like smoke across the troubled surface. In so far as white squalls are more wicked than black squalls, this unusual variety of squall was far worse than the worst of white squalls, being apparently continuous for hours, and not spasmodic. It sliced the surface off the sea like shavings from a plane, and blew it into spray and vapour.

No sail could possibly stand the fury of that hurricane, which made the ordinarily sheltered estuary into a seething pot. No steamer would have dared it at its worst. Till late in the afternoon, when an Irish boat came staggering up the Channel, no vessel showed, of any kind. At high tide, at eleven, enormous breakers swept the Greenock and Gourock esplanades; the tramcars were not running and the shoreside streets were practically impassable. Small boats adrift from the other side were thrown upon the shore and smashed to matchwood; ships' seats and other wreckage beat against the breast-walls. With nothing to wreak its venom on in the immediate sea, the storm made playful havoc on the shore. The Wemyss Bay pier was said to be destroyed, and a motor car from Greenock hydroplaned sensationally round the Cloch to make inquiries. The pier was still standing, with some berths still practicable, though seriously damaged, but it was not the motor car that discovered this; blown timber between the Cloch and Inverkip too soon put a stop to its hydroplaning.

A few folk went to church at the instant peril of their lives, but very few; and the preacher's voice was scarcely audible in opposition to the strident shouts of nature. To walk the pavement was to court disaster. Slates danced in the gutters of the roofs like withered leaves, and chimney-cans came crashing on the flagstones. Zinc ridges were peeled off as if they had been onion-skins or paper; roof hatches flew like kites.

There were narrow streets through which the gale went like a missile with an impact on opposing things that was appalling. Gas lamps burst and incandescent mantles dissipated into dust. Hoardings were levelled; front-plot trees uprooted; amazing debris was scattered everywhere. You had to hang on to lamp-posts or dodge into some friendly entry to evade the more furious gusts, which swept less cautious pedestrians off their feet. All day slaters and joiners wrought at the boarding-up of blown-in windows or the temporary repair of badly-damaged roofs.

In gardens, woods, and fields, the storm's supremacy was remarkable; all else in nature seemed to pause in a shuddering, mute expectancy. For hours the sheep – hogg winterers – stood jammed together in a solid mass behind an outhouse. Birds of all kinds were invisible; even the seagull seemed to have disappeared. Some days ago could be seen myriad thrushes feeding on the hedgerow hips and haws, and wood-doves battening on the acorns, which have never surely been more numerous or larger. In the storm's duration those birds were wholly absent; not a wing was stretched. Life seemed to have forsaken copse and hedgerow. Trees fallen and a roadway strewn with twigs marked the track of tempest. The last flowers perished in the gardens, loosened ivy trailed from walls.

But after all it was the Firth that was amazing – the Firth without a vessel on it, and the flying spume. The estuary, for all its summer smiles, from which alone so many judge its character, is the grave of many ships, from the second *Comet* of 1825, which sunk off Granny Kempoch with the loss of over seventy lives, to the recent *Portland*, now in some undiscoverable hole between the Cloch and Kirn. But they have been the victims of collision, not of storm.

The Dileas

from The Lonely Sea

ALISTAIR MACLEAN (1922–87)

A short story, The Dileas, *entered for a competition in* The Glasgow
Herald *in 1954 won its author, a thirty-four-year-old Glasgow school
teacher, the first prize of £100. More importantly, it attracted the notice
of Ian Chapman, an editor with what was then the Glasgow-based
publishing house of William Collins. Chapman contacted the school
teacher and invited him to consider writing a novel for Collins. Ten
weeks later the manuscript of* HMS Ulysses *was on Chapman's desk
and the spectacular career of Alistair MacLean was launched. Based on
his own wartime experiences in the Arctic convoys,* HMS Ulysses *became
one of the most successful British novels of all time – selling quarter of a
million copies in hardback in six months. The descriptions of gales and
men against the elements in* HMS Ulysses *have their echoes in* The
Dileas. *MacLean was to follow up his initial success with a string of
best-sellers – many of which were turned into films – such as* The Guns
of Navarone.*

*MacLean was born in Glasgow in 1922, but was brought up in
Inverness-shire, where his Gaelic-speaking father was a minister. This
background gave him a knowledge of Gaelic and a feel for the Gaelic
rhythms of speech which may be seen in* The Dileas. *After the War
he attended Glasgow University and started his career as a secondary
school English teacher – a career which the success of* HMS Ulysses
swiftly terminated. MacLean died in Germany in 1987.

*Dileas is a Gaelic word with a range of meaning including faithful,
dear, beloved, or related to. An appropriate choice, as you will come to
realise, for Seumas Grant's boat in this splendid, but surprisingly little
known, Scottish sea story by one of Scotland's most successful novelists.*

Three hours gone, Mr MacLean, three hours – and never a word of the
lifeboat.

You can imagine just how it was. There were only the four of us
there – Eachan, Torry Mor, old Grant, and myself. Talk? Never a

word among the lot of us, nor even the heart for a dram – and there on the table was a new bottle of Talisker, and Eachan not looking for a penny.

We just sat there like a lot of stookies, Seumas Grant with his expressionless face and yon wicked old pipe of his bubbling away, and the rest of us desperately busy with studying the pattern of the wallpaper. Listening to the screech of the wind we were, and the rain like chuckies battering against the windows of the hotel. Dhia! What a night that was! And the worst of it was, we couldn't do a thing but wait. My, but we were a right cheery crowd.

I think we all gave a wee bit jump when the telephone rang. Eachan hurried away and was back in a moment beaming all over. One look at yon great moonface of his and we all felt as if the Pladda Lighthouse had been lifted off our backs.

'Four glasses, gentlemen, and see's over the Talisker. That was the lightkeeper at Creag Dearg. The *Molly Ann* got there in time – just. The puffer's gone but all the crew were taken off.'

He pushed the glasses over, and looked straight at old Grant.

'Well, Seumas, what have you to say now? The *Molly Ann* got there – and Donald, Archie and Lachlan away over by Scavaig. Perhaps you would be saying it's a miracle, eh, Seumas?'

There was no love lost between these two, I can tell you. Mind you, most of us were on Eachan's side. He was a hard man, was old Seumas Grant. Well respected, right enough, but no one had any affection for him and, by Jove, he had none for us – none for anyone at all, except for Lachlan and Donald, his sons. For old Seumas, the sun rose only to shine on them alone. His motherless sons: for them the croft, for them the boat, for them his every waking thought. But a hard man, Mr MacLean. Aloof and – what's the word? – remote. Kept himself to himself, you might say.

'It's a miracle when anyone is saved on a night like this, Eachan.' Old Grant's voice was slow and deep.

'But without Donald and Lachlan?' Eachan pressed. Torry, I remember shifted in his seat, and I looked away. We didn't care for this too much – it wasn't right.

'Big Neil's weel enough in his own way,' Grant said, kind of quiet. 'But he'll never be the lifeboat coxswain Lachie is – he hasn't got the feel of the sea—'

Just then the hotel door crashed open, nearly lifted off its hinges by the wind. Peter the Post came stumbling in, heaved the door shut and stood there glistening in his oilskins. It only required one look at him to see that something was far wrong.

'The lifeboat, Eachan, the *Molly Ann*,' he jerked out, very quick and urgent. 'Any word of her yet? Hurry, man, hurry!'

Eachan looked at him in surprise.

'Why, surely, Peter. We've just heard. She's lying off Creag Dearg and—'

'Creag Dearg! Oh, Dhia, Dhia, Dhia!' Peter the Post sunk down into a chair and gazed dully into the fire. 'Twenty miles away – twenty miles. And here's Iain Chisholm just in from Tarbert farm – three miles in four minutes on yon big Velocette of his – to say that the Buidhe ferry is out in the middle of the Sound, firing distress rockets. And the *Molly Ann* at Creag Dearg. Mo creach, mo creach!' He shook his head slowly from side to side.

'The ferry!' I said stupidly. 'The ferry! Big John must be mad to take her out on a night like this!'

'And every boat in the fishing fleet sheltering up by Loch Torridon, like enough,' said Torry bitterly.

There was a long silence, then old Grant was on his feet, still puffing away.

'All except mine, Torry Mor,' he said, buttoning up his oilskins.

'It's God's blessing that Donal' and Lachie went to Scavaig to look over this new drifter.' He stopped and looked slowly around. 'I'm thinking I'll be needing a bit hand.'

We just stared at him, and when Eachan spoke it was like a man in a stound.

'You mean you'll take yon old tub out in this, Seumas?' Eachan was staggered. 'Forty years old if she's a day – and the seas like houses roaring straight down the Sound. Why, you'll be smashed to pieces, man – before you're right clear of the harbour mouth.

'Lachie would go.' Old Grant stared at the ground. 'He's the coxswain. He would go – and Donal'. I canna be letting my boys down.'

'It's suicide, Mr Grant,' I urged him. 'Like Eachan says, it's almost certain death.'

'There's no almost about it for the poor souls out on that ferry.' He reached for his sou-wester and turned to the door. 'Maybe I'll be managing right enough.'

Eachan flung the counter-flap up with a crash.

'You're a stiff-necked old fool, Seumas Grant,' he shouted angrily, 'and you'll roast in hell for your infernal pride!' He turned back and snatched a couple of bottles of brandy from the shelves. 'Maybe these'll come in handy,' he muttered to himself, then stamped out of the door, growling deep in his throat and scowling something terrible.

Mind you, the *Dileas* – that was old Seumas Grant's boat – was a deal better than Eachan made her out to be. When Campbell of Ardrishaig built a Loch Fyner, the timbers came out of the heart of the oak. And old Grant had added mild steel frames of his own and installed one of these new-fangled diesels – a 44 h.p. Gardner, I remember. But even so.

Outside the harbour wall – you couldn't imagine it and you'll never see the like, not even in your blackest nightmares. Bitter cold it was and the whistling sleet just flying lumps of ice that lanced your face open to the bone.

And the Sound itself! Oh Dhia, that Sound! The seas were short and desperate steep, with the speed of racehorses and the whole Sound a great sheet of driven milk gleaming in yon pitchy blackness. Man, it makes me shudder even now.

For two hours we headed straight up into it, and, Jove, what a wild hammering we took. The *Dileas* would totter up on a wave then, like she was falling over a cliff, smash down into the next trough with the crack of a four-inch gun, burying herself right to the gunwales. And at the same time you could hear the fierce clatter of her screw, clawing at the thin air. Why the *Dileas* never broke her back only God knows – or the ghost of Campbell of Ardrishaig.

'Are you seeing anything, boys?' It was old Grant shouting from the doghouse, the wind whipping the words off his lips.

'There's nothing, Seumas,' Torry bawled back. 'Just nothing at all.'

I handed the spotlight, an ancient Aldis, over to Eachan and made my way aft. Seumas Grant, his hands light on the wheel, stood there quietly, his face a mask of blood – when yon great, seething comber had buried the *Dileas* and smashed in the window he hadn't got out of the way quick enough. But the old eyes were calm, steady, and watchful as ever.

'It's no good, Mr Grant,' I shouted at him. 'We'll never find anyone to-night, and nothing could have lived so long in this. It's hopeless, just hopeless – and the *Dileas* can't last out much longer. We might as well go back.'

He said something. I couldn't catch it, and bent forward. 'I was just wondering,' he said, like a man in a muse, 'whether Lachie would have turned back.'

I backed slowly out of the wheelhouse. And I cursed Seumas Grant. I cursed him for that terrible love he bore for those two sons of his, for

Donald Archie and Lachlan. And then – then I felt the shame black and crawling, welling up inside me, and I cursed myself. Stumbling, I clawed my way for'ard again.

I was only halfway there when I heard Eachan shouting, his voice high and excited.

'There, Torry, look there! Just off the port bow. Somebody in the water – no, by God, two of them!'

When the *Dileas* heaved over the next crest, I looked along the beam of the Aldis. Torry was right. There, sure enough, were two dark forms struggling in the water.

In three quick jumps I was back at the doghouse, pointing. Old Grant just nodded, and started edging the *Dileas* across. What a skill he had with him, that old one! Bring the bows too far round and we'd broach-to and be gone in a second in yon great gullies between the waves. But old Seumas made never a mistake.

And then a miracle happened. Just that, Mr MacLean – a miracle. It was the Sea of Galilee all over again. Mind you, the waves were as terrible as ever, but just for a moment the wind dropped away to a deathly hush – and suddenly, off to starboard, a thin, high-pitched wail came keening out of the darkness.

In a flash, Torry had whipped his Aldis round, and the beam, plunging up and down, settled on a spot less than a hundred yards away – almost dead ahead. At first I thought it was just some wreckage, then I could see it was a couple of timber baulks and planks tied together. And lying on top of this makeshift raft – no, by God, *lashed* to it – were a couple of children. We caught only flying glimpses of them, up one minute, down the next, playthings of the devil in yon madness of a sea. The poor wee souls. Oh Dhia! The poor wee souls.

'Mr Grant!' I roared in old Seumas's ear. 'There's a raft almost dead ahead – two wee children on it.'

The old eyes were as quiet as ever. He just stared straight ahead; his face was like a stone.

'I canna be picking up both,' he said, his voice level and never a touch of feeling in it, damn his flinty heart. 'To come round in this would finish us – I'll have to quarter for the shelter of Seal Point to turn. Can the children be hanging on a while longer, do you think, Calum?'

He looked quickly at me, his eyes narrowing.

'The children are near gone,' I said flatly. 'And they're not hanging on – they're *lashed* on.'

'Lashed did you say, Calum?' he asked softly. 'Lashed?'

I nodded without speaking. And then a strange thing happened, Mr MacLean. A strange thing indeed. Yon craggy old face of his broke into a smile – I can see yet the gleam of his teeth and the little rivers of blood running down his face – and he nodded several times as if in satisfaction and understanding. And he gave the wheel a wee bit spin to starboard.

The little raft was drifting down fast on us, and we had only the one chance of picking them up. But with old Grant at the wheel that was enough, and Torry Mor, with one sweep of his great arm, had the children, raft and all, safely aboard.

We took them below and old Seumas worked his way up to Seal Point. Then we came tearing down the Sound, steady as a rock – for in a heavy stern sea there's no boat on earth the equal of a Loch Fyner – but never a trace of the two men did we see. A mile out from harbour old Seumas handed over to Torry Mor and came below to see the children.

They were sitting up on a bunk before the stove wrapped in blankets – a lad of nine and a fair-haired wee lass of six. Pale, pale they were, and frightened and exhausted, but a good night's sleep would put them right.

Quietly I told old Grant what I'd learned. They'd been playing in a wee skiff, under the sheltered walls of the Buidhe harbour, when the boy had gone too near the entrance and the wind had plucked them out to the open Sound. But they had been seen, and the two men had come after them in the ferryboat and then, they couldn't turn back. The rest they couldn't remember; the poor wee souls, they'd been scared to death.

I was just finishing when Eachan came below.

'The wind's backing, Seumas, and the sea with it. Perhaps there's a chance for yon two – if they're swimmers at all – of being carried ashore.'

Old Seumas looked up. His face was tired, lined and – all of a sudden – old.

'There's no chance, Eachan, no chance at all.'

'How can you be so sure, man?' Eachan argued. 'You never know.'

'I know, Eachan.' The old man's voice was a murmur, a million miles away. 'I know indeed. What was good enough for their old father was good enough for Donal' and Lachie. I never learned to swim – and neither did they.'

We were shocked into silence, I tell you. We looked at him stupidly, unbelievingly, then in horror.

'You mean—' I couldn't get the words out.

'It was Lachie and Donal' all right, I saw them.' Old Grant gazed sightlessly into the fire. 'They must have come back early from Scavaig.'

A whole minute passed before Eachan spoke, his voice wondering, halting.

'But Seumas, Seumas! Your own two boys. How could you—.'

For the first and only time old Grant's self-control snapped. He cut in, his voice low and fierce, his eyes masked with pain and tears.

'And what would you have had me do, Eachan? Pick them up and let these wee souls go?'

He went on, more slowly now.

'They'd used the only bits of wood in yon old ferry-boat to make a wee raft for the children. They knew what they were doing – and they knew, by doing it, that there was no hope for themselves. They did it deliberately, man. And if I hadn't picked the wee craturs up, it – it—'

His voice trailed off into silence, then we heard it again, the faintest shadow of a whisper.

'My two boys Lachie and Donal' – oh, Eachan, Eachan, I couldna be letting them down.'

Old Grant straightened, reached out for a bit of waste, and wiped the blood from his face – and, I'm thinking, the tears from his eyes. Then he picked up the wee girl, all wrapped in her blankets, set her on his knee and smiled down gently.

'Well, now, mo ghaol, and how would you be fancying a wee drop hot cocoa?'

6

PLEASURES OF THE SEA

For most of Scotland's history the concept of the 'pleasures of the sea' would have been one that her people would have found some difficulty in understanding. The sea was a means of earning a living, a means of carrying out essential journeys and, of course, a battleground. The sea was also an ever-present threat, an aspect we explore in other sections. To take pleasure from the sea requires one to have sufficient technology to exercise a measure of control over the element – and sufficient comfort in the technology to enjoy the experience.

The sea was most commonly seen, in Kipling's phrase, as 'the old grey Widow-maker' and much of the early literary reference to the sea is to be found in grateful references to the ending of storms and an escape from danger rather than a positive appreciation of the sea and its potential. Thus Gavin Douglas, writing in the early sixteenth century, praises the coming of Spring in his *Eneados*:

> For to behald, it was ane gloir to se
> The stabilit wyndis and the cawmyt sea.

Presumably even in those utilitarian times, men at sea, especially perhaps on the 'cawmyt sea', still found an aesthetic pleasure in the swift movement of a ship through the water, the play of light on sea, the satisfaction of a safe landfall and harbour reached. There is not, however, much literature, prior to the eighteenth century, of purely recreational sailing. There was of course a romantic landsman's view of the sea, for not all landsmen took the view of Dr Johnson, who, as James Boswell tells us, held that, 'No man will be a sailor who has contrivance enough to get himself into a jail; for being in a ship is being in a jail, with the chance of being drowned.' Johnson's realistic view is echoed by Tobias Smollett, who seems to have taken little pleasure in his voyage to Boulogne, '... tossed about by the sea, cold, and cramped, and weary...'

However the romantic school is well represented by Allan Cunningham (1784–1842), the Dumfriesshire-born contemporary of Walter Scott who waxed eloquent on the perceived joys of sailing:

> A wet sheet and a flowing sea,
> A wind that follows fast,
> And fills the white and rustling sail,
> And bends the gallant mast—
> And bends the gallant mast, my boys,
> While, like the eagle free,
> Away the good ship flies, and leaves
> Old England on the lee.

Greater control over the sea through the application of the steam-engine to ships seems to have had the paradoxical effect of stimulating interest in the recreational use of sailing ships. The extract from Walter Scott's diary comes from the very earliest days of steam power at sea – although his cruise was on a sailing ship he completed his journey on a steamer. Scott's voyage was as a passenger on a working ship and a similar relationship is to be found in the Neil Gunn extract.

Less orthodox pleasures of the sea should not be overlooked – and the bounty of the sea, celebrated by Compton MacKenzie, and the sea as last resting-place, memorably evoked by Eric Linklater, are worth recalling.

'A Packet-boat to Boulogne'

from Travels through France and Italy

TOBIAS SMOLLETT (1721–71)

Perhaps one of the under-rated pleasures of the sea, and indeed of travel in general, is complaining about the journey and the people and incidents encountered on it. Few travellers have left a better record of their atrabilious distaste for rascally ferrymen and dishonest inn-keepers and all the minor inconveniences of travel than the Scottish doctor, dramatist, poet and novelist, Tobias Smollett.

Born in Dumbartonshire in 1721, Smollett qualified as a doctor in Glasgow, then went to London to try his luck as a dramatist. This failed and he joined the navy as a surgeon's mate and served in the Cartagena campaign of 1741. Returning to London, he continued to practise medicine and embarked on a series of successful novels, starting with Roderick Random, *published in 1748. In 1763 he was ordered to go abroad for his health and the series of letters he wrote from France and Italy are caustically entertaining and reveal a positively hypochondriac approach to his health – confirming the popular view that doctors make the worst patients.*

If Smollett seems to foreshadow the twentieth-century novelist Nancy Mitford's view that 'abroad is bloody and foreigners are fiends' he, at least, is no more disposed to be sympathetic to his fellow-countrymen. Dover, he tells us, is a den of thieves whose inhabitants live by smuggling and fleecing strangers 'but I will do them the justice to say, they make no distinction between foreigners and natives.' Smollett is in a grumpy mood, and he has only reached Dover – things must and do get worse!

Despite his experiences and the problems of travel Smollett was to live for another eight years, dying in Leghorn in 1771.

On my arrival at Dover I payed off my coachman, who went away with a heavy heart. He wanted much to cross the sea, and endeavoured to persuade me to carry the coach and horses to the other side. If I had been resolved to set out immediately for the South, perhaps I should have taken his advice. If I had retained him at the rate of twenty guineas per month, which was the price he demanded, and begun my journey without hesitation, I should travel more agreeably than I can expect to do in the carriages of this country; and the difference of the expence would be a meer trifle. I would advise every man who travels through France to bring his own vehicle along with him, or at least to purchase one at Calais or Boulogne, where secondhand berlins and chaises may be generally had at reasonable rates. I have been offered a very good berlin for thirty guineas: but before I make the purchase, I must be better informed touching the different methods of travelling in this country.

Dover is commonly termed a den of thieves; and I am afraid it is not altogether without reason, it has acquired this appellation. The people are said to live by piracy in time of war; and by smuggling and fleecing strangers in time of peace: but I will do them the justice to say, they make no distinction between foreigners and natives. Without all doubt a man cannot be much worse lodged and worse treated in any part of Europe; nor will he in any other place meet with more flagrant instances of fraud, imposition, and brutality. One would imagine they had formed a general conspiracy against all those who either go to, or return from the continent. About five years ago, in my passage from Flushing to Dover, the master of the packet-boat brought-to all of a sudden off the South Foreland, although the wind was as favourable as it could blow. He was immediately boarded by a custom-house boat, the officer of which appeared to be his friend. He then gave the passengers to understand, that as it was low water, the ship could not go into the harbour; but that the boat would carry them ashore with their baggage.

The custom-house officer demanded a guinea for this service, and the bargain was made. Before we quitted the ship, we were obliged to gratify the cabin-boy for his attendance, and to give drink money to the sailors. The boat was run aground on the open beach; but we could not get ashore without the assistance of three or four fellows, who insisted upon being paid for their trouble. Every parcel and bundle, as it was landed, was snatched up by a separate porter: one ran away with a hatbox, another with a wig-box, a third with a couple of shirts tied up in a handkerchief, and two were employed in carrying a small portmanteau that did not weigh forty pounds. All our things were hurried to the custom-house to be searched, and the searcher was paid for disordering our cloaths: from thence they were removed to the inn, where the porters demanded half-a-crown each for their labour. It was in vain to expostulate; they surrounded the house like a pack of hungry hounds, and raised such a clamour, that we were fain to comply. After we had undergone all this imposition, we were visited by the master of the packet, who, having taken our fares, and wished us joy of our happy arrival in England, expressed his hope that we would remember the poor master, whose wages were very small, and who chiefly depended upon the generosity of the passengers. I own I was shocked at his meanness, and could not help telling him so. I told him, I could not conceive what title he had to any such gratification: he had sixteen passengers, who paid a guinea each, on the supposition that every person should have a bed; but there were no more than eight beds in the cabin, and each of these was occupied before I came on board; so that if we had been detained at sea a whole week by contrary winds and bad weather, one half of the passengers must have slept upon the boards, howsoever their health might have suffered from this want of accommodation. Notwithstanding this check, he was so very abject and importunate, that we gave him a crown apiece, and he retired.

The first thing I did when I arrived at Dover this last time, was to send for the master of a packet-boat, and agree with him to carry us to Boulogne at once, by which means I saved the expence of travelling by land from Calais to this last place, a journey of four-and-twenty miles. The hire of a vessel from Dover to Boulogne is precisely the same as from Dover to Calais, five guineas; but this skipper demanded eight, and, as I did not know the fare, I agreed to give him six. We embarked between six and seven in the evening, and found ourselves in a most wretched hovel, on board what is called a Folkstone cutter. The cabin was so small that a dog could hardly turn in it, and the beds put me in mind of the holes described in some catacombs, in which the bodies of the dead were deposited, being thrust in with the feet foremost; there was no getting into them but endways, and indeed they seemed so dirty, that nothing but extreme necessity could have obliged me to use them. We sat up all night in a most uncomfortable situation, tossed about by the sea, cold, and cramped and weary, and languishing for want of sleep. At three in the morning the master came down, and told us we were just off the harbour of Boulogne; but the wind blowing off shore, he could not possibly enter, and therefore advised us to go ashore in the boat. I went upon deck to view the coast, when he pointed to the place where he said Boulogne stood, declaring at the same time we were within a short mile of the harbour's mouth. The morning was cold and raw, and I knew myself extremely subject to catch cold; nevertheless we were all so impatient to be ashore, that I resolved to take his advice. The boat was already hoisted out, and we went on board of it, after I had paid the captain and gratified his crew. We had scarce parted from the ship, when we perceived a boat coming towards us from the shore; and the master gave us to understand, it was coming to carry us into the harbour. When I objected to the trouble of shifting from one boat to another in the open sea, which (by the bye) was a little rough; he said it was a privilege which the watermen of Boulogne had, to carry all passengers ashore, and that this privilege he durst not venture to infringe. This was no time nor place to remonstrate. The French boat came alongside half filled with water, and we were handed from the one to the other. We were then obliged to lie upon our oars, till the captain's boat went on board and returned from the ship with a packet of letters. We were afterwards rowed a long league, in a rough sea, against wind and tide, before we reached the harbour, where we landed, benumbed with cold, and the women excessively sick: from our landing-place we were obliged to walk very near a mile to the inn where we purposed to lodge, attended by six or seven men and women, bare-legged, carrying our baggage. This boat cost me a guinea, besides paying exorbitantly the people who carried our things; so that the inhabitants of Dover and of Boulogne seem to be of the same kidney, and indeed they understand one another perfectly well. It was our honest captain who made the signal for the shore-boat before I went upon deck; by which means he not only gratified his friends, the watermen of Boulogne, but also saved about fifteen shillings portage, which he must have paid had he gone into the harbour; and thus he found himself at liberty to return to Dover, which he reached in four hours. I mention these circumstances as a warning to other passengers. When a man hires a packet-boat from Dover to Calais or Boulogne, let him remember that the stated price is five guineas; and let him insist upon being carried into the harbour in the ship, without paying the least regard to the representations of the master, who is generally a little dirty knave. When he tells you it is low water, or the wind is in your teeth, you may say you will stay on board till it is high water, or till the wind comes favourable. If he sees you are resolute, he will find means to bring his ship into the harbour, or at least to convince you, without a possibility of your being deceived, that it is not in his power. After all, the fellow himself was a loser by his finesse; if he had gone into the harbour, he would have had another fare immediately back to Dover, for there was a Scotch gentleman at the inn waiting for such an opportunity.

Knowing my own weak constitution, I took it for granted this morning's adventure would cost me a fit of illness; and what added to my chagrin, when we arrived at the inn, all the beds were occupied; so that we were obliged to sit in a cold kitchen above two hours, until some of the lodgers should get up. This was such a bad specimen of French accommodation, that my wife could not help regretting even the inns of

Rochester, Sittingbourn, and Canterbury: bad as they are, they certainly have the advantage, when compared with the execrable auberges of this country, where one finds nothing but dirt and imposition. One would imagine the French were still at war with the English, for they pillage them without mercy.

Among the strangers at this inn where we lodged, there was a gentleman of the faculty, just returned from Italy. Understanding that I intended to winter in the South of France, on account of a pulmonic disorder, he strongly recommended the climate of Nice in Provence, which, indeed, I had often heard extolled; and I am almost resolved to go thither, not only for the sake of the air, but also for its situation on the Mediterranean, where I can have the benefit of bathing; and from whence there is a short cut by sea to Italy, should I find it necessary to try the air of Naples.

After having been ill accommodated three days at our inn, we have at last found commodious lodgings, by means of Mrs B—, a very agreeable French lady, to whom we were recommended by her husband, who is my countryman, and at present resident in London. For three guineas a month we have the greatest part of a house tolerably furnished; four bedchambers on the first floor, a large parlour below, a kitchen, and the use of a cellar.

These, I own, are frivolous incidents, scarce worth committing to paper; but they may serve to introduce observations of more consequence; and in the mean time I know nothing will be indifferent to you, that concerns – Your humble servant.

'Voyage on the *Pharos*'

from John Gibson Lockhart's Life of Sir Walter Scott

WALTER SCOTT (1771–1832)

In the late summer of 1814 Walter Scott sailed round Scotland as a guest on the annual inspection cruise of the Commissioners of the Northern Lights. Scott was Sheriff Depute of Selkirk and a Clerk of the Court of Session, he was also a poet of national reputation with works such as The Lay of the Last Minstrel, Marmion *and* The Lady of the Lake *to his credit – he had in fact refused the offer of the Poet Laureateship in 1813. Just three weeks before his trip he had published his first novel,* Waverley, *and seen it become an instant best-seller, although many years were to elapse before his authorship of this and subsequent novels would be publicly acknowledged.*

The Lighthouse Yacht Pharos *sailed from Leith on 29th July with three Commissioners, Scott and two other guests on board. However, in Scott's words, 'the official chief of the expedition is Mr Stevenson, the Surveyor-Viceroy over the Commissioners – a most gentlemanlike and modest man, and well known by his scientific skill.' This 'Mr Stevenson' was Robert Stevenson, the founder of the great Stevenson dynasty of lighthouse engineers – three generations of whose descendants were to be engineers to the Commissioners of the Northern Lights.*

The route of the Pharos *took Scott and his companions up the east coast to Shetland (where he was later to set his 1822 novel* The Pirate, *an extract from which we include in Chapter 3 – A Living from the Sea), back down to Orkney, through the Pentland Firth and on to the Outer Hebrides, Skye, Iona and Mull and across to Northern Ireland before ending their journey at Greenock on the Clyde on 8th September. Here Scott boarded one of the new steamships which had, within the last two years, started to ply on the Clyde between Greenock and Glasgow, and reported that this novel journey was '. . . performed at the rate of about eight miles an hour, and with a smoothness of motion which probably resembles flying.'*

Scott's cruise was not entirely without risk. Apart from the normal perils of the sea Britain was at war with the United States and the Pharos *had a Royal Navy escort through the Pentland Firth, an area where several vessels had recently been taken by American raiders. When they entered*

the Clyde they found that two American privateers had been operating
in the North Channel between Ireland and Scotland and had made many
captures.

Scott filled five notebooks with his journal of the cruise and the text
was published in his son-in-law John Gibson Lockhart's Life of Sir
Walter Scott, *first published in 1837/38. Scott's observations of manners*
and customs are well worth reading, as are his comments on social
conditions in the areas they passed through. Equally, his delight in
the picturesque scenery of the Highlands and Islands and the relaxed
adventure of an extended sea voyage with congenial company conveys
itself to the reader. Our first extract tells of the rounding of Cape Wrath,
the exploration of Smoo Cave and the passage to Scalpay in the Outer
Hebrides (18th–21st August). The second extract (27th August) recounts
the visit to Skerryvore, the isolated reef of rocks off Tiree, where Robert
Stevenson planned a lighthouse – a project triumphantly completed by his
son Alan in 1844.

The 'Bessy Millie', whose charm Scott refers to at the beginning of the
extract was a Stromness woman who sold favourable winds to sailors.

18th August 1814 – Bessy Millie's charm has failed us. After a rainy night,
the wind has come round to the north-west, and is getting almost
contrary. We have weathered Whitten-head, however, and Cape Wrath,
the north-western extremity of Britain, is now in sight. The weather gets
rainy and squally. Hamilton and Erskine keep their berths. Duff and I sit
upon deck, like two great bears, wrapt in watch-cloaks, the sea flying over
us every now and then. At length, after a sound buffeting with the rain,
the doubling Cape Wrath with this wind is renounced as impracticable,
and we stand away for Loch Eribol, a lake running into the extensive
country of Lord Reay. No sickness; we begin to get hardy sailors in
that particular. The ground rises upon us very bold and mountainous,
especially a very high steep mountain, called Ben-y-Hope, at the head of
a lake called Loch Hope. The weather begins to mitigate as we get under
the lee of the land. Loch Eribol opens, running up into a wild and barren
scene of crags and hills. The proper anchorage is said to be at the head
of the lake, but to go eight miles up so narrow an inlet would expose us
to be wind-bound. A pilot boat comes off from Mr Anderson's house,
a principal tacksman of Lord Reay's. After some discussion we anchor
within a reef of sunken rocks, nearly opposite to Mr Anderson's house
of Rispan; the situation is not, we are given to understand, altogether
without danger if the wind should blow hard, but it is now calm. In

front of our anchorage a few shapeless patches of land, not exceeding a few yards in diameter, have been prepared for corn by the spade, and bear wretched crops. All the rest of the view is utter barrenness; the distant hills, we are told, contain plenty of deer, being part of a forest belonging to Lord Reay, who is proprietor of all the extensive range of desolation now under our eye. The water has been kinder than the land, for we hear of plenty of salmon, and haddocks, and lobsters, and send our faithful minister of the interior, John Peters, the steward, to procure some of those good things of this very indifferent land, and to invite Mr Anderson to dine with us. Four o'clock – John has just returned, successful in both commissions, and the evening concludes pleasantly.

19th August 1814, *Loch Eribol, near Cape Wrath* – Went off before eight A.M. to breakfast with our friend Mr Anderson. His house, invisible from the vessel at her moorings, and, indeed, from any part of the entrance into Loch Eribol, is a very comfortable one, lying obscured behind a craggy eminence. A little creek, winding up behind the crag, and in front of the house, forms a small harbour, and gives a romantic air of concealment and snugness. There we found a ship upon the stocks, built from the keel by a Highland carpenter, who had magnanimously declined receiving assistance from any of the ship-carpenters who happened to be here occasionally, lest it should be said he could not have finished his task without their aid. An ample Highland breakfast of excellent new-taken herring, equal to those of Lochfine, fresh haddocks, fresh eggs, and fresh butter, not forgetting the bottle of whisky, and bannocks of barley, and oat-cakes, with the Lowland luxuries of tea and coffee. After breakfast, took the long-boat, and under Mr Anderson's pilotage, row to see a remarkable natural curiosity, called Uamh Smowe, or the Largest Cave. Stevenson, Marchie, and Duff go by land. Take the fowling-piece, and shoot some sea-fowl and a large hawk of an uncommon appearance. Fire four shots, and kill three times. After rowing about three miles to the westward of the entrance from the sea to Loch Eribol, we enter a creek, between two ledges of very high rocks, and landing, find ourselves in front of the wonder we came to see. The exterior apartment of the cavern opens under a tremendous rock, facing the creek, and occupies the full space of the ravine where we landed. From the top of the rock to the base of the cavern, as we afterwards discovered by plumb, is eighty feet, of which the height of the arch is fifty-three feet; the rest, being twenty-seven feet, is occupied by the precipitous rock under which it opens; the width is fully in proportion to this great height, being 110 feet. The depth of this exterior cavern is 200 feet, and it is apparently supported by an intermediate column of natural rock. Being open to daylight and the sea air, the cavern is perfectly clean and dry, and the sides are incrusted with stalactites. This immense cavern is so well proportioned that I was not aware of its extraordinary height and extent till I saw our two friends, who had somewhat preceded us, having made the journey by land, appearing like pigmies among its recesses. Afterwards, on entering the cave, I climbed up a sloping rock at its extremity, and was much struck with the prospect, looking outward from this magnificent arched cavern upon our boat and its crew, the view being otherwise bounded by the ledge of rocks which formed each side of the creek. We now propose to investigate the farther wonders of the cave of Smowe. In the right or west side of the cave opens an interior cavern of a different aspect. The height of this second passage may be about twelve or fourteen feet, and its breadth about six or eight, neatly formed into a Gothic portal by the hand of nature. The lower part of this porch is closed by a ledge of rock, rising to the height of between five and six feet, and which I can compare to nothing but the hatch-door of a shop. Beneath this hatch a brook finds its way out, forms a black deep pool before the Gothic archway, and then escapes to the sea, and forms the creek in which we landed. It is somewhat difficult to approach this strange pass, so as to gain a view into the interior of the cavern. By clambering along a broken and dangerous cliff, you can, however, look into it; but only so far as to see a twilight space filled with dark-coloured water in great agitation, and representing a subterranean lake, moved by some fearful convulsion of nature. How this pond is supplied with water you cannot see from even this point of vantage, but you are made partly sensible of the truth by a sound like the dashing of a sullen cataract within the bowels of the earth. Here the adventure has usually been abandoned, and Mr Anderson only mentioned two travellers whose curiosity had led them farther. We were resolved, however, to see the adventures of this new cave of Montesinos to an end. Duff had already secured the use of a fisher's boat and its hands, our own long-boat being too heavy and far too valuable to be ventured upon this Cocytus. Accordingly the skiff was dragged up the brook to the rocky ledge or hatch which barred up the interior cavern, and there, by force of hands, our boat's crew and two or three fishers first raised the boat's bow upon the ledge of rock, then brought her to a level, being poised upon that narrow hatch, and lastly launched her down into the dark and deep subterranean lake within. The entrance was so narrow, and the boat so clumsy, that we, who were all this while clinging to the rock like sea-fowl, and with scarce more secure footing, were greatly alarmed for the safety of our trusty sailors. At the instant when the boat sloped inward to the cave, a Highlander threw himself into it with great boldness and dexterity, and, at the expense of some bruises, shared its precipitate fall into the waters under the earth. This dangerous exploit was to prevent the boat drifting away from us, but a cord at its stern would have been a safer and surer expedient.

When our *enfant perdu* had recovered breath and legs, he brought the boat back to the entrance, and took us in. We now found ourselves embarked on a deep black pond of an irregular form, the rocks rising like a dome all around us, and high over our heads. The light, a sort of dubious twilight, was derived from two chasms in the roof of the vault, for that offered by the entrance was but trifling. Down one of those rents there poured from the height of eighty feet, in a sheet of foam, the brook, which, after supplying the subterranean pond with water, finds its way out beneath the ledge of rock that blocks its entrance. The other skylight, if I may so term it, looks out at the clear blue sky. It is impossible for description to explain the impression made by so strange a place, to which we had been conveyed with so much difficulty. The cave itself, the pool, the cataract, would have been each separate objects of wonder, but all united together, and affecting at once the ear, the eye, and the imagination, their effect is indescribable. The length of this pond, or loch as the people here call it, is seventy feet over, the breadth about thirty at the narrowest point, and it is of great depth.

As we resolved to proceed, we directed the boat to a natural arch on the right hand, or west side of the cataract. This archway was double, a high arch being placed above a very low one, as in a Roman aqueduct. The ledge of rock which forms this lower arch is not above two feet and a half high above the water, and under this we were to pass in the boat; so that we were fain to pile ourselves flat upon each other like a layer of herrings. By this judicious disposition we were pushed in safety beneath this low-browed rock into a region of utter darkness. For this, however, we were provided, for we had a tinder-box and lights. The view back upon the twilight lake we had crossed, its sullen eddies wheeling round and round, and its echoes resounding to the ceaseless thunder of the waterfall, seemed dismal enough, and was aggravated by temporary darkness, and in some degree by a sense of danger. The lights, however, dispelled the latter sensation, if it prevailed to any extent, and we now found ourselves in a narrow cavern, sloping somewhat upward from the water. We got out of the boat, proceeded along some slippery places upon shelves of the rock, and gained the dry land. I cannot say *dry*, excepting comparatively. We were then in an arched cave, twelve feet high in the roof, and about eight feet in breadth, which went winding into the bowels of the earth for about an hundred feet. The sides, being (like those of the whole cavern) of limestone rock, were covered with stalactites, and with small drops of water like dew, glancing like ten thousand thousand sets of birthday diamonds under the glare of our lights. In some places these stalactites branch out into broad and curious ramifications, resembling coral and the foliage of submarine plants.

When we reached the extremity of this passage, we found it declined suddenly to a horrible ugly gulf, or well, filled with dark water, and of great depth, over which the rock closed. We threw in stones, which indicated great profundity by their sound; and growing more familiar with the horrors of this den, we sounded with an oar, and found about ten feet depth at the entrance, but discovered in the same manner that the gulf extended under the rock, deepening as it went, God knows how far. Imagination can figure few deaths more horrible than to be sucked under these rocks into some unfathomable abyss, where your corpse could never be found to give intimation of your fate. A water kelpie, or an evil spirit of any aquatic propensities, could not choose a fitter abode; and, to say the truth, I believe at our first entrance, and when all our feelings were afloat at the novelty of the scene, the unexpected plashing of a seal would have routed the whole dozen of us. The mouth of this ugly gulf was all covered with slimy alluvious substances, which led Mr Stevenson to observe that it could have no separate source, but must be fed from the waters of the outer lake and brook, as it lay upon the same level, and seemed to rise and fall with them, without having anything to indicate a separate current of its own. Rounding this perilous hole, or gulf, upon the aforesaid alluvious substances, which formed its shores, we reached the extremity of the cavern, which there ascends like a vent, or funnel, directly up a sloping precipice, but hideously black and slippery from wet and seaweeds. One of our sailors, a Zetlander, climbed up a good way, and by holding up a light, we could plainly perceive that this vent closed after ascending to a considerable height; and here, therefore, closed the adventure of the cave of Smowe, for it appeared utterly impossible to proceed further in any direction whatever. There is a tradition that the first Lord Reay went through various subterranean abysses, and at length returned, after ineffectually endeavouring to penetrate to the extremity of the Smowe cave; but this must be either fabulous, or an exaggerated account of such a journey as we performed. And under the latter supposition, it is a curious instance how little the people in the neighbourhood of this curiosity have cared to examine it.

In returning, we endeavoured to familiarize ourselves with the objects in detail, which, viewed together, had struck us with so much wonder.

The stalactites, or limy incrustations, upon the walls of the cavern, are chiefly of a dark-brown colour, and in this respect Smowe is inferior, according to Mr Stevenson, to the celebrated cave of Macallister in the Isle of Skye. In returning, the men with the lights, and the various groups and attitudes of the party, gave a good deal of amusement. We now ventured to clamber along the side of the rock above the subterranean water, and thus gained the upper arch, and had the satisfaction to see our admirable and good-humoured commodore, Hamilton, floated beneath the lower arch into the second cavern. His goodly countenance being illumined by a single candle, his recumbent posture, and the appearance of a hard-favoured fellow guiding the boat, made him the very picture of Bibo, in the catch, when he wakes in Charon's boat:

> When Bibo thought fit from this world to retreat,
> As full of Champagne as an egg's full of meat,
> He waked in the boat, and to Charon he said,
> That he would be row'd back, for he was not yet dead.

Descending from our superior station on the upper arch, we now again embarked, and spent some time in rowing about and examining this second cave. We could see our dusky entrance, into which daylight streamed faint, and at a considerable distance; and under the arch of the outer cavern stood a sailor, with an oar in his hand, looking, in the perspective, like a fairy with his wand. We at length emerged unwillingly from this extraordinary basin, and again enjoyed ourselves in the large exterior cave. Our boat was hoisted with some difficulty over the ledge, which appears the natural barrier of the interior apartments, and restored in safety to the fishers, who were properly gratified for the hazard which their skiff, as well as one of themselves, had endured. After this we resolved to ascend the rocks, and discover the opening by which the cascade was discharged from above into the second cave. Erskine and I, by some chance, took the wrong side of the rocks, and, after some scrambling, got into the face of a dangerous precipice, where Erskine, to my great alarm, turned giddy, and declared he could not go farther. I clambered up without much difficulty, and shouting to the people below, got two of them to assist the Counsellor, who was brought into, by the means which have sent many a good fellow out of, the world – I mean a rope. We easily found the brook, and traced its descent till it precipitates itself down a chasm of the rock into the subterranean apartment, where we first made its acquaintance. Divided by a natural arch of stone from the chasm down which the cascade falls, there is another rent, which serves as a skylight to the cavern, as I already noticed. Standing on a natural foot-bridge, formed by the arch which divides these two gulfs, you have a grand prospect into both. The one is deep, black, and silent, only affording at the bottom a glimpse of the dark and sullen pool which occupies the interior of the cavern. The right-hand rent, down which the stream discharges itself, seems to ring and reel with the unceasing roar of the cataract which envelopes its side in mist and foam. This part of the scene alone is worth a day's journey. After heavy rains, the torrent is discharged into this cavern with astonishing violence; and the size of the chasm being inadequate to the reception of such a volume of water, it is thrown up in spouts like the blowing of a whale. But at such times the entrance of the cavern is inaccessible.

'Taking leave of this scene with regret, we rowed back to Loch Eribol. Having yet an hour to spare before dinner, we rowed across the mouth of the lake to its shore on the east side. This rises into a steep and shattered stack of mouldering calcareous rock and stone, called Whiten-head. It is pierced with several caverns, the abode of seals and cormorants. We entered one, where our guide promised to us a grand sight, and so it certainly would have been to any who had not just come from Smowe. In this last cave the sea enters through a lofty arch, and penetrates to a great depth; but the weight of the tide made it dangerous to venture very far, so we did not see the extremity of Friskin's Cavern, as it is called. We shot several cormorants in the cave, the echoes roaring like thunder at every discharge. We received, however, a proper rebuke from Hamilton, our commodore, for killing anything which was not fit for *eating*. It was in vain I assured him that the Zetlanders made excellent hare-soup out of these sea-fowl. He will listen to no subordinate authority, and rules us by the Almanach des Gourmands. Mr Anderson showed me the spot where the Norwegian monarch, Haco, moored his fleet, after the discomfiture he received at Largs. He caused all the cattle to be driven from the hills, and houghed and slain upon a broad flat rock, for the refreshment of his dispirited army. Mr Anderson dines with us, and very handsomely presents us with a stock of salmon, haddocks, and so forth, which we requite by a small present of wine from our sea stores. This has been a fine day; the first fair day here for these eight weeks.

20th August 1814 – Sail by four in the morning, and by half-past six are off Cape Wrath. All hands ashore by seven, and no time allowed to breakfast, except on beef and biscuit. On this dread Cape, so fatal to mariners, it is proposed to build a lighthouse, and Mr Stevenson has fixed on an advantageous situation. It is a high promontory, with steep sides that go sheer down to the breakers, which lash its feet. There is no landing, except in a small creek about a mile and a half to the eastward. There the foam of the sea plays at long bowls with a huge collection of large stones, some of them a ton in weight, but which these fearful billows chuck up and down as a child tosses a ball. The walk from thence to the Cape was over rough boggy ground, but good sheep pasture. Mr Dunlop, brother to the laird of Dunlop, took from Lord Reay, some years since, a large track of sheep-land, including the territories of Cape Wrath, for about £300 a year, for the period of two-nineteen years and a life-rent. It is needless to say that the tenant has an immense profit, for the value of pasture is now understood here. Lord Reay's estate, containing 150,000 square acres, and measuring eighty miles by sixty, was, before commencement of the last leases, rented at £1200 a year. It is now worth £5000, and Mr Anderson says he may let it this ensuing year (when the leases expire) for about £15,000. But then he must resolve to part with his people, for these rents can only be given upon the supposition that sheep are generally to be introduced on the property. In an economical, and perhaps in a political point of view, it might be best that every part of a country were dedicated to that sort of occupation for which nature has best fitted it. But to effect this reform in the present instance, Lord Reay must turn out several hundred families who have lived under him and his fathers for many generations, and the swords of whose fathers probably won the lands from which he is now expelling them. He is a good-natured man, I suppose, for Mr A. says he is hesitating whether he shall not take a more moderate rise (£7000 or £8000), and keep his Highland tenantry. This last war (before the short peace), he levied a fine fencible corps (the Reay fencibles), and might have doubled their number. *Wealth* is no doubt *strength* in a country, while all is quiet and governed by law, but on any altercation or internal commotion, it ceases to be strength, and is only the means of tempting the strong to plunder the possessors. Much may be said on both sides.[1]

Cape Wrath is a striking point, both from the dignity of its own appearance, and from the mental association of its being the extreme cape of Scotland, with reference to the north-west. There is no land in the direct line between this point and America. I saw a pair of large eagles, and if I had had the rifle-gun might have had a shot, for the birds, when I first saw them, were perched on a rock within about sixty or seventy yards. They are, I suppose, little disturbed here, for they showed no

[1]The whole of the immense district called *Lord Reay's country* – the habitation, as far back as history reaches, of the clan Mackay – has passed, since Sir W. Scott's journal was written, into the hands of the noble family of Sutherland.

great alarm. After the Commissioners and Mr Stevenson had examined the headland, with reference to the site of a lighthouse, we strolled to our boat, and came on board between ten and eleven. Get the boat up upon deck, and set sail for the Lewis with light winds and a great swell of tide. Pass a rocky islet called Gousla. Here a fine vessel was lately wrecked; all her crew perished but one, who got upon the rocks from the boltsprit, and was afterwards brought off. In front of Cape Wrath are some angry breakers, called the *Staggs*; the rocks which occasion them are visible at low water. The country behind Cape Wrath swells in high sweeping elevations, but without any picturesque or dignified mountainous scenery. But on sailing westward a few miles, particularly after doubling a headland called the Stour of Assint, the coast assumes the true Highland character, being skirted with a succession of picturesque mountains of every variety of height and outline. These are the hills of Ross-shire – a waste and thinly-peopled district at this extremity of the island. We would willingly have learned the names of the most remarkable, but they are only laid down in the charts by the cant names given them by mariners, from their appearance, as the Sugar-loaf, and so forth. Our breeze now increases, and seems steadily favourable, carrying us on with exhilarating rapidity, at the rate of eight knots an hour, with the romantic outline of the mainland under our lee-beam, and the dusky shores of the Long Island beginning to appear ahead. We remain on deck long after it is dark, watching the phosphoric effects occasioned, or made visible, by the rapid motion of the vessel, and enlightening her course with a continued succession of sparks and even flashes of broad light, mingled with the foam which she flings from her bows and head. A rizard haddock and to bed. Charming weather all day.

21st August 1814 – Last night went out like a lamb, but this morning came in like a lion, all roar and tumult. The wind shifted and became squally; the mingled and confused tides that run among the Hebrides got us among their eddies, and gave the cutter such concussions, that, besides reeling at every wave, she trembled from head to stern, with a sort of very uncomfortable and ominous vibration. Turned out about three, and went on deck; the prospect dreary enough, as we are beating up a narrow channel between two dark and disconsolate-looking islands, in a gale of wind and rain, guided only by the twinkling glimmer of the light on an island called Ellan Glas. – Go to bed and sleep soundly, notwithstanding the rough rocking. Great bustle about four; the lightkeeper having seen our flag, comes off to be our pilot, as in duty bound. Asleep again till eight. When I went on deck, I found we had anchored in the little harbour of Scalpa, upon the coast of Harris, a place dignified by the residence of Charles Edward in his hazardous attempt to escape in 1746. An old man, lately alive here, called Donald Macleod, was his host and temporary protector, and could not, until his dying hour, mention the distresses of the adventurer without tears. From this place, Charles attempted to go to Stornoway; but the people of the Lewis had taken arms to secure him, under an idea that he was coming to plunder the country. And although his faithful attendant, Donald Macleod, induced them by fair words to lay aside their purpose, yet they insisted upon his leaving the island. So the unfortunate Prince was obliged to return back to Scalpa. He afterwards escaped to South Uist, but was chased in the passage by Captain Fergusson's sloop of war. The harbour seems a little neat secure place of anchorage. Within a small island, there seems more shelter than where we are lying; but it is crowded with vessels, part of those whom we saw in the Long-Hope – so Mr Wilson chose to remain outside. The ground looks hilly and barren in the extreme; but I can say little for it, as an incessant rain prevents my keeping the deck. Stevenson and Duff, accompanied by Marchie, go to examine the lighthouse on Ellan Glas. Hamilton and Erskine keep their beds, having scarce slept last night – and I bring up my journal. The day continues bad, with little intermission of rain. Our party return with little advantage from their expedition, excepting some fresh butter from the lighthouse. The harbour of Scalpa is composed of a great number of little uninhabited islets. The masts of the vessels at anchor behind them have a good effect. To bed early, to make amends for last night, with the purpose of sailing for Dunvegan in the Isle of Skye with daylight.

27th August 1814 – The wind, to which we resigned ourselves, proves exceedingly tyrannical, and blows squally the whole night, which, with the swell of the Atlantic, now unbroken by any islands to windward, proves a means of great combustion in the cabin. The dishes and glasses in the steward's cupboards become locomotive – portmanteaus and writing-desks are more active than necessary – it is scarce possible to keep one's self within bed, and impossible to stand upright if you rise. Having crept upon deck about four in the morning, I find we are beating to windward off the Isle of Tyree, with the determination on the part of Mr Stevenson that his constituents should visit a reef of rocks called *Skerry Vhor*, where he thought it would be essential to have a lighthouse. Loud remonstrances on the part of the Commissioners, who one and all declare they will subscribe to his opinion, whatever it may be, rather than continue this infernal buffeting. Quiet perseverance on the part of Mr S., and great kicking, bouncing, and squabbling upon that of the Yacht, who seems to like the idea of Skerry Vhor as little as the Commissioners. At length, by dint of exertion, come in sight of this long ridge of rocks (chiefly under water), on which the tide breaks in a most tremendous style. There appear a few low broad rocks at one end of the reef, which is about a mile in length. These are never entirely under water, though the surf dashes over them. To go through all the forms, Hamilton, Duff, and I resolve to land upon these bare rocks in company with Mr Stevenson. Pull through a very heavy swell with great difficulty, and approach a tremendous surf dashing over black pointed rocks. Our rowers, however, get the boat into a quiet creek between two rocks, where we contrive to land well wetted. I saw nothing remarkable in my way, excepting several seals, which we might have shot, but, in the doubtful circumstances of the landing, we did not care to bring guns. We took possession of the rock in name of the Commissioners, and generously bestowed our own great names on its crags and creeks. The rock was carefully measured by Mr S. It will be a most desolate position for a lighthouse – the Bell Rock and Eddystone a joke to it, for the nearest land is the wild island of Tyree, at fourteen miles' distance. So much for the Skerry Vhor.

Came on board proud of our achievement; and, to the great delight of all parties, put the ship before the wind, and run swimmingly down for Iona. See a large square-rigged vessel, supposed an American. Reach Iona about five o'clock. The inhabitants of the isle of Columba, understanding their interest as well as if they had been Deal boatmen, charged two guineas for pilotage, which Captain W. abridged into fifteen shillings, too much for ten minutes' work. We soon got on shore, and landed in the bay of Martyrs, beautiful for its white sandy beach. Here all dead bodies are still landed, and laid for a time upon a small rocky eminence, called the Sweyne, before they are interred. Iona, the last time I saw it, seemed to me to contain the most wretched people I had anywhere seen. But either they have got better since I was here, or my eyes, familiarised with the wretchedness of Zetland and the Harris, are less shocked with that of Iona. Certainly their houses are better than either, and the appearance of the people not worse. This little fertile isle contains upwards of 400 inhabitants, all living upon small farms, which they divide and subdivide as their families increase, so that the country is greatly over-peopled, and in some danger of a famine in case of a year of scarcity. Visit the nunnery and Reilig Oran, or burial-place of St Oran, but the night coming on we return on board.

The Queen Mary

from Down to the Sea

GEORGE BLAKE (1893–1961)

One of the vanished 'pleasures of the sea' is the luxury transatlantic liner. Scotland's tradition in building ships for the Atlantic route was a long one – Samuel Cunard came to the Clyde for his first four steamships in 1839 and the great tradition continued into the twentieth century with ships like the Lusitania, Mauretania *and* Aquitania. Perhaps the high point in this story came with the Cunarder Queen Mary, *launched from the Clydebank shipyard of John Brown & Co. in September 1934.*

The Queen Mary, or No. 534 as she was known during her years of building and during the dark days of the Depression when work on her was suspended and her hull lay rusting, was a ship of some elegance and enormous presence. More importantly, she became a national symbol of hope when work on her recommenced with a Government subsidy in April 1934. Her maiden voyage across the Atlantic was in 1936 and her reputation was soon made. During the Second World War she was converted to a troop transport and conveyed hundreds of thousands of American servicemen across the Atlantic in speed and safety, if hardly in the style and comfort of pre-war days. Her post-war career was equally glamorous, when she shared the Cunard Atlantic service with her Clydebank-built sister-ship Queen Elizabeth. However the competition from jet aircraft meant the end of year-round scheduled transatlantic services and the Mary now rests dry-docked at San Diego, California.

George Blake was born in Greenock, very much a man of the Clyde. His first career was as a journalist in Glasgow and his novels and non-fiction work focus on the river and its shipbuilding industry. Our extract comes from his 1937 tribute to his native river 'Down to the Sea; the romance of the Clyde, its ships and shipbuilders.'

Blake's closing paragraph exists in another, slightly different, and perhaps more authentic form and well expresses the pride of the Clyde in their latest product, in its own way another pleasure of the sea. In the version given by Colin Castle in 'Better by Yards', John Brown's yard foreman, watching the launch, remarked:

Aye, she's no the Rex, *and she's no the* Bremen, *and she's no the*
Normandie, *but she's bluidy well oor idea o' a ship.*

Words, words, words ... and there may seem little enough excuse for
adding to the millions that have been lavished on the appearance of
the *Queen Mary*. Yet here was something decisive and, in its period,
final. The greatest ship of her time is assuredly not the last word in
ships, even if, measured against Henry Bell's *Comet*, she represents in
staggering form the advance of a science within the space of little more
than a hundred years. The contrast is so ludicrous that the bald figures
take on colour and liveliness – forty-three feet against a thousand; four
horse-power against two hundred thousand; five knots against thirty. It
is at the least permissible to surmise, having regard for economics and for
the possible developments of air travel, that the *Queen Mary* is indeed
a monument marking an era.

As for those millions of words, their justification seems obvious
enough. This thing, this ship, is in her time stunning in size and
efficiency. That men should be able to create so largely and beautifully
is in the order of poetry. That men concerned to see the ship prosper in
the mercantile adventure for which she was designed should stimulate
and swell the flow of words – that legitimately follows. And beyond
all that lies the very strange and symbolical history of the ship – how
work on the gigantic hull was stopped for years on end, so that when the
workmen went back at length they found the nests of colonies of rooks
and starlings in the fabric and in the interstices of the gantries about and
above it. That resumption of work had its drama, reaching its appropriate
climax in the blessing of the vessel by an ageing King and the christening
of her by his Queen. In short, the prides of a seafaring nation and of a
shipbuilding race were utterly engaged. This mass of metal had become
the symbol of a national self-respect. To leave her unfinished would have
been as unthinkable as, shall we say, to scuttle half the Fleet. To launch
and fit her out for service was the necessary satisfaction of a sentiment
more profound than some know it to be. There were never enough words
to express just what all that signified.

If this is an adding to the tale, belated and dead in the terms of
the newspaper men, it is still relevant to the topic with which this
narrative has been concerned. For in the appearance of the *Queen Mary*
one small wheel came full-circle, in that the boy who had forsaken a
piano-stool to gasp at the sight of the *Lusitania* coming down the
river lived and wrought so that he had an intimate, curious part in the

proceedings whereby the progress of the *Queen Mary* was conveyed, in still more words, and spoken words, to the world. Even the odd, irrelevant association of music coloured the end of the story as it had the beginning. If the *Lusitania* came down the Clyde to the feeble accompaniment of 'Woodland Whispers', the *Queen Mary* first crossed the Atlantic to the hardly more noble strains – to the sweet, nostalgic, trivial air – of 'These Foolish Things'. A song of the hour, transient and insubstantial as a cloud at dawn, yet inveterately woven into the texture of an abiding memory.

This record must be of little oddities of the sort – indeed, a tale of foolish things. But the sidelights are so often the most illuminating! Every experience has its atmosphere that may be lost among the exigencies of direct narration, and one whose function in the affair was at once privileged and obscure saw more than a great ship being launched and brought down the Clyde and despatched on her maiden voyage. His view was of the humanity involved in the proceedings; of follies and frivolities and the interplay of small ambitions; of little decencies and the abiding strength behind the undertaking. Shall we say at once that the affair was too public, too open to the intrusion of the pushful? Sometimes it was difficult to see the ship for the small people crawling about her. Sometimes it was impossible to believe that people of the sort could have produced such a lovely thing. And yet—

They launched the *Queen Mary* in a downpour of rain on the 26th of September, 1934, and the story of that daring exploit is safe and full in the records. There were memorable passages in King George's speech. The little hesitations of Queen Mary and the whispered promptings of Sir Thomas Bell, local managing director of the building firm, are now part of an oral legend. There were yards of ermine and gold braid, and a long roster of resounding titles, behind the rain-flooded glass of the launching dais. A bottle smashed high up on the precipice that was the port bow of the ship – a curiously feeble sound in the rain-filled space of the yard. Heavy hammers thumped on blocks of wood. One seems to remember the thin pipe of a whistle, probably blown by some bowler-hatted gaffer in the echoing chambers beneath the hull. One eye, matching the bow of the ship against a distant chimney, saw a gap of emptiness suddenly created between these fixed objects. Thirty thousand tons of steel, painted white, were moving, nay, plunging towards the water. Chains whipped and lashed like snakes. There was a spurt of flame, dowsed in clouds of oily smoke, over the greased ways. She seemed to move at terrific speed. She was surely rushing to disaster. The army of spectators was silent. Then it liberated itself in a roar. For there was the *Queen Mary*, no longer a number in the books, riding high and light in the narrow river, and the tugs bearing down on her with the purposefulness of terriers after a rat. The rain had suddenly, miraculously stopped. Had we really seen a man, high on the uttermost bow of the ship, waving his cloth cap like a madman? Anyhow, the ship was launched, securely water-borne. That was that part of the job done.

But the inwardness of the job, so elegantly withheld from the men in the silk hats and the fancy uniforms? That nerve-wracked man in the bowler hat under the hull, the whistle bitten into by his teeth? The yard manager on a little, separate platform of his own, and on him the intolerable fear that she might stick on the ways, or rush to destruction, or topple over on the open mouths of the mob of spectators? The inwardness seemed to be perceived by him who was then the Prince of Wales, now Duke of Windsor. The royal procession and the marshalling of it were stately, but then one saw a young man, fascinated by the spectacle of a huge ship ready for the launching, twisting his head and shoulders, and his body from the waist, to peer up at the frowning, formidable bows of the thing of which the launching was but an entry in the royal diary. The common humanity glowed there for a moment.

Another little thing. The broadcasting of this launching ceremony was a business of great moment since millions in all parts of the world would surely be listening, and the exact timing of the thing became therefore a matter of anxious concern. British royalty goes about its ceremonial affairs with an exact regard for the time factor, but while officials knew the probable order of events beforehand, there were in this case some awkward imponderables to be considered. No man could tell to a minute when the tide in the river would serve; and on such a day of rain the programme might be curtailed in the interests of an invalid monarch. (In the event, the omission of one small bit of ritual did throw the schedule out by an awkward minute and a quarter.) But the private problem of the broadcasters was to know when – and exactly when, to the quarter-minute – the royal procession would reach the gates of the shipyard. It was solved thus. The route from the city had been laid down; a royal car moves at a given pace on these ceremonial occasions. So a private car made an experimental journey at that stately rate of speed, establishing the fact that, from a certain post office on the way to the yard gates, the journey must occupy exactly nine and a half – or was it fourteen and a quarter? – minutes. Thus, if the postmistress could call a certain secret number precisely as the King's car passed her door, the rest would follow. And so it came to pass. Unseen by him who described his approach, a short, familiar figure in the uniform of an Admiral appeared above the heads of the crowd precisely as had been said it would.

That, however, was a trivial enough matter of staffwork behind the scenes. Something else, a much grander and more dramatic thing, happened in the open yard, and only a few had eyes to grasp its lovely significance. As has been told, the shipbuilder's yard manager stood apart that day on a little platform of his own to watch the great ship take the water. It was a delightfully characteristic figure he cut there – a sturdy man of Clydeside in the traditional bowler hat and familiar bow tie – but there were some to know what a burden was upon him in that moment. This was his essential, ineluctable responsibility – this hurtling of thirty thousand tons of metal into a canal that was in breadth less than half the ship's length. He was, in reality, the central figure on the stage. Yet the cameras of the Press did not turn that way. There were so many thundering titles, so much gold braid, within the dais. The yard manager stood alone and, alone, faced his trial.

The ship was launched. The tugboats took her in charge. Down from the dais streamed the party of notables, heading for cake and wine, the bloodhounds of the Press hot on the trail. Still the yard manager stood on his little platform watching his ship. It was as if he could not yet resign his responsibility to the pilots and the berthing foreman of riggers. But at last he turned away and stood down; and as he did so, a tiny group of shipyard workers, standing there to do some little job of their own, took off their tweed caps and cheered him. It was not a loud cheer, the bellow of a throng. It sounded a little feeble in the emptiness where the ship had been. It was a private affair – a few workers who knew their job saluting a worker of whose job they knew the significance. But to one watcher of the odd little scene it seemed the biggest thing of the day.

Those workers of Clydebank . . . It still seems impossible to understand them. The dramatic mind seeks continually to pin them down to type, and continually they elude characterisation. One could in the early stages of the ship's construction, when the interior of the hull seemed an iron foundry on the grand scale, discern the Clydeside artisan of the old tradition: the man of the Black Squad, with a terrific breadth of shoulder, a command of harsh language, a grim way of 'getting on with the job' and, no doubt, a noble capacity for glasses and pints. Yet that was a transient figure, perhaps a disappearing figure. A week later, and the army seemed to consist of halflin boys with such a passion for football in its sectarian aspects that, when they come at length to break up the *Queen Mary*, men will find chalked on the steel plates behind the elegant woods of the state-rooms gross insults to the Pope and praise of players long forgotten. At yet another stage, the alleyways hummed to the anxious debates of pale electricians, lovingly technical and deeply learned in the incredible intricacies of the circuits. Or one would see the army dispersing in the evening – a fleet of buses at the gates to take many of them to far-distant housing schemes, their gardens and their wireless sets. One could surmise of most of them that they were strictly sober, decently educated men of the new dispensation: the frivolity of the youngsters limited to prowess as Sunday cyclists or to expertise in the dance-halls. The abiding impression was of youth: of a new, clean, efficient youth, defying sentimentalisation as the rough diamonds of yesterday's fiction.

These men who built the *Queen Mary* defied sentimentalising to the end. There was an end to the ship so far as the rank and file were concerned on the 24th of March, 1936, when she was canted out of the builders' fitting-out basin and taken down to the sea, never, in any reasonable calculation, to return to the place of her making. That was a much less spectacular business than most people had anticipated. The tugs got her out of the basin in no time, and she bumped the mud of the channel when a strong wind from the east caught her on a bend at Dalmuir, and she was lying off Greenock at two in the afternoon. She filled the channel on her way down-river, as a cathedral dominates a city, and one may imagine that a lot of emotion followed her in the forms of pride in a job well done and regret that a vigorous spring of employment had dried up. But it was essentially a job of work: and Clydeside got on with it. If one looked for the satiating meed of melodrama the workers of Clydebank certainly did not provide it on that crisp and sunshiny morning of March. One may remember a queer encounter with the naval architect of the building firm, under the gantries. He, who had his own heavy load of responsibility for that day's work to bear, was so very anxious that the broadcaster should be at his post in time to see the ship move out earlier than had been expected: so fast was the tide running up the river that morning. Then the flash of humanity emerged when it was revealed that, in the background of the naval architect's mind, was a sick little boy at home, waiting eagerly to hear how the *Queen Mary* fared on her way to the sea.

That was a grand enough spectacle – an enormous mass being coaxed out of a box of water, as it were, into a rivulet. It was done with ease so apparent as to be preposterous. Tugs pulled at her stern and nuzzled into her sides. An antique winch ground at a wire hawse to assist her

away from the quay. The foreman rigger used powerful words. We saw
a sudden swirl of brown-creaming water under her stern – the first cut
of the mighty propellers under power. Yet the workers of Clydebank
let her go away from them for ever with hardly a cheer. The hooters
had called them from their jobs on other hulls to watch the pride of
the yard go out. They appeared in their hundreds, swarming up the
gantries and on to roofs. Again they seemed very young and insulated
against melodrama by a pervading facetiousness. One cheer they did
raise was half-hearted, semi-satirical, as if they must resist emotion.
Or they were not aware of emotion at all. One will never know.
In silence they let the *Queen Mary* go, and then they went back to
their jobs.

It could not have happened so in Italy, say, or even in England. The
phenomenon was of the racial or the professional order, or both. All one
knows is that it seemed to give a very strange atmosphere to the end of
a long and eventful story.

Yet there was about most of the major events of the *Queen Mary*'s
early days a curious lack of ostensible drama. It may be that she ceased to
figure as a curiosity and became just a fine, big, fast ship with a job to do.
The departure from Southampton on the maiden voyage must certainly
have been a secret disappointment to thousands who had dreamed of high
sensations. On the stroke of the appointed hour on that May afternoon
she backed like a car out of the Ocean Dock, canted handily in the
mouth of the Test, and went off on her voyage. The privileged crowd
on the pier might have been witnessing a fashionable wedding. There
were planes to roar above her as she went down Southampton Water,
and fast motor-boats to keep abreast, and excursion steamers to limp
behind, heeling over with the weight of their passengers. But Britain's
farewell to the ship of her pride was secretive compared with the lunacy
that burst about her when she passed the Ambrose Light early in the
morning of the fifth day thereafter.

Now, however, the events of departure and arrival seem separated by
a lengthy interregnum of unreality. The four days might have been four
weeks – or four months – so intense were the moods of the thousands
carried by the new ship, so frequent and confused and indecisive the
contacts among them. There is need for patience in any consideration
of the phenomenon, to be sure. This was one of the two greatest ships
of the world, and perhaps the faster of these two. She carried scores
of men who had had shares in her creation, even if it was only of
the water-bottles in the state-rooms. She carried an army of newspaper
men, British and American, hectic in competition to make news out of

the maiden voyage. Another international corps recorded in wirelessed words, English, American English, French, Dutch and Danish, the life and progress of the vessel at sea. Beyond these groups with their immediate interests in the ship's performance ranged a queer array of persons of title; of actresses, charmingly varied as to style and beauty and age, of the merely rich – all come on this voyage with motives of their own. One wonders if the *Queen Mary* took on her maiden trip a single passenger crossing the Atlantic for any of the quite ordinary reasons.

So the atmosphere of the proceedings was inevitably abnormal. The gantries and tenements of Clydebank – and the lighted spaces of the main lounge, with a dance band thrumming out the melodies of the moment, or a lady of the West End stage soulfully enunciating the words of the occasion's theme song . . . latterly to be described by Mr Larry Adler as 'the symphonic high spot of 1936'.

> A cigarette that bears a lipstick's traces,
> An airline ticket to romantic places,
> And still my heart has wings . . .
> These foolish things
> Remind me of you.

But not of Jock Campbell, the riveter in Dalmuir; any more than champagne cocktails in the observation lounge or the maître d'hôtel taking an order for penguin's eggs could conceivably be related to a mutton-pie and a pint in some pub along the Dumbarton Road.

For topic the company relied almost exclusively on comparisons with the French *Normandie*. What were the relative degrees of excellence in service, decoration, cooking, comfort? Over the air one night the French commentator sought to dispose of the question with exquisite Gallic grace. 'For who,' he asked of the ether, 'would think of comparing a beautiful blonde with a beautiful brunette?' The neutrality of Denmark, on the other hand, permitted Mr Carstensen to wireless to his distant listeners the *mot* of the trip. For him the Anglo-French jealousy was manna from on high, and thus he summed his conclusion: 'The French built a beautiful hotel and put a ship round it. The British built a beautiful ship and put a hotel inside it.' Wisdom and percipience there – but could we see the ship for the hotel?

Now and again it was indeed embodied in flashes of the talk that occasionally rose above the chatter of foolish things. The journalists got nearest to reality. They hymned two elements – Vibration and Speed. As to the first of them the *Queen Mary* was by common consent peerless among all big ships. But was she, even on this maiden voyage, to show a clean pair of heels to the *Normandie*? The question referred back directly to a lot of ordinary Clydeside men in oily overalls.

So, through this consideration, there prominently emerged the phenomenon of the American Journalist. . . . In every retrospect of that maiden voyage this interesting figure must stand out in the foreground. The American Journalist, haunted by the competitive elements in his profession and by the material and technical interests of his countrymen. The great question of Vibration settled, he was concerned only with Speed. That alone was News. The passion of the American Journalist was to have the *Queen Mary* beat the *Normandie* record and be done with it. This was not a matter of taking sides as between two friendly nations. But it would be News, a Beat, a Scoop.

Every day, at noon, an assembly of interested parties met in conference to hear the report from the bridge on the day's run. This was a curt affair of latitude and longitude, sea miles covered, average speed, and – a charming maritime irrelevance – the weather conditions we had endured, but its announcement was the little hour of the American Journalist. Towards record of latitude, longitude, and the weather he was tolerant but indifferent. Distance and Speed alone mattered; and as, day by day, the *Queen Mary* lagged behind the *Normandie* on the latter's record run, the face of the American Journalist grew longer, his comments more impatient. That a great new ship with terrific horsepower was not eating up the Atlantic seemed to him incredible, if not indecent. That she was not being run all out was for him a betrayal; nor was he willing to believe in the fact. They had to bring Sir Percy Bates into these conferences to soothe the American soul, and the encounters were dramatically illuminating. As against the urgency of the New World, the chairman of the owning company so perfectly represented the Old. This was a new ship, and her engines must be run in as with a new motorcar, he told the company. Nor had she been built to break records, but to maintain a schedule. The words were sensible, but it was not their sense that at length broke down the resistance of the American Journalist. It was the steel-rimmed spectacles of the chairman, far down towards the tip of his long nose, and his briar pipe, and his bland English wonder that there should be any fuss about this question of Speed. *This* was News – this vindication of a Scottish creation by a calm Englishman.

In the meantime, the day's run would be causing a stir in the smoke-room. Perhaps the pool had been auctioned for so much as £800 the night before. Would that vivacious little actress win it again? Anyhow, one of the army of stewards, in their holland jackets with red cuffs and

collars, would come in with cocktails; and no doubt somebody would
sing another verse of the song . . .

> The smile of Garbo and the scent of roses,
> The waiters whistling as the last bar closes,
> The song that Crosby sings—
> These foolish things
> Remind me of you.

For a day at least the Stowaway was a providential distraction for all,
a gift from heaven to the journalists. It was right that there should be
a stowaway; the great traditions must be maintained; but this one fared
more happily than the boys of the *Arran*. He was discovered in a lavatory
– a convenience probably unknown in Captain Watt's ship. He was a
sensible sort of fellow. Unemployed, he had tramped to Southampton
and, on a whim, had boarded the big ship with a squad of stokers. That
was all about it. When they put him to work in one of the galleys he
worked well. Then he was forgotten by all save the executive officers.
Not many passengers remembered the stowaway next day, and only
very few cared to discover that he was taken back to Southampton on
the return voyage and in due course 'dealt with'. The episode should
have been nobler than that; it should have ended more sentimentally.
Still, the novelty of it agreeably filled an hour or two until it was time
for cocktails about six.

The Fog was less directly in the romantic tradition, much nearer the
bone altogether. It came down on the afternoon of the third day out;
a wet and sickly mass of negation, closing in on the ship and wiping
out the spaces of the sea. More passengers than ever before became
aware of the fact that they travelled in a ship. Some who had hardly
seen the sea dared to step out on the wet decks to discover that the
hotel was indeed a shell of steel, suddenly lonely and helpless in face
of what might be lying ahead – icebergs, say, or some schooner out of
Newfoundland. Directional wireless, sounding machines, speed reduced
– but by how much? – and the intolerable roar of the monstrous siren
every forty-five seconds: all these things for safety; and yet the reality
of the living vessel had to dawn on almost all. That siren seemed to
blow you off the boat-deck. The long fabric of the ship quivered to
its vibrations. Three decks knew it as an imminent menace. Yet it was
reported to sound on B Deck only as a sort of distant shudder, while
the Tourist Cocktail Bar, they said, heard it not at all. It did not disturb
the run of the afternoon cinema show. Even in the Observation Lounge
right below the bridge, when the lights went up in the evening and the

chatter thickened in texture and the gin got to work, you could become used to it and forget it altogether. The very elements round the ship could be defied by the modern conveniences of the hotel.

Even so, the fog had played a larger part than the stowaway. It evoked from the siren an authentic noise of the ship that could be movingly broadcast to millions on shore. For the journalists it was news and for the American Journalist in particular an effective laying of the bogey of Speed that haunted him. There were thoughts at last for the Commodore as something more than a decorative figure with high social favours to bestow, and he drew to himself visions of the seaman on the bridge, frowning into the gloom as he stood face to face with responsibility. It was queer to learn that the man in the crow's nest rode high and alone above the besetting mists like an airman.

But the hotel had still its function of entertainment to fulfil. Deep down in the bowels of the ship, fog and icebergs the phantoms of quite another world, the compositors sweated over their thousands of menus and the setting of at least fifty special ones for private parties. Men in white jackets mixed and shook the glaucous Martinis and pallid White Ladies of two-score cocktail gatherings. The steward in the Library dealt suavely, patiently, with the fitful tastes in fiction of a dowager from Washington, D.C. The haberdasher's shop dealt in bathing trunks and frogged pyjamas. In his refrigerated cubby-hole aft, the ship's gardener, a Fellow of the Royal Horticultural Society no less, brooded over the thousand fresh spikes he must provide for the Main Dining-Room to-morrow, thought lovingly of the giant calceolarias that had been specially ordered for the ship long before she was ready for her trials, and set out a buttonhole or two for his favourites among passengers and journalists and broadcasters. Far down, in a pool of jade-green water that swung to the ship's slow motion, the fair exhibited their suave forms and the sinewy their strokes. The ornamental fish fluttered in the tank in the wall of the Children's Playroom. A lady stroked the frocks in the wardrobes of her state-room with thoughtful indecision, for was she not to dine in the Veranda Grill that night, as who, living in Claridge's, should go to sup at the Berkeley? Somewhere, for sure, somebody would be singing

> The winds of March that make my heart a dancer,
> A telephone that rings – but who's to answer?
> Oh, how the ghost of you clings!
> These foolish things
> Remind me of you.

That strain had a dying fall, reinforced by cunning fifths and cautious modulations in the accompaniment. It sang nostalgia – the mood of the civilised world that always goes back a little before civilisation for its sensations. The *Surprise* Symphony and 'These Foolish Things' – the *Queen Mary* at Clydebank and the *Queen Mary* at sea – sometimes one stepped out of the hotel for more than a breath of fresh air.

And the ship was always there for those who cared to look at it. Even a man with the earphones of radio clamped over his head could catch the echoes of infinity, as when, waiting to give the signal to a French or American or Dutch or Danish commentator, he heard over thousands of miles of empty, enigmatic sea the clipped, technical voices of Cockneys or New Yorkers saying, 'Hallo, *Queen Mary* . . . Speak up, *Queen Mary* . . . You're fading like hell . . . Speak up, *Queen Mary* . . . Copenhagen's waiting for you.'

It was best just to go out on deck, preferably on the open boat-deck, and realise it was truly a ship that cut through those meaningless seas. The darkness of night and the gleam of the wash breaking back from the ship's great bow-wave were reassurances of the true adventure and challenge of this maiden voyage. One could be alone with the ship, as it were, on the fo'c'sle head, from whence, looking aft, the lofty superstructure was in grace and intention the match of any cathedral. Awed and a little frightened, one could watch the slow swing of funnels and masts athwart the stars. Up in the dim-lit crow's nest the lookout-man would be singing softly to himself. Another row of lights, less dim but yet not bright, marked the line of the bridge, where, save for the clicking of the gyroscopic compass, it was always religiously quiet as if – perhaps because – the essential conduct of the ship was indeed a devotional exercise.

It was good to move from the fo'c'sle head to the very stern of the ship, there to gaze on the vehement churn of the propellers under the counter. From the bow the impression was of grace and easy speed, a gliding of beauty through the night. At the stern one's awareness was of implacable power – thousands of tons of water writhing, fuming, and rearing to the terrible drive of the mighty engines. Here was Clydeside vindicated in possession of the ship. This was the essential creation of a long line of builders and engineers. Was it too fanciful to imagine that the ghost of Robert Napier hovered there above the spray and the spume, smiling to see his work so superbly perfected?

Literally, the last word rested with a man of Clydeside, the doyen of the journalists and of the wits on board. He said it in retort to the American Journalist who, his nerves fraying, had taken to unfriendly comparisons between the *Queen Mary* and the other great ships on the Atlantic Ferry. There was no ostensible cracking of the surface of his urbanity, but perhaps one did detect the undertow of passion in his words.

'No,' he agreed. 'She's not the *Normandie*, and she's not the *Bremen*, and she's not the *Rex*. But she is Sandy's idea of a ship and' – the rider came relentless – 'Sandy has been building ships for a long, long time.'

Dawn at Sea

from Highland Pack

NEIL GUNN (1891–1973)

Neil Gunn came from a Caithness fishing family; he started to write while following a career as an exciseman, a period which saw his first great success with Morning Tide. *In 1937 he became a full-time writer and continued the exploration of his local and maritime heritage in classic works such as* The Silver Darlings.

'Dawn at Sea' is an account of a trip made by Gunn in a fishing boat off the Caithness coast near his childhood home of Dunbeath. Although the trip was, to the crew, an ordinary enough working voyage, we include it in this section on the pleasures of the sea because of Gunn's evident delight in all the details of the experience – from the working of the diesel engine and the cost of ropes to the passing gulls and the rising sun. 'Dawn at Sea' comes from Gunn's 1949 collection of essays on various aspects of Highland life, Highland Pack. *Originally written during the Second World War these essays together constitute Gunn's closest approach to a personal book about the Highlands he knew intimately and loved deeply. They were written, as he said, '. . . in simple gratitude for having been born and permitted to spend nearly all my life there.'*

Now and then a sudden craving comes for the sea, for the movement and tumult that the land has eternally frozen into valley troughs and mountain crests. From the sea one can come back to the quiet land as a child to its mother, but the old primitive father holds sway over the sea. 'The sea is in his blood' – but how seldom do folk say the same of the land!

So I reached the northern shore of the Moray Firth and at 4 a.m., as I was finishing a drop of hastily warmed milk, the skipper's tap came on the window. I blew out the paraffin lamp and joined him outside.

'I thought I'd take a walk past – in case you slept in!' There was no hurry in the voice nor in the still realm of moonlight and we walked over the tree-shadows and down by the stream. The cottages were asleep like sheep in a park. A small wind from the north brought a frost-chill to the air. The wind would go round with the sun. It was going to be a lovely morning.

A masthead light was coming in over the bar. The skipper named the boat. She had gone out at four o'clock the previous afternoon and had been fishing all night. As she came alongside we saw some open boxes full of haddock ready to be slung ashore. The haddock were gutted, and there were ten boxes altogether, each weighing six stone. Not much was said by way of greeting. A quiet word or two. A tidy forty-foot boat she was, all electrically lit, and the young skipper stood in his long white rubber boots by the wheelhouse.

And here is our own boat of about the same size and build, but with a Diesel instead of a Kelvin engine. The two lads who make up the crew are already on board, and I climb down the single rope, searching with my toes for crannies in the high stone wall, and land on the grey coils of the seine-net rope. In the engine-room aft there is the hiss of a blow-lamp, and presently the engine is running. We hang on to a mooring and the boat's head swings slowly round. Then the warp falls back against the harbour wall – for each boat has its own station – and we go ahead. The pulse of the sea meets us at the end of the cement quay and we stand straight out.

This is the moment one thinks about on land, this first lifting move-ment under the feet. The sea itself lifts to the horizon in an expansiveness that lifts the spirit with it. Eyes grow clear-sighted and muscles ready and prepared to be lively. The skipper ushers me into the slim wheelhouse where there is no room for two, lowers a glass panel, and stands outside by the opening. The compass is overhead in the roof. The throttle is no slim affair such as I had had on my own small motor cruiser but a tall T-shaped iron key thick as a forefinger. It takes eight or nine half-turns to reduce full speed to dead slow, so there is considerable flexibility. You can steer with one hand and put her out of and into gear with the other, for the gear lever is also a wheel and turns forward or backward with neutral midway. It is only a 26 h.p. engine but it is tough and can be left alone. Indeed no attention was paid to it, nor did it stop, from the moment we left harbour until we tied up over eight hours later.

These mechanical details I find refreshingly interesting. And in truth you cannot afford to neglect the smallest thing on a boat at sea. Moreover I was in the mood to ask questions, for war had not yet broken out, and the economic position of our fishing boats was growing steadily more desperate. The skipper, who was a very old friend, had a lot to say about this, even if I did not then realize how truly prophetic were his final words: 'It will take a war to bring back prices.'

We discussed every aspect of the problem as we made for the fishing ground. Than the boat we were on, it was difficult to conceive any kind of fishing craft that could be run more economically. The average daily fuel cost was round about ten shillings. She could carry a drift of up to fifty herring nets. True, her range of operations was restricted compared with that of the herring drifter, but then her running expenses were not a tenth of those of the larger vessel. Moreover, she was particularly suited for creek fishing and might revitalise the half-derelict little harbours along our coasts if reasonable prices and intelligent fishing regulations gave her half a chance.

It went deeper than that, too, for local knowledge, expensively gained, is required for inshore or coastal fishing. In the course of generations, as I well knew, the best spots for line-fishing came to be known very exactly, but in the recent change-over to the seine net everything was strange again, from the gear to the sea-bottom. Some of the best line-fishing spots for large haddock cannot be touched with the seine net, for the ground is 'hard' and on it a net may not only tear but become a total loss – not to speak of chafed or broken ropes. And the net and its coils of rope are expensive – with prices going up. 'Last year I paid 38s. 6d. for a single coil of rope, but this year it's £3.' And the coils of rope attached to a busy net do not last many months.

Thus as we gave ourselves to the sea we found our footing among the unstable and desperate elements which have to do with cash and markets, not with the sea and storm and hardly won knowledge and courage and endurance. It was a good kind of talk in this unearthly twilight; it made sure of the body; and I could already see it was going to be a remarkable dawn. The sea had a long easy rhythm, the sort of slow underswing that would send the first rays along the water in ever-vanishing cartwheels of spangled light. I was looking forward to this and cast an eye now and then towards the far horizon where the red rim of the great ball would come up behind the ocean. Some ghostly gulls were flying around but mostly they were riding the water, for now under the skipper's direction I was putting her about for the first drag.

And what an exact science it is, this business of dragging a seine net along a mathematically plotted strip of the sea's floor. From trial and error, the skipper had come to know the bottom twenty or more fathoms below him as an angler comes to know the bottom of a pool. Three miles out at sea he could with confidence say that if he were a fathom more inshore his net would stick. This may seem incredible to landsmen, but here is what exactly happened later on that morning. I was at the wheel and we were paying out the port rope when the skipper said casually: 'There's a smooth boss of rock down there, for sometimes our rope gets it and is dragged under. But we keep going ahead until there's a *twang*! – and up it comes again. We're very near it now.' Within three seconds the rope was gripped as by a great hand from below. I waited with more tension than was in the rope, then *twang*! and up it came to the normal angle. Yet now in this grey light before the dawn I could not have said whether we were two miles offshore or three – except that I knew it would be wise to be at least three or the Fishery cruiser might be down on us for inshore poaching.

'See Clyth Lighthouse yonder on the rock? See Bruan Kirk farther in against the sky? . . . Well, when you get the kirk just opening on the lighthouse, you're on the three-mile limit.'

And then he started putting me through the science of the 'meases' – an old local word for the plotting of two shore lines that meet in the boat, with as wide an angle between as possible. In this way a position is precisely fixed, and many narrow runs dragged by the seine net are named after some particular landmark in the meases, much as pools on a river are named from some prominent physical feature on their banks. The whole known landscape took on an added interest. Three miles out, too, all was on a smaller scale, map-like, so that the eye covered a long foot-journey in a short glance. The familiar became a little strange, strange as the toy cottages and the little chequered fields. The Rock of Ben-a-chielt was a knob on the horizon. The second park dyke east of the Latheron Burn was a straight line. When the straight line ran into the knob you had to find your second line among the hills that were opening west of the Scarabens. Mountain, plateau, glimpse of grey road, a house, a peat stack, headland, stream, hollow – all were pressed into service, while the engine never stopped and the wheel turned to port or starboard.

Moreover, over the more open ground the meases of each drag were mentally noted, so that, in the event of success, they could be at once repeated.

The skipper now held the flag – or 'dan' – ready to drop it overboard. It was a thin stick, longer slightly than himself, corked and weighted to keep upright, with a worn Union Jack at its peak and a herring buoy to float beside it. When he let it go I kept the boat going full speed on the given course. Swiftly the rope on the starboard side uncoiled, while one of the lads stood by ready to check it should it loop in going over.

As there are some 400 to 500 fathoms of rope attached to each end of the net, we travelled a considerable distance before the skipper made me alter course to about right angles, and shortly thereafter to throttle down to slow, for now the net was about to go out. The glass and the iron balls that acted as floats to the weighted net in order to keep it upright on the bottom hit the clearing board astern and bounded overboard like balls in a rattling game.

Soon the net was out, and when we had run a short way on the same course, the coils of rope on the port side now whisking out, the skipper told me to bring her round on the flag. But, stare as I would, I could not pick up the dan, until its slim line was pointed out against the sky at a distance, in that moment of illusion, that seemed fully ten miles!

By the time we had fetched the flag the port coil of rope was out, and now with the end of each coil made fast to its winch we went full speed ahead until the two ropes gradually came together as the wings of the net, like a moving fence along the bottom, slowly closed in, directing the fish into the long bag behind. After about twenty-five minutes the winches began to haul in, strongly checking our speed, and by a clever piece of mechanism the ropes were coiled on deck and left ready for the next drag.

At long last the floats of the net appeared, and my suspense as to our catch could be relieved. 'Not much,' said the skipper, for a heavy catch floats the net early to the surface. But it was not so fruitless as all that, for when the bag was untied a full box of prime haddock slithered on the deck. But I had not much time to look at them, for we were off again, leaving the skipper and one of the crew to gut the fish and grade them into boxes.

Immediately the winches had started, the gulls had left the sea, for they are the scavengers of the seine net. Later, I estimated our following at about 700 birds. When Kenn, for my obvious amusement, slung a gut high in the air, the strident din was terrific but the whole spectacle as an exhibition of concentrated flying was truly remarkable. Nor was Kenn satisfied until he had got four gulls doing an aerial tug-of-war over the one gut, with every other pair of wings wheeling to the attack.

Some greater black-backed gulls observed the proceedings warily from a little distance, while still farther out floated several gannets or solan geese apparently unconcerned with our fishing. When you come on a gannet asleep on the ocean, said the skipper, he lets out an unholy screech. A few fulmars passed swiftly – known locally as the 'St Kilda Maa'.

But now the starboard rope was nearly out and I was throttling back; round she came and over went the net, with the glass balls bouncing away after knocking on the stern board crisp and neat as flying feet in a fantastic ballet; and now the net was out, and round once more I brought her, opening throttle as the port rope slid over, on the run back for the dan.

I am quite sure that the dawn that morning must have been more wonderful, more vivid and beautiful, than most dawns that I have seen, but – for I try to be truthful here – I have no clear memory of it. All I see is a molten red, a red that is dazzling me. I cannot pick up the dan. I am steering blind, but haven't the courage to confess it. I could have swept that sun with pleasure from the sky. But I hold on, for I know that I must be roughly on course. Then I glimpse in a vanishing moment what seems a slim dark finger upright in the heart of the red and, with a breath of relief, I keep her dead on the rising sun.

'The *Cabinet Minister* Runs Aground'

from Whisky Galore

COMPTON MACKENZIE (1883–1972)

It is 1943, and one of the darkest periods of the Second World War is made even darker for the people of the Hebridean islands of Great and Little Todday by the whisky shortage. The Protestant folk of Great Todday and their Catholic neighbours on Little Todday are united in their despair. When salvation comes in the form of the stranding of the SS Cabinet Minister, *outward bound from the Clyde to America with 50,000 cases of dollar-earning whisky, they are equally united in their determination to save this Godsend of liquid gold from the perils of the sea and the unsympathetic grasp of the exciseman. A minor difficulty arises because the* Cabinet Minister *unfortunately runs aground on a Sunday – which gives something of a head start to the Little Todday men, less strict in their Sabbatarianism than the Presbyterians of Great Todday. However, the blessings of the steamer's hold – Stag's Breath, Stalker's Joy, Bonnie Doon, Auld Stuarts, King's Own, Deirdre's Farewell and the rest of the glorious treasure – proves ample for all. As Donald Macroon observes, 'Don't spare it, a bhalaich, you couldn't drink it all if you lived for ever.'*

This classic comedy of Hebridean life by Compton MacKenzie, imbued with the author's knowledge of and affection for the islands, was inspired by the wreck on the island of Eriskay in 1941 of the SS Politician, *which was also carrying a cargo of the water of life and which similarly comforted those islanders in their hour of need.* Whisky Galore *was first published in 1947 and was memorably filmed in 1949 by Alexander MacKendrick. Our extract tells of the wreck of the treasure-ship and the first stage in the 'rescue' of her cargo. Slàinte mhór!*

Chapter 9 The *Cabinet Minister*

'Now where we are I cannot tell
But I wish I could hear the Inchcape Bell.'

There is no need to waste sympathy on Sir Ralph the Rover as he paced the deck, because he himself some years earlier had cut the bell from the

Inchcape Rock merely to annoy the good old Abbot of Aberbrothock who had placed it there for the benefit of mariners. We can, however, commiserate with Captain Buncher who on that Sabbath morning in March paced the deck of the ss *Cabinet Minister*, outward bound to New York, when he expressed a passionate desire to hear the bell which warned mariners against the Skerrydoo, an unpleasant black reef awash at half tide to which ships proceeding down the Minch gave a wide berth. The reason why Captain Buncher could not hear the bell buoy of the Skerrydoo was that he was ten miles away from it and that in his anxiety to avoid it in the dense fog he had taken the *Cabinet Minister* into the Sound of Todday and thus right off his course.

The people coming out of church at Kiltod heard the siren of the *Cabinet Minister* sounding away to the north just as the people going into church at Snorvig heard it sounding to the north-west.

'That's queer right enough,' said Drooby to the Biffer, the expression of piety considered suitable for entering church lost for a moment in an expression of the liveliest curiosity.

'Sounding from the west,' the Biffer observed.

'Some ship's finding herself in trouble,' said Drooby. 'She's no business to be out there at all.'

Then the animation of curiosity which had been lightening their countenances died away to be succeeded by an expression of severely introverted piety as they turned into church and proceeded toward their accustomed seats.

Over on Little Todday the congregation, gathered in groups outside the towerless church of Our Lady Star of the Sea and St Tod, listened to the sound of the siren with as much attention as they had paid to the brief but eloquent sermon of Father Macalister whose view of Lent's rapid approach had perhaps never seemed quite so profoundly affected by the solemnity of the season.

'He was pretty fierce this morning Alan,' said one of his flock.

'*A Dhia*, what'll he be giving us on Wednesday?'

'Ay, he was fierce right enough,' agreed Alan Macdonald, a long, lean crofter with a trim square beard, as he slowly rolled some twist between his palms preparatory to filling a pipe. 'What do you make of that ship's siren, Hugh?'

Hugh Macroon, who was also preparing his after Mass pipe, stopped to listen more intently.

'I believe she's coming nearer.'

'Och, she's coming nearer all the time,' declared John Stewart positively.

'Will she be in the Coolish?' somebody asked.

'I believe she's more to the north,' said somebody else.

'I believe she'll be pretty near Bàgh Mhic Ròin,' said Hugh Macroon slowly.

A silence fell upon the group, not a man in which did not know the story of the black chest but not a man in which would have considered for one moment alluding to it.

'Ay, I believe you're right, Hugh,' said John Stewart. 'Ah, well, you and me had better be moving along towards home.'

The congregation was dispersing into the fog by the various tracks across the wet machair which led to the houses scattered all over the island. Presently Hugh Macroon and John Stewart could have fancied themselves the only people left in all Little Todday as they trudged northward. Their wives and families had driven on ahead.

'I'm not after hearing her blow for some time,' said John Stewart presently.

'I didn't hear nothing,' Hugh added in these deliberate tones of his which seemed to lend such weighty support of, or offer equally weighty opposition to, other people's assertions.

'There she goes again,' Jockey exclaimed.

'That's not a ship,' said Hugh. 'That's a stirk or a heefer.'

'Ay, ay, it would be a heefer right enough,' Jockey agreed as the melancholy mooing sounded somewhere in the distance of that silver-grey annihilation of figure and form, of sea and land.

They walked on for half an hour in silence, each preoccupied with the same dream which neither of them thought it would be decorous to put into words. At last they came to where the track forked to their respective crofts.

'I dare say dinner will not be ready for a while yet,' said Hugh.

'Och, it'll be a long while yet,' Jockey agreed.

'It's pretty quiet,' said Hugh.

'Ay, it's pretty quiet right enough,' Jockey agreed.

'She might have run into clearer weather,' Hugh suggested.

'Ay, she might, but it's kind of queer that she stopped hooting so sudden,' Jockey commented.

'Ay, it's queer right enough,' Hugh agreed. 'Maybe it wouldn't be a bad notion to walk on a bit and see if we could get a sight of her from the head of the *bàgh*.'

'*Ceart gu leoir*. Right you are, Hugh. Ay, we'll walk along to the head of the *bàgh*, and tinner will be chust about ready by the time we reach home.'

They had walked on for another twenty minutes when Hugh suddenly gripped Jockey's wet sleeve.

'*Eisd!*'

Both men stood still. From ahead of them through the viewless air there came thinly, remotely, but unmistakably the sound of someone hallooing at intervals.

'That's never a *Todach* shouting like that,' Hugh declared.

'Neffer!' Jockey agreed. 'Come on, let's hurry. I believe she iss. I was after thinking she wass all the way from church.'

At that moment the figure of a man running toward them along the track materialised from the fog. It was Willie Munro.

'There's a big steamer on the Gobha,' he gasped in excitement. 'I'm away to Kiltod to send word over to Snorvig.'

'What for?' Hugh Macroon asked.

'It's me that's the coast-watcher. The supervisor will want to send word to Nobost for the lifeboat.'

'Man, you're daft,' said Hugh contemptuously. 'What lifeboat could come from Nobost in such a fog? And the sea as smooth as glass. If they want to come ashore they don't want no lifeboat. Wass it you that was shouting just now?'

'I was never shouting.'

'Very well then,' said Hugh, 'I believe some of them will be ashore now. You'd have done better to wait where you were. Come on, Jockey. We'll be getting down to the *bàgh*.'

'Och, well, I'll be getting along to Kiltod,' said Willie Munro. He hurried on his way.

'Ay, he's cunning is Willie,' Hugh observed when he and Jockey had moved on. 'But he's a bit of a fool. Oh well, I don't believe this big steamer will be full of ashes.'

'*A Dhia*, I hope not,' Jockey exclaimed.

'She might be full of nothing,' Hugh suggested. 'If she's outward bound.'

'She would neffer be setting a course through the Sound of Todday if she was outward bound,' Jockey pointed out. 'No, no, she's homeward bound. *A Dhia*, she might be from Chamaica with plenty rum aboard. Parcels and parcels of it.'

'Stop your dreaming, Jockey,' Hugh Macroon advised. 'We were after dreaming of gold and it turned to ashes. If we go dreaming of rum it'll end up in grapefruits.'

A minute or two later two strangers emerged from the fog.

One of them was tall and lanky with red hair. The other was short and plump and also had red hair.

'Can you tell us where we are, mate?' the short seaman asked in the accent of Clydeside.

'You're on Little Todday,' John Stewart replied.

'Where in hell's that?' asked the lanky seaman in the same accent as his companion.

'I don't know at all where it is in hell,' said Hugh Macroon slowly. 'But I can tell you where it is on earth.' And this he proceeded to do.

'And you don't think she'll float off at high water?' asked the short seaman whose name was Robbie Baird.

'I'm pretty sure she won't,' said Hugh.

'What did I tell you, Robbie?' exclaimed his companion. 'Och ay, the old *Minister* will make a job for the salvage and that's about all she will do. Anyway, Fritz won't get her now.'

'Och, I'm not so sure myself she winna float,' Robbie Baird insisted.

'All richt, all richt. I'm not arguing aboot it,' Sandy Swan replied with a touch of impatience. Then he turned to the crofters.

'Look, will you two fellows come back on board with Robbie Baird and myself? The old man had better get word from strangers what's coming to him. He'll think he's gone plain daft when he hears where he is.'

'What port were you making for?' Jockey asked.

'New York.'

'Outward pound?' Jockey exclaimed in shrill amazement. 'How were you coming round the north end of Little Todday, and you outward pound?'

'Put the blame on the *Cabinet Minister*'s cargo,' Robbie Baird chuckled. 'The old ship was absolutely fou'.'

'There's cargo in her, is there?' Hugh asked. 'There's not much cargo outward bound these days.'

'Cargo in her?' Robbie Baird exclaimed with a wink. 'I'm telling you. There's fifty thousand cases of whisky in the auld *Cabinet Minister*,' he added with a triumphant toss of the head.

'What?' Jockey shrilled like a questing falcon.

Even the imperturbableness of Hugh Macroon was shaken by this news. He gulped twice.

'Fifty sousant cases of whisky?' Jockey lisped. He was never perfectly at case with 'th' and emotion now deprived him of any power even to attempt the combination of letters. 'She must be a huge crate ship.'

'Four thousand tons. Blue Limpet Line.'

'Fifty sousant! Fifty sousant!' Jockey murmured in awe. 'And twelf pottles in effery case? Oh, well, well, Clory be to Cod and to His Plessed Mother and to All the Holy Saints,' he ejaculated as he crossed himself in a devout rapture of humble human gratitude. '*Uisdein, eudail* wasn't it Mhaighstir Seumas who was saying we'd kept the Faith in Todaidh Beag and Almighty God would not be forketting us?'

The two red-haired Clydesiders grinned at the round sandy-haired Hebridean.

'Here's tae us,' said Robbie Baird, raising an imaginary glass.

The captain's cutter had been made fast to a rock, halfway up Macroon's Bay.

'You were pretty lucky to come in here,' Hugh commented. 'You might have lost yourselves.'

'The fog lifted for a while after we struck. That's why the old man sent us ashore. Then it came down thicker than ever, and we started to shout.'

'Ay, we heard you,' Hugh told them.

Now the fog lifted again, and presently the *Cabinet Minister* was visible.

'*A Dhia*, she's lying terribly crooket,' Jockey exclaimed.

'Och ay, the first big sea's likely to break her back,' Sandy Swan prophesied confidently.

'And there's a big sea running between Pillay and Todday when the tide's making and the wind is easterly,' Hugh observed thoughtfully.

'Ay, and you get a pick sea when the tide iss tropping and the wind is sou-west,' Jockey added.

'Och, you get a big sea whichever way the wind is or the tide either,' said Hugh. 'You'd better not be staying aboard any longer than you have to. You're in luck, too, because the mailboat got into Snorvig yesterday afternoon and couldn't leave again. I don't know if she'll go back to Obaig tonight if the fog clears right away. They're very strict about Sunday over in Great Todday. They're all Protestants there and we're all Catholics here; but still, I believe she will be going back tonight. The coast-watcher must have sighted you when the fog lifted for a bit. We were after meeting him on the way to Kiltod to get word to the Supervisor. But even if they won't send over for you from Snorvig on Sunday we'll get you across the Coolish.'

'Ay, and we'll get some carts over to the head of the pay and you'll be aple to take wiss you what you've a mind to,' Jockey added.

'You'd better tell the skipper all that,' Robbie Baird advised.

'Och, yess, we'll tell him right enough,' Jockey assured the two sailors. 'It wouldn't be ferry nice at all if the wind got up after this fock and you still on the Gobha.'

'Och, aye, it would be a bit gory,' Robbie Baird chuckled.

'It iss not *gobhar*. It iss *gobha*,' said Jockey. '*Gobha* iss a blacksmiss. *Gobhar* is a coat.'

'A coat, eh?' Robbie Baird nodded.

'No, not a coat. A coat.'

'A goat,' Hugh put in to help the seaman.

'Ah, a goat,' Robbie Baird repeated. 'And the name of this rock we're on is the Blacksmith, eh? Well, it's black all richt. All the same, goat widna hae been a bad name for the b–r the way he butted into us.'

The *Cabinet Minister* had been going dead slow when she struck the Gobha, but she was well on top of the submerged reef which extended for twenty yards on either side of the black fragment of basalt which thrust itself up out of the water. Two hundred yards ahead rose the dark cliffs on the eastern face of Pillay whitened by the droppings of the seafowl that nested upon their ledges.

The steamer was heeling over at enough of an angle to make the Captain's cabin seem as perilous a place in which to remain too long as the two crofters were anxious to persuade him it was.

'So that's where I am, is it?' said Captain Buncher, putting his finger on the chart. 'And you say there's no chance of floating off on the top of the tide?'

Hugh Macroon shook his domed head, and when Hugh did that onlookers were apt to be impressed. Captain Buncher, a small man with a small grizzled beard, a high complexion, and hair as dark as the rock on which his ship had struck, *was* impressed.

'But there's no need for you people to be bringing carts and wagons to this bay. We can row round in the ship's lifeboats to Snorvig. You say the mailboat is there now?'

'Ay, but she might not go back to Obaig till tomorrow morning, being Sunday,' Hugh replied. 'But you'll find good accommodation at the hotel. At least pretty good. There's very little beer just now. And no whisky at all.'

'No whisky, eh?'

'There's not been as much whisky as you'd get in a poorhouse for two months and more.'

'That's bad,' Captain Buncher clicked. He rang the bell, and when the steward came he bade him bring glasses. Then he went to a locker and produced a bottle of Stag's Breath, a brand which had been particularly favoured by the inhabitants of the two Toddays in the good old days of plenty.

'Stack's Press,' murmured Jockey, transfixed by the beauty of the sight before his eyes and under his nose and hardly a couple of feet away from his mouth.

'Help yourselves,' Captain Buncher commanded when the steward had brought the glasses. 'But no, that's not fair. I'll help you.'

'And, poys,' Jockey told them later that famous Sunday before Lent, 'it *wass* a help. It wass reeally powerful. Ay, and the man helped us twice. Neffer plinked an eye. Chust poured it out as if he was a *cailleach* pouring you out a cup o' tay. And mind you, the man's heart must have been sore inside of him, the way his ship was lying there on the Gobha. But he neffer plinked an eye. Chust poured it out.'

When Hugh and Jockey were raising to their lips that second glass Captain Buncher suddenly remarked:

'The glass is high and steady.'

'Ay, it's high right enough,' Jockey agreed. 'But it's not so steady as it wass the first time, Captain.'

Captain Buncher laughed.

'I was thinking, I might leave a couple of my chaps on board till the salvage people took over.'

'You know best, Captain,' Hugh Macroon allowed with grave courtesy. 'But you couldn't have a worse place than you are except when it's calm as it is just now, and when there's anything of a ground swell it's tricky right enough to get ashore at all.'

'Yes, well, I expect you're right, my friend. If she becomes a total loss there'll be no lives lost with her. Well, I'm much obliged to you for your help. Baird and Swan will put you ashore in the cutter, and then I think we'll make for Snorvig in the lifeboats. You don't think the mailboat will leave before evening, that is provided the fog doesn't come back, and she's able to leave at all?'

'Och, she'll never move on a Sunday afternoon,' Hugh assured him. 'Anyway, Jockey and me will go in to Kiltod and send word you'll be round before sunset. And you'll not be forgetting there's not a drop of whisky in Snorvig?'

'I won't forget,' Captain Buncher replied, with a smile. 'And as there isn't a drop of whisky in your island either, perhaps you'd like to take a bottle each with you ashore. Good-bye, and thanks very much for your help.'

When the two red-headed Clydesiders put Hugh and Jockey ashore inside Bàgh Mhic Ròin each pulled out his bottle of Stag's Breath to offer the seamen a dram.

'No, no, mates, we'll not rob you,' said Sandy Swan.

'It is not robbing us at all,' said Hugh in whom the two potent drinks he had had in Captain Buncher's cabin had induced that extreme deliberation of utterance which was the recognised sign that Hugh Macroon had had a hefty one. 'No, it is not robbing us. It is giving us pleasure to be able to offer a dram to a friend. Isn't that right, Jockey?'

'Right? Sure, it's right. It's a pleshure we've not been after having for munce, *a chàirdean*,' Jockey insisted, unfastening the stopper of his bottle.

The seamen saw that the islemen would be chagrined by their refusal. So each took a short swig from Jockey's bottle, and having wished and been wished good health and good luck they sheered off and pulled back to the *Cabinet Minister*.

The two crofters sat on an outcrop of rock and watched, now the cutter, now the two bottles of Stag's Breath. The sun like a great silver plate was visible again through the ever-lessening fog, and larger patches of pale-blue sky were spreading above them.

'Oh, well, who would have thought when we were walking to Mass this morning that we would be sitting here like this before two o'clock?' said Hugh. 'We'll just have a bite to eat and then we'll get the cart and drive along to Kiltod. I want to give my bottle to Father James.'

'Och, I want to give him my pottle,' Jockey protested.

'We've all had a dram out of yours. Och, one's enough for him just now,' Hugh decided firmly. '*A Dhia*, there's six hundred thousand bottles where this came from.'

'*Tha gu dearbh, Uisdein. Tha gu dearbh*,' Jockey agreed, in his voice a boundless content. '*Uisge beatha gu leòir, taing a Dhia*. We'll chust be saying three Hail Marys, Hugh.'

'Ay,' the other agreed, 'for favours received.'

The two crofters knelt down, and mingling with the murmur of their prayers was the lapping of the tide along the green banks of Bàgh Mhic Ròin and a rock pipit's frail fluttering song.

Chapter 10 Whisky Galore

The strict Sabbatarianism of Scotland has been the target for a good deal of satire. Some have not hesitated to suggest that it encourages among its devotees a Pharisaical observance of the letter of the Divine Law without any corresponding observance of its spirit. Scoffers are invited to contemplate the behaviour of the people of Great Today on that

Sunday in March when the ss *Cabinet Minister* became a wreck a few hundred yards from Little Todday.

Not one man was willing to break the Sabbath by crossing the Coolish to investigate that wreck: if cynics demand a lower motive, let it be said that not one man was brave enough to flout public opinion by doing so. The weather was fine. The sea was dead calm. Captain Buncher and the whole of his crew were going off with the *Island Queen* when she left for Obaig at dusk. There was for the moment nobody with authority over the wreck. Excise and salvage had not yet appeared upon the scene. The supervisor of the coast-watchers was John Macintosh the piermaster at Snorvig, known as Iain Dubh, but his only job was to notify the head of the coastguards at Portrose eighty miles away that a ship had been wrecked or to summon the lifeboat from Nobost if a ship was in danger of being wrecked. After that his responsibility ceased. Constable Macrae was charged with the invigilation of crashed aircraft and with notifying Rear-Admiral, Portrose, if he saw an enemy submarine. Wrecks were not his pigeons.

Captain Paul Waggett was profoundly convinced that the war would not be over until he had been granted authority to deal in the manner he considered appropriate with crashed aircraft, enemy submarines and wrecks, but this authority he had not yet been able to acquire. He was not even allowed to put Home Guards in charge of the stores of food locked up in the now disused old school at Snorvig as emergency rations for the island in the event of invasion. Most of these stores had been removed by what Captain Waggett declared he had no hesitation in calling common thieves, and this was just as well, because the rest of them had gone bad in the course of over two years.

It was obvious to the people of Great Todday that for once in a way there was no time like the present, but the present being the Sabbath their principles would not allow them to take advantage of it. Tribute must be paid to the staunchness of those principles. Mental agony is hardly too strong a term to describe what many of the people of Great Todday went through on that Sabbath evening when they thought of the people of Little Todday not merely breaking the Sabbath but encouraged to do so by the tenets of their religion.

The Biffer was one of those who suffered most acutely. He had seen the lifeboats of the *Cabinet Minister* coming round into the Coolish. He had been down on the pier when they landed. He had been almost the first man in Snorvig to know what cargo the wrecked ship was carrying. For the rest of that afternoon he was jumping up and going to the door of his house built not far from the water's edge on the rocky point that protected the harbour from the north. At last even his large placid wife protested.

'Will you not be sitting quiet for more than one minute, Airchie?'

'I'm keeping a sharp look-out on the weather,' he replied. 'If it came on to blow when the sun goes down she might break in two before morning the way they tell me she will be lying on the Gobha.'

'The weather won't change one way or the other because you're for ever jumping up and running to the door,' his wife observed. 'For goodness' sake be still for a moment. It's the only quiet time I have in all the week.'

'I might take the *Kittiwake* round the north side of Todaidh Beag and have a look at her,' Airchie suggested. 'No one could call that breaking the Sabbath.'

'Couldn't they?' said his wife, shaking her head in compassion for such self-deception. 'You know as well as I do, Airchie, what everybody would say when they saw you out there in the Coolish on a Sabbath afternoon. Indeed, what would yourself be saying if you saw Alan Galbraith out there just now?'

'If I saw Drooby out there I'd be out there myself pretty quick,' the Biffer replied emphatically.

'And a fine sight you'd be giving the neighbours, the pair of you.'

'Och, well, he isn't there.'

'No, indeed, I hope he has more sense, and if he hasn't the sense himself Bean Ailein will have the sense. Goodness me, you're like a child, Airchie. Let the ship bide till Monday.'

'Do you think they'll let the ship bide till Monday on Little Todday? Och, Ealasaid, you're talking very grand about my sense. But where is your own sense, woman?'

'If the poor *papanaich* on Todaidh Beag don't know better than to break the Sabbath, is it you that's wanting them to lead you by that great nose of yours into breaking it with them?'

'I'm not so sure if it would be breaking the Sabbath just to have a bit of a look round,' the Biffer ventured to speculate.

'Are you not? Ah well, I'm not going to argue with you, Airchie. We'll have been married twenty-five years next July, and if I'd argued with you every time you were wrong I don't know where we'd have been today. No, indeed. You'll just go your own way, and if you want to be breaking the Sabbath you'll be breaking it.'

Such recognition of his obstinacy took all the relish out of being obstinate. That had always been Ealasaid's method with him. He felt almost inclined to be aggrieved by her reasonableness.

'I believe I'll go along and see what's doing on the *Queen*. Maybe Captain MacKechnie won't be leaving till tomorrow. He may be afraid of what everybody will say if he goes to Obaig tonight.'

The sarcasm was lost on his wife. She was sitting placidly back in her chair, her hands folded in her lap, her eyes closed.

The Biffer found Drooby standing on the pier in contemplation of the *Island Queen*, aboard which there was no sign of life.

'Is she going tonight?' he asked.

'Ay, six o'clock, the Captain said. They're all up at the hotel now,' Drooby replied. 'They brought a tidy bit of stuff with them in the boats. It's all safe aboard now.'

'What will they do with the boats?' the Biffer asked.

'Och, the salvage men will have them.'

'I was thinking, Alan, I'd go along in the *Kittiwake* after twelve o'clock and see what's doing over yonder.'

'Not a bad idea,' Drooby observed.

'Will you be going along yourself with the *Flying Fish*?'

'I don't believe I will. Two of the crew went home yesterday till tomorrow. I wouldn't be able to get hold of them tonight. And anyway I wouldn't want to take the *Flying Fish* round there. Iain Dubh and me are not very good friends just now. He made a proper mess of that last lot of whitefish I sent over to Obaig.'

'Ay, I heard about that.'

'We lost a lot of money over him being so obstinate the way he was. Ay, and nothing would give him more pleasure than to be reporting me to the Navy up at Portrose if he thought I was doing anything on the side with the *Flying Fish*!'

'Would you like to come along with me tonight in the *Kittiwake*?' the Biffer asked. 'Just you and me, and young Jimmy to stand by while we get aboard?'

'*Ceart gu leoir*. Right you are, I'll come along with you, Airchie.'

'It would be a pity to let them have all that whisky over yonder.'

Drooby shook his head.

'They'll never get it all, Airchie. There's thousands and thousands and thousands of bottles in the *Cabinet Minister*. Some say there are fifty thousand cases. Others say it's fifteen thousand cases. Whichever it is, it's a lot of whisky. And it's wonderful stuff too. Not a drop under proof, they tell me. That's the kind of whisky you and me drank before the last war. And we didn't pay twenty-five shillings a bottle for it in those days.'

'Were you having a crack with some of the crew?'

'Ay, and I had a couple of drams too,' said Drooby.

'Ach, I thought you were looking a bit pleased with yourself, Alan, when I came on the pier.'

'Ay, it's only when you haven't had a good dram for a long while that you're knowing how important it is not to go without it.'

A golden decrescent moon was hanging in a clear blue sky below Ben Sticla and Ben Pucka when Drooby, the Biffer, and the Biffer's youngest boy Jimmy went chugging up the Coolish in the *Kittiwake* soon after midnight. The strait was glassy calm, and even when they rounded the north-easterly point of Little Todday the Atlantic itself was almost without perceptible motion.

'I believe this weather will hold for a few days yet,' said the Biffer.

'Unless it comes on thick again,' Drooby qualified.

'Ay, it might do that.'

The *Kittiwake* was now approaching the entrance of Macroon's Bay, and a minute or two later the 4000-ton steamer loomed before them in the tempered moonshine.

Presently they were hailed by a sizeable fishing-boat.

'Who are you?'

'That's the Dot,' said Drooby.

Donald Macroon, generally known as the Dot, owned the largest of the Little Todday craft; it was called the *St Tod*, except by Father Macalister, who always called it the *St Dot*.

'Hullo, hullo,' the Biffer shouted back. 'This is Airchie MacRurie and Alan Galbraith in the *Kittiwake*.'

He slowed down the engine and presently drew alongside the *St Tod*.

'You've been a very long time coming,' said the Dot, a small, swarthy, and usually taciturn fisherman. Tonight he was, for him, voluble.

'Ay, we had to wait till the Sabbath was over,' the Biffer explained.

The Dot laughed.

'Ay, that's what we were thinking. Never mind, boys, there's enough for everybody from the Butt of Lewis to Barra Head. You'd better have a dram right away now before you get on board. How many crans did you catch last week, Alan?'

'We had nine.'

'Och, well, *a bhalaich*,' said the Dot, 'there's thousands of crans of whisky on board of her. There's more bottles of whisky on board of her than the biggest catch of herring you ever made in your life, Alan. But have a dram with me before you go aboard.'

The Dot thrust a bottle of Islay Dew at the Biffer.

'Don't spare it, *a bhalaich*, you couldn't drink it all if you lived for ever.'

'*Slàinte mhór*,' said the Biffer, and then took a deep swig. '*A Chruithear*,' he commented reverently, 'that's beautiful stuff.' He wiped his mouth and passed the bottle to Drooby.

'Oh, well, well,' said Drooby when he too had drunk deep, 'that stuff would put heart into anybody.'

'When were they saying in Snorvig that the salvage men were coming?' asked the Dot.

'They might be here with Tuesday's boat,' the Biffer told him.

'Och, well, we must do our best to make their job as easy for them as we can,' the Dot chuckled. 'You'd better get on board and help yourselves. We've shifted quite a lot of it. I've been backward and forward loaded with cases a dozen times already, but you wouldn't see what we're after taking, there's so many thousands of cases.'

'You're pretty lucky over here,' said the Biffer. 'It won't be so easy to land it on the other side.'

'You'd better take back a good load with you tonight,' the Dot advised. 'You needn't worry to pick and choose. It's all beautiful stuff. We've rigged a rope-ladder to get down into the hold. It took a bit of doing, too. Still, so long as the weather keeps good for a bit, we ought to get a tidy few cases out of her the way she's lying now. Take another dram before you go, boys. It's pretty hard work coming up with those cases from the hold.'

'Well, I've known the Dot for forty years and more, Drooby,' the Biffer told his friend as they took the *Kittiwake* alongside the wreck. 'But I never heard him say so much in all those years as I heard him say tonight.'

'Nor I either,' said Drooby. 'Mostly it's just "*tha*" or "*chan 'eil*" and a big spit and you've heard all he has to tell you. Islay Dew,' he added reflectively. 'I hope we'll hit on a case of that.'

Many romantic pages have been written about the sunken Spanish galleon in the bay of Tobermory. That 4000-ton steamship on the rocks of Little Todday provided more practical romance in three and a half hours than the Tobermory galleon has provided in three and a half centuries. Doubloons, ducats, and ducatoons, moidores, pieces of eight, sequins, guineas, rose and angel nobles, what are these to vaunt above the liquid gold carried by the *Cabinet Minister*? It may be doubted if such a representative collection of various whiskies has ever been assembled before. In one wooden case of twelve bottles you might have found half a dozen different brands in half a dozen different shapes. Beside the famous names known all over the world by ruthless and persistent advertising for many years, there were many blends of the finest quality, less famous perhaps but not less delicious. There were Highland Gold and Highland Heart, Tartan Milk and Tartan Perfection, Bluebell, Northern Light, Preston Pans, Queen of the Glens, Chief's Choice, and Prince's Choice, Islay Dew, Silver Whistle, Salmon's Leap, Stag's Breath, Stalker's Joy, Bonnie Doon, Auld Stuarts, King's Own, Trusty Friend, Old Cateran, Scottish Envoy, Norval, Bard's Bounty, Fingal's Cave, Deirdre's Farewell, Lion Rampant, Road to the Isles, Pipe Major, Moorland Gold and Moorland Cream, Thistle Cream, Shinty, Blended Heather, Glen Gloming, Mountain Tarn, Cromag, All the Year Round, Clan MacTavish and Clan MacNab, Annie Laurie, Over the Border, and Cabarféidh. There were spherical bottles and dimpled bottles and square bottles and oblong bottles and flagon-shaped bottles and high-waisted bottles and ordinary bottles, and the glass of every bottle was stamped with a notice which made it clear that whisky like this was intended to be drunk in the United States of America and not by the natives of the land where it was distilled, matured and blended.

'Ah, well, Jockey,' said Hugh Macroon when he and John Stewart were coming back with the last boat load of the *St Tod*, 'we were after thinking we had found plenty gold last Sunday and it turned to ashes; but it was a sign right enough that a better kind of gold was on its way.'

The grey of dawn was glimmering above the bens of Todaidh Mór, and the high decrescent moon, silver now, was floating merrily upon her back across the deep starry sky toward the west.

'I believe I never worked so hard and enchoyed myself so much in all my life,' Jockey averred.

Over on Great Todday, Drooby and the Biffer were conveying a dozen cases of whisky up the rocky path to the Biffer's house while Jimmy kept watch against any sign of curiosity from the pier house and the police station.

'It's a good beginning, Drooby,' the Biffer said when the cases were stowed away at the back of his shed under a heap of old nets. 'But we mustn't be wasting tomorrow night. There's the weather to think about and the salvage, and I'm sure Ferguson will be along from Nobost, and there's the pollis. Och, you'd better take the *Flying Fish* over and get a big load aboard.'

'I'll do that right enough,' Drooby vowed. 'I'm just wondering where will be the best place to store it.'

'There's the old curing-shed down by your place.'

'Ay, there's that; but, if it got about that the stuff was there, some of my bold fellows who never put foot or hand to bring it across might be helping themselves.'

'That's right enough,' the Biffer agreed. 'How would it be to take the stuff up Loch Sleeport? There's a fine big loft in Watasett School. We used to climb up there when we were children.'

'Not a bad idea, Airchie. And Norman Macleod would likely come along with us tomorrow night. There's bound to be a lot of them over from Todaidh Mór tomorrow. Well, I'll just take half a dozen bottles along with me now.'

'Ay, we'll open a case and I'll take the other half-dozen into the house,' said the Biffer.

'I believe a dram would do us both good just now,' Drooby suggested. 'It'll keep the cold air out of our *stamacs*. Is there any Islay Dew in that case?'

The Biffer looked at the bottles.

'No, this is Lion Rampant and Tartan Perfection. We'll try Lion Rampant.'

'Well, I don't believe anything could be better than that,' Drooby decided, putting down the bottle with a sigh. 'Still, we might as well try Tartan Perfection. Ah, well, I don't know which is best,' he declared after the second dram. 'I'll take another dram of Lion Rampant just to make sure. And now I'm not sure, after all,' he said.

'And I'm not so sure,' the Biffer echoed. 'We'd better try Tartan Perfection again.'

'Ay, it's a pity not to know which really is the best,' Drooby agreed. 'I don't know what's the matter with me, Airchie, but I'm feeling much better.'

'Ay, I'm feeling much better myself, Alan. Och, I don't believe the war will last for ever at all. *Slàinte mhath!*'

'*Slàinte mhór!*' Drooby wished in return. 'I don't believe anybody could find out which was best. Well,' he went on, 'some people say they're close in Little Todday. I wouldn't say that, Airchie.'

'I wouldn't say that myself,' the Biffer agreed. He poured himself out another dram, but whether it was Lion Rampant or Tartan Perfection he was hardly aware. 'I wouldn't say it at all. *Slàinte mhór* to all friends on Little Todday.'

'*Slàinte mhór!*' Drooby echoed, with a hiccup like the castanets at the beginning of a cachucha. 'They never grudged us a bottle. "Help yourselves, boys," that was the spirit. I'll never see a Little Todday man go without a dram so long as there's whisky in the country. Never.'

'Never,' the Biffer echoed. 'What about a song, Alan?'

Drooby rose to his feet and, swaying to the combined effect of the whisky and the tune, delivered *Mo Nighean Donn* (My Nutbrown Maid) in the very resonant but slightly raucous tenor that hardly suited his bulk, to which a profound bass would have been more appropriate.

'*Glè mhath! Glè mhath*. Very good, Drooby,' the Biffer applauded. 'Let's have another.'

Drooby had started *Mo Run Geal Dìleas* (My Faithful Fair One) even more resonantly when Jimmy appeared in the doorway of the shed.

'*Istibh!*' the boy warned them sharply. 'Are you wanting to wake up everybody in Snorvig?'

'I don't want to wake up nobody,' his father replied with dignity. 'I'm feeling pretty sleepy myself. Is Iain Dubh about?'

'There's nobody about, but it's getting light,' Jimmy pointed out.

'Ay, I'd better be making my way back home,' said Drooby.

'You'd better see that there's nobody about, Jimmy,' his father told him.

The boy went off again.

'Only two of my boys left in the home, Alan,' the Biffer went on sentimentally. 'Four of them serving in the Mairchant Navy.'

Drooby poured out another dram.

'*Slàinte mhór* to the Merchant Navy,' and his toast was followed by a hiccup that rivalled the performance of a xylophone. He then planted bottles in all his pockets and proclaimed his intention of going home immediately in case his wife should be worrying where he was.

'You'd better have a *deoch an doruis* before you go, Alan,' the Biffer advised.

'Ay, I believe you're right, Airchie. I'm just beginning to feel a little tired out. Och, we did a hefty night's work. Up and down, up and down.'

Drooby swallowed the *deoch an doruis*; but it took him no further than the heap of nets on which he was sitting, and leaning back, all his bottles chinking, he fell asleep at the same moment as the Biffer tipped backwards off the lobster-pot on which he was sitting and lay on the cork-strewn floor.

Ten minutes later Jimmy looked in to say that no time was to be lost if Alan Galbraith wanted to get home without being observed. He eyed the two sleepers with a grin. Then he pulled a tarpaulin over them and went off to his own bed.

'A Funeral At Sea'

from The Merry Muse

ERIC LINKLATER (1899–1974)

*Burial at sea may seem, at first sight, an unlikely subject for a section
headed 'The Pleasures of the Sea'. However Eric Linklater's marvellously
comic novel* The Merry Muse – *which relates the effects on post-war
Edinburgh of the discovery of a unknown, and highly erotic, Burns
manuscript – certainly merits inclusion.*

*The manuscript's unlikely owner, Charlie Youghal, a retired school
teacher, has died and been cremated but has revealed an unexpectedly
romantic side to his character by requesting that his ashes be scattered at
sea. His much more successful brother-in-law, Max Arbuthnot, a wealthy
Edinburgh lawyer with varied business interests and an equally varied
and lively interest in the pleasures of the flesh, arranges for a tug under
charter to one of his firms to be made available to carry out Charlie's last
wishes. Max's sisters Jessie (Charlie's widow) and Annie, together with
a group of Max's friends and the Youghal's neighbours from Peebles
(attracted by the novelty of the ceremony) set out from Leith into an
increasingly rough Firth of Forth to take their last leave of Charlie – but
the event does not pass off with the expected degree of dignified solemnity.*

*The Merry Muse was published in 1959 and its black comedy and sharp,
though affectionate, portrayal of Edinburgh earned it a reputation as one
of Linklater's best and funniest novels.*

On Wednesday, exactly half an hour after noon, a party of some
twenty people moved from the drawing-room in Max Arbuthnot's
house, where they had been drinking sherry, to the dining-room, where
a buffet-luncheon of cold salmon, cold grouse and trifle awaited them.
Mrs Arbuthnot had argued that so lavish a meal was inappropriate to the
occasion, but Max had replied, 'If they've got to come and eat here – and
it was you who said I had to accept some responsibility – then they're
going to eat well. And this is Scotland, remember that! And in Scotland
we've always enjoyed a funeral more than a wedding, because there's
no fear of having to buy a christening-mug nine months later. So they'll

drink Traminer with the salmon and Nuits St Georges with the grouse, and then we'll be in a proper mood to face the open sea.'

The mortal remains of old Charlie Youghal had been duly cremated – his ashes lay in a small urn that Max, a little impatient of his burden, had left in the downstairs lavatory and some of the assembled mourners were thinking, uneasily, of the voyage that would conclude the obsequies. In obedience to old Charlie's wishes, and his widow's determination to respect them, Max had arranged that one of the tug-boats under charter to his shipping-firm should be free, that afternoon, for a short trip to sea. At the port of Leith the tug lay ready, and in Leith, as on Corstorphine Hill, there were those who lifted a questioning eye to the south-east, and listened with a calculating ear to the wind. The morning had been fair, but now the wind was rising.

Mrs Arbuthnot had insisted on there being some of Max's own friends at the funeral: that was the proper way, she had said, in which to show respect for his sister, and sympathy with her in her loss. So Max had asked Tom and Mona Murdoch, with whom he had lately been stalking, and their friend Hugh Burnett, whose name his daughter Jane had failed to remember when they met at the Gargoyle Restaurant. They, with Max, enjoyed a substantial luncheon, but some of the widowed Jessie's friends from Peebles thought the richness of their entertainment out of place, and showed their displeasure by refusing to eat anything but some bread-and-butter and the smallest possible helping of salmon. The cold grouse, and the burgundy, they refused with quiet indignation, as being wholly unsuited to the occasion.

Jessie herself was an impressive picture in her small and shrivelled dignity. She was in full control of her feelings, and even Mrs Arbuthnot spoke to her with a visible deference, while Max avoided her in barely hidden fear of the authority in which sorrow had dressed her. Her sister Annie, though wearing mourning as deep as Jessie's, was less responsive to the funerary mood. After she had drunk a glass of Traminer, Annie began to show signs of enjoying herself, and among her friends from Peebles there were those who – unlike the disapproving minority – saw no reason in the death of an old man, whom death had shouldered for some years, for refusing good food and drink. There was the doctor who had attended Charlie Youghal, and the banker who had guided him in his small investments; there was the secretary of a bowling club, and the secretary of a golf club; there was a retired inspector of schools – and they, who rarely drank burgundy at lunchtime, took sensible advantage of an unusual pleasure. They encouraged Annie to drink a little more, and were loudly amused by the freedom with which she discussed their neighbours.

By half-past one the party had split into three separate groups. Jessie and Mrs Arbuthnot, with those who disliked a festive air at funerals, had retired to the drawing-room; and with them were Jane, who was feeling dutiful, and the Rev. Mr Myrtle, the very young vicar of St Mungo's in Peebles. Max and his friends had joined Annie and the heartier guests from Peebles, and Max was expounding the virtues of the great canvas, painted by William Etty, that hung on the west wall. The women who so proudly showed their glowing nakedness within its frame were indeed the creation of a brush that could almost put the pulse of life into painted flesh, and for that reason the picture may well have been a salutary assertion of life's indomitable will, even in the presence of death. But the third group of mourners did not see it in so favourable a light. They thought it shocking, but they accepted it as a necessary part of the outing to which they had committed themselves.

This small group consisted of four of Jessie's female friends from Peebles. They had told each other, with some repetition, that it was by no means their habit to attend funerals – that, as they well knew, was a masculine function – but this was so unusual an occasion that they had felt they could not miss it. It was not every day that an old acquaintance enjoyed the dignity of being buried at sea, and it was a privilege, not to be spurned, to attend him at the last rites. But now they felt isolated, and increasingly uncomfortable. They had not wanted to leave the party with those who disapproved of it, but they found it impossible to join the hearty group that was admiring the luscious quality of Etty's painting – and they listened, nervously, to the sound of the rising wind.

Then Mrs Arbuthnot came to say it was time to go, and at once a silence fell upon the party as all remembered the solemn circumstances of their presence at it. They turned away from Etty and his nudes, and went to find their coats and tall black hats; and Max, retrieving the ashes from the downstairs lavatory, took his seat beside Jessie in the first of the several motor-cars that waited for them.

At a smooth decorous pace they drove along Ravelston Dykes, by Orchard Road and Comely Bank to Fettes Avenue, past park and playing-fields into the long length of Ferry Road and the assertive, commercial earnestness of Leith. At the dock gates a policeman saluted Max, who gravely acknowledged the courtesy, and a young man, employed by his firm, got in beside the driver to guide the cortège to the waiting tug. Leaning forward in his seat, Max surveyed with a proprietary interest the grey and busy roads, a glimpse of water in steep-sided basins, the funnels of ships from Hamburg or Copenhagen, and told Jessie which was which: for this (or some small part of this) was his domain, and it was time to make Jessie aware of his knowledge and importance: throughout the long drive she had been talking, with a drably egotistical insistence, of nothing but her own affairs. – Behind them, in the motor-cars that followed, their fellow-mourners, though well-fed and comfortably carried, were thinking, not that they were important, but vulnerable. They looked out and saw flags flying stiffly, smoke flowing flatly, and realised that the wind was blowing strongly.

The tug-boat lay near the entrance to the Victoria Dock, and her captain, clad smartly in dark blue, waited at the shoreward end of the gangway. He shook hands with Max, he was introduced to Jessie, and while the others gathered uncertainly behind them – none eager to assert precedence – Jessie was escorted to the captain's cabin, followed by Max, who, with an air of some distaste, carried the ashes.

The moorings were cast off, and the tug steamed slowly past the long West Pier into the Firth of Forth. Ahead lay Inchkeith, and then, as they turned to the east, the broadening gulf that led to the rough North Sea. And not until they reached the open sea could old Charlie's ashes be committed to the deep. Such had been his wish, and by Jessie's insistence his wish would be respected.

The wind was from the south-east, and from Leith to the light on Fidra they were in shelter of the land. But the land was not a shelter so near as to prevent the sea from dancing a little, and those who were nervous from the start soon became physically unhappy and lost the brightness of their cheeks. Indifferent to her surroundings, Jessie sat in the captain's cabin, still and silent; while beside her, on a cushioned settee, the Rev. Mr Myrtle pursed his lips, tried to think of nothing but the service he must soon conduct, and wiped a little perspiration from his forehead. Mrs Arbuthnot sat on a swivel-chair and read *The Times*.

On the deck outside, Annie, well wrapped up, was excited by her trip to sea, and talked with great animation, now to Hugh Burnett and Tom Murdoch, now to her friends the banker and the doctor from Peebles.

She pointed to a grey blur of buildings on the shore, over which blew a canopy of smoke, and archly enquired, 'Now where is that? Who can tell me where we are now?'

'Portobello,' she was told – and brightly she exclaimed, 'But I've been there! I used to go and swim there, when I was just a girl. I was *very* good at duck-diving. They have a splendid swimming-pool in Portobello – I know it well! Oh, what a pity poor Charlie isn't with us! Well, in a way he is, of course, but not so as to enjoy it. He *would* like to see all this.'

Three of the mourners sat in the mate's cabin, two in the engineer's; while half a dozen, in a very small saloon, felt the air grow oppressive and wondered how long the voyage would last.

Jane stood in a corner of the bridge and talked quietly to the captain. Neither of them spoke to Max, who, in the other corner, sat on a tall stool and proclaimed by his attitude and his glum expression that his thoughts were private and profound. Enisled in solitude he contemplated his responsibility, and death.

The ship in which they sailed was his – or temporarily his, by right of charter – and old Charlie's ashes had become his care. Old Charlie, for the last time, was his guest, and now he let himself feel sorry for that grey atomy of a man, who had lived so thinly, who had held so small a parcel of life within his veiny, greyish hands. And therefore, like the very poor who cherish their few possessions, had held fiercely to all he owned, and struggled bitterly with death.

How would he face it, thought Max, when his own time came? – But no, it was futile to speculate on that. True, he had memorized a brace of resounding epigrams, so that he might leave some good 'last words' if he retained his consciousness till near the end; but apart from that one could plan neither strategy nor tactics against death. Better not to think of it.

Think of his youth instead: and how bitter was that loss! He was still strong enough, in wind and limb, in mind and desire, to fall sometimes into a rage of sorrow when he remembered the fleetness of his legs and the tireless energy of forty years ago. Unlike old Charlie, he had taken his fun and drunk its aftermath of bitterness – but less, far less than he could have swallowed! If only he had his time again!

He looked at a long, pale scar on the palm of his left hand. That was the memento of an escapade in his last year at school, when he and another boy, both at Corstorphine College, had been given leave to spend Sunday afternoon at home. But they had not gone home. They had gone to a small and discreet brothel which, in those days, catered for unruly appetites a little way down Leith Walk. It was their first visit – the other boy's older brother had recommended it – and, arriving before the normal hours of business, they had found the young ladies – there were five of them – unprepared for customers. But the good woman who kept the house had saved the boys from embarrassment. She had not complained of their ill manners or ignorance in coming so early but, turning to her girls in a great pretence of wrath – 'What!' she exclaimed, 'Fower o'clock on a Saabbath efternoon, and nae a hoor painted! Oh, think shame on yourselves!'

She had given them tea, good woman – boiled eggs and toast – and it was late when they returned to school. The college gates were locked, but in the darkness of a February evening they thought it possible to climb them unobserved. They might have done, if Max had not slipped and torn his hand on one of the sharp iron spikes that topped the gates.

They had, until then, both been prefects, but now they were stript of rank, and for the rest of the term Max was unable to play Rugby football. Worse than that, his parents were told of his accident, and though he lied stoutly to cover his failure to spend the afternoon with them, they did not believe his excuses. This was one of several family quarrels that disturbed his youth.

The most serious occurred in the Easter vacation after his second term at Cambridge; but the start of it was laid in the Christmas holidays. His parents had lived more modestly than he – though his father, when the pound sterling was still worth almost as much as it pretended, had left £60,000 – but they kept a cook and two maids, and that Christmas there had been a new maid, a young and very pretty girl, with whom Max had fallen rashly in love. To exchange endearments, they found it convenient to meet in a sort of large cupboard immediately behind the baize-covered door that divided the front of the house from the kitchen quarters. The cupboard held brooms and pails, and so strict was old Mrs Arbuthnot's discipline – so orderly her housekeeping – that it was never entered after nine in the morning, when work of that sort was finished. Though small and stuffy, it was ideal for clandestine meeting, and in Max's remembrance it had become a grotto dedicated to romance, or the Grecian cave where Juan woke to find young Haidée bent above him.

But for the Easter vacation he came home, frightened and ashamed, to a house of wrath. His father was a mild and gentle man, but now, as though an innocent and familiar hill were to surprise its neighbours by erupting like Vesuvius, from his father's leniency there broke such a flame of anger that Max stood before him tremulous and tearful, and for a month lived quiet and docile.

His father's anger lasted a few days only, but his mother's pervasive sorrow endured longer. She was a woman of great strength of character, and she could make her sorrow felt. The house of wrath, of initial wrath, became for most of the vacation a house of mourning: of mourning for Max's lost virtue. The poor girl, of course, had gone before he returned and for the rest of his time at Cambridge – so his father had told him – a pound a week would be deducted from his allowance to pay for her keep. But this deprivation was the least of his punishment.

On his last day at home when he thought recrimination had come to an end – when his mother's sorrow had worn itself out, he supposed, as had his father's anger – she said to him, at the breakfast-table, 'I want you to come for a walk with me, Max. I have something to say to you.'

It was a fine morning under a bright sky on which small clouds marched briskly to the south. She took him uphill from India Street, where they lived, along Heriot Row by the gardens and into Hanover Street. They went up the Mound, climbing still, to the Castle; and on its heights beside the great gun called Mons Meg she halted and looked down across the city, sprouting its many spires.

'You have been guilty of a great sin,' she said, 'but if you truly repent it may be forgiven you. For you're young yet, and you've time to atone for it. But there's something even worse than what you and that bad girl did together – and that's back-sliding! You haven't been going to church, Max, and that will never be forgiven you, and you'll never succeed in your profession. There's a rich heritage waiting for you, and you can make it richer still – but only if you go to church, go regularly, and take Communion. You'll never be a success without that. But if you're a good church member, and take Communion, success will be added unto you.'

At that time the Arbuthnots worshipped in the Presbyterian mode. A few years later, when they moved from India Street to Randolph Crescent, old Mrs Arbuthnot found it more agreeable to attend the Church of St John, and having, with stubborn importunity, persuaded her husband to go with her, had little trouble in transferring the allegiance of her children to the episcopal rites. She pretended to have found that God's authority rested more securely on Bishops than on Elders – for how could an absolute Divinity live happily in the noisy democracy of a synod? – and her new belief may have been genuine; though most of her friends asserted bitterly that Bishops and it were both born of mere snobbery.

But Max took her advice, and went with her to St John's. He repented deeply of his misdemeanours with the pretty little maid in the broom cupboard, and became for some years a pattern for youth; and then, for many years, an example of probity which some of his contemporaries in Edinburgh deeply resented. For his probity was accompanied by a conspicuous success in his profession.

And I owe it all to her, he thought, wiping away a tear as he sat on his high stool in a corner of the bridge. I did as she told me. I went to church and took Communion – not too often, but enough for propriety – and now the £60,000 that my father left isn't far short of a quarter of a million – or wouldn't be, if those damned Americans could keep their feet on the ground and not let hysteria play mischief with the stock-market. A quarter of a million – and I owe it to her . . .

At Cambridge he had won his Rugby Blue, and later he had played for Scotland. When he returned to Edinburgh he had given generously of his time to youth clubs, and for ten years had served as an officer in the Boys' Brigade. He had worked hard, married wisely, and shown a seemly devotion to his own welfare as well as to others'. For a quarter of a century he had lived beyond reproach, and prospered. All due to his mother, to her insistence and her advice.

And what a narrow-minded, self-centred, domestic tyrant she had been, he thought! With what unrelenting egotism she had gone her own way, and compelled others to follow her sanctified example!

Through the broad windows of the bridge he could see the sands and low shore about Gullane and Aberlady – beyond them North Berwick Law and the Bass Rock – and far away, in a sudden gleam of light, the cloudy heights of the Lammermuirs. Beneath him the sea was now more profoundly rolling. The squat and sturdy tug-boat rose and pitched, lay over on her side and lifted again, and Max found the movement exhilarating. The grey scene woke in him a hunger for more and yet more of the world's richness. Over the Lammermuirs the sun was hidden, but a ragged cloud divided its radiance into shafts of light, and with the change of mood that was common to him, the sentimental memory of his mother gave way to a harder and more realistic view of her intransigence and stubborn temper. He thought more kindly of his father: that mild and gentle man who would never have made £60,000 had he not been driven to it by the fierce persuasion of his wife.

And though I, thought Max, but for her would never have made my quarter of a million – less what the Americans are throwing away – I might have had more time for love in a cupboard and the girls in Leith Row. What did I lose – and what have I got that's worth more?

The sea, now turbulent, and the land, an alluring haze with sun-dogs dancing on its farthest hills, seemed in his present mood – his mood of revulsion against both sentiment and the sourness of success – to be nature inviting him to live as broadly as the view. But for a quarter of a century he had lived with propriety, with a narrow subservience to convention – and a handsome profit for conformity. But oh, how much had he lost?

Since turning fifty he had increasingly repented of his wasted years – as now they seemed – and done a good deal to wipe out their reproach. He spent less time at his office, and more on pleasure. At home, his voice became assertive, his insistence on comfort explicit. He discovered a taste for wine, and for the last ten years had kept a good cellar; though for most of his life a few bottles in a cupboard – whisky for visitors, champagne for birthdays – had served his simple needs. He found that hearty drinking suited him: his temper grew more expansive, his behaviour a little eccentric. His attendance at church became infrequent, but he travelled more widely and formed the habit of taking holidays abroad. He was especially fond of Copenhagen, a city with which his shipping-firm did business, and he remembered with perfect clarity the very moment in which Denmark had first engaged his heart.

It was ten years ago now. He had celebrated his fiftieth birthday there, on a business trip, and in the gaiety of Tivoli – his Danish hosts were generous – he admitted the inclinations he had long suppressed, and decided to give them a run before it was too late. A day or two later he was sitting outside a small restaurant a few miles south of Helsingör, watching a full-rigged ship come over the Sound from the opposite shore of Sweden. It was a day of warm and brilliant weather, and the ship, with the wind behind her, showed as a tall, diminishing white tower of billowing canvas rising from a bleached bone of surf on the crumpled gentian sea. She came nearer, grew larger, and as she turned to the north her sheets were hauled, the yards swung round, and all her three masts were visible, clothed to their topmost spars with a pattern of tautly filled and palely shining sails.

It was a picture of rare and moving beauty – and then, for Max's private view, a figure of smaller, commoner grace came into the foreground. Her coming was heralded by the staccato tap of her high-heeled shoes, and announced by a cry of anger. She had been leading a clipped white poodle, but opposite the restaurant the dog broke loose and ran towards Max's table. She followed, then halted with a pretty show of embarrassment. She wore only a white bathing-suit – and her high-heeled shoes – and her arms and her long legs were darkly sun-burnt. The sun had bleached her hair, and sun-glasses hid her eyes. Slender and briefly clad in white, she stood against the background of the white and leaning ship, and when Max had caught the poodle she thanked him – in English. Her voice was a little hoarse, her accent a little guttural; but she had a ready command of the language. Presently she sat down to drink a glass of beer. For the day was uncommonly warm . . .

The tug-boat rolled heavily, and recovered so quickly that Max, on his high stool, had to reach forward and grasp an oaken rail to keep his balance. They were, by now, north-west of the Bass Rock, and beyond shelter of the land. The movement of the sea was considerable, and the wind cried angrily above the waves. Perhaps, he thought, they had gone far enough – and as remembrance came back of his task and responsibility, of his duty to poor Jessie and the ashes of her late husband, he remembered also the matter of her rich legacy. And what had happened to it? Where was it? Twice he had telephoned to Hector Macrae, to ask if he had completed his enquiries and established the authenticity of the pages in manuscript, and what Hector had said in reply was far from satisfactory. He had said that Max must be patient for a few days. Scientific tests were necessary – chemical analysis of the paper and ink – and when Max asked him who was doing the analysis, and where, he had answered, with nervous resentment, that he was employing an old friend, who could be trusted. He had refused to give his name, or the address of his laboratory, and while Max was still talking, he had rung off.

It was worrying. No, not truly worrying – for he had entire trust in Hector – but a pin-prick on the edge of worry. Hector should have been more explicit. He should have explained frankly what he had been doing . . .

The captain came towards him, and said, 'I think we've gone far enough, Mr Arbuthnot. You told me to go out beyond the Isle of May, but the weather won't get any better, and some of our passengers are not looking very well.'

Indeed, the tug was now lurching steeply, and Max, as he stood up, had again to grasp the oaken rail. He looked to the south and east, and saw grey seas rearing to ragged crests. It was nothing like gale weather – the wind was no more than fresh – but the sea was turbulent, and away to the north-east the Isle of May was hidden by a plume of white feathers as the waves broke over it. 'All right,' he said. 'We'll have the service here. Can you get the parson out? And tell someone to warn the others?'

'In just a moment,' said the captain, and telling the man at the wheel to turn her head to the wind, rang the engine-room telegraph for half-speed, then less than that, and quickly had his ship pointing to the south-east and almost stationary in the wild flux of the sea: stationary, that is, except for a violent and irregular vertical motion.

She was a large, ocean-going tug, originally chartered by Max's firm to bring home a ship that had gone ashore in the Oslo Fjord, and held for a week more, with another of the same sort, to tow a floating-dock from Grangemouth to the Clyde. She had a small well-deck between the bridge and the fo'c'sle-head, and it was there that the service was to be held. The captain, in his wisdom, had had life-lines made fast across it, and when the mourners emerged from shelter – half of them the colour of wet dish-cloths or winter-shrivelled cabbage leaves – many clung to the ropes with convulsive effort and a pathetic gratitude. Of the original twenty-two who had gathered for luncheon in Max's house on Corstorphine Hill, no fewer than seventeen came on deck; and none who had seen their condition could blame the remainder for staying below.

The mourners, however, even the sturdiest, presented a less dignified appearance than they had worn ashore. Most of the men had been so thoughtful as to bring tweed caps, as well as their top hats, and now, with their caps pulled fiercely down, they looked coarsely proletarian or aggressively sporting; while the women, hooded closely in scarves or mufflers, were like weather-beaten, dissipated gipsies.

Jessie, supported by Max and the captain, retained her dignity with no apparent effort; but the Rev. Mr Myrtle, whom the mate and the engineer held upright, was white as bog-cotton and limp as grass. He was a young man of resolute temper, however, and with a truly heroical contempt for physical weakness he began to recite in a loud voice the psalm *Domine, refugium*. He had got as far as the verse, 'In the morning it is green, and groweth up; but in the evening it is cut down, dried up, and withered' – when he was aware of an interruption.

Annie, whose attention had been wandering, had just seen a great wave break in wild white plumage over the distant Isle of May. She stood on the port side of the well-deck, in the shelter of the fo'c'sle-head, and nearby were Tom Murdoch and Hugh Burnett, the banker and the doctor from Peebles. – Another wave broke, and rose in a prodigious high fountain above the drenched island.

'Oh, look!' she cried. 'What's that? What is it called?'

'The Isle of May,' she was told.

'The Isle of May? I never heard of it! Has it always been there?'

'Always.'

'And I never knew! Well, isn't that funny. What a lot you learn by going to sea.'

Mr Myrtle's attention wandered, his resolution faltered, and *Domine, refugium* came untimely to an end. A fan of spray opened above the blunt bow of the tug, and closing as it fell, revived Mr Myrtle's failing spirit with a cold salt douche. Bravely he began to read, and now in a stronger voice, 'There is one glory of the sun, and another glory of the moon, and another glory of the stars; for one star differeth from another star in glory.'

Against the clamour of the wind the Corinthian mystery was very nobly stated; but again Mr Myrtle felt his strength ebbing, and when he declared 'Man that is born of woman hath but a short time to live, and is full of misery,' it was impossible to doubt either the truth of what he said or his own conviction of it.

The captain gave an order that brought the bow of the ship from south-east to east, and Jessie, cautiously holding the urn and carefully guided by Max, took a hesitant step towards the port side, which was now the lee side. The men took off their caps, and the wind made their hair look like ludicrous wigs.

'We therefore,' said Mr Myrtle, 'commit his ashes to the deep' – and at that moment Jessie, very foolishly, took the lid off the urn to pour the remnants of old Charlie over the side. But the wind got at them first.

The wind still blew from the south-east, but about the tug there were innumerable draughts and eddies, there were counter-winds and wilful airs, and one such vagrant breeze or opposing gust scooped out the ashes, blew them about like a lunatic storm of hail, and then, in a momentary calm, let them settle, for the most part, on the wet heads and shoulders of the dispirited mourners.

Jessie herself was unaware of the mishap – her eyes were closed, her thoughts far off – and neither Max nor Mr Myrtle, by word or movement, let her know that anything had gone wrong.

'Lord, have mercy upon us,' said Mr Myrtle, and it was with exceptional fervency that several of the mourners made the response, 'Christ, have mercy upon us.'

The service came to an end, and quickly Max took his sister back to the captain's cabin. Then he went on deck again, and in a very bad temper began to pick fragments of old Charlie from his wet coat.

On the well-deck the other mourners were all similarly engaged. They helped each other – 'Do my back and I'll do yours' – and gradually the morsels of incinerated bone were gathered together and carefully thrown overboard. Old Charlie, or the greater part of him, was eventually given the burial he had desired, but his ashes were scattered over an uncommonly wide area; for now the tug-boat was heading for home again, and making good speed.

Though deeply regretted by all there, the unfortunate conclusion of what should have been a dignified ceremony had a happy effect on those who had suffered most from the roughness of the sea: they were given something to talk about, something so unusual in its impact that it made them forget their physical unhappiness, and this, together with the comforting knowledge that they were homeward bound, let them recover their customary poise and normal spirits. The tug rolled boisterously, sending out great hissing surges from its lee side, but their voices grew louder and more confident, and long before they reached Leith they were walking the deck with the assurance of old salts, and talking of other days when all but they, and a few of the ship's officers, had succumbed to the

anger of the Channel, or the Pentland Firth, or the Bay of Biscay. Even
the worst of the invalids, the poor quintet that had failed to attend the
service, were revived by hearing of what had happened, and now ventured
on deck to look hopefully for any scraps that might yet remain as visible
evidence of the fiasco. They were encouraged in their search by Annie,
who assured them that she, for one, had not been at all surprised by
what had happened.

'It was just what I expected,' she said. 'Poor Charlie, he was always
so clumsy.'

All but the Arbuthnots were in good spirits when they went ashore in
Leith, and physically in better shape than anyone could have anticipated
who had seen them an hour or two before. But none of the Arbuthnots
was happy. Mrs Arbuthnot was indignant about what she saw as an insult
to poor Jessie, and though she was in doubt about whom to blame for
it, she felt – obscurely, but with the acquired instinct of a woman who
had been married for more than thirty years – that her husband must
be culpable; while Max and Jane were both deeply upset by an affront
to their dignity.

Jane showed her displeasure by snubbing Hugh Burnett when he asked
her to have a drink with him, later that evening, at the Gargoyle; and
Max refused to talk to his sister Jessie when she said, as they went
down the gangway and walked towards the waiting motor-cars, 'And
now that poor Charlie is buried as he wished to be – and how well
you have managed everything! I am deeply grateful to you, Max. You
have arranged everything in the most dignified way. – But now we
must talk about the book. That book, you know, which may be worth
so much . . .'

'I have no time to talk about it now,' said Max. 'I have spent the better
part of a day looking after your affairs, and what's left of it I'm going to
devote to my own. I'm sorry, but I'm not a man of leisure, like Charlie.
I have to work for my living. And work damned hard! But I'll see you
later – perhaps. Anyway, there's nothing to worry about. You've buried
Charlie, so now go home and have a good rest.'

Mrs Arbuthnot took charge of Jessie, and Max, having curtly said
good-bye to the mourners, got into his car and was driven by Thomson
to his office in Hill Street. He had, in fact, no excuse for leaving the
party so abruptly except his disgust with what had happened, and his
unwillingness to stay longer with the people who had witnessed it. The
whole voyage, the orderly embarkation and the concluding ceremony,
ought to have been distinguished by flawless solemnity – heaven knows
it had cost him plenty to take an ocean-going tug to sea! – but instead

of that there had been farcical calamity and a grotesque mishandling of what should have been the impressive climax. Jessie was an old fool, of course – she always had been – but he blamed Charlie even more than her. Charlie had never known how to live, and even the scorched remnant of his bones had been so maladroit as to refuse a decent burial. At this very moment, he thought, Tom and Mona Murdoch, and Hugh Burnett, would be laughing loudly, laughing coarsely, over the tale they would tell, with ornament and addition, to a dozen dinner-tables within the next month. The whole thing had been a mistake, and he should never have listened to Jessie and her nonsense.

Thomson drove slowly past the National Portrait Gallery, turned into St David Street – David Hume the atheist, he thought. He was the St David it commemorated – and from there into Thistle Street and Hill Street. Max had no reason for returning to his office so late in the afternoon – it was after five – but he was thankful for the shelter it offered from a memory of humiliation.

It was not an impressive building that he entered. There was no dignity in its appearance, nothing of distinction in the neighbouring architecture – it was, indeed, a rather mean-looking street, a utilitarian, servile thoroughfare – but within its secret walls he and his fellow-lawyers managed great estates, handled or mis-handled large fortunes, and made for themselves a very comfortable living as they shook the tremulous branches of the Stock Exchange with their buying and selling.

His clerk met him as he went in, and said, 'There's a lady waiting for you, Mr Arbuthnot. She's been here for half an hour or more. I told her I didn't know if you'd be coming back, but she said she would take the chance of seeing you, for it's urgent, she says . . .'

'Who is she?'

'Mrs Moberley.'

'God Almighty, what does she want? I told her not to come here . . .'

'I asked if she had an appointment . . .'

'Well, she hadn't. And another time, if she comes again . . .'

'Shall I tell her you're engaged?'

'Oh, never mind, never mind. I'll deal with her. – All right, Hoyle, I'll let you know if there's anything I want.'

Hoyle, his clerk who had been with him for thirty years, had followed Max upstairs, and now, as Max stood for a moment at the door of his room, he waited with a look of disapproval on his old, pale face – but as Max had no more to say, he went slowly and disapprovingly down again.

'I've been waiting a hell of a long time for you,' said Paula, as

Max went in. 'And there aren't many men I'd wait for: do you realize that?'

He closed the door, and she, moving quickly, came and kissed him
lightly, three or four times, on cheeks and mouth.

'Where have you been?' she demanded. 'And what have you been
doing? You smell of salt, you taste of salt, like an old pirate – though in
those clothes you look more like the undertaker's man. What have you
been doing?'

Disengaging himself, Max laid his top hat on a table, and took off his
thick, dark overcoat. 'I've been burying my brother-in-law,' he said. 'He
wanted to be buried at sea, so I had to go to sea with him.'

'At heart,' said Paula, 'you're a pure romantic. Burying people at sea!
How old are you?'

'Just the right age for you,' said Max. 'But in spite of that, I'm a
respectable Edinburgh lawyer, and I've told you that you're not to
come here.'

'But I had to! That man Bruce you sent me to – you said he was very
clever, and the best man for divorce in Scotland . . .'

'So he is.'

'But I don't like him. He won't believe me. He doesn't believe a thing
I tell him.'

'Who would?'

'Anyone with decent feelings! Oh, what a brute you are!'

'I told you he was the best man for your purpose, but I said you would
have to find a convincing story . . .'

'I told him the truth!'

'I find it difficult to believe that.'

With an expression of returning enjoyment on his grim face, Max
sat down behind his table. It was a large and ponderous table, adorned
with a large and ponderous silver inkstand and a silver cigar-box. His
arm-chair, upholstered in green leather, was made for comfort. 'Very
difficult,' he said, and taking a cigar from the box, began carefully to
remove the band. But Paula, in a sudden turbulent advance, knocked
the cigar from his fingers, and sat herself on his knee.

'I don't know why I put up with you,' she said. 'You're cruel – you're
bloody cruel – but if only I'd met you three years ago . . .'

'Would your Mr Moberley have been saved a lot of trouble?'

'Don't talk about him! He isn't a man, he's a collector. Like a stamp
collector. He looks for nice, new specimens, all in mint condition, and
buys them. But after he's stuck them in his album, he loses interest
in them.'

'He shouldn't have got tired of looking at you.'

She bent and kissed him again. 'My God,' she said, 'you're as salt as old seaweed!'

She stood up, and undoing her coat, swept it back to show her figure tautly displayed in a tightly fitting jersey and a short tweed skirt. 'It's worth a little attention, isn't it?' she said. 'More than he gave it, after six months: that American bastard!'

Max looked at her with a lively approval. She was uncommonly like the beautiful Mrs Moncrieffe whom Raeburn had painted, and he prided himself on having discovered the resemblance. In expression she was bolder, as in temper she was much the harder; but the likeness was indisputable.

'You're a beauty,' he said. 'The first time I saw you, I thought your proper place was on canvas in the National Gallery. But the next time I thought of a better place. Not on canvas, but a sheet.'

'That's a compliment,' she said, 'but what's it worth? I could fall in love with you – but, oh, hell, there's no point in that. What I want is my freedom. I'm young yet . . .'

'Come here,' said Max.

'No, I won't! I've admitted too much, and I know what you think. You think it's the old men – old men like you – who get the best girls nowadays, because young men can't afford to give them what they want. But you needn't think I belong to you, just because – well, because of that time in the shooting lodge, and then the other night after dining with Tom and Mona. I'm not your property, and you'd better not think I am.'

'Come here,' said Max.

'I won't! Or if I do . . .'

'What are you going to ask for now?'

'The other night, after we'd dined with Tom and Mona, you told me about that book you had. The book that's worth – so you said – ten thousand pounds. But do you know where it is now?'

'Do you?'

'Perhaps I do and perhaps I don't. And if you want me to tell you . . .'

'Where is it?' demanded Max, rising from his chair and leaning forward on his table with menace in his eyes and posture.

'Wouldn't you like to know?' said Paula, in a tone of schoolgirl's disdain.

'You'll soon tell me,' he said, and pursued her across the room. She retreated, and deftly avoiding him dodged to the other side. Again he advanced, and she, with a dancing step that mocked his heavy figure and three-score years, let him come close before she dodged him again. But she underestimated him, for now he swerved, moving swiftly and swaying from his knees, as many times in his youth he had swayed to bring down a fast-running, jinking three-quarter – and taking her round the middle brought her down with a crash on to the fine Axminster that covered his floor . . .

In the room below his office, Hoyle his clerk, and Atkinson a young accountant, looked up with some anxiety to the ceiling. The houses in Hill Street were old, and many of their upper floors depended on timbers whose original stability had weakened, whose strength dry rot and worms had eaten. The clerks and lesser people who sat on the ground floor were accustomed to the shaking tread of their seniors overhead. But this was a shock beyond all previous experience, and as a few flakes of plaster descended from the ceiling, and fell upon the deed that Hoyle was copying, on the domestic accounts that Atkinson was balancing, the younger man looked up and said, 'Well, Mr Hoyle, what do you think they're doing now? Is she teaching him dancing, or all-in wrestling?'

'Mr Arbuthnot,' said Hoyle, 'may have dropped a book. There is no need for a more fanciful explanation. And if you want to finish your work before six o'clock—'

'All right, all right,' said the young accountant. 'I was just wondering – if I were a rich man I'd be doing the same – but don't take offence, Mr Hoyle, I was only making a joke.' And brushing from his ledger a flake of plaster, he resumed his work.

As Max and Paula lay on the floor, wrestling with a fierceness that was half pretence but half the recurrent dawn (that bright perennial miracle) of simple passion, she said to him, 'If I tell you where it is, and who's got it . . .'

'I know,' he said.

'Oh, no, you don't,' she answered.

'But there's something else I want to know . . .'

'No, no!'

'You want it too. And this – I tell you this – this is what's in my mind. I want something else, something better, than a day-to-day dullness of life. These dull, damned people that I've lived with all my life – I'm sick and tired of them – I want something better, more, than they have ever thought of. Will you come with me if I go? I don't know where. Jamaica for a start, or the Bahamas. Anywhere you like. If I say, let's cut and run, will you come too?'

'Yes, if you want me to. But you wouldn't dare!'
'I would – if you'll come with me.'
'Now – or any time you like.'

In the room below, the attention of Hoyle and the junior accountant was again directed to the curious, rhythmic movement of the ceiling. For a little while they stared at it with bewilderment and a wild surmise; and then, as another flake of dislodged plaster fell on his ledger, Atkinson let out a wistful sigh.

'If I know anything,' he said . . .

'You know very little,' said Hoyle, 'but if your figures agree, I think you can close your ledger and go home. And remember this: that no one who wishes advancement in his profession, ever says anything about what he has seen or heard during office hours.'

'Darling!' said Paula, on the floor above, and caressing her elderly lover, ran affectionate fingers through his thick crop of silver hair. 'You darling!' she said again. And then, 'My God, what's this? What the hell is this?'

Between thumb and forefinger she held a small fragment of some hard, sharp substance that she had discovered in his hair; and sitting up, she invited his inspection of it.

'I found it in your hair,' she said, and showed him a spicule of bone.

'By God,' said Max, 'it's a bit of poor old Charlie!'

THE AGE OF STEAM AND IRON

Although Scotland had built many famous ships before the nineteenth century it is with the coming of steam power and the development of iron and steel construction that Scotland, and in particular, the River Clyde, came to prominence and fame.

Now all but vanished, the shipbuilding industry of the Clyde, based on the somewhat improbable and uncertain foundation of Henry Bell's little *Comet* of 1812, grew to dominate the world's seaways – both in sheer numbers and in technological innovation. Wherever there was water to float a ship, from the rivers of Burma to the lakes of Central Africa, from the Arctic to the Pacific, there would be found a Clyde-built ship. When iron replaced wood and steel replaced iron – the Clyde yards were to the fore. When the steam engine was improved and perfected with double and triple expansion systems the innovations came from the Clyde. Clyde-built became a symbol and guarantee of quality; whether sailing ship or steamer, the mark of her home river was to be seen on her. Joseph Conrad the Polish-English ship's captain and novelist recognised this, writing of his first command, the iron barque *Otago*, built in 1869 by Alexander Stephen of Linthouse, he commented:

> Her hull, her rigging, filled my eye with great content . . . At the first glance I saw that she was a high-class vessel, a harmonious creature in the lines of her fine body, in the proportioned tallness of her spars. Whatever her age and history, she had preserved the stamp of her origin.

If the Clyde-built ship became a familiar sight in all parts of the world, then the Clyde-built man, the ship's engineer, became an equally kenspeckle figure in the engine-rooms and harbour bars of the world. The Scottish engineer has indeed outlasted the age of the steamship and it is no chance that the USS *Enterprise*, boldly going into outer space in the television series *Star Trek*, had her warp-drive engines in the careful and concerned charge of a Scottish chief engineer.

Perhaps the greatest celebration of the omnipresent Scottish chief engineer comes in a poem by that quintessentially English writer, Rudyard Kipling. *McAndrew's Hymn*, a long reflection during a middle watch by the 'auld Fleet Engineer' who hears his engines sing their ordained refrain:

'Law, Orrder, Duty an' Restraint, Obedience, Discipline!'

and who glories in the power of the technical innovation he has seen since he started as a 'boiler-whelp'.

Ten pound was all the pressure then – Eh! Eh! – a man wad drive;
An' here, our workin' gauges give one hunder sixty-five!

McAndrew, the stern Calvinist that he is, has his doubts however:

What I ha' seen since ocean-steam began
Leaves me na doot for the machine: but what about the man?
The man that counts, wi' all his runs, one million mile o' sea:
Four time the span from earth to moon ... How far, O Lord, from Thee

Henry Bell's own account of his part in this story is a little known document, worth reprinting here, as is the narrative of one of the earliest long-distance steamboat voyages – the passage made by the *Thames* from Glasgow to London. Two men who were friends and colleagues, although a generation apart, complete our picture of the Clyde. Neil Munro in 'The Ship-shop' paints it at the start of the twentieth century, at the zenith of its success and fame. The bustling River Clyde in those brave days could be a dangerous place, and Munro, writing under his journalistic pen name of 'Hugh Foulis', tells a tale of a collision in the harbour involving a French cargo ship and 'the most uncertain puffer that ever kept the Old New Year in Upper Lochfyne' – the immortal *Vital Spark*. George Blake, in an extract from his novel *The Shipbuilders*, writing in the depression of the 1930s, shows the industry in decline and his elegy for a once-great industry makes a fitting, if sad, conclusion to our selection of writing on Scotland and the seas that surround her.

McAndrew's Hymn

RUDYARD KIPLING (1865–1936)

Lord, Thou hast made this world below the shadow of a dream,
An', taught by time, I tak' it so – exceptin' always Steam.
From coupler-flange to spindle-guide I see Thy Hand, O God—
Predestination in the stride o' yon connectin'-rod.
John Calvin might ha' forged the same – enorrmous, certain, slow—
Ay, wrought it in the furnace-flame – *my* 'Institutio'.
I cannot get my sleep to-night; old bones are hard to please;
I'll stand the middle watch up here – alone wi' God an' these
My engines, after ninety days o' race an' rack an' strain
Through all the seas of all Thy world, slam-bangin' home again.
Slam-bang too much – they knock a wee – the crosshead-gibs
are loose,
But thirty thousand mile o' sea has gied them fair excuse. . . .
Fine, clear an' dark – a full-draught breeze, wi' Ushant out o' sight,
An' Ferguson relievin' Hay. Old girl, ye'll walk to-night!
His wife's at Plymouth. . . . Seventy – One – Two – Three since
he began—
Three turns for Mistress Ferguson . . . and who's to blame the man?
There's none at any port for me, by drivin' fast or slow,
Since Elsie Campbell went to Thee, Lord, thirty years ago.
(The year the *Sarah Sands* was burned. Oh, roads we used to tread,
Fra' Maryhill to Pollokshaws – fra' Govan to Parkhead!)
Not but they're ceevil on the Board. Ye'll hear Sir Kenneth say:
'Good morrn, McAndrew! Back again? An' how's your bilge to-day?'
Miscallin' technicalities but handin' me my chair
To drink Madeira wi' three Earls – the auld Fleet Engineer
That started as a boiler-whelp – when steam and he were low.
I mind the time we used to serve a broken pipe wi' tow!
Ten pound was all the pressure then – Eh! Eh! – a man wad drive;
An' here, our workin' gauges give one hunder sixty-five!
We're creepin' on wi' each new rig – less weight an' larger power;
There'll be the loco-boiler next an' thirty mile an hour!
Thirty an' more. What I ha' seen since ocean-steam began

Leaves me na doot for the machine: but what about the man?
The man that counts, wi' all his runs, one million mile o' sea:
Four time the span from earth to moon. . . . How far, O Lord,

from Thee

That wast beside him night an' day? Ye mind my first typhoon?
It scoughed the skipper on his way to jock wi' the saloon.
Three feet were on the stokehold-floor – just slappin' to an' fro—
An' cast me on a furnace-door. I have the marks to show.
Marks! I ha' marks o' more than burns – deep in my soul an' black,
An' times like this, when things go smooth, my wickudness

comes back.

The sins o' four an' forty years, all up an' down the seas,
Clack an' repeat like valves half-fed . . . Forgie's our trespasses!
Nights when I'd come on deck to mark, wi' envy in my gaze,
The couples kittlin' in the dark between the funnel-stays;
Years when I raked the Ports wi' pride to fill my cup o' wrong—
Judge not, O Lord, my steps aside at Gay Street in Hong-Kong!
Blot out the wastrel hours of mine in sin when I abode—
Jane Harrigan's an' Number Nine, The Reddick an' Grant Road!
An' waur than all – my crownin' sin – rank blasphemy an' wild.
I was not four and twenty then – Ye wadna judge a child?
I'd seen the Tropics first that run – new fruit, new smells, new air—
How could I tell – blind-fou wi' sun – the Deil was lurkin' there?
By day like playhouse-scenes the shore slid past our sleepy eyes;
By night those soft, lasceevious stars leered from those velvet skies,
In port (we used no cargo-steam) I'd daunder down the streets—
An ijjit grinnin' in a dream – for shells an' parrakeets,
An' walkin'-sticks o' carved bamboo an' blowfish stuffed an' dried—
Fillin' my bunk wi' rubbishry the Chief put overside.
Till, off Sambawa Head, Ye mind, I heard a land-breeze ca',
Milk-warm wi' breath o' spice an' bloom: 'McAndrew, come awa'!'
Firm, clear an' low – no haste, no hate – the ghostly whisper went,
Just statin' eevidential facts beyon' all argument:
'Your mither's God's a graspin' deil, the shadow o' yoursel',
'Got out o' books by meenisters clean daft on Heaven an' Hell.
'They mak' him in the Broomielaw, o' Glasgie cold an' dirt,
'A jealous, pridefu' fetich, lad, that's only strong to hurt.
'Ye'll not go back to Him again an' kiss His red-hot rod,
'But come wi' Us' (Now, who were *They*?) 'an' know the

Leevin' God,

'That does not kipper souls for sport or break a life in jest,

'But swells the ripenin' cocoanuts an' ripes the woman's breast.'
An' there it stopped – cut off – no more – that quiet, certain voice—
For me, six months o' twenty-four, to leave or take at choice.
'Twas on me like a thunderclap – it racked me through an' through—
Temptation past the show o' speech, unnameable an' new—
The Sin against the Holy Ghost? . . . An' under all, our screw.

That storm blew by but left behind her anchor-shiftin' swell.
Thou knowest all my heart an' mind, Thou knowest, Lord, I fell—
Third on the *Mary Gloster* then, and first that night in Hell!
Yet was Thy Hand beneath my head, about my feet Thy Care—
Fra' Deli clear to Torres Strait, the trial o' despair,
But when we touched the Barrier Reef Thy answer to my prayer! . . .
We dared na run that sea by night but lay an' held our fire,
An' I was drowsin' on the hatch – sick – sick wi' doubt an' tire:
'*Better the sight of eyes that see than wanderin' o' desire!*'
Ye mind that word? Clear as our gongs – again, an' once again,
When rippin' down through coral-trash ran out our moorin'-chain:
An', by Thy Grace, I had the Light to see my duty plain.
Light on the engine-room – no more – bright as our carbons burn.
I've lost it since a thousand times, but never past return!

Obsairve! Per annum we'll have here two thousand souls aboard—
Think not I dare to justify myself before the Lord,
But – average fifteen hunder souls safe-borne fra' port to port—
I *am* o' service to my kind. Ye wadna blame the thought?
Maybe they steam from Grace to Wrath – to sin by folly led—
It isna mine to judge their path – their lives are on my head.
Mine at the last – when all is done it all comes back to me,
The fault that leaves six thousand ton a log upon the sea.
We'll tak' one stretch – three weeks an' odd by ony road ye steer—
Fra' Cape Town east to Wellington – ye need an engineer.
Fail there – ye've time to weld your shaft – ay, eat it, ere ye're spoke;
Or make Kerguelen under sail – three jiggers burned wi' smoke!
An' home again – the Rio run: it's no child's play to go
Steamin' to bell for fourteen days o' snow an' floe an' blow.
The bergs like kelpies overside that girn an' turn an' shift
Whaur, grindin' like the Mills o' God, goes by the big South drift.
(Hail, Snow and Ice that praise the Lord. I've met them at
                                                  their work,
An' wished we had anither route or they anither kirk.)

Yon's strain, hard strain, o' head an' hand, for though Thy
　　　　　　　　　　　　　　　　　Power brings
All skill to naught, Ye'll understand a man must think o' things.
Then, at the last, we'll get to port an' hoist their baggage clear—
The passengers, wi' gloves an' canes – an' this is what I'll hear:
'Well, thank ye for a pleasant voyage. The tender's comin' now.'
While I go testin' follower-bolts an' watch the skipper bow.
They've words for every one but me – shake hands wi' half the crew,
Except the dour Scots engineer, the man they never knew.
An' yet I like the wark for all we've dam'-few pickin's here—
No pension, an' the most we'll earn's four hunder pound a year.
Better myself abroad? Maybe. *I'd* sooner starve than sail
Wi' such as call a snifter-rod *ross* . . . French for nightingale.
Commeesion on my stores? Some do; but I cannot afford
To lie like stewards wi' patty-pans. I'm older than the Board.
A bonus on the coal I save? Ou ay, the Scots are close,
But when I grudge the strength Ye gave I'll grudge their food to *those*.
(There's bricks that I might recommend – an' clink the fire-bars cruel.
No! Welsh – Wangarti at the worst – an' damn all patent fuel!)
Inventions? Ye must stay in port to mak' a patent pay.
My Deeferential Valve-Gear taught me how that business lay.
I blame no chaps wi' clearer heads for aught they make or sell.
I found that I could not invent an' look to these as well.
So, wrestled wi' Apollyon – Nah! – fretted like a bairn—
But burned the workin'-plans last run, wi' all I hoped to earn.
Ye know how hard an Idol dies, an' what that meant to me—
E'en tak' it for a sacrifice acceptable to Thee. . . .
Below there! Oiler! What's your wark? Ye find it runnin' hard?
Ye needn't swill the cup wi' oil – this isn't the Cunard!
Ye thought? Ye are not paid to think. Go, sweat that off again!
Tck! Tck! It's deeficult to sweer nor tak' The Name in vain!
Men, ay, an women, call me stern. Wi' these to oversee,
Ye'll note I've little time to burn on social repartee.
The bairns see what their elders miss; they'll hunt me to an' fro,
Till for the sake of – well, a kiss – I tak' 'em down below.
That minds me of our Viscount loon – Sir Kenneth's kin – the chap
Wi' Russia-leather tennis-shoon an' spar-decked yachtin'-cap.
I showed him round last week, o'er all – an' at the last says he:
'Mister McAndrew, don't you think steam spoils romance at sea?'
Damned ijjit! I'd been doon that morn to see what ailed the throws,
Manholin', on my back – the cranks three inches off my nose.

Romance! Those first-class passengers they like it very well,
Printed an' bound in little books; but why don't poets tell?
I'm sick of all their quirks an' turns – the loves an' doves they dream—
Lord, send a man like Robbie Burns to sing the Song o' Steam!
To match wi' Scotia's noblest speech yon orchestra sublime
Whaurto – uplifted like the Just – the tail-rods mark the time.
The crank-throws give the double-bass, the feed-pump sobs an' heaves,
An' now the main eccentrics start their quarrel on the sheaves:
Her time, her own appointed time, the rocking link-head bides,
Till – hear that note? – the rod's return whings glimmerin' through
                                                    the guides.
They're all awa'! True beat, full power, the clangin' chorus goes
Clear to the tunnel where they sit, my purrin' dynamoes.
Interdependence absolute, foreseen, ordained, decreed,
To work, Ye'll note, at ony tilt an' every rate o' speed.
Fra' skylight-lift to furnace-bars, backed, bolted, braced an' stayed,
An' singin' like the Mornin' Stars for joy that they are made;
While, out o' touch o' vanity, the sweatin' thrust-block says:
'Not unto us the praise, or man – not unto us the praise!'
Now, a' together, hear them lift their lesson – theirs an' mine:
'Law, Orrder, Duty an' Restraint, Obedience, Discipline!'
Mill, forge an' try-pit taught them that when roarin' they arose,
An' whiles I wonder if a soul was gied them wi' the blows.
Oh for a man to weld it then, in one trip-hammer strain,
Till even first-class passengers could tell the meanin' plain!
But no one cares except mysel' that serve an' understand
My seven thousand horse-power here. Eh, Lord! They're grand –
                                                    they're grand!
Uplift am I? When first in store the new-made beasties stood,
Were Ye cast down that breathed the Word declarin' all things good?
Not so! O' that warld-liftin' joy no after-fall could vex,
Ye've left a glimmer still to cheer the Man – the Arrtifex!
That holds, in spite o' knock and scale, o' friction, waste an' slip,
An' by that light – now, mark my word – we'll build the Perfect
                                                    Ship.
I'll never last to judge her lines or take her curve – not I.
But I ha' lived an' I ha' worked. Be thanks to Thee, Most High!
An' I ha' done what I ha' done – judge Thou if ill or well—
Always Thy Grace preventin' me. . . .
Losh! Yon's the 'Stand-by' bell.
Pilot so soon? His flare it is. The mornin'-watch is set.

Well, God be thanked, as I was sayin', I'm no Pelagian yet.
Now I'll tak' on. . . .
'Morrn, Ferguson. Man, have ye ever thought
What your good leddy costs in coal? . . . I'll burn 'em down to port.

Observations on the Utility
of Applying Steam Engines
to Vessels etc.

HENRY BELL (1767–1830)

Henry Bell pioneered steam navigation in Europe. Although others in Scotland, like Patrick Miller and William Symington, had succeeded in building steamships to sail on lochs and canals, none of these earlier vessels were put into commercial service and none ventured into the open sea or even the stormy waters of the Firth of Clyde, where Henry Bell's Comet *traded from 1812 onwards, providing the first commercial steamship service in Europe.*

Bell, a millwright to trade, had established a business as a wright in Glasgow, before moving to the new planned seaside town of Helensburgh and building the Baths Inn there in 1807 to cater for the current fashion for sea bathing. Elected the first provost of the new town, his enthusiasm for progress seems to have outstripped the cautious conservatism of his fellow citizens and, leaving municipal politics behind, he devoted himself to steam navigation. The Comet *found its first employment carrying guests down from Glasgow to take the waters at the Baths Inn, but as other and larger steamships came into service,* Comet *was transferred to the Forth and later, in 1819, was lengthened and commenced the first steamer service to the Highlands and Islands, trading between Greenock and Fort William.* Comet's *pioneering career ended in December 1820 when she was wrecked off Crinan.*

Bell's 'Observations' (dedicated to another great Scottish enthusiast for progress, Sir John Sinclair of Ulbster, the force behind the Statistical Account of Scotland) was sent to the Admiralty, accompanied by a letter from Bell offering to bring the Comet *down to the Thames to demonstrate her to their Lordships. The ever-ingenious Bell also offered the Admiralty a bombproof vessel and a non-lethal secret weapon designed to prevent ships being boarded by the enemy. Inundated by letters from enthusiasts convinced that their pet plan could win the war at sea, and deeply conservative by instinct, the Board of Admiralty*

*decided not to trouble Bell and rejected all his offers. However sus-
picious the Admiralty might have been, one does feel that they might
have shown sufficient intellectual curiosity to accept Bell's offer to show
them the* Comet – *which was, unlike war-winning secret weapons, an
accomplished reality.*

*Unfortunately, despite all his enthusiasm and pioneering zeal, Bell
never made a great commercial success of his involvement in steam
navigation. A small Government grant, and a pension from the Clyde
Navigation Trustees, made his latter days more comfortable but his
impulsive nature and appetite for ambitious and ingenious plans made
him a poor businessman. Nevertheless, as that great engineer of the age,
Isambard Kingdom Brunel, observed, 'Bell did what we engineers all
failed in – he gave us the sea steamer, his scheming was Britain's
steaming.'*

Bell's pamphlet describes his steamship Comet *and also gives some idea
of his vision for the future of steam power at sea. It would be many years
before exclusively steam-powered vessels had developed sufficiently to
sail the longer routes and Bell's thoughts are confined to coasting vessels
and cross-channel ferries, with steam power as a supplementary means
of propulsion in larger, ocean-going vessels. However, there is other
evidence to suggest that Bell had, from an early time, an all-embracing
vision of the triumph of marine steam power, a vision that was to
be made reality by subsequent generations of Clyde shipbuilders and
engineers.*

As a ship is the noblest, and one of the most useful machines that ever
was invented, every attempt to improve it becomes a matter of the greatest
importance, and merits the particular attention of every British subject.

In the year 1809 I attempted to make a small model, in which I
succeeded so far, that I was convinced an engine could be made, on
such a construction, so as to drive a vessel in all weathers.

But for further information, before I attempted any thing on a large
scale, in the year 1810, I built a small boat 13 feet long, and 5 feet of
beam, in which I tried a great many experiments, by erecting a number
of different machines; and in the year 1811, I succeeded so far in my
views, that I was fully convinced a vessel of any size could be wrought
by steam.

Being thus satisfied; in the year 1812, I built a vessel 40 feet long and
10½ feet beam, and hold eight feet deep, which I fitted up solely for
Passengers in the following manner:

1st, In the stern there is a cock-pit of 6 feet, seated all round, with six lockers, neatly fitted up. On each side there is a stair, by which you ascend to the cabin.

2nd, The Cabin is 10 feet 4 in length, and 7 feet 6 in breadth, elegantly furnished with sofas all round, &c. There are, also, moveable divisions, by which it can be divided at pleasure into three different apartments, two of which contain each two handsome beds. The third is formed into a small neat cabin, with seven lockers for holding stores, &c.

3rd, Next to the cabin is an apartment of 12 feet 6 in length, and 10 feet 6 in breadth, in which the engine and machinery are placed. And in the steerage (which is 10 feet in length, and 7 feet in breadth) are 4 beds, two on each side, has also 6 lockers, and seated all round, &c.

The upper deck above cabin and steerage is seated all round; on each side there is a projection of 1 foot 10 inches, being a recess for the paddles, which form part of the deck; and in each projection are a water closet.

This vessel has been running between Glasgow and Greenock for 6 months past, and is found very commodious for passengers. The distance between Glasgow and Greenock by water is about 26 miles, which she runs, (in ordinary weather) with ease, in 4 hours and a half – The engine is a small portable one, on only 3 horse power; a vessel of her size would require an engine of 5 horse power, by which she could run the same distance in 3½ hours.

In this country many attempts have been made to apply steam engines to the purpose of driving vessels; and vessels have been set agoing, and even patents obtained for them, but never one of them was found to answer the end.

The above vessel is the first that ever answered the purpose; the engine of which is so constructed, that no change of position can have any effect upon it. It goes as well when the vessel is tossed with a heavy gale, as in a calm. This has been experienced; for the *Comet* (which is the name of the above vessel) has run between the island of Bute and Greenock in very stormy weather, with high seas, which is known to be a more dangerous passage than out in the open ocean.

These portable engines are by far the most useful that have yet been invented, as they can be applied to almost any purpose; they can be applied with equal advantage to carriages on rail roads, &c. As no change of position, as above mentioned, can have any effect upon them, and the room which they occupy is so small, that one of 10 horse power requires only 8 feet of height, 8 feet of length, and 5 feet of breadth.

The utility of those engines when applied to *coasting* vessels, &c. will be seen from the following observations.

1st, Coasting vessels are very often detained by contrary winds, &c. and the people to whom their cargoes belong are much disappointed in not receiving their goods at the time expected. This obstacle would in a great measure be removed by adopting steam; for those vessels requiring no rigging, the wind (although straight a-head of them) would have less effect in retarding their progress,

2nd, They would be more *safe* than other vessels – How often do we hear of vessels being run ashore by those sudden gusts of wind, which are so frequent on the coast, and so unexpected, that the most experienced seamen are taken at unawares, and often before their sails can be reduced, the vessels are laid on their beam-ends.

3rd, They are easier fitted out and managed than other vessels – An engine will not cost so much as the *rigging* of a vessel, and all the machinery required besides, is only a pair of spur wheels, and cross shaft, by which the paddles are attached to the engine, and then they are not liable to go wrong, nor will they require the tenth part of the repairs which are necessary to keep up the rigging of other vessels.

Portable engines could also be applied with great advantage to ferries, such as Portpatrick, Queen's ferry, &c. as those vessels not having any rigging, could easily be made on such a construction that they would not upset, which would prevent the loss of many lives. It would be of particular advantage to the public were a passage to be obtained at ferries in all weather, without people being obliged to expose their lives to such imminent danger as at present. As this is a matter of such great consequence, and the mode of improvement so simple, I would hope to see, in a short time, the plan universally adopted.

A steam engine could be erected on a punt or vessel, and used with great advantage in deepening of rivers, harbours, &c. and could also be applied for the purpose of breaking ice in the winter season.

One of these engines would be particularly useful on board large vessels at sea.

1st, In case of a vessel being becalmed, by setting her engine agoing, she would always be kept on her way; or with a slight breeze of side-wind, by applying the paddles to the lea-side, she would be wrought two points to windward.

2nd, The engine could be used at all times when a vessel required pumping – It could be attached to the same lever by which the pumps are at present wrought on board large vessels, and with so little machinery, that the incumbrance would be but trifling. In case of the vessel springing a leak, the engine would do more in clearing her of water than all the hands on board together; and at the same time, the hands could be employed at something else. By this means many a valuable ship and cargo might be saved. The same machinery could be attached to the capstan is loading and discharging the vessel, or for any purpose in which the capstan is used. How quick could a vessel be warped out of harbour by this method – In short, the number of different purposes for which the engine could be used are many, and require only a little time and experience to evince its utility.

Since the *Comet* was set agoing on the Clyde, two vessels have been built on nearly the same construction; the one handsomely fitted up for Passengers, and the other, a vessel of about 70 feet long, intended for conveying *Goods* and Passengers: this last will be found very advantageous to the public, as she will be a much more regular trader than any vessel that must wait for fair wind. Goods sent by this conveyance will not cost above one-third of land carriage; and as they can be delivered on board any vessel in Greenock harbour, the vast expense of cellarage and porterage, &c. will be saved to the public.

'The Voyage of the *Thames*'

from The Scots Magazine March 1816

ISAAC WELD (1774–1856)

In May 1815 an advertisement appeared in the Glasgow Courier:

MARINE EXCURSION FROM THE CLYDE TO THE THAMES

A select party, not exceeding six, may be accommodated in the *Thames* schooner, late the *Argyll* steam engine packet. This vessel has received many improvements, is perfectly sea worthy, and enabled to proceed either by steam or sails, separately or united.

Those who wish to enjoy this novel and interesting trip along the Coast of Scotland, Wales and England, will please apply to William Ker, the Agent, Broomielaw. The vessel will start early next week.

This, the first advertisement for a long-distance sea excursion, marks the dispersion of steam power technology from its first British home on the Clyde. The Argyll *had been launched at Port Glasgow in April 1814 and had traded on the Clyde for almost a year before being purchased by George Dodd, a civil engineer and former naval officer, and renamed* Thames, *in anticipation of her service on that river.* Argyll/Thames *was not the first Clyde-built steamer to go south – the* Margery *had in 1814 gone via the Forth and Clyde Canal and the East Coast to the Thames, before being sold on to French owners. The entrepreneurial Henry Bell, seldom uninvolved in early steamship matters, was concerned in some unspecified way in the sale of both the* Margery *and the* Thames.

Dodd's plan to take the Thames *south by way of Land's End and expose her to the full force of the Atlantic, and to sell tickets for the voyage, marks an unprecedented level of confidence in the new technology.*

The voyage of the Thames *attracted much interest and is well documented – our version comes from an account published in* The Scots Magazine, *which copied it from the* Journal de Physique. *The author, Isaac Weld, a Dublin-born topographical writer, also contributed a somewhat fuller account to the* Journal des Mines, *which George Dodd reprinted in his 1818* Dissertation on Steam Engines and Steam Packets. *Dodd was also interviewed by a Parliamentary Committee looking into improvements to the mail service across the Irish Channel and gave the*

Committee a very positive picture of the Thames' *pioneering voyage, 'I found her more sea-worthy than any vessel I ever was in; she is fully capable of going head to wind in violent gales, and over high seas . . .'*

Naturally the rThames also attracted attention on her way round the coast – the Plymouth and Dock Telegraph *reported:*

> . . . in her passage along the Cornish coast, the fishermen and others, who perceived her rapidly gliding on without masts or sails, and vomiting forth flame, and smoke from her bows, conceived her to be a sea devil and made a precipitate retreat.

and at Portsmouth her arrival caused the abandonment of a naval court martial to allow the members of the court the opportunity to inspect this novel phenomenon.

On reaching the capital, Dodd put the Thames *into service between London and Margate where she proved highly successful. By 1817 Dodd had five steam boats operating on the Thames.*

The command of the vessel had been given to Mr G. Dodd, a young man of great resolution, who had gone to Glasgow expressly to bring it to London. He had made his apprenticeship in the English navy, and had afterwards distinguished himself as a civil engineer, an architect, and even a topographer. His equipment consisted merely of a master, four sailors of the first class, a smith, a fireman and a cabin-boy. It was the first embarkation of the kind which had ever been attempted on the stormy sea which terminates St George's Channel; but, full of confidence in his vessel and his equipment, he put boldly to sea.

The beginning of his voyage was not fortunate; the weather was very unsettled; and in the narrow channel which separates Scotland from Ireland, the swell is sometimes rendered terrible by the meeting of the ebbtide with the strong swell which comes from the Atlantic Ocean. After having vainly attempted to advance, he was forced to seek shelter in Loch Ryan. A second attempt did not succeed much better than the first; he gained, however, the coast of Ireland; but there he had nearly lost his vessel, from the ignorance or awkwardness of a pilot, who, mistaking one cape for another, was like to cast it on shore. Captain Dodd affirmed to me, that no force but that of steam could have pushed the vessel against wind and tide, and saved it amid rocks. It halted at Dublin for rest and repairs.

On the 25th May, I learned by mere accident the arrival of a steam ship at Dublin. I immediately went to see it, and found it ready to set out, with a great number of curious persons, to exhibit its passage across the bay. I was so enchanted with what I witnessed, and what I learned of its passage from Glasgow to Dublin, that, intending to go over to London, I immediately formed the resolution of trying the adventure of this voyage. The following Sunday, being the 28th, at noon, we put to sea. Many persons embarked along with us, through curiosity, only to cross the bay, and land at Dunleary, at seven miles distance. Some naval officers who were on board, agreed in thinking that this vessel could not long sustain a heavy sea, and that there would be great danger in venturing far from the coast. Nothing, however, suffered in this passage, and the vessel went through the waves in less time than the best sailer could have done. My wife and I spent some hours on shore at Dunleary, and then set sail, the only passengers.

The shore was covered with many thousands of spectators, who wished us a happy voyage. The sea was very calm, and we reckoned on an agreeable sail through the night; but when no longer sheltered by the coast, we found a great swell. In fact, the movement of the vessel differed entirely from that of one pushed by sails or oars; the action of the wheels upon the water on both sides prevented rolling; the vessel floated on the summit of the waves, like a sea-bird. The most disagreeable movement took place when the waves struck the ship crossways; but here too its particular construction gave it a great advantage; for the cages which contained the wheels acted like so many buoys. On these occasions, the sudden arrival of the water in the windward cage, and the compression of the air caused an alarming noise, and a shock like what is experienced from a high sea. After having received this shock on one side, we commonly experienced another, by way of reaction, on the opposite; then a third, much slighter, on the first side; after which the vessel preserved a regular motion for some minutes. I do not recollect to have experienced more than three of these shocks in rapid succession; and their constant effect was to put a stop to that rolling, which continues often so long in sailing vessels. It cannot be denied that they were unpleasant at the first moment, from the noise which accompanied them, and from their force of percussion, which made the whole vessel tremble; but no lasting inconvenience resulted from them; on the contrary, the equilibrium was immediately restored; and, during the rest of the voyage, the vessel made what the sailors call a dry way, that is, it danced so lightly over the waves, that it never took in one; and in all the passage we were not once wet, even by their foam; a most rare case, and which could not be expected in any common ship.

We left far behind us all the vessels that left Dublin by the same tide; and next day, about nine in the morning, we passed Wexford. The inhabitants, from the heights which rise over the city, had remarked the thick smoke that issued from our mast, and had thence concluded that the vessel was on fire. Instantly all the pilots put to sea, to fly to our aid; and on the arrival of the first, we could judge, by their attitude, of their extreme surprise, mingled with disappointment, at seeing us in good condition, and themselves frustrated of the dues of *salvage*.

The same day we reached Ramsay Passage, between the island of that name and Cape St David. Although the coast is broken by very abrupt rocks, we were not long of seeing, from some little creeks, round which there appeared no habitations, a number of boats issue, the rowers as usual taking us for a vessel in distress. We had then to cross the bay of St Bride, where a great swell was produced by the meeting of spring tide with the current which came out of Ramsay Passage. The turbulence of the waves, when we were in their power, was truly alarming; we were often so low between two of them, that we lost sight of the coast, though very high; but the vessel made its way across all these obstacles, in the most alert manner; and we left far behind us a fleet of merchant vessels which attempted to follow.

We now crossed a narrow, and very dangerous passage, called Jack Sound. Our situation at one time would have been very perilous on board a vessel which had only sails to trust to; but our powerful and indefatigable wheels soon drew us out of this danger, and brought us safe and sound into Milford Road.

Two days were employed at Milford in satisfying the curiosity of a number of marine officers, in examining the interior of the machine, and in cleaning the boiler – an operation which had not been performed since the departure from Glasgow.

We set sail in the evening of Thursday, and sailed through the middle of the Bristol Channel. In the evening, we discovered the high coasts which form the western extremity of England; and as it would have been imprudent, this night, to have doubled the land's end, we turned into the Bay of St Ives. Our appearance caused the usual alarm; and in an instant every disposable sail was in motion towards us. The pilots on this station are the finest I ever saw. As we entered the bay, the appearance of our vessel appeared to cause as much surprise to the inhabitants, as that of Captain Cook produced on its first appearance in the South Sea Islands.

We spent a day or two on shore, and went to examine those curious masses of rock which form St Michael's Mount. On Monday the 5th

June, at four in the afternoon, the weather appearing favourable, we re-embarked. But, in doubling Cape Cornwall, the first of the two great promontories which terminate England to the west, we soon saw that appearances had deceived us; a tremendous swell came upon us from the whole depth of the Atlantic; while the current which came down St George's Channel, met these waves, and raised them to a height which it seemed impossible to pass. The vessel appeared to suffer; and the repeated shocks against the cage of the wheels alarmed the pilot, who heard them for the first time. Night approached, and no harbour presented itself, except that which we had quitted, and which was already too distant. In this state of things, Captain Dodd remarking, that the vessel sailed better against the wave than otherwise, caused it to make a long stretch in that direction, till we were out of the quarter where the swell struggled against the tide; we hoisted sail, which contributed always to the equilibrium of the vessel; and, at the end of some hours, we had at length doubled the land's end, and found a tranquil sea. From this moment the voyage presented nothing painful or formidable; we were at the entrance of Mount Bay, which is said to be always more tranquil than the Irish Sea; the sun shone upon us, the sea sparkled with light, and the coast displayed all its beauties; we distinguished its woods, its villages, and its rich cultivation.

We arrived at Plymouth on Tuesday the 7th June. We were an object of astonishment to the sailors, who all collected on the sides of their vessels, to gaze upon us, and make their observations. We had no sails; our wheels were invisible; and as the fire happened at the moment to burn without smoke, it was certainly difficult to divine the cause of our rapid motion.

From Plymouth we sailed without interruption to Portsmouth, where we arrived on Friday 9th June, at nine o'clock in the morning, having made 150 miles in 23 hours. At Portsmouth, the admiration was still more marked than elsewhere. The spectators crowded by tens of thousands, and the numbers of craft that pressed around us, became so considerable and inconvenient, that we were obliged to apply to the Admiral for a guard to maintain the police.

Our next stop was at Margate, at the mouth of the Thames. We arrived on Sunday morning the 11th, and spent twenty-four hours there. We then concluded our voyage, by sailing up the river to Limehouse, at the entry of London, in nine hours. We had made 760 miles in 121½ hours.

The notice which I have given leaves not the least doubt as to the usefulness of steam vessels, in every case when it is of importance to make a quick voyage, and where the distance to be passed over is not very considerable; but the immense quantity of combustible matter which this process requires (two tons in twenty-four hours for a vessel of 75 tons) is an insurmountable obstacle to the employment of them in a long voyage; the great outlay required for constructing the machine, added to the value of the materials which it consumes, will not allow them to be employed with advantage in the conveyance of goods; but in situations like Dublin and Holyhead, where nothing is spared to accelerate the dispatches from London, these vessels might be of great service, particularly in the summer months, when calms are very frequent, and stop all ships that use the sail. In the same manner, between Dover and Calais; and wherever passengers are in haste to cross, these vessels will be used with much advantage.

This first voyage in open sea has proved that the wheels perform their functions very well in the roughest weather; and that the movement of the steam-boat, tho' certainly slower amid waves than in a calm, will always be more rapid than that of an ordinary boat. As *avisos*, or sea courriers, their merit is incalculable; and in time of war – but I stop; too many miseries mingle with these recollections; we breathe at last the balsamic zephyr of peace; let us enjoy it.

The Ship-shop

from The Clyde, River & Firth

NEIL MUNRO (1863–1930)

Neil Munro was a poet, novelist and journalist, but he was, perhaps, above all a man of the Clyde. Born at Inveraray, on one of the Clyde's sea lochs, a community linked to the outside world by MacBrayne's steamers, Munro wrote:

Along the western sea-board, from Tarbert, Loch Fyne, to Lochinver, and throughout the Inner and Outer Isles from Port Ellen in Islay to Stornoway in the Lews, generations of young Highlanders have grown up with the idea that their very existence was more or less dependent on MacBrayne. But for MacBrayne, most of them would never have seen bananas or the white fish of the lowlands; might still be burning coalfish oil in cruisies, and getting no more than sixpence a dozen for their eggs.

Like many another Highlander Munro moved to Glasgow to further his career and the Clyde, Glasgow's river, continued to be an important element in his journalistic work, most obviously in his Para Handy stories, but much of his other writing takes account of the great river that lay at the heart of the 'Second City', providing it with so much of its employment, wealth and fame.

In 1907 Munro wrote The Clyde, River & Firth – *a handsome and discursive work which follows the Clyde from its Lanarkshire headwaters to the sea. His chapter on 'Harbour Life' vividly conveys the great days of the port of Glasgow:*

One must see the ships disgorge themselves under mighty derricks, of ore from New Caledonia, timber from Oregon, nitrates from Iquique; crates of odorous fruit from Spain, tuns of wine from France and Portugal; palm oil and ivory from South Africa; cotton, tea, spice, and jute from India; tea from China; cattle, corn, flour, beef, scantlings, and doors and windows ready-made from the United States; wheat from Canada, Egypt, and Russia; sugar, teak and mahogany from the West Indies, tinned food and gold from Australasia.

Chapter 11 – 'The Ship-shop' is Munro's tribute to the Clyde's shipyards and to their dominant position in world shipping in the early years of this century.

If the native of Glasgow, travelling abroad and advertising himself vaingloriously as of the 'Second City in the Kingdom', is often vexed to find it adds nothing to his importance, he is almost always sure of some solace to his wounded pride when he goes on steamers. He finds so often there, above some flashing mass of enginery, or on a not too unobtrusive panel, a brazen legend that informs him what he looks upon was made upon the Clyde. I have known a Glasgow child, in the streets of Cairo, gaze transported on a boiler, which, carted through Eastern traffic, seemed the embodiment of ugliness or incongruity, but had for her a charm because it showed, white-painted on its ends, the name of 'Polmadie'. 'I should like to hug that old boiler!' she exclaimed, and it is perhaps in search of some such happy pang of home association that Glasgow men, steam-sailing anywhere, are so prone to go below to 'see the engines'. They really want to be assured that all is well with the workmanship of the crafts to which they trust their precious lives.

> Glasgow ships come sailing in, come sailing in,
>   Come sailing in,

says our old school-time rhyme, and indeed Glasgow ships come sailing into every open harbour in the world. They are found in the oddest waters; they have been taken by the Kara Sea and the Yenisei River to Lake Baikal in the heart of Asia; in parts, like nursery picture-blocks, they have been put together on the inland seas of North America. There are twin-screw awning deckers on the Amazon, Khedival yachts on the Red Sea, stern-wheelers in South African rivers, Rajahs' paddle-galleys on the shores of Sarawak, and nondescripts for gospel purposes or for worldly trade in the lakes of Central Africa, which came to life under our smoky northern sky, beneath the hands of Glasgow rivet-boys. Clyde clippers have broken records and held them long in the days of the 'wind-jammer', when each trip from China or Australia was a feverish race, and Clyde steamers, since the marine engine came to being, have had a *cachet* like Sheffield cutlery or the buns of Bath, so that the praise of them is a convention of English literature, and Kipling and Conrad, voicing the sentiment of the seaman, credit their heroic ships, their shrewdest engineers, to Clyde; our very dredgers keep innumerable ports and rivers navigable in countries where the name of Glasgow, or Simons & Co., is unpronounceable. So much for the ships of peace; Clyde-built men of war, like the old Scots soldiers of fortune, have fought under strange flags, and there has probably been no sea-fight in the last half-century, in which a grimy Scottish engineer could not be found deep in the hot heart of some furious combatant, careless, maybe, of the cause his vessel fought for, but cherishing his beloved engines, which knew only his language, best understood his touch, ministering most willingly to him because he came from the place of their conception. Strange men, foreign-looking, anti-Christian to our suspicious Presbyterian eyes, though maybe to be found with human qualities under the ameliorative influence of the senior partner's bottle, come from all the sea-beat borders of the world to buy Clyde boats, as women go to market, certain of finding all they want so long as they have the money to pay for it. To-day it is a Californian owner – half Scot, half Irish, now of Nob Hill, but once of Paradise, Port Glasgow – who wants, in ten months, a 5000 ton cargo steamer for the Pacific. He will register her, when he gets her, as of Glasgow, and take her home tariff free, to change her port of registry to Vancouver as soon as may be convenient. To-morrow it will be a sun-bronzed, crisp-haired, Spanish-spoken gentleman with an order in his pocket for a cruiser for Peru or San Domingo. Again, it is a stranger seeking 'tramps', and the provision of cargo-carriers classed under that eloquent appellation is so easy a task to the lower Clyde, and carried out so expeditiously, that the builders are said to construct hulls by the mile, and saw them up in the requisite lengths to order with a dent at the ends to finish them. The dent is always water-tight. It would be a marvellous taste in vessels that could not be accommodated in this ship-shop; its keepers have plans and models (the latter made at incredible cost by artists of the miniature) comprising every new development, anticipating the requirements of to-morrow; even if freaks be your foible they will make you them – Fairfield built the *Livadia*, weirdest of marine monsters, for the Czar. You may find sometimes that the very ship you want is ready waiting for you, since the builders, knowing the world must move, knowing what it ought to have, and certain it must have it sooner or later, build ships 'on spec' in slack seasons, and so keep their men employed.

So much for ships at first hand; Clyde ships, second-hand, grown obsolete for Glasgow passengers, go, at the end, to less fastidious quarters, so that 'crocks' from the Clyde have glorified the lower Thames and provided a standard of elegance for the traveller to Clacton and Southend; and elsewhere in English waters the Scotsman often comes upon old friends of the 'Fair' holidays working under aliases. Such good stuff are those old Clyde passenger steamers that they seem immortal, and their owners buff out the natal dates on their bells and engine brasses, ashamed, perhaps, to be found demanding the labour of youth from such veterans.

For two reasons the Clyde can claim to be the greatest of shipbuilding centres in a shipbuilding age. She is the mother-lodge in the freemasonry of men who build fleets, whether it be on Thames, Belfast or Stettin, for the first passenger steamboat in Britain was launched upon her waters and almost all the great discoveries in marine engineering were made or tested first upon her banks. If Stettin and Belfast, having borrowed her brains for a while in recent years, have challenged her supremacy in the production of ocean liners that should be bigger and faster than all others, she has again, by the advent of the *Lusitania* recovered such prestige as lies in tonnage and speed. 'When you want apples,' said Yarrow of Poplar, 'you go to Covent Garden; for meat to a meat market, and for ships you go to the North.' The four chief reasons are that here we have cheap coal, cheap iron, cheaper labour, and cheaper rates, so men like Yarrow leave the Thames and establish themselves in the Scottish ship-shop.

I have said the first passenger steamboat ever built in Britain was launched upon the Clyde; it was the forty-two feet *Comet* of 1812, with a three horse power engine, working at a pressure of five pounds to the square inch, built in Port-Glasgow for Henry Bell, an enterprising inn-keeper of Helensburgh, whereto she sailed deliberately three times a week from the Broomielaw. The sloop-sailors of the time, looking at her puffing seaward, fervently thanked God they went by 'the Almichty's ain win' and no' wi' the deevil's sunfire and brimstane.' The story of the Clyde since then is the story of the steamer. Having proved the practicability of propelling ships by steam-driven paddles, local genius sought at once, with Scottish thrift, to do it economically. Men rose then who seemed to give themselves as with poetic ecstasy to the revelation of the power of this new agent in the destiny of man – the Napiers, the Dennys, and the Cairds; John Elder, John Wood, William Pearce; the Thomsons, Tod & McGregor, Russells, Stephens, Connells, Scotts, Hendersons, Rodgers, Barclay Curles, Simons, and Inglis. By the earliest of them were invented and applied the surface condenser and the compound, triple, and quadruple engine: the screw propeller for ocean steaming, and the change of hull material from wood to iron and from iron to steel if elsewhere first suggested, were developments which for years were in the hands of Clydeside men. A Partick firm no longer in existence, Tod & McGregor, inaugurated the age of the deep sea iron steamer sixty years ago, and Wingate of Whiteinch made the engines of the *Sirius*, the first vessel to cross the Atlantic under steam, and virtually reduce the breadth of that waterway by one-half, to the great gain of the sufferer from *mal-de-mer*. From 1840 to 1899 (with coquettish intervals of no great duration, during which they went elsewhere) the great ship companies remained constant to the Clyde, and here by Napier were built the first Cunarders – wooden paddle ships of about 1100 tons; midgets compared with the *Lusitania*; the first of the Inman Liners and the Royal Mail Steam Packets; the pick of the Orient line, the Castle, Union, Pacific, British India, P.&O., Allan, Anchor, Canadian Pacific. Continental fleets of merchantmen came for long from the same river; the Norddeutscher-Lloyd started with seven Fairfield ships; Caird alone has built a score of Hamburg American packets, and second-hand Clyde liners pioneered the enterprise of the Compagnie Generale Transatlantique.

To-day, nearly all the high-speed cross-channel services are maintained by Clyde-built vessels, and the summer fleets of the Thames, the Solent, Bristol Channel, and Belfast Lough have, at their best, the same origin, as of course have also the swift luxurious passenger boats of our own estuary. As a centre of yacht designing and yacht building the Clyde has no serious rival in the world; the fame of G.L. Watson and the Fifes of Fairlie rests upon racers and steam yachts here constructed; *Shamrocks* grown on our banks persistently struggle for an elusive America's Cup, and American millionaires come here for the floating pleasure palaces of which Gordon Bennett's *Lysistrata* and Drexel's *Marguerita* may be looked upon as the 'top notch' in luxury. These for peace; for war the Clyde has provided the British Admiralty with almost every class of fighting ship, and contributed to the navies of nearly every maritime state in the world.

It may well astound the stranger, passing for the first time down the narrow ribbon of murky water between the clamorous yards, that any ship at all should find her way from the stocks to the safe entrance of what we call her 'native element'. In other quarters hulls are sometimes built broadside to rivers, and so in due time slide to life: here they grow at an angle on keel-block and cradle, and at the release of triggers, a mammoth like the *Lusitania* slides down the well greased ways to float in 86 seconds, yet with a velocity so moderate that she is brought up to her 1000 ton drags with her bow about 110 feet from the shore.

The *Vital Spark*'s Collision

from Para Handy, Complete Edition

NEIL MUNRO (1863–1930)

In 1905, when he was working on The Clyde, River & Firth, *Munro started to delight the readers of his 'Looker-On' column in the* Glasgow Evening News *with the adventures of Captain Peter Macfarlane – Para Handy – and the crew of the steam lighter, or puffer,* Vital Spark *– 'the smertest boat in the tred'. Munro continued to record the adventures of Para Handy in the* News *for close on twenty years. The stories have never been out of print and their west coast setting, charm, humour and wry social comment have continued to attract readers in each generation. In newspaper and book Munro's creation has become one of the enduring comic characters – as long-lasting as Bertie Wooster and Jeeves, as evergreen as Jerome K. Jerome's* Three Men in a Boat. *Apart from their continuing life in book form the Para Handy stories have been successfully translated into television programmes and stage plays and inspired the 1954 Alexander Mackendrick film* The Maggie.*

The story chosen for this anthology is one of eighteen tales, written throughout the course of Munro's journalistic career, which escaped inclusion in any of the collections he saw through the press, or the posthumous complete edition of 1931. These eighteen stories, unearthed (or perhaps more appropriately dredged up) from the files of the* Glasgow Evening News, *were first published in book form in our edition of the* Complete Para Handy Stories *(Birlinn 1992) and range from very early stories – such as 'The* Vital Spark's *Collision' – to the very last Para Handy tale, a 1924 story called 'Wireless on the* Vital Spark *– Intercourse with the Infinite'. However, this latter venture into the Telecommunications Age seemed to take us well beyond our remit in 'The Age of Steam and Iron' so we have chosen the story of the* Vital Spark's *unfortunate collision with the French steamer* Dolores *and its dramatic sequel in the Glasgow Marine Police Court.*

Without wishing to detract from the tension of the courtroom scene the editors would like to remind readers of a nervous disposition that this is a Scottish sea anthology and that Scots law enjoys the

*unique distinction of having a third verdict available to its courts –
'not proven'.*

✿

There was a haze, that almost amounted to a fog, on the river. The long,
unending wharves on either hand, and the crane-jibs, derricks, masts,
hulls, and sheds looked as if they had all been painted in various tones
of smoky grey. From the vague banks came the sound of rivet-hammers,
the rumble of wheels, and once, quite distinctly, from out of the reek
that hung about a tar-boiler at the foot of Finnieston Street, The Tar,
who was standing by the Captain at the wheel, heard a gigantic voice
cry, 'Awa', or I'll put my finger in your e'e!'

'We'll soon be home noo,' said The Tar. 'Man, it's a fine cheery place,
Gleska, too.'

Para Handy gave one knock as a signal to the engineer, then bent
down and said to that functionary, who was really within whispering
distance, 'I think you can give her another kick ahead, Macphail, there
iss nothing in the road, and I would be aawful sorry if you lost the
wife's tea-pairty.'

'There's no' another kick in the old tinker,' said Macphail, viciously,
wiping his perspiring brow with a wad of waste, and spitting on his
engine.

'"Tinker" 's no' a name for any boat under my cherge,' said Para
Handy, indignantly. 'She's the smertest in the tred, if she chust had a
wise-like enchineer that kent the way to coax her.'

As he spoke there loomed out of the haze ahead the big hull of
a steamer going much more cautiously in the same direction up the
river, and threatening to block, for a little at least, the progress of the
Vital Spark.

'Keep on her port and you'll clear her,' said Dougie.

'Do you think yoursel' we can risk it?' asked the Captain, dubi-
ously.

'We'll chust have to risk it,' said Dougie, 'if Macphail's going to get
to his wife's tea-pairty this night.'

And so the accident happened.

The case was tried at the Marine Court before River Bailie Weir,
the charge being that, on the afternoon of the 3rd inst., Captain Peter
Macfarlane, of the steam lighter *Vital Spark*, had, between Lancefield
Quay and Anderston Quay, while going in the same direction as the
steamer *Dolores*, of Havre, and at a greater rate of speed (1) caused the
Vital Spark to pass the Dolores on the port side; (2) failed to signal to

the master of the Dolores that he was approaching; and (3) attempting to cause the *Vital Spark* to pass the Dolores before she had given the *Vital Spark* sufficient room to pass.

The Captain of the French boat, who gave his evidence through an interpreter, said, in the course of it, that the *Vital Spark* was steering very badly.

Para Handy, the accused, interrupting – 'Holy smoke! and me at the wheel mysel'!'

Witness, resuming, testified that he saw the skipper of the *Vital Spark* once leaving the wheel altogether, with the result that she took a sheer away and could not recover herself. More than once the crew of the *Vital Spark* shouted to him, and gesticulated wildly, but he did not understand their language. So far as he could guess, it was not English.

Para Handy, violently – 'Not English! There iss not a man on my boat that hass wan word of any other language than English.'

The Magistrate – 'with a Scotch or Hielan' accent, of course.' (Laughter.)

Para Handy – 'Hielan' or Scotch is chust a kind of superior English.'

Witness went on to say he told accused to come up on the starboard side, and he would try to make room for him to pass. But the *Vital Spark* came in on the port quarter and kept there, boring in under the *Dolores'* belting, with the result that there was a collision, and the *Dolores* had a plate bent, some stanchions broken at the aft port gangway, and pipes damaged.

The first witness for the defence was the mate of the *Vital Spark*, Dugald Cameron. On being requested by the agent for the defence to tell his story in his own way, Dougie coughed, cleared his throat, took in his waist-belt two holes, rubbed the palms of his hands together till they creaked, and said – 'We were comin' up the ruver at a medium speed, not sayin' a word to nobody, and the Captain himsel' at the wheel, when the French boat backed doon on the top of us and twisted two of her port-holes against the bow of oor boat. I cried to the French boat—'

The Magistrate – 'What did you cry?'

Witness, addressing the accused – 'What wass it I cried, Peter?' (Laughter.)

The Magistrate – 'You must answer the question yourself.'

Witness – 'Ay, but the Captain helped me at the crying.'

The Magistrate – 'Never mind if he did; what did you shout to the *Dolores*?'

Witness, bashfully – 'I would rather no' say; would it do to write it on a piece of paper?' (Renewed Laughter.)

The witness, being allowed to proceed without the question being pressed, said – 'The *Fital Spark* at the time wass going with consuderable caaution, not more than three knots or maybe two-and-a-half, and everybody on board keeping a smert look-oot.'

The Assessor – 'Did the Captain leave the wheel at any time before the collision occurred?'

'Iss it Peter? Not him! he wass doing splendid where he wass if it wass a Chrustian he had to do with in front and not wan of them foreigners.'

'Did you blow your steam-whistle?'

'Hoo could we blow the steam-whustle and the Captain's jecket hanging on it? Forby, there wass no time, and Macphail needed aal his steam for his enchines anyway. There wass not mich need for a whustle wi' The Tar and me roarin' to them to keep oot of the road. Anybody would think to see them that they owned the whole ruver, and them makin' a collusion without wan word of English! They chust made a breenge down on the top of us.'

Colin Dewar (The Tar) was the next witness for the defence. He deponed that he was standing close beside the Captain of the *Vital Spark* when the collision took place. The *Vital Spark* was hardly more than moving when the French steamer suddenly canted to the left and came up against the lighter's bow. She gave a good hard knock. Just before the collision the Captain and the Mate cried out to the Frenchman.

The Magistrate – 'What did they cry?'

The Tar, after a moment's deliberation, 'I don't mind very weel, but I think they said, "Please, will you kindly let us past?"'

The accused – 'Holy smoke! Colin; the chentleman that's tryin' the case will think we're a bonny lot of dummies.' (Great laughter.)

The Tar, continuing his evidence, said there was a sort of fog on the river at the time. They had come up from Greenock to Govan at a pretty fair speed for the *Vital Spark* because the engineer was particularly anxious to get to his house early in the evening, but above Govan they slowed down a good deal. Could not say what rate of speed they were travelling at when the collision with the *Dolores* took place. Might be six knots; on the other hand, might be two or three knots; he was not a good counter, and would not care to say.

The Assessor – 'Do you know the rules of the road at sea?'

The Tar – 'What? Beg pardon, eh?'

'The rules of the road at sea?'

'It wass not in my depairtment; I am only the cook and the winch; the Captain and Dougie attends to the fancy work. It iss likely the Captain would know aal aboot rules of the road.'

The accused – 'I ken them fine—

    Green to green and rud to rud

    Perfect safety, go aheid!'

The Magistrate – 'Did the Captain of the *Dolores* say anything when he found you butting under his port quarter?'

The Tar – 'He jabbered away at us in French the same ass if we were pickpockets.'

'You're sure it wass French?'

'Yes. If you don't believe me, ask Captain Macfarlane. And the very worst kind of French.'

The Assessor, humorously – 'What was he saying in French?'

The Tar – 'Excuse me. I wouldna care to repeat it. I wish you saw his jaw workin'.'

The charge was found not proven, and the accused was dismissed from the bar. The crew of the *Vital Spark* promptly transferred themselves to a judicious hostelry near the police court, and in the gratitude of his heart at having got off so well, Para Handy sent The Tar out to look for the French captain to invite him to a little mild refreshment. 'There's no doot,' he said, 'we damaged the poor fellow's boat, and it wass aal Macphail's fault cracking on speed to get up in time for his wife's tea-pairty.'

Macphail, looking very uncomfortable in his Sunday shore clothes, sat gloomily apart, contemplating a schooner of beer.

'It's a waarnin',' said Para Handy, 'no' to obleege onybody, far less an enchineer. All the thanks I got for it wass a bad name for the *Vital Spark*. She'll be namely aal over the country now.'

'Ach! it wass only a – Frenchman!' said Dougie.

'Still and on a Frenchman hass feelings chust the same's a Chrustian,' said Para Handy. 'Here's The Tar; did you get him, Colin?'

'He wouldna come,' said The Tar, 'and I gave him every chance in the two languages.'

'Weel, chust let him stay then,' said the Captain. 'Seein' we got Macphail into Gleska in time for his wife's tea-pairty at the cost o' the *Vital Spark*'s good name in the shipping world, perhaps he'll stand us another round.'

Whereupon Macphail looked gloomier than ever, and contributed the first remark he had made all day.

'To the mischief wi' the tea-pairty,' he said. 'I was a' wrang wi' the date; it's no till the next Friday, and when I got hame my wife was in the middle o' a washin.'

The Trial Trip

from The Shipbuilders

GEORGE BLAKE (1893–1961)

George Blake was born in Greenock on the River Clyde. After commencing legal studies at Glasgow University and war service he went into journalism, working on the Glasgow Evening News *under the editorship of Neil Munro. Blake had been friendly with Munro's son Hugh, killed during the First World War, and this friendship extended to Munro himself. Blake edited two posthumous collections of Munro's journalism. After his newspaper career Blake became editor of various literary journals and was a director of the Porpoise Press, which played a very significant role in the Scottish cultural renaissance of the 1930s.*

Blake's 1935 novel The Shipbuilders *looks at a Glasgow shipyard through the parallel lives of the yard owner Leslie Pagan and the riveter Danny Shields. The novel opens with the launch of the last ship on the yard's order book – the* Estramadura – *and our extract comes from her trial trip down river. Leslie Pagan is on board and reflects on what Blake calls 'the high, tragic pageant of the Clyde' as the* Estramadura *sails slowly past the empty yards and desolate slips of the depression-hit Clyde. Although published in 1935 the setting is a year or so earlier – passing Clydebank Pagan sees the great rusting hull of No. 534 'looming in its abandonment like a monument to the glory departed.' No. 534, which would become the* Queen Mary, *had been laid down in 1930 but work was suspended on her in 1931, not to be resumed until April 1934 and her desolate hull was, for these years, a symbol of despair, just as the order to recommence work was the occasion for national rejoicing.*

Leslie Pagan's reflections on the memories of past glories and the tragic sights to be seen from the deck of his own yard's last order from a moving threnody for the vanishing industry of a great river. 'Never again, in any calculation of which the human mind was capable, would the Clyde be what it had been.'

❀

The *Estramadura* went down the river on the Wednesday afternoon, and Leslie Pagan travelled with her.

He was busy and preoccupied while the tugs moved her from the basin in their fussily efficient way. She was still his own, and the more precious for being the last he had in that kind. His heart was in his mouth when her cruiser-stern cleared the pierhead with only a foot to spare. He was haunted by daft fears that this winch would not function and that bollard fail to hold the pull of the tow-ropes. The extinction of a series of lights on the promenade deck at one moment gave him the panic notion that the dynamos had broken down. Knowing well that the apprehension was excessive, he was haunted by a sense of the fallibility of the intricate and interdependent mechanisms of the ship; her security, the thousands of pounds of value she represented, resting perhaps on an abraded inch of insulation on a mile or so of electric cable.

As soon, however, as she was fair in mid-channel, her head down-stream and her beautiful light hull towering over the riverside buildings, he suddenly resigned his creation to chance and the skill of the pilot. At another time he would have been fretfully active until her anchor-chain rattled over the Tail of the Bank, dodging now into the engine-room, now up steel ladders to where the steering-gear churned forward and back again with its own queer air of independence, and then hurrying to the bridge and the battery of telltale lights up there. But now he did nothing, keeping in a mood of uneasy detachment out of the way of busy men in overalls. He found a corner for himself on A deck, well forward below the navigating bridge, and in that retired position stood for a long time – watching, as it were, the last creation of his own hands pass forever beyond him.

It was in a sense a procession that he witnessed, the high, tragic pageant of the Clyde. Yard after yard passed by, the berths empty, the grass growing about the sinking keel-blocks. He remembered how, in the brave days, there would be scores of ships ready for the launching along this reach, their sterns hanging over the tide, and how the men at work on them on high stagings would turn from the job and tug off their caps and cheer the new ship setting out to sea. And now only the gaunt, dumb poles and groups of men, workless, watching in silence the mocking passage of the vessel. It was bitter to know that they knew – that almost every man among them was an artist in one of the arts that go to the building of a ship; that every feature of the *Estramadura* would come under an expert and loving scrutiny, that her passing would remind them of the joy of work and tell them how many among them would never work again. It appalled Leslie Pagan that not a cheer came from those watching groups.

It was a tragedy beyond economics. It was not that so many thousands of homes lacked bread and butter. It was that a tradition, a skill, a glory, a passion, was visibly in decay and all the acquired and inherited loveliness of artistry rotting along the banks of the stream.

Into himself he counted and named the yards they passed. The number and variety stirred him to wonder, now that he had ceased to take them for granted. His mental eye moving backwards up the river, he saw the historic place at Govan, Henderson's of Meadowside at the mouth of the Kelvin, and the long stretch of Fairfield on the southern bank opposite. There came Stephen's of Linthouse next, and Clydeholm facing it across the narrow, yellow ditch of the ship-channel. From thence down river the range along the northern bank was almost continuous for miles – Connell, Inglis, Blythswood, and the rest: so many that he could hardly remember their order. He was distracted for a moment to professionalism by the lean grey forms of destroyers building for a foreign Power in the sheds of a yard that had dramatically deserted Thames for Clyde. Then he lost himself again in the grim majesty of the parade. There came John Brown's, stretching along half a mile of waterfront at Clydebank, the monstrous red hull of Number 534 looming in its abandonment like a monument to the glory departed; as if shipbuilding man had tried to do too much and had been defeated by the mightiness of his own conception. Then came, seeming to point the moral, the vast desolation of Beardmore's at Dalmuir, cradle of the mightiest battleships and now a scrapheap, empty and silent forever, the great gantry over the basin proclaiming stagnation and an end.

Even where the Clyde opened out above Erskine, with the Kilpatricks green and sweet above the river on the one hand and the wooded, fat lands of Renfrewshire stretching to the escarpment of Misty Law on the other, the sight of a legend – FOR SALE – painted large on the walls of an empty shed reminded him with the effect of a blow that Napier and Miller's were gone, shut down, finished, the name never to appear again on a brass plate below the bridge of a good ship. And he suddenly remembered that there lay on his desk at the office a notice of sale of the plant at Bow, Maclachlan's on the Cart by Paisley. His world seemed visibly to be crumbling. Already he had been appalled by the emptiness of Lobnitz's and Simons's at Renfrew, and the sense of desolation, of present catastrophe, closed the more oppressively upon him.

As they rounded the bend by Bowling, passing close under the wooded crags of Auchentorlie on the one hand and, as on a Dutch canal, past the flats of Erskine on the other, his eye was taken by the scene ahead. The jagged, noble range of the Cowal hills made a purple barrier against the glow of the westering winter sun. Now he was lost for a space in wonder that this cradle and home of ships enjoyed a setting so lovely. Through the gap of the Vale of Leven he could see the high peak of Ben Lomond, and his fancy ranged up those desolate, distant slopes. But then the dome of Dumbarton Rock, the westernmost of the chain strung across the neck of Scotland, brought him to think of the mean town at its base, and of Denny's yard in the crook of the Leven behind it, and of the lovely, fast, small ships they could build, and of the coming of the turbine. And another yard there, Macmillan's, derelict.

Past Dumbarton, the river opening to the Firth, the scene took on an even more immediate grandeur. The sands of the Pillar Bank were showing in golden streaks through the falling tide. The peninsula of Ardmore was a pretty tuft of greenery thrust out towards the channel. Dead ahead lay the mouth of the Gareloch, backed by the jagged peaks on the western side of Loch Long. A man could almost feel the freshness of the open sea coming to meet him over the miles of island, hill and loch; and Leslie Pagan marked how the fresher and larger waves slapped against the sides of the *Estramadura* and could almost imagine that the ship responded with quiver and curtsey to their invitation.

That openness of the river below the derelict timber ponds of Langbank, however, is deceptive; for still the channel must run round the end of the bank and close into the Renfrewshire shore. There are miles of waste space there over the shallows, and Glasgow is more than twenty miles away before a ship of size has more than a few feet of water between her keel and the bottom. Port Glasgow and Greenock look across miles of sand and sea to the Highland hills, but the yards there must launch their ships into narrow waters; so that the man who had built the *Estramadura*, scanning the shores, saw thereabouts an even thicker crowding of berths than he had marked on the upper reaches.

It was another roster of great names, older, more redolent even than those that had become namely about Glasgow with the deepening of the Clyde. Ferguson's, Duncan's, Murdoch's, Russell's, Hamilton's. ... Even he could not be sure that he had them right; there had been so many changes. Out on Garvel Point, under the old marooned Scots mansion-house, stood Brown's – the 'Siberia' of the artisan's lingo. There came Scott's East Yard – was it not once Steele's, where the clippers were built? There came the Greenock and Grangemouth, once the artisan's 'Klondike'. Then Scott's Mid Yard; then Caird's, the last of the lot – closed down. It was queer to see how Newark Castle survived in its pink grace and antiquity among the stocks and gantries.

Here history went mad – the history of the countryside and the history of shipbuilding in fantastic confusion. Here they had moved a sixteenth century church stone by stone that a yard might be extended, and with it carted away the poor bones of a poet's love. This town of Greenock, sprawling over the foothills of Renfrewshire, had had its heart torn out to make room for ships. It was as if a race had worshipped grim gods of the sea. And now the tide had turned back. Greenock's heart lay bare and bleeding – for the sake of a yard that had never cradled a ship since strangers, afire with the fever of wartime, took it and played with it and dropped it. Never again, in any calculation of which the human mind was capable, would the Clyde be what it had been.

That was incredible, surely. The fall of Rome was a trifle in comparison. It was a catastrophe unthinkable, beside which the collapse of a dynasty or the defeat of a great nation in battle was a transient disturbance. How in God's name could such a great thing, such a splendid thing, be destroyed?

As they swung the *Estramadura* to anchor at the Tail of the Bank, Leslie Pagan wrestled with this enormity. He saw the million ships of the Clyde as a navy immortal and invincible. Launches, yachts, tugs, hoppers, dredgers, tramps in every conceivable shape and size, tankers, destroyers, cruisers, battleships, liners, and now the largest and last of them all, the Cunarder on the stocks at Clydebank – there was nothing the Clyde could not do in this business of ships. Out of this narrow river they had poured, an endless pageant, to fill the ports of the world.

Why had he forgotten, passing Port Glasgow, that John Wood had built there the *Comet*, the first effective thing using steam of all? Or, sailing by Denny's, that there were shaped the perfect historic lines of the *Cutty Sark*? The last, mightiest Cunarder of all up at Clydebank; and here in Greenock Robert Duncan had built the first – the *Britannia*, all of wood, a mere two hundred odd feet long, only fit to cross the Atlantic in fourteen days under the drive of her two primitive engines. (She could have been housed handily on the boat-deck of the *Estramadura*.) He remembered – for the great stories came crowding – how the name and tradition were immortalised by that *River Clyde*, built in Port Glasgow, which carried the soldiers to the bloody and splendid assault on the heights above V Beach.

But the story was to end. So the fates indicated in terms unmistakable. To-morrow, the day after, the dagoes would take away the *Estramadura*. Then there would be nothing left to him and little left to the Clyde, with its few poor hulls building here and there and its indentations packed with idle vessels. Perhaps it was just another phase, an ill turn of the wheel. But the flashing thought left him uncomforted.

He had to resist the eagerness of Señor Martinez and a bevy of olive-skinned officers to have him accompany them on the search for pleasure in the improbable region of Greenock, and that night he dined quietly in the ship with his own technical staff, and was happy enough hearing them discuss their problems. He took a turn on deck before going below. The sou'-westerly wind blew fresh from the open sea, and there was something in the tang of it that touched him to a sweet melancholy. He could see across the dark levels of the anchorage the ceaseless winking of buoys and beacons and over a distant, black hillside the unresting beam of the lighthouse at the Cloch. A phrase, a tag, something subconsciously remembered, glowed in letters of sombre fire before his mind's eye: 'Good-bye to all that' ran the legend. And was it a final message?

Through the proceedings of the next two days he went automatically. There was everything to interest him and nothing to touch him. They swung compasses off the Powder Buoy. On a morning of winter sunshine the ship bore down on the Cloch and, at a signal from him, went racing past the white poles that mark the measured mile. Up and down and up again she went past the shores of red rock set in green fields, and between the Cumbraes and Bute they swung the ship about like a car to see how she steered. These were hours of high and eager concentration, but they suddenly became bleak when he learned from hard-faced men in overalls that she had topped her scheduled speed by a good knot, and that all her intricate mechanism functioned as perfectly as man could make it. He realised then that he had not expected anything else.

He had to drink a glass of wine in the upper lounge. He had to make a facetious speech. He had to listen to flowery ones from Señor Martinez and the new captain. The *Estramadura* was theirs at last, and he drove back to Glasgow empty-handed.

Dakers was waiting for him in the office, full of questions. He answered him impatiently and asked some on his own behalf.

'So it's a pretty clean sweep,' he concluded grimly. 'Only a maintenance squad in the yard and a skeleton in here. We'll keep two or three draughtsmen going, of course, but I suppose it's just a waste of money. It's these clerks and girls that worry me, Dakers. God Almighty, it's awful! But what can we do?'

'Nothing, sir. But there's nothing new in unemployment.'

'I know that. But, good God, man, don't you see that you and I are unemployed, too? I dare say we can live, but there's no work. I'm telling you, Dakers, there's no *work!*'

Index of Authors

Acknowlegdements

Sealskin Trousers *from* Sealskin Trousers and other stories, The Earldom *from* The Ultimate Viking, and 'A Funeral at Sea' *from* The Merry Muse, reprinted by permission of The Peters Fraser and Dunlop Group Limited on behalf of Eric Linklater © 1947, 1955, and 1959 respectively;

Skule Skerry *from* The Runagates Club and Various Doings in the West *from* Mr Standfast reprinted by permission of AP Watt Ltd on behalf of The Lord Tweedsmuir and Jean, Lady Tweedsmuir;

Ships of Julius Agricola Sail into the Pentland Firth *from* The Wreck of the Archangel reprinted by permission of John Murray (Publishers) Ltd;

Iolaire *from* Collected Poems by Iain Crichton Smith reprinted by permission of Carcanet Press;

Basking Shark *from* Collected Poems reprinted by permission of the estate of Norman MacCaig and Chatto & Windus;

'Shark-fishing in Soay' by Gavin Maxwell reprinted by permission of House of Lochar, publishers of Harpoon at a Venture (1998);

Clann Nighean an Sgadain (The Herring Girls) reprinted by permission of the author;

The Derelict Boat *from* The Silver Darlings reprinted by permission of Faber and Faber;

Christie Christison *from* Charity published by Gerald Duckworth & Company Ltd. Copyright © The Estate of R.B. Cunninghame Graham 1912;

Da Sang o Da Papa Men reprinted by permission of The New Shetlander;

Translation of Bha mi og ann an Strathghlais (I Was Young in Strathglass) by Margaret Macdonell *from* The Emigrant Experience: Songs of Highland Emigrants in North America reprinted by permission of University of Toronto Press;

'Maiden Voyage' taken *from* Adventures in Two Worlds (Chapter 4) published by Victor Gollancz Ltd, copyright © 1952 by AJ Cronin;

The Canal Boatman by J–h C–nr–d *from* Glasgow Evening News 24/11/1898, 'The Clyde Gale of 1911' *from* Glasgow Evening News 6/11/1911, The Ship-Shop *from* The Clyde, River & Firth, and The Vital Spark's Collision *from* Para Handy, Complete Edition, reprinted by permission of the Estate of Neil Munro;